P9-ARZ-095

SOCIAL PSYCHOLOGY

OTTO KLINEBERG

Columbia University

NEW YORK

HENRY HOLT AND COMPANY

COPYRIGHT, 1940,
BY
HENRY HOLT AND COMPANY, INC.

September, 1950

PRINTED IN THE
UNITED STATES OF AMERICA

44668

TO MY
MOTHER AND FATHER

PREFACE

THE rapid changes which have occurred in the content of social psychology, both in its concepts and in its data, have seemed to me to justify the appearance of a new textbook in the field. More particularly, the increasing concern of psychologists with other cultures has suggested that there might be some interest in an attempt at integration between psychology and ethnology. This integration is by no means complete, but I have the hope that some at least of the findings of ethnology and comparative sociology have been brought within the psychologist's frame of reference. At the same time the traditional content of social psychology has also been taken into consideration, although to a somewhat reduced extent because of the inclusion of materials from neighboring social sciences.

With the increasing variety of courses offered in psychology, it is inevitable that social psychology will trespass upon related fields. As far as the present text is concerned, this is true especially of the sections dealing with Differential Psychology and with Personality. In spite of possible overlapping it was decided that these materials do belong legitimately within the scope of social psychology.

References have been appended rather liberally at the end of each chapter for the convenience of the student or teacher interested in supplementary reading. It may be worth while to mention some of the texts which I would regard as particularly helpful. Among the writings of psychologists the revised edition of *Experimental Social Psychology* by Murphy, Murphy and Newcomb is especially valuable, but there is excellent material also in *A Handbook of Social Psychology,* edited by Murchison, in G. W. Allport's *Personality,* in Anastasi's *Differential Psychology,* and in Doob's *Propaganda.* The 39th Yearbook of the National Society for the Study of Education, *Intelligence: Its Nature and Nurture,* was published too late

v

for inclusion in the present text, but it should be consulted. For data from ethnology and comparative sociology, Thomas' *Primitive Behavior* and Sumner and Keller's *The Science of Society* are rich source-books, and the writings of Boas, Linton, Benedict, Lowie, Mead, Malinowski and Goldenweiser give an understanding of culture which is of real value to the psychologist.

In connection with the actual preparation of this book, it is a pleasure to record my indebtedness to Gardner Murphy, who read the first draft of the manuscript and made valuable suggestions for its improvement; to G. W. Allport, who performed a similar service at a later stage; to Ralph Linton, J. G. Peatman, George Herzog and E. L. Horowitz, who read portions of the manuscript in proof; to Edward Arluck, who assisted with the bibliographies; and to Lillian Dick, Allan Fromme and Louis Long, who gave so generously of their time in the painstaking tasks of proof-reading and preparing the index.

Throughout this undertaking my wife has been my partner. She has collaborated at every stage from the writing of the first draft to the completion of the book in its present form. Her name should really appear as co-author.

O. K.

April 15, 1940
Columbia University

CONTENTS

PART ONE. INTRODUCTORY

PART TWO. SOCIAL FACTORS IN HUMAN NATURE

CONTENTS   xi

CONTENTS

PART ONE

INTRODUCTORY

CHAPTER I

BACKGROUND AND HISTORY

INTRODUCTION

SOCIAL psychology may be defined as the scientific study of the behavior of the individual as related to other individuals. It is concerned with the individual in the group situation. Usually it is distinguished on the one hand from general psychology which deals at least in theory with the activities of the individual as such, and on the other hand from sociology which is concerned primarily with the group.

Actually both of these distinctions are difficult to maintain. In connection with the former, there is a growing recognition among psychologists of the importance of the group in determining the characteristics of the individual. In particular the discoveries of the ethnologists have revealed the extent to which personality is shaped by the cultural and social environment in which it develops. It would be difficult to point to any substantial amount of psychological description of the individual which does not reveal social influences at least to some degree. It may not be entirely true that "all psychology is social psychology," but we shall have occasion to see that this statement contains little exaggeration.

It has been said that the psychoanalysts have not been sufficiently aware of the part played by culture in the formation of the individual. It is probably true that they have paid too little attention to the varieties of behavior for which culture may be responsible. Freud himself does, however, admit that the activities of the individual can be understood only in relation to the group.

The contrast between Individual Psychology and Social or Group Psychology, which at a first glance may seem to be full of signifi-

3

cance, loses a great deal of its sharpness when it is examined more closely. It is true that Individual Psychology is concerned with the individual man . . . but only rarely and under certain exceptional conditions is Individual Psychology in a position to disregard the relations of this individual to others. In the individual's mental life someone else is invariably involved, as a model, as an object, as a helper, as an opponent, and so from the very first Individual Psychology is at the same time Social Psychology as well—in this extended but entirely justifiable sense of the words (*1*, pp. 1-2).

For purposes of convenience, however, some line will have to be drawn between the material usually included in a textbook of general psychology and that which will be our concern in the present volume. In the descriptions, for example, of many of the phenomena of memory or of sense perception, the social component enters only indirectly, and most of the material may be understood with little reference to social factors. It has been demonstrated, however, by Bartlett (*2*) in the case of memory, and by Sherif (*3*) in connection with sense perception (see Chapter VIII), that there are also social influences of a much more direct kind acting upon both these types of phenomena. Our procedure will be to take for granted on the part of the reader a knowledge of the usual textbook material, and emphasize here merely those aspects which are primarily social-psychological.

This absence of any sharp dividing line holds also for the relation between social psychology and sociology. It is true that sociology supposedly deals with groups and psychology with individuals, but as groups are obviously made up of individuals, overlapping is inevitable. It is surely no accident that so many of the textbooks in social psychology have been written by men who are technically labeled sociologists.[1]

We may perhaps make the distinction in this manner. Suppose, for instance, our interest is in the problem of gangs and gang behavior. The sociologist would presumably be concerned with the social and economic causes of gang life, the relation of the gang to law and order and institutions like the school

---

[1] For example, Ross (*4*), Bogardus (*5*), Folsom (*6*), Krueger & Reckless (*7*) Reinhardt (*8*), and others.

and the church, the distribution of gangs, their effect on the life of the community. The social psychologist, on the other hand, might be expected to study the nature of the individuals in the gang, their intellectual and personal characteristics, the effect of the gang on the individuals composing it, the life history of individual members, etc. When, however, a sociologist writes a book on "The Gang" [Thrasher (9)] he certainly makes no such artificial distinctions, and many of his findings belong properly in the field of social psychology. Similarly, when the Lynds (10) give us a sociological account of "Middletown," they tell us a great deal also about the attitudes and the personality of the individuals in that community. At the same time, difficult though it may be to maintain the distinction in practice, it remains true that the primary concern of the sociologist is group behavior, and that of the social psychologist is the behavior of the individual in the group situation.

Psychology and Anthropology. The science of anthropology, particularly cultural anthropology or ethnology, bears a similar relation to social psychology. Wissler (11) regards psychology as concerned with individual performances, and anthropology with group behavior. The anthropologist, according to him, is not greatly concerned with the function of the individual in the group; if he were, he would be indistinguishable from a psychologist. It is certainly true, however, that on occasions the individual may be of great importance to the anthropologist. The description of the Ghost Dance, a religious movement among the Plains Indians during the latter part of the last century, is clearly incomplete without some attention to the personality of Wovoka, its founder (12). The autobiography of Crashing Thunder, a Winnebago Indian, although edited by an anthropologist [Radin (13)], is obviously concerned much more directly with the individual than with the group. Lowie's (14) distinction between ethnology as the science of culture, and psychology as the science of individual minds, and his further insistence that psychology "deals on principle exclusively with *innate* traits of the *individual*" (p. 16), have to us now a somewhat antiquated flavor, but the distinction between culture and individual personality is still being made on all sides. At the same time the recent book by Thomas (*15*), *Primitive Behavior*, written primarily from the ethnological standpoint, is hailed as a contribution to social psychology.

The writings of many ethnologists reveal this difficulty of separating their material and their problems from those of social psychology. Radin (*16*, p. 267) writes: "Let me refer . . . to what is perhaps the core of all investigations of cultures: can we ever arrive at any satisfactory knowledge of what constitutes human nature?" It is clear, however, that the knowledge of what constitutes human nature is also the central problem of the social psychologist. Seligman (*17*) states that he "has become convinced that the most fruitful development—perhaps indeed the only process that can bring social anthropology to its rightful status as a branch of science and at the same time give it the full weight in human affairs to which it is entitled—is the increased elucidation in the field and integration into anthropology of psychological knowledge" (p. ix). Linton (*18*) in *The Study of Man*, a textbook in social anthropology, devotes considerable space to a discussion of such problems as the relation between instinctive and learned behavior, and the nature of man's inherent qualities— problems usually associated with the content of psychology. Rivers (*19*), who was himself both psychologist and ethnologist, expresses the belief that "the ultimate aim of all studies of mankind, whether historical or scientific, is to reach an explanation in terms of psychology, in terms of the ideas, beliefs, sentiments, and instinctive tendencies by which the conduct of man, both individual and collective, is determined" (p. 3).

We have here sufficient proof of the intimate relation between the two sciences. This relation has two main aspects. In the first place, the materials collected by ethnologists may be of tremendous value in clarifying many psychological problems. Kantor (*20*) pointed out in 1925 that psychologists were oblivious of the fact that much of the data they require

could be found in the writings of the ethnologists, but it is safe
to say that at the present time this oblivion no longer exists.
In recent years psychologists have become increasingly "culture conscious." They have made considerable use of such
materials whenever possible,[2] and when they have reported the
results of an experimental study they have come to realize
that the conclusions may be applied only in our own culture,
and not universally.[3] Though it is probably not unfair to say
that the majority of psychologists are unfamiliar with anthropological research in any detail, most of them would nevertheless be willing to concede its importance in connection with the
attempt to separate the accidental from the universal in
"human nature."

The second aspect of the relation between the two sciences
lies in what psychology can do to explain certain ethnological
problems. In spite of Lowie's insistence on the separate aims
and methods of psychology and ethnology, he does not hesi-
tate to make use of some of the findings of abnormal psychology in his interpretation of primitive religion (25). In some
cases, psychologists [4] and psychoanalysts [5] have applied their
techniques to the understanding of ethnological phenomena;
in other cases, ethnologists [6] have taken from psychology those
modes of interpretation which they have found most useful.

This account of the way in which psychology and social
anthropology are interrelated may perhaps serve as an introduction to the present textbook, and as a justification for the
method which is here adopted. The writer has for some years
felt the need of a closer integration between the contents of
these two disciplines; he is here attempting to write a social
psychology mainly from the standpoint of the relation of the
individual to his culture, and to effect at least a partial synthesis of the science which deals with culture and the science

[2] See, for example, Freeman (21), Murphy, Murphy & Newcomb (22), Katz
& Schanck (23).
[3] See Terman & Miles (24).
[4] For example, Bartlett (26).
[5] Freud (27), Abraham (28), Rank (29), Roheim (30).
[6] Benedict (31), Mead (32), Malinowski (33), etc.

which deals with the individual. That seems to him to be the only way in which one can write a "social psychology" which may legitimately be termed "social."

It follows that in one important respect this textbook differs from others in the same field. The usual concern is with the constants of human behavior, the present one at least as much with its varieties. The method is comparative, but the purpose of the comparison is to show the wealth of possible social patterning rather than to reduce behavior to a common human denominator. There is no real opposition between these two points of view. Social psychology does have implications for all societies, but at the same time the cultural variations which influence human behavior must not be neglected. In a sense then, this book may be described as an attempt to write a Comparative Social Psychology.[7]

HISTORICAL OUTLINE

As psychology grew out of philosophy, so were many of the problems of social psychology anticipated by the philosophers. More particularly, speculations as to "human nature" or "the original nature of man" are apparently as old as philosophy itself. Aristotle and Plato, for example, were both very much interested in this problem. The former looked upon man primarily as a biological animal, to be explained largely on the basis of hereditary organic dispositions; Plato, on the other hand, thought that man was mainly a product of a certain type of society, and in his Utopian "republic" believed it possible to mold human nature in any direction by the proper use of educational and social institutions. It is not a very comforting reflection that after the lapse of so many centuries we are still debating this same problem.

In more recent times, interest was directed to the problem of original human nature by the writings of the English phi-

---

[7] The word "comparative" has acquired a special meaning because of its use by animal psychologists. It is applied with at least equal propriety to a comparative study of human behavior. The term "comparative sociology," which is devoid of animal implications, may be regarded as setting the necessary precedent.

losopher Thomas Hobbes, who published his *Leviathan* in
1651. Hobbes described the "natural" state of man without
organized society as "solitary, poor, nasty, brutish and short."
Although his concern was primarily with the problems of politics, he did seek to understand human nature, and he has sometimes been called the first social psychologist [Murphy (*34*)].
Somewhat after the manner of the modern "instinct" psychologist he listed the dominant motives of man—according to
him, hunger, thirst, sex, fear and the desire for honor; through
all of these ran the search for pleasure and the avoidance of
pain. Original human nature is selfish and self-interested, and
must be curbed and controlled by society if men are to live together in peace.

It is usual to contrast Hobbes with Jean Jacques Rousseau.
The latter also was concerned with the problem of original
human nature, which was of importance to him from the point
of view of educational as well as political theory. His portrait of the "noble savage" is too well known to require much
comment; it is perhaps sufficient merely to mention that his
theory was in many ways the opposite of that of Hobbes. For
Rousseau natural man is essentially good, unselfish and pure
and it is only when civilization has had its effect upon him
that vice and defect appear. It may be of interest to add that
this conflict of opinion as to whether man is originally good
or bad occurs also among other peoples; in ancient Chinese
philosophy Mencius adopted on this point a position similar
to that of Rousseau, and Hsün Tsu anticipated Hobbes.

The publication of Darwin's *Origin of Species* in 1859 was
of great significance in the development of social psychology.
Among other things it stimulated Francis Galton's study of
hereditary factors in individual mental differences (*35*). Galton was particularly interested in the hereditary transmission
of genius, but he believed also that individuals are born to im-
becility, criminality and other defects as well as to virtues.
He was responsible for the use of the pedigree method of
studying mental endowment and his emphasis resulted in the
genealogical histories of the Jukes (*36*), the Kallikaks (*37*),

the Edwards family (*38*), and others. Although there has been great criticism of Galton for his relative indifference to social and environmental factors, and especially for his one-sided emphasis on a rather narrow theory of eugenics, he must still be regarded as the founder of the study of individual differences, which now represents an exceedingly important subdivision of social psychology.

Another important effect of Darwin's theory was the introduction of the evolutionary viewpoint into social science. There had been attempts to develop such a viewpoint before Darwin, as in Auguste Comte's *Law of the Three Stages* (*39*) and in the theory of economic evolution developed by Marx (*40*), but it is not probable that these had any very important influence on the main stream of social psychology.[8] Darwin's theory, particularly as it was developed by Herbert Spencer (*41*), for a long time played a decisive part in shaping the theoretical approach to the social sciences.

In general Herbert Spencer's view was that social behavior is to be understood as a series of stages the succession of which obeys certain fundamental laws of development. Just as in biology the later more evolved forms may be understood only in the light of what has preceded them, so in social science the complex institutions of modern society require an evolutionary explanation. Largely as a result of Spencer's influence it became fashionable to erect schemes of evolution in connection with the various aspects of culture. Tylor (*42*) explained the development of religion from its origin in animism, through polytheism to the ultimate belief in one God; Morgan (*43*) attempted to demonstrate that economic life passed through stages of hunting, pastoral life and agriculture; Haddon (*44*) believed that geometric art grew out of realistic; Lubbock (*45*) thought that marriage began with primitive promiscuity which was followed by group marriage, polygamy and finally monogamy. Although this evolutionary standpoint is not now

[8] It should be added, however, that in recent social psychology not only in Russia, but also in America and in western Europe, a Marxian point of view has entered to an increasing degree.

widely accepted, it has had unmistakable historical significance.

A more direct contribution to the development of social psychology was made by a number of French writers toward the
end of the nineteenth century. Their aim was to explain the
way in which groups control the behavior of the individuals of
which they are composed as well as the way in which individuals act upon one another. Tarde's (46) discussion of the
laws of imitation and Gustave LeBon's analysis of crowd
mentality (47) may be taken as representative of this trend.
Both were very much influenced by the psychiatry of Charcot,
especially by his studies of extreme cases of suggestibility and
hypnosis. It was believed that suggestion furnished the key
to the explanation of mass behavior, and it was so used by
these and other French writers. Tarde believed that a proper
application of the laws of imitation was all that was needed in
order to understand the phenomena of social change, progress,
religious hysteria and all other varieties of group effects.
LeBon, on the other hand, gave impetus to the notion of a
crowd psychology, relatively independent of the psychology of
the individuals of which it is composed, and constituting an
entity *sui generis*. This theory in turn is related to the viewpoint of the French sociologist Émile Durkheim (48) for
whom the individual has no existence except as a member of a
society. LeBon's book marks a turning point in the discussion
of the relation between the group and the individual, and it
has initiated a controversy which still continues, and to which
we shall have occasion to refer later (Chapter XII). Some indication of LeBon's influence may be seen in the fact that
when the phrase "social psychology" is used by the layman he
almost invariably thinks of a "mob psychology" in LeBon's
sense of the term.

The first book to be titled *Social Psychology* was written
by Professor E. A. Ross, and appeared in 1908 (4). Ross was
greatly influenced by Tarde, and his book consists largely of
an application of the "laws of imitation" to the events of his
day. Almost at the same time there appeared William Mc-

Dougall's *Introduction to Social Psychology* (*49*) which gave a tremendous impetus to the development of this field. The book is one of the most popular ever written in the field of psychology and went through fourteen editions in the first thirteen years. Greatly influenced by the evolutionary point of view, McDougall postulated certain primitive urges or "instincts" which were the prime movers of action both in animals and man. Whatever we may think now of McDougall's instinct theory (see Chapter IV) the fact remains that in its time it laid the foundation of much of the work in the social sciences and became the guiding concept in the application of psychology to the understanding of social phenomena.[9]

Recently there has been a marked reaction against the use of instinct as a fundamental concept in social science. Many writers particularly among the sociologists have emphasized the social factors in human behavior, as contrasted with the biological ones upon which McDougall insisted. The attack by the behaviorists probably went too far, but they helped to bring about a re-examination of McDougall's assumptions and a rephrasing of the problem. Still more important in this connection has been the contribution of the anthropologists, who have given to the psychologists an insight into the variations in human behavior and into the manner in which culture may determine activities formerly regarded as instinctive.

Another important development in the field of social psychology has been the gradual extension of the applicability of the experimental method. There were early attempts in this direction by German educators who compared the work done by school children when alone and in the presence of others. Moede (*52*) was perhaps the first to make careful experimental studies of the effects of rivalry and competition, and F. H. Allport (*53*) carried this whole trend further in an important series of experiments the results of which were first published in 1920. The extent to which the experimental method has been carried in this and related fields is shown by

---

[9] The books by Graham Wallas (*50*) and Ordway Tead (*51*) are examples of this tendency.

the examination of this material in *Experimental Social Psychology* by Murphy and Murphy (*54*) in 1931, and also in the revised edition by Murphy, Murphy and Newcomb (*22*) in 1937. It is doubtful whether the whole of social psychology lends itself to an experimental approach, but there can be no doubt about the important contributions which this method has made and the promise which it holds for the future.

This historical sketch would not be complete without at least some mention of a few of the special developments in the psychological field which have direct pertinence to the material of social psychology. These include among others the psychology of religion, the science of criminology, the study of differences between racial and national groups, psychoanalysis and allied approaches, the application of psychology to some of the phenomena of culture and certain of the recent developments in sociology, economics and other social sciences. It is hoped that the following chapters will succeed in showing the way in which at least some of these may be integrated with the content of social psychology.

SUMMARY

Social Psychology is concerned with the individual in the group situation. There is, however, no strict line of demarcation from general psychology on the one hand, or from sociology and anthropology on the other. For this reason the attempt is here made to bring about an integration between the material collected by students of society, particularly the anthropologists, and the material referring more directly to the individual. The aim is not merely to arrive at the constants of human nature, but also to indicate the variations in behavior resulting from social and cultural factors. The method may be described as that of a Comparative Social Psychology.

The history of this field of investigation begins with the speculations of the philosophers. More recent developments include the application to society of evolutionary and hereditarian principles, the emphasis on the psychological characteristics of groups as distinct from individuals, the instinct theory and the reactions against it, the application of the experimental method to the problems of social psychology, and the increasing realization of the part played by society in determining the behavior of the individual.

REFERENCES

1. Freud, S. *Group Psychology and the Analysis of the Ego.* 1922.
2. Bartlett, F. C. *Remembering.* 1932.
3. Sherif, M. *The Psychology of Social Norms.* 1936.
4. Ross, E. A. *Social Psychology.* 1908.
5. Bogardus, E. S. *Social Psychology.* 4th ed. 1923.
6. Folsom, J. K. *Social Psychology.* 1931.
7. Krueger, E. T., and Reckless, W. C. *Social Psychology.* 1931.
8. Reinhardt, J. M. *Social Psychology.* 1938.
9. Thrasher, F. M. *The Gang.* 2d ed. 1937.
10. Lynd, R. S. and H. M. *Middletown,* 1929; *Middletown in Transition,* 1937.
11. Wissler, C. *Introduction to Social Anthropology.* 1929.
12. Mooney, J. "The Ghost-Dance Religion," *Annual Report of the Bureau of Ethnology,* vol. 14, Part 2, 1896.
13. Radin, P. *Crashing Thunder: The Autobiography of an American Indian.* 1926.
14. Lowie, R. H. *Culture and Ethnology.* 1929.
15. Thomas, W. I. *Primitive Behavior.* 1937.
16. Radin, P. *The Method and Theory of Ethnology.* 1933.
17. Seligman, C. G. Introduction to J. S. Lincoln's *The Dream in Primitive Cultures.* 1935.
18. Linton, R. *The Study of Man.* 1936.
19. Rivers, W. H. R. *Kinship and Social Organisation.* 1914.
20. Kantor, J. R. "Anthropology, Race, Psychology and Culture," *Amer. Anthrop.,* 1925, 27: pp. 267-283.
21. Freeman, E. *Social Psychology.* 1936.
22. Murphy, G., Murphy, L. B., and Newcomb, T. M. *Experimental Social Psychology.* Rev. ed. 1937.
23. Katz, D., and Schanck, R. L. *Social Psychology.* 1938.
24. Terman, L. M., and Miles, C. C. *Sex and Personality.* 1936
25. Lowie, R. H. *Primitive Religion.* 1924.
26. Bartlett, F. C. *Psychology and Primitive Culture.* 1923.
27. Freud, S. *Totem and Taboo.* 1927.

28. Abraham, K. "Dreams and Myths," *Nerv. and Ment. Dis. Mono.*, Ser. 15, 1913.

29. Rank, O. "The Myth of the Birth of the Hero," *Nerv. and Ment. Dis. Mono.*, Ser. 18, 1914.

30. Roheim, G. "Psychoanalysis of Primitive Cultural Types," *Internatl. J. Psychoanal.*, 1932, 13: pp. 2-224.

31. Benedict, R. F. *Patterns of Culture.* 1934.

32. Mead, M. *Coming of Age in Samoa,* 1928; *Growing up in New Guinea,* 1930; *Sex and Temperament in Three Primitive Societies,* 1935.

33. Malinowski, B. *Sex and Repression in Savage Society.* 1927.

34. Murphy, G. *An Historical Introduction to Modern Psychology.* 3d ed. 1932.

35. Galton, F. *Hereditary Genius.* 1869.

36. Dugdale, R. L. *The Jukes,* 1910; Estabrook, A. H. *The Jukes in 1915.* 1916.

37. Goddard, H. H. *The Kallikak Family.* 1912 and 1921.

38. Winship, A. E. *Jukes-Edwards.* 1900.

39. Comte, A. *Cours de Philosophie Positive.* 6 vols. 1835-1852.

40. Marx, K., and Engels, F. *The Communist Manifesto,* 1848; Marx, K., *Zur Kritik der Politischen Oekonomie,* 1859.

41. Spencer, H. *Principles of Sociology.* 1880-1896.

42. Tylor, E. B. *Primitive Culture.* 1874.

43. Morgan, L. H. *Ancient Society.* 1907.

44. Haddon, A. C. *Evolution in Art.* 1914.

45. Lubbock, J. *The Origin of Civilization.* 1870.

46. Tarde, G. *Les Lois de l'Imitation.* 1890.

47. LeBon, G. *La Psychologie des Foules.* 1895.

48. Durkheim, E. *Les Formes Élémentaires de la Vie Religieuse.* 1912.

49. McDougall, W. *An Introduction to Social Psychology.* 1908.

50. Wallas, G. *Human Nature in Politics.* 3d ed. 1921.

51. Tead, O. *Instincts in Industry.* 1918.

52. Moede, W. *Experimentelle Massenpsychologie.* 1920.

53. Allport, F. H. *Social Psychology.* 1924.

54. Murphy, G., and Murphy, L. B. *Experimental Social Psychology.* 1931.

CHAPTER II

ANIMAL SOCIAL PSYCHOLOGY

INTRODUCTION

IT is interesting to note that in *A Handbook of Social Psychology*, edited by Murchison (*1*), there are no fewer than eight chapters out of twenty-two devoted directly to aspects of subhuman social behavior. This may seem to be an undue amount of emphasis, but there can be no doubt that the study of animal behavior has a very real significance for the understanding of human social psychology.

This significance has several aspects. In the first place, social phenomena may be observed in rather simpler form, and it is possible to study the development of in-groups and out-groups, of leadership, of habits of courtship and mating, of social habituation and other forms of social behavior common to animals and man. In the second place, the study of animal behavior may be particularly useful as an aid in the separation of hereditary and environmental factors in human life. It seems reasonable to suppose that whenever a form of behavior is found which man shares with a number of animal species, and particularly with those most closely related to him, such behavior may with some certainty be regarded as having a biological basis. On the other hand, when a form of behavior is found in man and is completely lacking throughout the rest of the biological kingdom, it is more probably the result of cultural factors. In connection with the theory of instincts this approach is of particular value (see Chapter IV). In addition, the fact that social psychological experiments of various kinds may be carried out on animals much more quickly than among human beings, and that changes may be introduced into the conditions of their life much more effectively, makes it possible to conduct among them investigations of direct pertinence to human social psychology. Finally it may be urged that animal social psychology is of interest for its own sake, just as is animal psychology in general, and not merely for the comparisons which it makes possible.

This chapter attempts to summarize some of the most important findings in this field. It would be an artificial division, however, to separate the animal material completely from the human, since in so many cases both are required for the understanding of a particular problem. Much of the data, therefore, collected from observation and experiment among animals will be discussed in later chapters whenever pertinent.

GROUP BEHAVIOR

If we adhere strictly to our definition of social psychology as dealing with the influence of the group on the behavior of the individual, we find the rudiments of a social psychology among the very simplest biological forms. It may seem farfetched to speak of a social psychology of plants, yet Clements (2) states that the first definite families are found among the unicellular algae, arising as the result of multiplication by fission, accompanied by sufficient pressure to prevent separation, or by the production of a mucilage that serves a similar purpose. Such families may be temporary, but while they last there is among them something approaching a division of labor, with special cells developing for the tasks of dividing the thread, of apical growth, and of spore production. There is even among plants a rudimentary parental care in some cases, as may be seen in juvenile families enclosed within the adult *volvox* and in many other species in which the young remain attached to the parents until they are able to support themselves. Among bacteria also (3) may be seen some of the simplest examples of living things working together to their mutual advantage, as well as all grades of parasitism and antagonism.

These examples are of course "social psychological" only in a very broad sense. When we turn, however, to relatively simple biological forms like the insects, we find social phenomena of the greatest intricacy and complexity. Wheeler (4) expresses the opinion that human and insect societies are so similar that it is difficult to detect really fundamental differences between them. Warden (5), on the other hand, believes that the differences are so great that the similarities appear altogether trivial and superficial. Whether they are similar to human societies or not, however, the study of insect societies is of particular interest. Ants, for example, show very definite lines of demarcation between the in-group and the out-group, the distinction apparently being due to scent, since ants of the same species will devour each other if some have been bathed in the juices extracted from an enemy group. Ants also have many "guests" in their territory. These are usually plant lice or aphids, which supply their hosts with a sweet excretion in exchange for care and food; this excretion is exuded in drops at a signal from the "host," and immediately imbibed. The "guests" are carefully guarded and reared in large numbers.

Even below the level of the social insects, group behavior of a highly integrated type may be observed. The degree of integration within a group varies widely, and its beginnings may be difficult to perceive. It is shown most clearly when the individuals composing the group give reactions over and above those which they would give as individuals. As Allee (6) points out, some of the most primitive integrations are shown in the modification of the timing of individual behavior to give rise to group synchronization. This is observed in the synchronist flashing of fireflies as well as in the singing of tree crickets.

At a higher level social behavior may be seen in the life of birds. The migration of birds in groups is difficult to explain, but represents a highly integrated pattern of group activity. The intricate courtship and mating activities of birds, as well as the frequent occurrence of family relationships among them, are further evidence of the importance of social life. Reports from zoological gardens also describe behavior in birds which is strikingly similar to what we regard as nostalgia or homesickness in ourselves (7).

In the case of the great apes, there appears to be wide variation in the amount of social behavior. The gibbons are said to be gregarious and to move about treetops in groups. The orang-utan, on the other hand, is not very sociable, and males apparently keep away from the females except in the mating season. The gorilla is found in groups which are said to consist of a single adult male with one or more females and their offspring; other observers insist that bands numbering as many as thirty individuals and including several adult males may be found together.

The social behavior of the chimpanzee has been described in considerable detail, and it has been pointed out (7) that social dependence is a fundamentally important fact in chimpanzee existence. From birth through infancy and into early childhood it may or actually does powerfully direct development and expression. Enforced separation from customary companions may bring about marked physiological reactions comparable to loneliness or homesickness in man. This condition may even lead to a disturbance in the processes of digestion, and in extreme cases not relieved by restoration to companionship, serious illness or even death may result. Köhler (8) states that a chimpanzee kept in solitude is not a real chimpanzee at all. When taken from the group the smaller animals are terribly frightened and the larger ones cry and scream in rage. When an animal is returned to the group, the other members rejoice; they put their arms around him and greet him with enthusiasm.

One important form of social relationship found in chimpanzees as well as in other animals is the habit of grooming. It has been urged that grooming in the chimpanzee is a form of social service accompanied by strong feelings and a definitely altruistic quality. This service may be eagerly and persistently solicited. The social relation which it establishes favors the development of disinterestedness, friendliness and confidence; among captive chimpanzees it is a favorite and engrossing occupation. "It is our opinion that no pattern of social behavior which involves the cooperation of at least two individuals is at all comparable with it in social significance" (7, p. 1027).

Tinklepaugh (9) lists the factors which he regards as important in determining social relationships. There is in the first place the physical environment; for example, protozoa with negative phototropism will respond similarly to the presence of light and will therefore be found in groups wherever there are shadows. Climatic factors will bring about the common behavior of migration or hibernation in many species. In the second place, social behavior may be determined by structure. The complex social organization of the ants, for instance, is to be understood in the light of their morphology; the anatomical differences between the egg-laying queens, the males and the sterile females or workers determine the pattern of social relationships. Thirdly, physiological factors may be important as in the courtship and mating relationships determined by the mutual attractiveness of the sexes. Finally, there may be psychological factors, particularly of an emotional type. One sheep in a herd may become startled and throw all the others into a panic.

THE IN-GROUP AND THE OUT-GROUP

The phenomenon of friendliness within the group and hostility against those outside it has been described for many species of animals. It has already been referred to in the case of ant societies in which lines of demarcation seem to be due to differences in odor. Among birds it has been noted (10) that there is almost invariably fighting against a newcomer. As among human beings, this common attack upon the stranger may obliterate hostilities within the group and at least temporarily unite all its members. The in-group phenomenon has been noted among chimpanzees who immediately attacked a newcomer introduced among them (8). Little by little, however, they tolerated her and finally became friendly.

This hostility against the stranger has sometimes been regarded as evidence for the biological nature of the "conscious-ness of kind" (*11*), or the "ethnocentrism" or "dislike of the unlike" (*12*), which is alleged to exist among human beings. It is important to note, therefore, that the in-group among animals is not necessarily made up of members of the same species. It has been pointed out that in a great many in-stances a herd may be made up of very heterogeneous ele-ments. Wild zebras may follow domestic horses and graze among them, or they may accompany various species of ga-zelles and ostriches. Wild buffaloes may be found with ele-phants, and horses with antelopes of different types. If there is an "urge to company" among animals it is not necessarily for company of their own biological kind. Alverdes (*13*) cites the case of a young captive rhinoceros which was appar-ently much comforted by being given a grown-up goat as a companion; the two animals soon were such good friends that the goat frequently rested on the rhinoceros. It would seem that familiarity rather than "consciousness of kind" is the basis for the in-group relationship.

Alverdes further illustrates this artificial determination of the in-group in connection with sexual behavior. A young donkey brought up with mares will later mate only with mares, and not with donkeys. Whitman (*14*) has shown that a male passenger-pigeon reared by ring-doves will always be ready to mate with ring-doves and not with other passenger-pigeons. In these cases also, familiarity rather than biological similarity determines the pattern of social relationships.

LEADERSHIP AND DOMINANCE

The phenomenon of leadership has been observed among a large variety of animal species. Anecdotal material is rich in examples of the manner in which two members of a mam-malian herd may fight for dominance, the victor usually being accepted as the leader of the whole group. In the case of gorilla societies, the leader is almost invariably the adult male who is followed by a number of females with their immature offspring, and in this case the sexual relationship is undoubtedly the most important factor determining dominance. This is, however, not necessarily the case in other groups, and the pattern of following a leader is widespread altogether apart from the sexual factor.

The question of dominance has been studied most carefully in the case of birds, among whom Schjelderup-Ebbe (*10*) noted a definite order of precedence or social distinction. Between any two birds of each species in a large number of different species examined, one individual invariably had precedence over the other, which was thus forced into a subordinate position. "A generalization may be made from the observation of these various species to the effect that there are no two individual birds of any given species which, when living together, do not know which of the two has precedence and which is subordinate" (p. 949). Both birds display characteristic reactions. The subordinate one shows apprehension, fear, and occasionally even terror of the other. There is also a pattern of avoidance and a distinctive variety of vocalization. The despot, on the other hand, may completely ignore the other's existence, but more frequently will peck at him and drive him away. The order of despotism is decided at the first meeting, and revolts rarely occur.

Strength is an important factor in the hierarchy, but it is by no means the only one operative. This is demonstrated by the curious fact that the pecking may be of a triangular variety, that is to say, bird *A* will peck *B, B* will peck *C,* and *C* in turn will peck *A.* There is evidently, as among human beings, a specific personality relationship which makes an individual act differently in different company.

Dominance is not primarily a matter of sex. In some species of birds, for example the silver pheasant and the turkey, it is the male which is the despot over the female, whereas in many sparrow species it is the female which is dominant. Among certain birds, for example the half-wild mallards of Sweden, the remarkable circumstance is found that the female has the upper hand at one time of the year, and the male at another.

Older birds are usually dominant over younger, and this

despotism may continue even after the older ones have lost their strength. The wrath of the old birds gives them so martial and so uninviting an appearance that this acts as a substitute for their former strength. Force of habit also appears to keep the young in a subordinate position. "We can in this connection not help thinking of how many analogies there are between the position of the old human in social life and that of the old among birds" (*10*, p. 961). This whole question has been subjected to careful analysis by Murchison (*15*) in a series of experimental investigations upon domestic fowl. By varying the conditions in a number of ways, Murchison was able to determine with greater precision the factors creating dominant and subordinate behavior.

In an interesting series of studies Maslow (*16*) has described the patterns of dominant and submissive behavior among baboons. In their case also, two animals placed together very quickly determine which one is to be the despot. The relationship shows itself not only in the harsh physical punishment often meted out to the subordinate, but also in the despot's tendency to take the greater share of the food placed in the cage and in the supplicant behavior of the subordinate animal. One of the most important of Maslow's observations shows the manner in which dominant behavior may be altered by the social situation. He tells of the case of one animal, *A*, who was dominant over animals *B* and *C*. Once when all three animals were placed in the same cage, *B* and *C* joined forces and gave *A* a severe pummeling. Ever after, *A* was subordinate to the others even when alone with either one of them. Personality characteristics of this type seem therefore to be determined not merely by the nature of the individual, but by the whole social situation.

Among chimpanzees also it is a matter of common observation that every group of captives more or less promptly and definitely displays the principle of dominance. Yerkes and Yerkes (*7*) mention age, sex, vigor, alertness, resourcefulness, and temperamental characteristics as determiners of this relationship. It is not merely a matter of leadership of one individual over the group, but a system of relationships extending to all individuals and constituting an order or hierarchy.

THE INDIVIDUAL IN THE GROUP SITUATION

In Chapter XII we shall have occasion to summarize the experimental material bearing upon the manner in which the behavior of an individual is modified by the presence of others. It may be of interest here to note that in the case of a number of animal species comparable modifications have been described. Katz (17) has shown, for example, that when a domestic hen has eaten her fill of seed, she may start to eat all over again when another hungrier animal begins to eat in her vicinity. A chimpanzee which has refused to eat cellulose may accept a piece after he has seen the experimenter eat it (7).

In experiments on conditioning, the effect of the group situation seems to vary from species to species and from one situation to another. A cockroach when isolated may be conditioned with less time and fewer errors per trial than when the same cockroach is a member of a pair or of a group of three. In the paired and group condition activity is reduced and the number of errors per trial is increased (18). There is a similar group retarding of conditioning when mud-minnows are trained to jump out of the water if a red light is turned on and to seize a bit of earthworm loosely impaled on a wire. In this case there is apparently a direct interference in motor activity, since it often happened that as one fish would assume a jumping attitude, another would attack it with a vigorous jab (19). On the other hand, common goldfish become conditioned more rapidly to run simple mazes in the group situation than when alone. The larger the group, the quicker the conditioning. This appears to be due in part to group cohesion, as well as to interstimulation and the quieting effect of the presence of others.

Allee (6) concludes from this material that the only safe generalization to be drawn is that the nature of the group effect, even in fish, depends in part on the problem set and

in part on the experimental conditions. He believes that when
research in this field will have been completed, a similar relation may be found to hold with regard to the effect of group
size upon the rate of learning in man. In his opinion animal
and human social psychology are intimately related and exhibit the same fundamental tendencies.

ANIMAL "CULTURE"

There is a difference of opinion as to whether animals may
be regarded as possessing culture, or whether culture is rather
to be thought of as an exclusively human product. This question has considerable significance in connection with the possibility of using animal psychology in order to determine the
relative importance of hereditary and cultural factors in
human behavior. It is usually believed that if any activity
is found both in human beings and the higher apes, this activity must be due mainly to biological causes, without any appreciable cultural influence. For example, F. H. Allport (20)
writes,

In order to discover what part human beings really do play in forming and using their culture pattern, we must discover what the behavior of human beings might be if divested of all culture. We
cannot learn this directly because there are no human tribes without a culture of some sort. Recourse must therefore be had to a
comparative study using as control groups the lower animals, particularly those most closely related to man (p. 459).

Although not explicitly stated, the underlying assumption in
Allport's position is that animals have no culture. This point
of view is expressed more directly by Warden (5) in a recent
book dealing with this question. Warden proposes a threefold
criterion of culture—invention, communication, social habituation. That is to say, culture involves some new form of behavior which is communicated to other members of the species
so that it becomes a habit common to a large number of them.
This is not found in his opinion among any animals below
man. What seems like culture among them is "biosocial" in
character, determined phylogenetically or by heredity, whereas

culture in man is ontogenetic, developing during the lifetime of individuals as the result of social factors. Although it is true that domestic animals display marked social traits and a high intelligence in submitting to man's cultural regime, they are unable, says Warden, to take over human cultural traits and impress them upon their progeny by social habituation. They are the wards of human culture and would revert to the wild state if man cast them off.

Kroeber (21) expresses similarly the opinion that even the beginnings of culture are not found in existing anthropoid apes. Boas (22), on the other hand, believes that phenomena analogous to those of human culture occur in animal society. He regards culture as embracing "all the manifestations of social habits of a community, the reactions of the individual as affected by the habits of the group in which he lives, and the products of human activities as determined by these habits" (p. 79). In spite of the inclusion of the word "human" in this statement, Boas states that the nature of animal social behavior is such that "there is no absolute gap between many of the aspects of human culture and the life habits of animals" (p. 79).

The decision in this question may turn out to be a matter of terminology, but the more reasonable position appears to be one which finds the same continuity in animal and human social behavior as has been demonstrated in animal and human morphology. There is evidence that in many cases a new pattern of animal behavior is established in a manner closely parallel to social change among human beings. Such an instance has recently been reported in the case of African lions. All African lions belong to a single species, and throughout most of Africa they hunt alone or at most in pairs accompanied by their partly grown offspring. In Kenya, however, they have taken to hunting in packs with a regular division of function. The pack spreads out in a surround and closes in, roaring, thus driving the game within the circle to a point where one lion lies quietly in ambush. "Old hunters say that this is a recent development and that, within the memory of persons still living, the Kenya lions hunted in the ordinary way" (*23*, p. 78). Why the change occurred is not entirely clear, but the fact that it did occur is significant.

A similar modifiability of group behavior has been noted in the case of beavers, apparently in response to the nature of their environment. It is stated that the few beavers still living in Europe usually live in couples, but beavers in rather quiet countries, for instance in Canada, may live in small or large groups. In thickly populated countries they usually live in simple underground tunnels, but in sparsely settled regions they frequently build houses (*13*).

The evidence in the case of bird society is perhaps the most striking. In the classical experiment by Scott (*24*), very young orioles were separated from the parents and were given no opportunity to learn the usual oriole song from them. The result was that they developed a song of their own, what Scott calls "a new school of oriole music." When other young orioles were placed among these, they too learned this new song. It is true that in this case there has been some human interference, but the results do indicate the possibility of invention, communication and social habituation, and therefore satisfy Warden's criteria. The equally important experiment by Conradi (*25*) showed that when sparrows are placed among canaries they imitate the canary song, and in spite of their vocal limitations there is an unmistakable resemblance. It is of course well known that canaries, nightingales and other birds all improve their song when in the presence of a good "teacher," and that such teachers are kept by bird fanciers for this very purpose. It seems a reasonable conclusion that the song of birds has ontogenetic as well as phylogenetic elements, or in other words, that culture does play a part.

The statement that domestic animals are unable to impress human cultural traits upon their progeny cannot be accepted without some question. Unfortunately we have here only anecdotal material, but it has frequently been pointed out by those who have had experience with domestic animals that the mother does "train" the young to observe certain of the rules which have been imposed upon her. Apart from such human rules of behavior, there are many ways in which animal mothers of various species train their young. The bird mother teaches her offspring to fly, and in the case of the eagle the training period may be long and arduous. Both the orang and the chimpanzee mothers have been observed teaching their offspring to walk.

Yerkes and Yerkes (7), in referring to this and similar material, insist that to "refrain from the use of such terms as educate, teach, train, merely because the subject is infrahuman would seem indefensible, since as a fact the chimpanzee mother, apparently with definite intent, encourages and in many ways aids her infant to achieve locomotor independence, to walk, climb, and eventually to run about and play in a variety of ways and freely" (p. 1013). Systematic exercise of the infant by the mother may appear during the first year of its life, continue for a time and then disappear. The youngster may be restrained from doing certain things until he has reached a definite stage of development, and then he is encouraged and aided to do them. These writers conclude that if we are unwilling to attribute the beginnings of culture to the anthropoid apes, we must at least admit that tradition and experience function in the social life of the chimpanzee as do cultural accumulations in man.

It was stated above that this problem may depend upon the definition of culture. Even if we accept Warden's criteria, there can be no doubt that the phenomena of invention and social habituation are certainly found in animal societies. There may be some argument, however, about the fact of communication. Is it communication when a sparrow learns a song from a canary? Or does communication depend upon the existence of a language? At this point it may be of interest to examine the whole question of the language of animals.

LANGUAGE AMONG ANIMALS

It is first necessary to make a distinction between "active" and "passive" language. By the latter, we mean the ability of an animal to respond with appropriate behavior to sounds, such as those made by a human being. We know that a dog, for example, may quite easily be trained to carry out orders of various kinds and to distinguish clearly between the auditory impressions he receives from the human voice. In the case of the young chimpanzee studied by the Kelloggs (26) this passive language reached a high degree of complexity, and the investigators give an impressive list of the words and phrases which the chimpanzee "understood." By "active" language we refer rather to the sounds made by the animals themselves as a means of communication or of control of the action of other animals. This presents a more serious problem and it is important to understand its extent and its limitations.

Alverdes (13) points out that animals frequently produce sounds in common; these may be regarded as due to imitation, to rivalry in the case of males, or to the expression of greeting. When two or more animals meet, it is by no means rare for them to make some sound. When a lion roars, others nearby usually join at once in the roaring. One donkey may cause all the donkeys in the neighborhood to bray. Two bats may call to each other in passing.

Sounds of this type may have no "meaning," that is to say, they may not partake of the nature of language as we understand it. There is, however, a large group of vocal expressions which may in certain situations serve to elicit characteristic responses in other animals. These have been called "signalling reflexes" (27). It must be noted that the effect of such cries is due only in part to the cry itself; the total context is also important. This is true of human language also, but not to the same extent as in the case of animal cries. Their biological significance lies in the fact that they make possible the co-ordination of activities of two or more individuals. As the result of the cry, stimuli acting on one individual may indirectly act on others, so that the sense organs and motor organs of one individual are placed at the disposal of other members of the group. Esper (*28*) describes four main type-responses in this connection. (1) The Flight Response—certain sights and smells may cause flight plus a cry; other animals respond to the cry with flight. The striking phenomenon of "sentinels" is an example of this form of behavior, and makes it possible for a large number of animals to be calmly feeding while one of their number stands on guard. (2) Feeding Behavior—the cry on finding food or prey brings other animals to the scene. (3) Sex Behavior—the cries of one animal prepare another for sex responses and co-ordinate such behavior. (4) Aggressive Behavior—the cries may be preliminary to or substitutes for combat.

In the case of the infrahuman primates, there are several careful studies of the most important types of vocalization. Carpenter (*29*) was able to distinguish a large variety of separate sounds in the "vocabulary" of the howling monkey. (1) The males give a low-pitched and sonorous barking roar, and the females a terrier-like bark in response to disturbing stimuli. (2) In connection with group progression, the leading male may produce at regular intervals a deep metallic cluck. (3) When slightly disturbed or apprehensive, the animal may give a series of gurgling grunts or crackling sounds which prepare the group for defensive behavior. (4) If the offspring falls to the ground, the mother may produce a wail ending in a grunt or groan. (5) A youngster out of its mother's reach may utter a series of cries, usually consisting of three notes. (6) A young infant may emit a prolonged purr which influences the mother-young relation. (7) In play, the young howling monkeys utter low chirping squeals. (8) When the youngsters play at fighting, an old male may make a grunting sound of reprimand or warning. (9) When confronted by a strange situation, the males grunt who! who! who!

Baboons (*30*) make a low chattering sound as part of their friendly advances. In sex activity as well as in all states of well-being there is a series of deep grunts, and in case of danger the young animals and the female give a high-pitched screech and the adult male makes a similar sound in anger. After the death of a baby its mother was heard making a series of deep barking sounds.

For the chimpanzees, Nissen (*31*), who made a careful study of them in French Guinea, describes (1) an excitement or panting cry, (2) a fear-pain cry—a high-pitched scream, (3) a loud barking cry—anger, defiance or exasperation, (4) a whimper or a whining cry—disappointment or frustration, (5) food muttering—a low soft bark expressive of satisfaction. There is also much noise-making by "drumming" on hollow logs or trees, but Nissen was not able to discover its precise significance.

These careful studies show that animals below man can and do make a number of distinct sounds in a variety of situations. It may be added that at least so far as chimpanzees are concerned, there are so many phonetic elements in the vocal expression that any limitations to their articulate speech cannot be ascribed to deficiencies in the glosso-labial apparatus. That is to say, there is nothing in their vocal cords, the mouth, the larynx, etc., to prevent their using language as human beings do; if there is any deficiency, it appears to be somewhere in the higher nervous centers. The main difference between human language and that of all other animals seems to lie mainly in the fact that the language of animals can express only what is present at the time; it occurs mainly in response to an emotional situation; it may on occasions indicate desires or types of object or action (*7*). As far as we can tell, however, it can have no abstract or symbolic meaning, nor can it to any extent describe what has happened in the past or what is to happen in the future.

In this connection Esper (*28*) concludes that the deficiency in animal language imposes two limitations of the utmost importance. In the first place, co-operation in communal undertakings is radically limited, and in the second, social tradition, the accumulation of useful techniques and discoveries, is possible only to a slight degree. The material which we have summarized seems to show, however, that the difference between human beings and animals in this respect is not an absolute one, and that the rudiments of language, like the rudiments of culture in general, certainly have pre-human beginnings. We may at the same time conclude that the special qualities of human communication do give to human societies a unique character, and it is therefore important to understand as well as we can the psychological phenomena underlying the use of language.[1]

SUMMARY

Social interaction of varying degrees of complexity is found among the simplest as well as the most advanced biological species. Although the most striking phenomena occur among the social insects, many other animal forms also illustrate the dependence of individual behavior on the group situation. Among the conditions determining social relationships are the physical environment, the morphological structure of the individuals, physiological and psychological factors. In-groups are formed, but these may consist of members of different species. Within any one group, particularly among the vertebrates, the individuals frequently arrange themselves in a hierarchy with well-defined patterns of dominance and submission. These and allied phenomena indicate some of the close parallels to be found between human and animal social groups.

There is no sharp dividing line between the social behavior of animals and the culture of human societies. The suggested criteria of culture—invention, communication and social habituation—are satisfied in rudimentary form by the observed changes in the song of birds, as well as in the behavior of lions, beavers and other species. Special studies have been made of communication among infrahuman primates, and these have shown that baboons, howling monkeys and chimpanzees make a number of distinguishable sounds in a variety of different situations. It seems certain, however, that animal language

[1] For a recent review of the social psychology of vertebrates, with an extensive bibliography, see *32*.

occurs mainly if not exclusively in response to stimuli in the external or internal environment, and that it does not refer to the past or the future. The superiority of human language in this respect creates the possibility of a definite accumulation of social traditions.

REFERENCES

1. Murchison, C. *A Handbook of Social Psychology* (editor). 1935.

2. Clements, F. E. "Social Origins and Processes among Plants," *Hdbk. Soc. Psychol.* (ed. by C. Murchison). 1935.

3. Buchanan, R. E. "Population Behavior of Bacteria," *Hdbk. Soc. Psychol.* (ed. by C. Murchison). 1935.

4. Wheeler, W. M. *Social Life Among the Insects.* 1923.

5. Warden, C. J. *The Emergence of Human Culture.* 1936.

6. Allee, W. C. "Relatively Simple Animal Aggregations," *Hdbk. Soc. Psychol.* (ed. by C. Murchison). 1935.

7. Yerkes, R. M., and Yerkes, A. W. "Social Behavior in Infrahuman Primates," *Hdbk. Soc. Psychol.* (ed. by C. Murchison). 1935.

8. Köhler, W. *The Mentality of Apes.* 1925.

9. Tinklepaugh, O. L. "Social Psychology of Animals," *Comparative Psychology* (ed. by F. A. Moss). 1934.

10. Schjelderup-Ebbe, T. "Social Life of Birds," *Hdbk. Soc. Psychol.* (ed. by C. Murchison). 1935.

11. Giddings, F. H. *The Principles of Sociology.* 1896.

12. Sumner, W. G. *Folkways.* 1906.

13. Alverdes, F. "The Behavior of Mammalian Herds and Packs," *Hdbk. Soc. Psychol.* (ed. by C. Murchison). 1935.

14. Whitman, C. "The Behavior of Pigeons," *Carnegie Inst. Publ.*, 1919, No. 257.

15. Murchison, C. "The Experimental Measurement of a Social Hierarchy in *Gallus domesticus,*" *J. Gen. Psychol.*, 1935, 12: pp. 3-39; *J. Soc. Psychol.*, 1935, 6: pp. 3-30; *J. Genet. Psychol.*, 1935, 46: pp. 76-102.

16. Maslow, A. H. "The Role of Dominance in the Social and Sexual Behavior of Infra-Human Primates," *J. Genet. Psychol.*, 1936, 48: pp. 261-277.

17. Katz, D. *Hunger und Appetit.* 1932.

18. Gates, M. F., and Allee, W. C. "Conditioned Behavior of Isolated and Grouped Cockroaches on a Simple Maze," *J. Comp. Psychol.*, 1933, 13: pp. 331-358.

19. Welty, J. C. "Experimental Explorations Into Group Behavior of Fishes," *Physiol. Zool.*, 1934, 7: pp. 85-128.

20. Allport, F. H. "Introduction: the Hanover Round Table—Social Psychology of 1936," *Soc. Forces*, 1937, 15: pp. 455-462.

21. Kroeber, A. L. "The Superorganic," *Amer. Anthrop.* N.S., 1917, 19: pp. 163-213.

22. Boas, F. "Anthropology," *Encycl. Soc. Sci.*, 1930, 2: pp. 73-110.

23. Linton, R. *The Study of Man.* 1936.

24. Scott, W. E. D. "Data on Song in Birds," *Science.* N.S., 1901, 14: pp. 522-526.

25. Conradi, E. "Song and Call-Notes of English Sparrows When Reared by Canaries," *Amer. J. Psychol.*, 1905, 16: pp. 190-199.

26. Kellogg, W. N., and Kellogg, L. A. *The Ape and the Child.* 1933.

27. Meyer, M. F. *Psychology of the Other-One.* 1922.

28. Esper, E. A. "Language," *Hdbk. Soc. Psychol.* (ed. by C. Murchison). 1935.

29. Carpenter, C. R. "A Field Study of the Behavior and Social Relations of Howling Monkeys," *Comp. Psychol. Monog.*, No. 10, 1934.

30. Zuckerman, S. *The Social Life of Monkeys and Apes.* 1932.

31. Nissen, H. W. "A Field Study of the Chimpanzee," *Comp. Psychol. Monog.*, No. 8, 1931.

32. Crawford, M. P. "The Social Psychology of Vertebrates." *Psychol. Bull.*, 1939, 36: pp. 407-446.

CHAPTER III

LANGUAGE

INTRODUCTION

NOTHING can be said with certainty about the origin of human language. As we have seen in the last chapter, there is reason to believe that the beginnings of language are pre-human, and that some at least of its important aspects find their counterparts in the communicative behavior of animals. There are several theories, however, as to how human speech originated.

One of the best known of these is the onomatopoeic theory, usually attributed to the German philosopher Herder, and nicknamed the "bow-wow" theory. According to this, words arose in imitation of natural sounds. So, to use familiar English examples, we speak of the "hiss" of a snake or of escaping steam, the "twitter" of birds, the "rustling" leaves, "whirring" wings and the sound of a "gong." It is suggested that out of these beginnings a language might very well have arisen. Boas (1) points out in this connection that in some languages, for example Chinook (American Indian) and many Bantu (South African) dialects, the formation of new words by sound imitation is a very live process. In criticism of this theory, however, it has been urged in the first place that only a small proportion of the words in any known language appear to have an onomatopoeic derivation, and secondly that this theory does not account for the symbolic or abstract quality which is characteristic of human speech.

Similar criticisms may be leveled against the interjectional or "pooh-pooh" theory. It is true that there are certain sounds and words in our language which have an interjectional quality; we say "oh" and "ah" and "whew," but it is difficult to see in these examples a general basis for language. On the other hand, it seems reasonable to regard the vocalization of animals as having at least in part an interjectional quality, and as predisposing to similar linguistic activity among human beings.

A third theory suggests that man possesses a faculty which makes it possible for every impression from without to receive its vocal expression within the body by a kind of predetermined resonance. This has been called the "natural ringing" or "ding-dong" theory. It was first proposed by the philologist Max Müller, but was later abandoned by him and has today very little scientific support.

John Dewey (2), commenting on these theories, expresses the opinion that they are not true theories of language, but mere "accounts, of some plausibility, of how and why certain sounds rather than others were selected to signify objects, acts, and situations." In other words, they may explain the nature of the sounds used, but not the reason why sounds were used in the first place, nor the manner in which they attained any symbolic significance.

Another theory of a somewhat different type is that the first language was a language of gestures, which gradually gave way to vocal speech. Paget (3) suggests that there were probably fully developed gesture languages which served as the first means of communication. He points to the sign language of the American Indians, of the Cistercian monks and of deaf-mutes as examples of the extent to which communication may be carried on by gesture alone. His theory is that after the gestures were developed, occasions would arise when men were busy working with their hands, and yet wished to communicate with their fellows; they would then make the great discovery that this could be done by means of the voice. The many advantages of vocal communication would soon become apparent and gradually supersede pantomime or gesture. The fact that gestures are obviously useless in the dark, for example, would impose an immediate limitation upon their use.

There is of course no doubt that gestures may be used very effectively as a means of communication. The best known of all sign languages, that used by the American Indians of the Plains, was a sort of international language common to a large number of American Indian tribes whose spoken languages were mutually unintelligible. The sign language was valuable in all inter-tribal contacts, especially in commerce and in peace-making ceremonies. It probably served as an important agent in the process of acculturation, or the transmission of culture traits from one tribe to another. To the White man in his first contacts with the Indians of the Plains it proved particularly valuable, since it made it possible to learn one language which would serve over a wide area. It is interesting to note that this language, in spite of its pantomimic character, was not restricted to the expression of concrete situations, but by means of a wide use of metaphors was able to convey abstract ideas as well. There is no proof, however, that this gesture language antedates the spoken languages of the Plains. It is not possible to use its occurrence as evidence for the priority of gesture language, since there are so few parts of the world in which a gesture language appears, even in legend. There is, however, one argument in favor of Paget's theory, namely, that the expression of meaning through gesture is much more direct than through voice and may very often be understood even when we have had no previous experience with these particular gestures. It is possible, for example, because of its pantomimic character to understand something of the Indian sign language, though by no means all, the first time it is seen. On the other hand, perhaps the strongest argument against the theory is that animals below man make some use of vocal expression for communication.

That the interest in the origin of language is by no means a recent one is shown by a report of the Greek historian Herodotus (4). He tells of an Egyptian king Psammetichus who was interested in discovering whether Egyptian was really the first language of mankind. He therefore had two young children put by themselves on an island before they had a chance to learn to speak, and fed and cared for by a herdsman. After the passage of some years they were visited, and they ran up to the newcomers shouting "becos." Unfortunately the Egyptian scholars could not find that word in their language. They did, however, discover that this sound means "bread" in the Phrygian language, so they reluctantly decided that this must be the oldest language, and Egyptian the second. It is reported that a similar experiment was tried by the Mogul emperor Akbar in order to determine the first religion of mankind, but the children isolated by him had no speech at all when they were discovered.

PHONETIC SYMBOLISM

Allied to the onomatopoeic theory of the origin and nature of language is the fact that certain words appear to convey something of their meaning by the nature of their sound. This phenomenon has been called phonetic symbolism. Jespersen (5), for example, has pointed out that the vowel "i" serves very often to indicate what is small, insignificant or weak, or, on the other hand, what is refined and dainty. It is also symbolic of brief duration. Paget (3) believes that the "i" sound also indicates what is near; he cites the example of the Javanese "iki," "ika" and "iku," representing respectively three degrees of distance from the speaker.

Recently Sapir (6) has subjected this theory to an experimental attack. One of his studies concerned the contrast between "large" and "small." He presented to his subjects the following two words, "mal" ("a" as in German "Mann") and "mil" ("i" as in French "fini"). He arbitrarily assigned to these two nonsense syllables the meaning of "table," but one of them was to mean a large table and the other a small one. The subjects were asked to decide which was which, and in the great majority of cases "mal" was chosen as the larger. There were seven Chinese students among the subjects and their choice was also in the same direction. Newman (7) carried this experiment further, and established a scale of size for a number of different vowel sounds. He found that "i" vas the smallest, with the other vowels following in this order—"e" (as in French "été"), "ε" (as in English "met"), "ä" (as in English "hat"), "a" (as in German "Mann"), "u" (as in English "put"), "ɔ" (as in English "note"), and finally "o" (as in French "tôt").

Newman also conducted experiments on other types of phonetic symbolism, and in connection with consonants as well as with vowel sounds. He found, for instance, that vowel sounds had a "symbolism" with reference to the opposition between bright and dark, as well as between small and large; "i" was the brightest vowel, and "u" the darkest. Among the consonants, "p" apparently was smallest and "br" the largest; "s" was the brightest and "br" the darkest.

It has been suggested that many of these results may be due not to phonetic symbolism as such, but to some sort of assimilation to the sounds of actual familiar words expressing the meaning of "large," "small," etc. For example, the French words "petit" and "grand" or the English words "little" and "large" might conceivably be responsible for the findings in the "mil, mal" experiment. Boas (1), while admitting some relation between sound and concept, regards it as by no means certain that the same impressions are conveyed by all languages through the medium of similar phonetic elements. He gives several illustrations of the manner in which size or intensity may be expressed by variations in sound.

Thus Nez Percé, an Indian language spoken in Idaho, changes "n" to "l" to indicate smallness; Dakota has many words in which "s" changes to "sh," or "z" to "j," indicating greater intensity. . . . Undoubtedly the particular kind of synesthesia between sound, sight and touch has played its role in the growth of language (p. 132).

What is clearly needed here is a series of studies on subjects ignorant of any of the common European languages. Sapir did have a small group of Chinese subjects, but they were familiar with English; in any case a larger number of subjects would be needed. It is important to keep in mind that there are many words in English as well as in related languages which would tend to have an influence in the opposite direction—for example, "big" and "small," "infinity," and others. Newman made a careful survey of a number of English words denoting largeness and smallness, and concluded that they take practically no account of the magnitude symbolism revealed by his and Sapir's experiments. He concludes that experience with actual language probably plays little or no part in the phenomenon of phonetic symbolism. In any case the investigation should be carried further.

In explanation of these results, three possible factors have been invoked. There may be a difference in the kinesthetic sensations arising from the size of the oral cavity; in making the "i" sound the resonance chamber (the mouth, etc.) is smaller than in the case of the vowel "a." A second possibility is that the difference is acoustic, due to unequal vibration frequencies in the actual sounds. A third, which is allied to the first, is the difference in the position of the tongue in the mouth. The first of these suggestions seems by far the most reasonable. Mauthner, for instance, writes:

If we are in a foreign country and, not knowing its language, want to express bigness, we shall open our arms wide; if the opposite, we shall press the palms of the hands together. Now suppose the whole vocal apparatus desired to share in the gesture; suppose the glottis and the mouth pressed themselves together to articulate an "i" in imitation of a small space, or opened wide into an "o" to imitate a big one (8, p. 237).

There is no doubt that the actual sensations experienced in the two cases are quite different, and they would certainly help to account for the "feeling" of size which these vowel sounds give us.

It is not suggested that phonetic symbolism can help in the understanding of the origin of language. It is not even probable that it accounts for the actual nature of more than a small part of our vocabulary. The fact that it occurs at all, however, does constitute an important psychological problem, and shows the possibility that sound in itself may have "meaning," apart from the conventional significance which attaches to it.

In poetry this may have special importance. Coleridge spoke
of the "loud bassoon," and was later criticized because actually
the bassoon is not an especially loud instrument. There is,
however, something about the word which suggests loudness,
and which at least explains, if it does not justify, his use of
this expression.

There is an allied problem which may be mentioned at this
point. Languages differ very markedly in the phonetic elements out of which words are composed, although there is of
course a great deal of overlapping between one language and
another. When a language contains a large number of words
with the same vowel or consonantal sound, it is probable that
the facial expression of the speaker may to some extent be
affected by this constant repetition. In other words, if the
muscles of the face are used habitually in a certain manner,
the consequence is that even in repose there is still sufficient
contraction of these muscles to differentiate the members of
one linguistic group from another. For example, as Bloomfield (9) points out, English in contrast to French or German,
retracts the jaw; German and French advance the jaw and
use the muscles more vigorously—German in large sweeping
movements, French in smaller and more precise ones, especially in the front of the mouth; Danish draws the muscles
in toward the median line. It is obvious that such language
habits would affect facial expression only after a considerable
period of time, and it is therefore not likely that a person who
merely learned another language in addition to his own would
show any such influence. Nor is it suggested that this is the
only factor which determines facial expression. It is, however,
probable that when a German is recognized as different from
an Englishman of the same racial stock, one feature which
makes this recognition possible—in addition to such extraneous
factors as posture, clothing, haircut, etc.—is the expression
of the face due to the effect of language on facial musculature.

LANGUAGE AND THOUGHT

The problem of the exact relation between language and thought has been the subject of considerable discussion by psychologists. The behaviorist Watson (*10*) has even gone so far as to regard them as identical. For him thinking is merely speech which remains subvocal; it is laryngeal rather than vocal language. When we think, we really speak, though this speech cannot be heard. Watson's theory has stimulated a number of experimental studies in this field, which have demonstrated that during the process of thinking, movements do take place in the tongue, the palate, and other portions of the vocal and laryngeal apparatus. Against Watson it has been urged, however, that even though we habitually think by means of language, it is also possible to think in images and without giving expression to the thought in words; it has been pointed out also that we may be thinking of one thing while saying another, so that subvocal speech is not a prerequisite of the thought process. Very recently, important experiments by Max (*11*) have shown that in the case of the deaf, thinking produces action currents in the muscles of the hands and arms, that is to say, in the organs ordinarily used in communication.

Whether or not language is to be identified with thought, there can be no doubt that thinking in the large majority of cases does require the use of language, and that the nature of language has an important influence on the nature of thought. Sapir (*12*) points out that the forms of our language predetermine for us certain modes of observation and interpretation; we must learn in a great many cases to fight the implications of language. When we use the expression "the grass waves in the wind" or "friction slows up a moving body," we are in danger of personalizing or reifying words which have no such meaning. This process is clear also in much of the work of Piaget (*13*) on the relation between the language and thought of the child. Piaget finds among children a marked tendency to personalize inanimate objects, and to speak of them as if they were living things. This "animistic" tendency is regarded by him as universal among children and overcome gradually as they grow older. He himself recognizes, however, that linguistic habits are at least in part responsible. If we speak of the sun as "rising" and "setting," or ask, "What are the wild waves saying?" or refer to a ship as "she," we are clearly encouraging children in our society to give expression to this personalizing or anthropomorphic tendency. Margaret Mead (*14*) has suggested that the absence of this tendency among the Manus children of New Guinea may be due at least in part to the relatively more matter-of-fact language they speak. Piaget believes that the tendency would persist even if the language did not encourage it, but he is willing to admit that language does have some influence.

Language may affect the nature of thought in many ways. It has been pointed out, for example by Trendelenberg, that Aristotle's categories and similar distinctions which play a large part in his system cannot be studied apart from the peculiarities of the Greek language. Mauthner states that Aristotle was superstitiously devoted to words. In his logic he is absolutely dependent on the accidents of his mother tongue. "If Aristotle had spoken Chinese or Dacotan, he would have had to adopt an entirely different logic, or at any rate an entirely different theory of categories" (*15*, p. 50).

In this connection it is not always possible to determine the exact nature of the causal relationship. It may be that language determines thought; it may also be that the thinking of a people and the problems which interest them determine the form and character of the language. Dr. Hu Shih believes [1] that the relatively concrete and matter-of-fact character of the Chinese language is unfavorable to the development of metaphysical subtleties or hair-splitting distinctions, and that this accounts for certain characteristics of Chinese philosophy. It might be argued, however, that a lack of interest in such subtleties might be responsible for a vocabulary defective in this respect. At the other extreme it has been pointed out

[1] Personal communication.

that Sanskrit is a particularly rich language from this point of view. With reference, for instance, to the training in concentration there is a special word for the state of concentration "when the name of the object alone is in the mind, another when the object is thought of with its predicate relations, still another when it is merely a point, and so on. It is significant that more words for philosophical and religious thought are to be found in Indian literature than in the Greek, Latin and German languages combined" (*16*, p. 93).

We shall probably never be able to decide which came first. It is likely that an interest in certain problems or objects develops a vocabulary capable of dealing with them adequately; but it is also likely that an individual born into any particular culture will think in terms of the medium of expression current in his society, and that the nature of his thinking will be affected thereby. For the culture as a whole, however, it does seem possible to learn something about the mental life of the people from an analysis of its language. Dunlap (*17*) says:

In studying the structure of the language of a people, we are studying the forms and methods of their thinking. In studying their vocabulary, we are finding their types of discrimination. The description of a language as the crystallized thought of a people is far from wrong (p. 310).

This may seem a somewhat extreme statement, but there can be no doubt that differences in the vocabulary of peoples tell us something about their culture. In some languages, for example, it is impossible to differentiate between "to kill" and "to murder" (*12*). The distinction that we make in this regard is based on a certain legal philosophy which considers intent or motivation to be an important aspect of the act; that is to say, killing accidentally or without intent is entirely different from deliberate murder. Other societies emphasize the result; intentionally or not someone has been killed, and that is the only thing that matters.

One of the most striking examples of the manner in which vocabulary may mirror the interests of a people is to be found

in the words for "camel" in Arabic (*18*). There are said to
be about six thousand names connected in some way with
"camel," including words derived from the camel and attributes
associated with it. These include, for instance, names of
classes of camels according to function—milk camels, riding
camels, marriage camels, slaughter camels, etc.; names of
breeds of different degrees of nobility of lineage, derivation
from different lands, etc.; names of camels in groups, as several, a considerable number, innumerable, and with reference
to their objectives—grazing, conveying a caravan, war expedition, etc.; as many as fifty words for pregnant camels, states
of pregnancy, stage at which movement of the fetus is first
felt, mothers who suckle and those who do not, those near
delivery, etc. This list might be continued almost indefinitely,
and it is hardly necessary to point out that it reflects the exceptional importance of the camel in Arab civilization.

In the same manner the large variety of words for "snow"
among the Eskimos clearly results from the need to discrimi-
nate between numerous aspects of what is to most of us a
single phenomenon. "In the life of the Eskimo *snow* means
something entirely different as falling snow, soft snow on the
ground, drifting snow or snowdrift. Fresh water ice, salt
water ice, an iceberg, play quite different rôles in their life
and all these are designated by distinctive terms" (*1*, p. 130).
Similarly the Chuckchee of Northeastern Siberia have a wide
array of designations for the reindeer.

There are other types of linguistic distinction which are important in this connection. For example, in the Hupa (California Indians) language whenever a statement is made a suffix
is employed to indicate the source of authority. There is one
suffix for what is perceived by hearing, another when the
transaction is in sight, another for things conjectured from
circumstantial evidence (*19*). We cannot conclude that the
Hupa are necessarily more accurate than we are, but it is probable that their language does avoid certain misunderstandings
which are common in English.

It has frequently been argued that the absence of certain

words from a vocabulary may point to a deficiency in the type of thinking represented by such words. More particularly, the fact that many of the languages of primitive peoples have few or no abstract words has sometimes led to the conclusion that the thinking of primitive peoples is restricted to the concrete, and that they have no power of abstraction. This is undoubtedly a faulty conclusion. The paucity of certain abstract terms is probably due to a lack of interest in these abstractions, rather than to an inability to deal with them. Boas (20) has shown that it is possible to convey an abstract notion to a member of a tribe whose language normally makes no use of it; the native may on such occasions even decide what the word should be in order to express such a notion. The present writer had a similar experience among the Huichol Indians. Their language has words for "my father," "your father," "his father," but no word for "father." The informant, however, was perfectly capable of understanding the idea of "father," and supplied a word which he thought could be used with that meaning.

In general we may conclude that language and thought are intimately related and mutually influence each other. The vocabulary in particular can give us valuable information as to the content and the interests of the culture. The argument from the absence of certain words to corresponding defects of the intellect is, however, more than questionable. Vandryès (21), for instance, notes that modern Greek and Bulgarian have no infinitive, and yet no one could possibly say that Greeks and Bulgarians therefore lack the faculty of conceiving a verbal action in an abstract way.

LANGUAGE DEVELOPMENT IN THE CHILD

Esper (22) describes five stages in the acquisition of language. The first is the stage of screaming, which begins with the birth cry; this was formerly interpreted as expressing the infant's wrath or joy at entering the world, but it is now more prosaically regarded as a reflex activity, an incidental result of the mechanism of blood oxygenation. In the early period of life the sounds are reflex in character and uttered without any conscious intent. It has been suggested that in this early stage various organic conditions—hunger, pain, anger, etc.— are each accompanied by its own specific cry, and may be distinguished from one another. An interesting series of experiments by Sherman (23) demonstrated, however, that observers were not able to tell from the cry what condition it accompanied. When they heard the cry but could not see what caused it, they were just as likely to be wrong as right in their interpretation. It is quite possible, however, that whereas there is no common "language" for all infants, each particular infant may have a specific and characteristic cry for each condition, and that this cry may be successfully interpreted by the mother or nurse.

The second or babbling stage occurs usually toward the end of the second month, when consonantal sounds appear for the first time. During the whole of the first year the infant makes use of a great multiplicity of sounds, many of which do not occur in the adult language. This large variety of sounds shows that any infant could with equal facility learn any human language, and that racial heredity is of no importance in this connection. The babbling of these early months is probably due to intra-organic stimulation, and occurs especially after meals, after waking from sleep, etc.

The third is the stage of sound imitation, which usually begins during the second six months of life, but may occur somewhat earlier. One aspect which has received particular attention is the so-called circular reaction, characterized by the child's repetition of the same sound over and over again. This has been explained on the principle of the conditioned response (24). Some organic condition causes the child to make the motor response resulting in the sound; at the same time he hears the sound of his own voice, so that this auditory experience may become the conditioned stimulus setting off the same motor response. The following diagram may serve as an illustration.

$$S_1 \text{ (organic condition)} \rightarrow R_1 \text{ (producing the sound)}$$
$$S_2 \text{ (hearing the sound)}$$

The hearing of the sound, which is the consequence of the motor response, may at the same time serve as the conditioned stimulus because of its coexistence with the original unconditioned stimulus. It may therefore bring on the motor response; this in turn results in the hearing of the sound, which again produces the motor response, and so on in this circular fashion until some new condition intervenes.

$$S_2 \text{ (hearing the sound)} \rightleftarrows R_1 \text{ (producing the sound)}$$

At the age of eight or nine months there may be imitation of sounds made by others. This may be understood on a basis similar to the preceding. Once the sound itself has served as a stimulus for the associated vocal reaction, the same or associated sounds made by the parents may have a similar effect. It has been pointed out by the Sterns (25), however, that what has been called "sound imitation" in the speech development of children refers to a number of distinct forms of activity, of which that described above is perhaps the simplest. True imitation of new vocal patterns introduced by adults appears usually toward the end of the first year or at the beginning of the second. The Sterns describe also a type of "imitation" to which they have given the name *metalalia;* when the child has had frequent experience with a complex situation which includes certain sounds produced by the adults (e.g., "good night"), he may himself in a similar context supply the sound before anyone else has spoken it. This phenomenon is closely associated with the origin of true vocal utterance—the final stage in the developmental process (26, p. 46).

The fourth has been called the stage of verbal understanding, and has its beginnings toward the latter part of the first year. The child now begins to respond with specific movements to sounds made by others. This stage also may be explained on the principle of the conditioned response. For example, the child may be playing in the bath and splashing, and at the same time the parent says, "Splash, splash!" In time, this word becomes the conditioned stimulus which sets off the same response. In the same way such a conditioned response may be established when the child is put through certain movements which are invariably accompanied by the same words. This stage may also be described as the acquisition of a passive vocabulary, and as was pointed out in the preceding chapter, it may reach a high degree of complexity among many species of animals.

The final stage is that of verbal utterance, usually beginning in the first half of the second year. It is the stage of the acquisition of an active vocabulary and is described by Esper as "the establishment of conventionalized speech reactions as specific responses to socially presented stimulus patterns" (p. 442). It may perhaps best be explained as the result of a combination of the conditioning process described above and the pattern of imitation which was noted in the third stage. The child, for instance, hears the sound "bow-wow" when he sees a dog, and later produces it by himself in the same situation. Further development in language is essentially a continuation of the same process, as well as of the processes of sound imitation and of verbal understanding which have had an earlier start.

THE IMPORTANCE OF LANGUAGE IN SOCIAL PSYCHOLOGY

It is hardly possible to overestimate the part played by language in the development and control of social behavior. It represents what is specifically human in social life. It is an instrument of thought and of communication. It serves as a cohesive force uniting human groups and setting them apart from others; as Sapir (12) points out, the fact of common speech is an index of the social solidarity of a group. Much of the opposition between the in-group and the out-group reported for the most primitive as well as for the most complex societies may probably be explained by the fact that the groups cannot understand each other. It is no exaggeration to say that language is one of the fundamental facts of human social life.

SUMMARY

There are several theories of the origin of language, but they account for the particular sounds used rather than for the phenomenon of communication. The suggestion that the first language was a language of gestures conflicts with the fact that vocal expression occurs in animals below man. The experimental evidence for phonetic symbolism supports the theory that onomatopoeia may account for some of the actual sounds used in spoken language. More important is the demonstration of a relationship between language and thought; the forms of language determine certain modes of observation and interpretation. This may be seen not only in the animistic thinking of young children, but also in the complex speculations of philosophers. The content of a vocabulary reflects the interests of the corresponding culture, but does not justify any conclusions as to the intellectual capacity of a people.

In the acquisition of language by the child, five stages of development may be distinguished—(1) the stage of screaming, which begins with the birth cry; (2) the babbling stage toward the end of the second month; (3) sound imitation, beginning usually during the second six months of life, characterized by the circular conditioned response, resulting also in imitation of sounds made by others; (4) verbal understanding toward the end of the first year; (5) verbal utterance, or the acquisition of an active vocabulary, usually beginning in the first half of the second year.

Language serves as an instrument of thought and of communication, as a means of controlling the actions of others, and as a cohesive force uniting the members of a particular community.

REFERENCES

1. Boas, F. *General Anthropology.* 1938.
2. Dewey, J. *Experience and Nature.* 1925.

3. Paget, R. *Human Speech.* 1930.

4. Kroeber, A. L., and Waterman, T. T. *Source Book in Anthropology.* Rev. ed. 1931.

5. Jespersen, O. *Language, Its Nature, Development and Origin.* 1923.

6. Sapir, E. "A Study in Phonetic Symbolism," *J. Exp. Psychol.,* 1929, 12: pp. 225-239.

7. Newman, S. S. "Further Experiments in Phonetic Symbolism," *Amer. J. Psychol.,* 1933, 45: pp. 53-75.

8. Mauthner, F.; quoted in Rank, O., *Art and Artist.* 1932.

9. Bloomfield, L. *Language.* 1933.

10. Watson, J. B. *Behaviorism.* 2d ed. 1930.

11. Max, L. W. "An Experimental Study of the Motor Theory of Consciousness," *J. Comp. Psychol.,* 1937, 24: pp. 301-344.

12. Sapir, E. "Language," *Encycl. Soc. Sci.,* 1933, 9: pp. 155-169.

13. Piaget, J. *The Language and Thought of the Child.* 1926.

14. Mead, M. "An Investigation of the Thought of Primitive Children with Special Reference to Animism," *J. Roy. Anthrop. Instit.,* 1932, 62: pp. 173-190.

15. Ogden, C. K., and Richards, I. A. *The Meaning of Meaning.* 2d ed. 1927.

16. Behanan, K. T. *Yoga.* 1937.

17. Dunlap, K. *Civilized Life.* 1934.

18. Thomas, W. I. *Primitive Behavior.* 1937.

19. Goddard, P. E. "Life and Culture of the Hupa," *Univ. Cal. Publs. Amer. Archaeol. & Ethnol.,* 1903, 1: pp. 1-88.

20. Boas, F. *Handbook of American Indian Languages. Bull. Bur. Ethnol.,* No. 40, 1911.

21. Vendryès, J. *Language.* 1925.

22. Esper, E. A. "Language," *Hdbk. Soc. Psychol.* (ed. by C. Murchison). 1935.

23. Sherman, M. "The Differentiation of Emotional Responses in Infants," *J. Comp. Psychol.,* 1927, 7: pp. 265-284; 335-352.

24. Allport, F. H. *Social Psychology.* 1924.

25. Stern, W. and C. *Die Kindersprache.* 1922.

26. Lorimer, F. *The Growth of Reason.* 1929.

PART TWO

SOCIAL FACTORS IN HUMAN NATURE

CHAPTER IV

THEORIES OF HUMAN NATURE

INTRODUCTION

IT is customary for textbooks in social psychology as well as for many in the field of sociology to include a discussion of the characteristics of human nature. This has usually been done on the theory that any science which deals with the behavior of groups of individuals or with that of the individual in the group situation should begin with some statement of the nature of the individual as such. In other words, it is admitted that this problem belongs in the field of general psychology, but that some consideration of it is essential as a preliminary to all social science.

The point of view adopted here is somewhat different. The very problem of human nature and its characteristics seems rather to be one which belongs to the social at least as much as to the individual aspects of psychology. If human nature is in whole or in part created or affected by social factors, it is of direct, not only of indirect, concern to the social psychologist.

Theories of human nature have of course practical as well as theoretical implications. Discussions of possible changes in our economic system frequently center upon the question of whether "acquisitiveness" is natural to man, or whether he would be willing to work in other than a competitive system. The possibility of the abolition of war is frequently questioned on the ground that "aggressiveness" is a fundamental human trait. It becomes of the greatest importance therefore to discover what are the essential characteristics of human behavior, as well as the limits of their variability. There is implicit here the controversy between those who believe in an original

55

human nature relatively fixed and immutable, and those who hold that what we call human nature is socially determined and modifiable. As has already been pointed out, this controversy is not a new one; Aristotle and Plato defended the opposing viewpoints many centuries ago.

THE INSTINCT THEORY

Much of the discussion of human nature centers upon the instinct theory. In the earlier uses of the concept of instinct, it was regarded as referring to the behavior of animals, not of men. For Descartes, for example, there was a sharp dichotomy between the instinct of animals and the intelligence of man; man had intelligence because he had a soul. Descartes' successors, says Brown (*1*), left God out of it. "In place of God, gradually, came the concept of heredity" (p. 86). The question of the origin of behavior was passed on to the biologists. It was noted that animals might show the same type of modifiability of behavior that was called intelligence in human beings, and that conversely, men sometimes behaved like the beasts. The transition between human and animal behavior, or between intelligence and instinct, was seen to be a gradual one, and the Darwinian viewpoint was extended to the continuity of behavior as well as of morphology.

The instinct theory in its modern form is usually associated with the name of William McDougall, whose *Social Psychology* was first published in 1908 (*2*). He presented the theory that instincts are the prime movers of all human activity; take them away and the organism would be incapable of activity of any kind. They are the forces that shape the life of individuals and societies. An instinct was described as an innate disposition which determines the organism to perceive or to pay attention to any object of a certain class, to experience in its presence a certain emotional excitement, and to act or have an impulse to action which finds expression in a specific mode of behavior in relation to that object. An instinct, therefore, had three aspects—cognitive, affective and conative; the association between instinct and emotion was of particular importance.

McDougall gave a list of thirteen major instincts, including such activities as curiosity, self-assertion, submission, food-seeking, mating, acquisitiveness, and others, and six minor instincts, such as sneezing, coughing, laughing and eliminating waste products from the body. In making up this list he looked on the one hand at the behavior of animals, and on the other to the exaggeration of instincts found in psychopathic individuals; he turned, according to his critics, "to the menagerie and the insane asylum" for his material. It has also been said that "he does a great deal of packing for a journey on which he never starts"; for he describes his instinct theory as an "introduction" to social psychology, but he makes almost no use of it when he deals with social phenomena. This last criticism is not quite fair, since McDougall's treatment of group behavior is associated with his theory of "sentiments," which are more complex systems of behavior and attitude erected upon an instinctive basis. He may be said, therefore, to have continued the journey in *The Group Mind* and other volumes.

Many psychologists accepted the instinct theory with one modification or another. Thorndike (3) and Warren (4), for instance, gave their own lists of instincts, somewhat longer and more complicated than McDougall's. It became fashionable in psychology to use instinct as a principle of interpretation of all sorts of behavior. As one critic of this theory (5) put it,

Man is impelled to action, it is said, by his instincts. If he goes with his fellows, it is the "herd instinct" which actuates him; if he walks alone, it is the "anti-social instinct"; if he fights, it is the instinct of pugnacity; if he defers to another, it is the instinct of self-abasement; if he twiddles his thumbs, it is the thumb-twiddling instinct; if he does not twiddle his thumbs, it is the thumb-not-twiddling instinct. Thus everything is explained with the facility of magic—word magic (p. 4).

As was pointed out in the first chapter, there has been a marked reaction against the instinct hypothesis. Serious criticisms have been leveled against it on the basis of observations of animals and young children who apparently showed simple reflex patterns of behavior rather than the more complex ones which McDougall had postulated. Many social scientists came to a similar negative conclusion in the light of their sociological analysis of the various factors influencing and determining the so-called instincts.[1] Because of these and other criticisms the very term "instinct" has fallen into disrepute as denoting something mystical and intangible which has no place in the field of science. The one important exception is to be found in the writings of Freud and his followers, who refer to the sex instinct, the instinct of self-preservation, the death instinct, the aggressive instinct and others. Even among psychoanalysts, however, there has been a distinct reaction against Freud's biological and "instinctual" orientation.[2]

Although the term is now rarely used by academic psychologists, however, it appears still to be the fashion to speak of certain underlying motivating factors in behavior common to human beings in general. Dunlap (10) uses the term "desires"; according to him, the primary desires are important everywhere for the preservation of the life and welfare of the individual and the life of the race. They have an organic basis and are subject to perversions. He lists the primary desires as alimentary, excretory, protection, activity, rest and relaxation, amorous or erotic, parental or philopedic, pre-eminence and conformity. This list may certainly be criticized in the same manner as McDougall's and it hardly seems as if much has been gained by the substitution of "desire" for "instinct." The same may be said for Gurnee's (11) discussion of "motives," which are described as internal stresses disposing the organism to restless activity until that stress is relieved. These motives include food seeking, temperature,

---

[1] Cooley (6), Bernard (7), and others.
[2] Horney (8), Fromm (9), and others.

escape and avoidance, sex, protection of other living things, gregarious tendencies, social approval and disapproval, self-assertion, negativism and submission. The books by Gurnee and Dunlap are relatively new, and they indicate that the kind of psychology for which McDougall is mainly responsible has by no means disappeared from the field.

Many other terms have been used in this same connection, frequently without any preconception as to the innate or instinctive nature of the corresponding behavior. The word "drive," for example, is preferred by Holt (5) in his *Animal Drive and the Learning Process* as well as in the studies of animal motivation by Warden and his associates (12). Woodworth (13) speaks of "dependable motives" and we shall later make use of this expression in our own analysis. In a recent publication Murray (14) has used the word "need," and distinguishes between *viscerogenic* needs which are presumably "provoked by internal conditions regardless of the environment," and *psychogenic* needs which "though found to operate without obvious dependence upon the viscerogenic needs, were perhaps once subsidiary to the latter," and are influenced to a great extent by cultural forms (pp. 74-75). As we shall see later, however, the line between these two is difficult to maintain, since cultural factors affect the specific expression of viscerogenic phenomena as well. Murray's list is a long one and includes most, if not all, of the motives which have been described in other publications. He discards the term "instinct" because it is limited to those needs which can be proved innate. Murphy, Murphy and Newcomb (15) list four groups of motives or drives: visceral drives (hunger, thirst, etc.), activity drives (exercise, novelty, exploration, etc.), aesthetic drives (color, tone, rhythm, etc.) and emotions.

All attempts to define the fundamental characteristics of human nature have recently been challenged by Brown (1), who has written a social psychology from the point of view of the "field theory" developed by Kurt Lewin (16). In essence, the field theory maintains that behavior is to be understood as due not so much to the nature of the individual as to his relationship to the physical and social environment acting upon him and in which his behavior occurs. From this standpoint, says Brown, there is no such thing as human nature independent of the existing structure of the social field. There are no specific reaction forms inherent in the human as such. "From our primitive ancestors to us as modern men, change in 'human nature' has occurred and it seems only reasonable to suppose that change will continue to occur in the lives of our issue" (p. 261). Even such apparently fundamental tendencies as those toward self-preservation and race-preservation may not be said to belong to human nature. Suicides and homosexuals are still human and cannot be explained away as special cases; under selected field conditions any individual may be caused, according to Brown, to develop homosexuality or to commit suicide.

Although much of Brown's criticism of the usual concept of human nature is justified, his own point of view appears to go too far in the other direction. There can be no doubt as to the great importance of the "field" in shaping human behavior. It is still necessary, however, for us to inquire into the nature of this human animal who is part of the field. To put it another way, we might say that if human nature were different, behavior would differ accordingly; the social field itself would be changed as a result. In a brilliant essay by Clarence Day (17) there is some amusing speculation as to what human beings would be like if they were descended from the great cats or from the social insects, instead of from a primate stock. Many of the characteristics of "this simian world" are to be understood precisely in the light of our biological ancestry.

In all fairness to Brown, it should be pointed out that in a more recent statement (18) he does emphasize clearly the biological characteristics of man as important aspects of the total field. "Implicit in field theory is the idea that social behavior depends on the biological nature of the individual as an integral part of groups whose characteristics are intimately connected with cultural phenomena" (p. 863). In that case, the problem of the essential characteristics of human nature remains a real one. We may prefer the term "fundamental drive" to that of "instinct," but we have still to ask what drives there are, and what evidence there is that they are fundamental. In what follows we propose to examine those forms of behavior which have been alleged to be fundamental or dependable and attempt to determine to what extent they may be so regarded.

Criteria of Dependability. In general the procedure will be to employ a threefold criterion. The first is the existence of continuity between a particular form of behavior and that of other biological species, particularly the anthropoid apes. In the light of the close biological relationship as well as the similarity observed in their activity, it seems reasonable to assume that such continuity may be used as evidence for an unlearned component in such behavior. In the second place, the discovery of a biochemical or physiological basis for any specific activity will also be evidence in the same direction; it will show that there is in the organism a condition predisposing to such an activity. Finally, a significant criterion will be that of universality. The discovery of a form of behavior common to all human societies in spite of the variations in their culture will constitute strong evidence in favor of its dependability. This last criterion need not be applied too strictly. If the universality is disturbed by no more than a few exceptions which may be explained in the light of special circumstances operative in those communities, the behavior may still have a fundamental basis. To return to one of Brown's examples, the fact that some individuals or even some groups commit suicide by no means proves that it is as "natural" to wish for death as for life.

In connection with this third criterion, liberal use will be made of the material collected by anthropologists, whose reports show something of the varieties of human behavior determined by culture. It is important to point out that examples from primitive communities are not employed in an evolutionary sense; that is to say, they are not to be regarded as stages of behavior prior to our own. The evolutionary point of view with reference to culture is in general no longer accepted by the large majority of competent anthropologists. In other words, we use primitive material as illustrating *varieties*, not *stages*, of human behavior.

The use of this threefold criterion makes possible a treatment of the problem of motivation which differs in one important respect from previous analyses with which the writer is familiar. The customary procedure has been to present lists of drives or motives on what may be described as an "all or none" basis. That is, a particular motive was either dependable or not; there was no intermediate ground. The view adopted in the present text is that dependability is a relative concept, permitting of marked variations in degree. For any particular motive we must determine not merely whether it is dependable or not, but also how dependable it is. We must place it somewhere in a hierarchy of dependability, so that we may know how it stands in comparison with other motives. To put it another way, motives differ in their degrees of compulsion; some have an imperative character, others may be more easily suppressed or neglected. In this connection the amount of variation found in different cultures will be of special significance.

THE ORIGINS OF CULTURE

Culture may be defined as consisting of the capabilities and habits acquired by man as a member of society (*19*). How culture arose and how it developed are problems outside the scope of this discussion; we must take culture for granted. It may perhaps be sufficient to point out that those cultural phenomena which are universal have been explained on the basis of (1) the psychic unity of man (to be discussed in the following chapters), (2) the identity in the basic needs of life, (3) the fact that man's physical environment, broadly speaking, is always the same (*20*). Linton (*21*) also speaks of the constants (to be found mainly in human nature) which affect the development of all social systems. The cultural phenomena which are variable, on the other hand, must be understood historically.

The specific form of any pattern or institution is mainly the result of social inventions, culture contacts, and the total environment, natural as well as cultural, in which the pattern or institution develops and functions. Since all these factors are inherently variable, patterns and institutions, when treated as discrete phenomena, can only be explained on a historic basis (p. 268).

Linton points out further that pure chance may also enter. The Mohammedan rule that a man may marry the divorced wife of his adopted son is due to the fact that the Prophet wished to marry the divorced wife of his adopted son and had a revelation that this was permissible. There is a clan among the Tanala in Madagascar which prohibits the taking of sisters as plural wives, although all other clans (as well as most polygynous peoples) permit it; this prohibition resulted from an actual case of poisoning among sisters who were plural wives in this group about fifty years ago.

Variations in culture may thus be due to differences in the physical environment, to economic factors, to contacts with other peoples, to accident, perhaps also to the nature of the individuals composing the group. Whatever their origin, however, our concern is with the variations in human behavior for which they are responsible, and with the uniformities that may still be found in spite of the cultural variations.

SUMMARY

The determination of the characteristics of human nature, as well as of the limits within which they may vary, is of practical as well as theoretical importance; attempts to bring about fundamental changes in social institutions or to eliminate war and other evils must meet the challenge that "human nature" makes certain forms of behavior inevitable. The instinct theory of McDougall assumes the existence of innate dispositions to specific modes of behavior, but there has been a marked reaction among social scientists against this view, and the term *instinct* is now rarely used. Recent texts speak of *desires, motives, drives* or *needs,* but the assumption of underlying common-human characteristics is still frequently made.

The procedure followed here is to examine the allegedly dependable motives through the use of a threefold criterion— (1) phylogenetic continuity, (2) physiological basis, (3) universality. Motives may differ in their degree of dependability, and this procedure makes possible a decision not merely as to whether a motive is dependable, but also as to how it compares with other motives in this respect. Ethnological material helps to make such a comparison possible, since the variations in culture, whatever their origin, are responsible for a wide range of human activities. The extent of this range, and the existence of uniformities in spite of it, must be determined before any decision may be reached about the nature of human motivation.

REFERENCES

1. Brown, J. F. *Psychology and the Social Order.* 1936.
2. McDougall, W. *Introduction to Social Psychology.* 1st ed. 1908.
3. Thorndike, E. L. *Educational Psychology.* 3 vols. 1913.
4. Warren, H. C. *Human Psychology.* 1919.
5. Holt, E. B. *Animal Drive and the Learning Process.* 1931.
6. Cooley, C. H. *Human Nature and the Social Order.* 1922.
7. Bernard, L. L. *Instinct.* 1924.
8. Horney, K. *New Ways of Psychoanalysis.* 1938.
9. Fromm, E. "Über Methode und Aufgabe einer analytischen Sozialpsychologie," *Ztschr. f. Sozialforschung,* 1932, 1: pp. 28-54.
10. Dunlap, K. *Civilized Life.* 1934.
11. Gurnee, H. *Elements of Social Psychology.* 1936.
12. Warden, C. J. *Animal Motivation.* 1931.
13. Woodworth, R. S. *Psychology.* Rev. ed. 1929.
14. Murray, H. A., et al. *Explorations in Personality.* 1939.
15. Murphy, G., Murphy, L. B., and Newcomb, T. M. *Experimental Social Psychology.* Rev. ed. 1937.
16. Lewin, K. *Principles of Topological Psychology.* 1936.
17. Day, C. *This Simian World.* 1936.

18. Brown, J. F. "Individual, Group, and Social Field," *Amer. J. Sociol.*, 1939, 44: pp. 858-867.

19. Tylor, E. B. *Primitive Culture.* 1874.

20. Goldenweiser, A. A. *Anthropology.* 1937.

21. Linton, R. *The Study of Man.* 1936.

CHAPTER V

THE DEPENDABLE MOTIVES

INTRODUCTION

WE turn now from the theoretical discussion of motivation in general to a specific examination of individual motives, particularly in their social implications. The procedure will be to apply to each motive in turn the criteria developed in the preceding chapter, and to determine in that way the nature and the extent of its dependability. The presentation does not follow any systematic order, because it seems preferable to postpone the classification of motives to the end of the discussion after the pertinent material has been reviewed. The motives are then assigned their position in the list on the basis of the assembled evidence. The reader who wishes to know in advance the precise nature of the classification will find it on page 160.

THE PARENTAL DRIVE

The Maternal Drive.[1] The maternal drive constitutes one of the forms of behavior for which universality has been claimed. Obviously it is not peculiar to our own society. As a matter of fact there are probably many cultures in which it has a strength and importance greater if anything than among ourselves. There are many peoples among whom the respect in which a woman is held is proportionate to her fecundity, and as Westermarck (1) points out, a barren wife is frequently despised as an unnatural and useless being.

In this as well as in what follows, it is important to keep in mind that there is a distinction, psychologically, between the desire to have children and the urge to care for them.

[1] The words "motive" and "drive" are used interchangeably.

These have both been included in most discussions of the maternal drive, but they are by no means identical. Although clearly related biologically, they are distinct as motives. For convenience, we shall use the terms *pre-maternal* motive for the attitude or behavior related to the desire for children, and *post-maternal* motive for that which follows conception and comes to its fullest expression after the child is born. There is reason to believe that the latter is a far more dependable motive.

As far as concerns the care of offspring, there is ample evidence for its existence among many animals besides man. In fact, it has been shown in a series of experiments by Warden and his associates (2) that in the white rat this drive at its height is stronger than any other. The strength of the drives was measured by means of an apparatus composed of three compartments, the central one consisting of an electric grill. The experimental animal was placed in the compartment to one side of the grill, and the object representing its "goal," on the other. The number of times the animal crossed the grill to the goal measured directly the amount of punishment it received, and therefore indirectly the strength of its drive toward the goal. In this way comparison could be made of the strength of various drives by putting in at different times a hungry animal separated from food, a thirsty animal separated from drink, a mother from her young, a female in heat from a male, etc. The results were as follows:

Drive	Av. No. of Crossings (optimum conditions)
Maternal	22.4
Thirst	20.4
Hunger	18.2
Sex	13.8
Exploratory	6.0
No incentive	3.5

It is important to add that although at its maximum the maternal drive is the strongest, it decreases as the age of the mother increases, and even more markedly as the age of the litter increases. While it lasts, it includes also a strong urge to retrieve the young when they have wandered away, and to bring back even members of other litters and small lifeless objects. It begins to decrease in strength from twelve to twenty days following parturition, and usually has disappeared by the twenty-fifth day. It apparently parallels closely the duration of the lactation period. As P. T. Young (3) points out, the demand of the mother for her offspring seems to be due to the fact that the young are required for the free and normal functioning of the mammary glands; without them a congested condition of the breasts arises which the animal finds painful. This need normally persists until the young are weaned, and it largely explains the urge of the mother to return to her litter.

There are undoubtedly other physical or biological factors operative. "Maternal behavior" was induced, for example, in adult male rats through the implantation of anterior pituitary. These animals made nests, cared for young rats, licked them in a maternal way, etc. There was no apparent development of the mammary glands (4). There is also some indication of the production in the female organism of certain hormones which may contribute to the strength of the drive. In any case, there can be no doubt that post-maternal behavior satisfies our first two criteria—continuity with lower animals and a physiological basis.

Adoption. When, however, we turn to an examination of maternal behavior in various human societies, we find a number of striking phenomena which require consideration. In our culture, for example, parents prefer to have their own rather than adopted children; adoption occurs, but it is definitely a second-best. There are many societies among which this is apparently a matter of complete indifference. Rivers (5) reports that it was very difficult to obtain genealogies in Murray Island in the Torres Straits and that the islanders were reticent about this whole subject. The chief difficulty arose from the great prevalence of adoption. It was a common practice to adopt a child, in some cases the arrangement being made before its birth, and it was customary then to keep the child ignorant of his true parents. Even after reaching adult life, the child would give the name of his adoptive father. After Rivers left the island, one of the White residents continued the effort to determine true family relationships, but with little success.

In the Andaman Islands, adoption was similarly prevalent. In an early account by Man (6) it is reported to be of rare occurrence to find any child above the age of six or seven residing with its parents, "because it is considered a compliment and also a mark of friendship for a married man, after paying a visit, to ask his hosts to allow him to adopt one of their children. The request is usually complied with, and thenceforth the child's home is with his (or her) foster-father" (p. 125). In this case there is apparently no ignorance of the true parentage, but it seems a matter of little moment. A man may adopt as many children as he pleases on the understanding that he will treat them kindly.

Adoption was also very common in Borneo (7). Frequently it was the child of a relative who was adopted, but it might also be a captive or a slave child whose parents were willing to relinquish him. The adoption was always accompanied by an elaborate ceremony. For some weeks the adoptive mother observed all the prohibitions of pregnancy; at the end of that time the child was pushed forward between her legs, and if very young was put to her breast. So complete was the adoption that the new parents regarded the child as entirely their own, and it was very difficult to obtain from them any admission to the contrary.

There were also cases in which adults were adopted. Among the Omaha Indians, when a war party took a captive, he might be adopted by anyone who had lost a child or who was childless. In an early account by Tanner (8) it is reported that there was among many Indian groups a strong feeling about the replacement of lost members. He cites one incident which in our own society would certainly seem incredible, namely, that an Indian mother proposed to adopt a young man who had murdered her son in a drunken brawl. When we consider how a mother among us would feel about having in her own home the man who had killed her son, we realize the extent to which the manifestations of "maternal love" may vary from one community to another.

The many instances of adoption reported in the ethnological literature appear to indicate that the attachment of parents to their own children is determined by the folk-ways of the community. It is important to note, however, that the ethnologist frequently fails to inform us of the attitudes of the persons involved. If adoption occurs because of the dictates of the community and in spite of the objections of the parents, it would constitute no argument against the universality of the maternal drive. For example, adoption occurred with considerable frequency in the Gilbert Islands (8), and the request to adopt a child could not be refused by the parents. It is reported, however, that "the parents are often extremely unwilling to part with their child, and it is probably only the force of native custom and the fear of social ostracism which makes them do so" (p. 141). This is of course an interpretation by the ethnologist, and it may be the correct one, although it is not made clear why the custom should persist if it conflicts with the wishes of the people.

It must not be assumed that all primitive peoples are alike in their attitude toward adoption. There are many communities in which it is relatively rare, and others in which a sharp distinction is made between adoption and blood kinship. This is true of Dobu, for instance, where a foster-parent will refer freely and publicly to an adopted child as a "bastard" or an "orphan," and where the relationship is not regarded as particularly binding (9).

Infanticide. The prevalence of adoption has been interpreted by Lowie (10) as due to the fact that "savages commonly have a generic love of children in no way dependent on the sense of consanguinity" (p. 460). This interpretation is in conflict, however, with the existence of another behavior pattern which is widespread among primitive peoples, namely, infanticide. This occurs so frequently that it is easy to multiply examples (*11*). The reasons for infanticide varied. In the Murray Islands in the Torres Straits it was considered proper to have the same number of boys and girls in the family, and if there were too many of the same sex, some were put to death. In the New Hebrides women had a great deal of work and could not attend to more than two or three children; they buried the rest as soon as they were born. Infanticide was practiced in Australia for similar reasons of convenience. In other cases, as in China, infanticide appears to occur only as a last resort when economic conditions have made it impossible to rear all the children.

Here also the psychologist would like to know very much more about the emotions and attitudes of the parents who put their children to death. If they are driven to it by economic necessity and are unhappy as a result, their action by no means implies an absence of the maternal drive. If on the other hand, they do it calmly and willingly, the probability is that the nature of the maternal drive in general is socially determined. Some of the examples in the literature appear to point in this latter direction. It is reported that an Australian woman was asked why she had killed her baby; she pointed to a child two years old and said with apparent indifference that she could not look after two babies at once (*11*). There is no indication that any great emotional conflict was here involved, but negative evidence is not satisfactory. In a case of this kind it is of the utmost importance to know how the woman felt about the act she had committed. Unfortunately the ethnologist who made the report was more interested in the behavior than in the emotion which may have accompanied it.

It might be argued that infanticide is by no means absent from our own society. The practice of abortion is not uncommon. In the eyes of the Catholic Church at least it is in exactly the same category. It seems certain, however, that psychologically the two acts are entirely different. Many people who calmly proceed with an abortion would be completely revolted at the thought of killing the child after it was born. The fact that infanticide does occur in the case of births out of wedlock, is to be explained by the social disapproval of illegitimate motherhood rather than by the absence of a maternal impulse.   There is certainly nothing in our society to parallel the attitude of the Arioi in Tahiti, among whom special privileges were acquired by membership, but who had a rule enforced without exception that all their children should be immediately put to death (*12*).   A woman who failed to kill her child was known as "a bearer of children," which was a term of reproach, and she was immediately expelled from the society.   It seems clear that if there is a maternal drive, the customs of a people may not only alter its direction, but even cause its apparent disappearance.

Even apart from ethnological evidence of the type which we have just summarized, the existence of a maternal instinct has been questioned on the basis of an analysis in terms of our own society.   Bernard (*13*), who has made one of the most thorough criticisms of the whole concept of instinct, expresses the opinion that social and traditional factors have been mistaken for apparently instinctive behavior.   The little girl, for instance, plays with dolls not because of the presence of an incipient biological drive, but because she imitates her mother.   Boys do the same until they learn that such behavior is not fitting for them.   This observation is borne out by the experience of Margaret Mead (*14*) in the Manus tribe in New Guinea.   In this community the women are usually occupied with regular work in the house and the fields, whereas the men are busy for a time with their hunting and fishing, but have more leisure.   As a consequence, after the initial care of the baby it is the father rather than the mother who spends time with the child.   These children have no dolls.   It happened, however, that Miss Mead brought them some small wooden figures from a neighboring tribe, and found that it was the boys rather than the girls who showed an interest in them and a desire to play with them.   Apparently in this case social factors have produced behavior in boys which in our community is often regarded as "instinctive" in girls. Bernard believes further that the mother's affectionate behavior toward the child grows out of her contact with it and that an initial biological basis for this affection is of no great importance.

In summary it may be said that there is a physiological or biochemical basis for post-maternal behavior in the changes occurring in the maternal organism during the period of gestation and after parturition. The enlargement of the mammary glands, as well as other glandular changes affecting the presence of hormones and other products in the organism, prepare the expectant mother for maternal behavior. In any case, however, this physiological condition explains the presence of a maternal drive only in those cases where the child is expected or where it has already arrived. It offers no basis for the desire to have children, i.e., for what we have called the pre-maternal drive.

The Desire for Children. If we apply to this pre-maternal drive the criteria of dependability, we find no evidence either for continuity with animals below man or for a physiological basis. The presence of such a drive in female animals might be expected to reveal itself in a willingness to accept punishment in order to get to the young of the species before parturition or even conception. In the studies by Warden and his associates no such tendency was observed. Among human beings, on the other hand, the desire for children is widespread.

Leta Hollingworth (*15*) has discussed what she calls "social devices for impelling women to bear and rear children." She mentions the forces of public opinion; the fact that governmental leaders like Mussolini, Theodore Roosevelt and the former Kaiser encourage and in some cases subsidize large families; the law that sterility in the wife may be a cause for divorce; the law against dissemination of birth control information; the drastic laws against abortion, infanticide and infant desertion. She believes that the very existence of these laws testifies against the "instinctive" nature of the maternal drive, and that we cannot imagine laws forcing us to feed our-

selves or to give ourselves sex satisfaction.[2] She points also
to the religious forces behind the bearing of children as well
as to the myriad madonnas by means of which art holds up
the ideal of motherhood. In the light of this and similar material she concludes that the maternal drive would not be very
effective if left to itself.

Sumner (*16*) comes to a similar conclusion for somewhat
different reasons. "Children add to the weight of the struggle
for existence of their parents. The relation of parent to child
is one of sacrifice. The interests of parents and children are
antagonistic. The fact that there are or may be compensa-
tions does not affect the primary relation between the two. It
may well be believed that if procreation had not been put
under the dominion of a great passion, it would have been
caused to cease by the burdens it entails" (p. 309).

There is an apparent contradiction in this point of view.
To the biologist, for example, the causal relationship would
appear to be exactly the reverse of that which Sumner suggests. That is to say, the biologist would regard the sexual
impulse as subordinate to the preservation of the race, or in
other words, to the bearing of children. It may still be true,
however, that for the *individual* the primary motivating force
is the sex drive, and that at least in a large number of cases
procreation is a by-product.

When children are desired, either by men or women, a variety of reasons may be operative. In a great many instances
an economic motive is clearly responsible, for the child may
be a practical asset to the entire family. Stefansson (*17*), for
example, writes that "the nearest thing to an investment
among the Stone Age Eskimos, the one means of providing
against old age, is children. For that reason a widow without a child would have to be loved for herself alone. A widow
with one child would be a desirable match. To marry a widow
with three or four children was, among the Stone Age people

---

[2] It should be pointed out, however, that we do have laws against homosexual practices, so that on this basis we should have no right to assume that
heterosexual behavior is innately determined.

of Coronation Gulf, the New York equivalent to marrying the widow of a millionaire" (p. 164).

The motive may not always be directly economic. The women of the Pilaga tribe in the Gran Chaco of the Argentine are said not to care very much for children but they are glad when children come, because they know that is the best way to keep their husbands.[3] This mechanism is of course not unknown in our own society.

The material from primitive societies is not to be understood as indicating that maternal love is always subservient to practical considerations. It is rather that culture determines the extent to which children are loved and the reasons for which they are desired.

Paternal Behavior. So far we have said little about the attitude of the father and the existence of a "paternal" drive. There is considerable evidence that the father's interest in the offspring is found far down in the animal scale, and is by no means confined to human beings. In the case of many species of birds the male usually remains with the female even after the breeding season, helps build the nest, brings food for the young and defends the mother and the offspring against enemies. In mammals the male commonly does not concern himself with the progeny, though there are many exceptions. The evidence regarding the anthropoids is contradictory on this point. Some observers describe the male parent as relatively indifferent to the welfare of the offspring. Yerkes (*18*), however, states that the chimpanzee father helps look after the young one, amuses and exercises him, protects him and supplies him with food. There appears to be some indication therefore that the human family may be an inheritance from anthropoid ancestors.

On the other hand, the anthropologist Malinowski (*19*) states that at least in higher cultures the necessity for imposing the bond of marriage is practically and theoretically due to the fact that a father has to be made to look after his chil-

[3] Jules Henry, personal communication.

dren. Culture forces the male to keep guard over the pregnant female and to share in her anticipatory interest in the child. Once forced into this position, however, the male responds with strong interests and positive feelings for the offspring. This furnishes the raw material out of which culture fashions paternal love. In other words, society imposes upon the man the duty of caring for his children as a sort of payment for the rights he has in his wife.

This theory offers an explanation of paternal behavior which does not depend upon the presence of any biological factors. Malinowski is himself inconsistent on this point. He insists that there must be an anatomical basis for paternity before it may be regarded as instinctively determined. Without finding such a basis, he still concludes that paternity is determined by biological elements, and that culture merely emphasizes natural tendencies. If we apply our threefold criterion, we see that paternal behavior must be denied the status of complete dependability, since no visceral or biochemical basis has ever been discovered which might explain its existence.

The criterion of universality is also not fulfilled. Whereas most families do consist of mother, father and offspring, there are a few striking exceptions. It is reported of a warrior tribe in India, the Nayars (20), that immediately after marriage divorce occurs on the theory that warriors must not be burdened by wives and families who might constitute a responsibility for them. After the divorce the wives are permitted intimacies with any number of other men and the children belong to the mothers alone. The institution of "professional husbands," also found in India (8), is another exception. As one aspect of the caste system there exists the practice of "hypergamy," which means that a woman may marry a man of her own or of a superior caste, but not of an inferior one. Frequently her father may not be able to pay the dowry needed to obtain a husband who satisfies these requirements. In that case he may marry his daughter to a professional husband who has a number of wives, and who makes periodical visits to each one of them. The children belong entirely to

the mother and her family. It is true that these exceptions
to the more usual family pattern are rare and due to special
circumstances, so that they should not be overemphasized.
The absence of any known physiological basis for the paternal
drive, however, constitutes a more serious objection to the assumption that it is an innate part of human nature.

The desire for children is of course present in men as well
as women. It may perhaps be adequately explained on the
basis of the values attached to children by the particular culture. These values may be economic, as mentioned above;
they may be religious, as in China, where sons are necessary
to insure the immortality of the parents by attending to their
shrines and burning incense to their memory. Children may
be desired as a form of immortality in another way, by insur-
ing the continuity in others of what is really ourselves. They
may also be welcomed by men as a tangible proof of their
virility. It is interesting to note in this connection that in our
society the inability to procreate is regarded as much more
"shameful" in a man than in a woman; this is in direct contrast to the attitude in many other cultures where the worst
thing that may be said of a woman is that she is unable to
bear children.

A behavior pattern similar in some respects to the phenomenon of adoption and also expressive of an attitude diametrically opposed to our own is the claim of the husband to all
the offspring of his wife, even when he knows that he is not
the father. This has been reported for a large number of
communities in Africa, Melanesia, Siberia, etc. (11). An especially interesting case is found in the Sakalava tribe in Madagascar. There the bride price is considerable, and in case of
divorce there is no refund or substitution. The divorced wife
may not remarry, however, without the permission of her husband, who usually enters into an agreement with the new husband by which he receives the first three children of the new
union. He is said to take as much interest in them as if they
were his own (20). The fact that children are an economic
asset undoubtedly explains this attitude, but for our present

purposes the cause is less important than the existence of a point of view which seems to be opposed to "human nature" as we know it.

In connection with the attitude toward children, there is a final point to be made. The familiar adage "spare the rod and spoil the child" played a more prominent part in the life of our society a hundred years ago than it does today, but it still reflects a not-uncommon practice. To a large number of "primitive" groups it represents something quite unthinkable. Among many American Indians, for example, corporal punishment in any form was severely condemned. It is reported that Eskimos do not consider that White people deserve to have children, since they are so heartless as to strike them. In Tahiti a White man who beat his own child was almost put to death by the natives. Among the Buka people in Melanesia (21) any kind of punishment of children was unknown. It is interesting to speculate on what an Eskimo or Melanesian psychologist would say about such behavior in our society; he might decide that we were lacking in the parental instinct.

The evidence here assembled permits the following conclusions. What we have called the post-maternal drive has a physiological basis, shows continuity with animal behavior and a very wide, though not universal, distribution among human beings. The pre-maternal drive, on the other hand, has apparently no physiological basis, cannot be demonstrated in animals below man, and its distribution among human societies appears to be determined by the economic and social motives operative in the community. The same is true for the attitudes of the father. In any case, whether they have a physiological basis or not, the functioning of these motives is clearly influenced by cultural patterning and conditioning.

AGGRESSIVENESS

The problem of the innateness or universality of aggressive behavior is one of obvious practical significance. It would probably be agreed that the occurrence of war and the threat of war in our society represent its worst feature—one which may even contain the germs of the destruction of our whole civilization. It is frequently asserted that war will never be abolished because it is rooted in an instinct of pugnacity which is natural to man. It is important to see what psychology and ethnology have to offer in connection with this problem.

Aggressive behavior is of course found widely in the animal kingdom. It must be borne in mind, however, that it is by no means an invariable rule of behavior. Cases of mutual help and co-operation also occur in abundance, even between members of different species. When aggressiveness is found it is frequently in association with other drives, such as self-preservation, sex and maternal love, and probably is not to be regarded as an end in itself.

On the physiological side no basis has been discovered for the existence of aggressiveness as such. It has been amply demonstrated by Cannon (22) that in anger there is a whole series of biochemical and physiological changes under the influence of the sympathetic nervous system and the adrenal glands. These changes prepare the organism for an emergency; they include the liberation of glycogen from the liver so that in the form of glucose it may be used as a source of energy; the more rapid elimination of the products of fatigue; the quicker clotting of blood, so that wounds will not be so dangerous; the movement of blood from the digestive system to the muscles, so that these may act more efficiently, and so on. The general result of these changes is that in the presence of an enemy the organism may respond with an unusual output of energy over an unusually long period of time. These changes do occur in anger, but they occur also in fear and in excitement; they constitute an organic basis for violent emotional behavior in general, rather than for aggressiveness itself (see also Chapter VII).

War. There are some human groups among whom aggressive behavior was apparently indulged in for its own sake. An Iroquois chief is reported to have proposed to a neighboring ruler that their young men be allowed to have a little war. On the second chief's refusal, he was asked, "With whom then

can my children play?" (23). However, this may not be an
example of aggressiveness as such, since the Iroquois chief
was concerned with the need of his young warriors for practice. Of the Lango it is said—"They are brave and venturesome warriors, who have won the fear and respect of their
neighbors, delighting in war not only for the plunder which it
brings, but also for its own sake" (24, p. 68).

These examples do not necessarily prove that aggressive behavior is innately determined. It may become an end in itself
even though it originated as a means to an end. In all cases
we have a long previous history of warfare and the possibility
therefore that warlike habits have been developed. As we
shall see later much of the warfare of primitive peoples is to
be understood as similar to athletic contests or trials of
strength, and that may be the primary motivation responsible.

On the other hand, it has been noted that warfare is by no
means universal and that there are many societies to which
it is foreign. In their survey of the cultural characteristics
of a large number of groups, Hobhouse and his associates (25)
report that there were at least ten tribes which had no war.
The Arctic explorer Nansen quotes an Eskimo letter of 1756
which is pertinent to this discussion. The writer of the letter
cannot understand how it is that men of the same faith are
hunting each other like seals and stealing from people they
have never seen or known. Fighting about land seems to him
sheer greed. He apostrophizes his own country. "How well
it is that you are covered with ice and snow! How well it is
that, if in your rocks there are gold and silver, for which the
Christians are so greedy, it is covered with so much snow that
they cannot get at it. Your unfruitfulness makes us happy
and saves us from molestation" (26, p. 180). The writer was
surprised that the Europeans had not learned better manners
among the Eskimo and proposed to send medicine men as
missionaries to the Whites to teach them the Eskimo way of
life.

There are many writers who feel that aggressive warfare,
far from being native to man, develops only when culture

has reached a certain degree of complexity. Letourneau (27) states that at the beginning of society, when men were few in number and did not trouble each other, war was as strange to them as until recently it was among the Eskimo of the far north. Van der Bij (28) also believes that the simplest and most primitive peoples were not warlike; they had no offensive war and were even unwilling to engage in defensive wars. He cites cases from a number of very simple societies in support of this point of view, and believes that war comes only with greater cultural development and an increase in the size of the groups. Elliot Smith (29) is substantially of the same opinion. It may be that these writers tend unduly to glorify the "noble savage" and to attribute all the ills of mankind to an interference with the state of nature, and we must certainly be careful not to exaggerate the purity and nobility of primitive man. There is no doubt, however, that there were many groups who were not at all warlike, and that therefore aggressiveness, at least to the extent that it expresses itself in war, does not satisfy our criterion of universality.

Wars do of course occur with great frequency, but they may usually be understood in terms of certain very definite motives. Obviously, most peoples will defend themselves when attacked. Clearly too, they will fight for food and in many cases for plunder. Examples of this type of warfare are numerous. As Bunzel (30) indicates, war raids for profit are characteristic of many primitive societies; even the peaceable Zuñi formerly conducted raids on the sheep of their Navajo neighbors. The Crow raided on horses, as this was their favorite form of wealth, and a stolen horse was the only acceptable bride gift. Among the Kiowa, the whole economic system hinged upon warfare, the objective of which was the acquisition of horses; the enemy was killed only when it was absolutely necessary. In parts of West Africa slave-raiding was one of the main causes of war. Hobhouse and his associates (25) found also that in forty or more peoples, where marriage by capture occurred, the possession of women was the direct object of a warlike raid.

War has often been due to religious causes. Eating a dead man was interpreted by many peoples as giving the conqueror his virtues. Among the Yoruba hearts were regularly sold in order to give courage, and the procuring of them often led to battle. In Aztec Mexico religious factors were responsible for the major part of aggressive behavior. One of the important beliefs was that the gods, particularly the Sun, would die if deprived of food, and the only satisfying nourishment consisted of human hearts. The victim of the sacrifice was identified with the god, and his killing and eating meant a resurrection of the god and the renewal of his strength. There was a Mexican legend to the effect that the gods themselves had formerly been sacrificed to the Sun in order to endow him with strength to do his work, and they bequeathed the duty to the human representatives, directing them to fight and kill each other to provide the necessary food. There was almost perpetual warfare with the neighboring Tlaxcalans for the sole purpose of obtaining captives to serve as sacrificial victims (*31*).

When the great temple of Huitzilopochtli was dedicated in 1486, the chain of victims sacrificed on that occasion extended for the length of two miles. In this terrible massacre the hearts of no less than 70,000 human beings were offered up. . . . These victims were nearly always captive warriors of rival nations. . . . (*32*, p. 41.)

Among the Wyandot Indians it was believed that an increase in the size of the clan would please the animal god from which it was descended. Every effort was made to keep the clan full, that is, to keep in use the complete list of names belonging to all. For this purpose war was carried on in order to secure women and children, and occasionally men for adoption. Connelley (*33*) writes:

The old Wyandots have often told me that their tribe made war on the Cherokees for the express purpose of securing women and children with which to make good the wasting clans. To allow a clan to become extinct was sure to call down the displeasure of the animal-god for which the clan was named and from which it was supposed it was descended (p. 237).

The glory motive, or the quest for prestige, is one of the most frequent causes of aggressive behavior. Head hunting, for example, although sometimes the result of religious practices, may also be due to the intense desire for a trophy which will elevate its possessor to a higher position in the community. Among the Asaba on the Niger River a man receives the honorary title of Obu if he has done a brave deed, and he most clearly earns this title if he has killed another man (*34*). In parts of New Guinea a youth must have "fetched a head" before he may be counted an adult, and the badges of distinction for warriors depend on the number of lives taken (*35*). Distinguished Masai warriors had the right to wear bracelets and bells. Among the Bagobo of the Philippines a man's clothing indicated his status, which was determined by the number of deaths for which he was responsible (*36*).

Among the Plains Indians the desire for military renown was hypertrophied. The Crow, for example, regarded four events as honorable and as conferring the title of chief upon the warrior—(1) cutting loose and stealing a horse picketed in the camp of the enemy, (2) taking an enemy's bow or gun in a hand-to-hand encounter, (3) striking "coup"—touching an enemy with a weapon or with the hand, and (4) leading a victorious occupation or attack. A man's standing was proportional to his war record, and at tribal gatherings he recounted his exploits and was honored by his fellows. Warriors often courted death in foolhardy adventures, and a coward was the object of supreme contempt (*36*). In Plains Indian warfare in general, killing an enemy was relatively unimportant; the bravest act was to count coup by touching or striking a living unhurt man without killing him. It was an evidence of bravery to go into war without any weapon that could harm the enemy at a distance, and the most courageous warrior was the one who was armed only with a coup stick. This does not mean that economic motives played no part, since booty was also the frequent reward of the warrior, but there can be no doubt that the added prestige concerned him most.

It should be pointed out further that when primitive peoples do fight they seem not to be giving expression to a spontaneous and uncontrolled pugnacious drive, but rather to a form of behavior which is regulated and modified by social conventions. In general, primitive warfare was not very destructive of human life and the casualties were frequently insignificant. When two groups of Australian aborigines fought, the battle was over as soon as one warrior on either side had been killed. Sometimes the first wound ended the combat. Sumner and Keller *(35)* state that conflicts among primitive people were generally brief and relatively bloodless. "A savage would stand aghast before the wholesale slaughter of civilized warfare, and beside some of its methods his own are those of a gentleman" (Vol. I, p. 370).

As a matter of fact, war was really in many cases a sort of duel or game, and the attitude toward it was frequently sportsmanlike. It is said that the Arkansas Indians once gave a share of their powder to the Chickasaw with whom they were at war; an Algonquin tribe refrained from pressing an attack upon the Iroquois when it was pointed out that night had fallen. Australian tribes have been known to provide unarmed Europeans with a set of weapons before attacking. The Maori are reported to have filled canoes with food for their hungry enemies so that they might fight on more equal terms. On the other hand, sudden raids without any warning are by no means unknown in primitive warfare.

Quarrels Between Individuals. William James *(37)* once spoke of a "moral equivalent for war." There are many primitive communities which have worked out some such equivalent, particularly in the case of quarrels between individuals. The Indians of the Northwest Coast settle disputes by means of the institution of the potlatch. If two men have a quarrel one of them may give a potlatch or feast, at which the aim is to give away or destroy as large an amount of property as possible. His rival is humbled as a consequence and regarded as having lost status in the community until he can do likewise. A Kwakiutl chief once said, "The White man fights with his hands, but we fight with property" (38). This fighting with property may also take place under much more informal conditions. There is a story to this effect told of the Tlingit of Alaska. "Two women were quarreling. In a rage one of them said to the other, 'I'll shut you up!' At that she rushed into her house, came out with both hands full of silver money, and scattered it to the crowd that was watching the proceedings. This did shut the mouth of her opponent as she could not do likewise" (39, p. 95). Goldman (40) reports a case among the Alkatcho Carrier Indians in which a man had been insulted by being placed in a position of inferiority at a feast. He went out with his relatives, returned with a number of articles which he presented to his host, thereby humbling him and wiping out the insult.

A particularly interesting method of settling a quarrel is reported for various groups of Eskimos, from the Aleuts at one geographical extreme to the Greenland tribes at the other. An Eskimo who has suffered some injury may compose a satirical song in mockery of his enemy and challenge him to a public singing contest. The village group assembles, and the two contestants take turns mocking each other to the best of their ability. The spectators decide the victor. Sometimes this is not possible until the contestants have been recalled many times.

One example of this Eskimo "duel" may be of interest. Eqerko had married the divorced wife of Marratse. The marriage reawakened the old love and jealousy of Marratse, who challenged his rival to a singing contest. Marratse sings:

> Words I shall split
> little sharp words, like wood splinters
> from under my axe.
> A song of olden days
> a breath of the ancestors.
> A song of longing

for my wife.
A song that brings
forgetfulness.
A cheeky braggart
has stolen her.
He has tried
to belittle her.
Miserable wretch
who loves human flesh.
A cannibal
from famine days.

Eqerko answers:

Cheek which amazes one!
Laughable fury
and sham courage.
A song of derision
which proclaims my guilt.
You want to frighten me!
Me who defy death
with indifference.
Hei!   You sing to my wife
who once was yours.
Then you were not so worthy
of love.
While she was left alone,
you forgot to exalt her
in song,
in challenging, fighting
song.
Now she is mine,
nor will she ever be visited
by song-making, false lovers,
abductors of women
in strangers' tents (*41*, pp. 97-99).

These examples indicate that aggressiveness, whether or not
it has an innate basis, may be modified by the culture in many
ways.   It may be stimulated in one society and relatively lacking in another.   It may arise as the result of any one of a
number of different causes.   It may express itself in violent
physical combat or in a socially regulated contest in which no

one is harmed. There is no justification, therefore, for the
attempt to explain any specific type of aggressive behavior on
the ground that it has a biological basis. To the question as
to whether war is inevitable because of the existence of such
an aggressive instinct, the ethnologist and the social psychologist have reason to give a categorical negative. War is an
institution, and must be explained in relation to the whole
social structure in which it occurs. After a somewhat similar
survey of the pertinent material, Sumner and Keller (35) come
to the conclusion that "There is no 'instinct of pugnacity.'
What there is is a set of life conditions demanding adjustment" (Vol. IV, p. 369).

To the more specific question as to what does cause war in
our society, it is not an easy matter to give a definite answer.
There is a growing conviction backed up by a large amount
of concrete evidence, that economic factors play by far the
most important part. There is also within our culture a
marked development of the sentiment of patriotism, which
easily leads to a supernationalism committed to the ideal of
expansion and aggrandizement for one's own people. It is
certainly no accident that in the Fascist countries an attitude
of almost religious adoration of the Fatherland has been accompanied by a greater readiness to resort to war. It may
be that this too is to be explained on an economic basis, but
whatever its origin, the cult of nationalism is a phenomenon
which predisposes to war. In general we may say with certainty that whatever may be the causes of war, they are rooted
in society and not in human nature.

In the writings of the psychoanalysts the notion of an aggressive instinct—sometimes called the death instinct—has
been revived in a somewhat different form. The Freudians
believe that there is in all of us an unmistakable, though often
latent, aggressiveness. This may express itself during infancy
in the hostility against the father; later it may be directed
against a whole group. It is stimulated and aggravated by the
controls and inhibitions which society imposes upon the individual, and it develops in him the desire to "get even." War

may furnish a socially approved outlet for this aggressiveness, and may therefore be welcomed by a substantial proportion of the community. One writer (*42*) states that during a long process of sublimation the anger and resentment of a child toward the father becomes successively directed upon various substitute objects.

In some cases the sublimation may be carried on and on until at last the hatred becomes directed upon an object that the whole community agrees in disliking. What more likely object is there than "the enemy," who thus fulfils the extremely important function of providing intense expression for the repressed father-hate of childhood? The desire to "punish" the enemy then becomes a consuming passion, and a harmless citizen becomes a fanatical supporter of a ruthless war policy (p. 129).

Other psychoanalysts stress the fundamental character of aggressiveness without such direct reference to father-hatred.

We shall return to this theory later in the discussion of group conflict as expressed in the phenomenon of race prejudice. At this point it may suffice to say that the Freudian explanation of war is definitely inadequate. Perhaps the best disproof of the theory is to be found in the fact that in every modern war the number of those who volunteer for service (and who may therefore be expressing this latent aggressiveness) always represents a small minority. Every large nation has had to depend upon some form of conscription or draft to form its armies. Aggressiveness, whether overt or latent, is apparently far from universal and must be stimulated by every artificial means at the disposal of governments and army staffs and propaganda experts. Aggressiveness as an end in itself is of no help as a principle of explanation, either in the form of one of McDougall's instincts or in the more recent formulation of Freud and his followers. It should be added that the recent statements by certain psychoanalysts, particularly Horney (*43*) and Kardiner (*44*), lay less emphasis upon the innateness and inevitability of aggressive behavior and more upon the socially-determined conflicts and strains which lead to violence.

We may conclude that aggressive behavior shows continuity with animals, that it has an indirect though probably no direct physiological basis, and that in one form or another it has a wide distribution. The exact nature of its expression varies from one group to another, and no particular form of aggressiveness, e.g., war, may be regarded as inevitable. Social factors determine the amount, the nature and to a large extent the very existence of aggressiveness.

ACQUISITIVENESS

The phenomenon of acquisitiveness may with considerable justification be regarded as central to the social structure of the Western world. It is probable that the larger number of our institutions are to be understood only in connection with acquisitive behavior. As we noted in the preceding section, the institution of war may be at least partly explained from this standpoint. It becomes of prime importance therefore to analyze the nature of this phenomenon from both ethnological and psychological points of view.

The problem of variations in acquisitive tendency was noted by W. H. R. Rivers (45), who in a great deal of his work applied ethnological categories to the understanding of psychological behavior. He took the position, which is in complete agreement with our own, that only that behavior may be regarded as instinctive which is common to mankind in general. He then analyzed the attitudes toward property among the people of Melanesia, and reported that there are a great many objects, particularly those made by the united efforts of the community, which are regarded as owned in common. A canoe, for example, is the common possession of the group, and land though individually cultivated is always common property.[4] There are rules concerning the use of produce taken from land which has been cultivated by others, and disputes do not arise. Even those objects like weapons and uten-

---

[4] It may be noted here that whereas primitive groups differ widely from one another in the distinctions made between private and common property, it is rare for land to be owned outright by an individual.

sils produced by an individual and regarded as his own are used by others much more frequently than would be the case in our society. Rivers concludes: "Melanesia shows that the instinct of acquisition in the interest of the individual can be so greatly modified in response to gregarious needs that it practically disappears or only appears under special circumstances" (p. 272).

If it "practically disappears," should we still speak of it as an instinct? Since Rivers himself applied the criterion of universality and found it not to be satisfied by his Melanesian data, it would have been more reasonable to question the instinctive nature of the phenomenon. This is precisely what is done by Beaglehole (46), who has written the best analysis of this whole question. In his introduction to a very careful survey of the pertinent literature, he writes:

That, in general, my conclusions are not favorable to the acquisitive instinct theory I should perhaps state at the outset. The biological facts are too complex to be explained away in terms of an innate acquisitive tendency. One is sometimes tempted to wonder how many more of McDougall's instincts would survive an equally rigid biological examination! (p. 28).

Beaglehole begins with an examination of the evidence for acquisitive behavior among various animal species, from insects up to anthropoids. His general conclusion is that although acquisitive behavior is found in considerable frequency it is to be explained not as an end in itself, but as a means of satisfying the more fundamental needs of the organism. Objects are appropriated when they are required for some specific purpose. The fundamental forms of acquisitive behavior have to do with the demand for food, for a mate, for a nest or territory. Most cases of acquisitiveness among animals are due to the operation of the more powerful drives of hunger, sex and care of offspring.

An exception to the above is noted in the behavior of certain birds like the magpie and the raven, who apparently collect objects for their own sake. Beaglehole's explanation of this phenomenon is not entirely satisfactory. He believes that in the case of these intelligent birds, their curosity and interest are easily aroused by bright portable objects. "Curiosity rather than a blind desire to collect is the motive of their behavior" (p. 119). In the meantime, curiosity has not been established as a "dependable motive," and until we have subjected it to the same critical analysis which Beaglehole has directed toward the concept of acquisitiveness, we can hardly use it as a principle of explanation.

As far as our first criterion of dependability is concerned, namely, continuity with lower animal forms, we conclude that such continuity undoubtedly exists. With a few rare exceptions, however, the acquisitive behavior of animals may be shown to be subordinate to other apparently more fundamental drives.

On the physiological side we can find no basis whatsoever for acquisitive behavior, except in the indirect manner referred to in the preceding paragraphs; that is to say, to the extent that acquisitiveness is subordinate to the hunger drive as it clearly is in the case of squirrels, for example. The hunger contractions might then be regarded as the visceral basis of the behavior. It is clear, however, that we have here an organic basis for hunger and not for acquisitiveness, and it seems safe to conclude in general that our second criterion is definitely not fulfilled in this case.

The question of the universality of acquisitive behavior has already been mentioned in connection with Rivers' analysis. There can be little doubt that culture may determine any degree of emphasis on the principle of private ownership, from its almost complete absence in one society to its all-pervasiveness in another. It was formerly believed, largely as the result of the work of Morgan (47), that primitive peoples were communistic and that there had been a gradual evolution from that condition to our present one of private property. This evolutionary scheme is no longer taken seriously by the majority of ethnologists. In the Torres Straits Islands, for example (48), private property was present in an extreme form.

Every rock and water hole had its owner, the only piece of common land being the village street. There were, however, many societies in which the economic system could be described as partial or complete communism.

Attitudes Toward Property. One example of a society in which the essentials of life are communally owned is to be found in the people of Lesu (*49*). In this Melanesian group there is abundance of land and no private ownership of it, nor are there any private fishing or hunting rights. Food may be obtained by a moderate amount of industry, shelter is easy to provide, and clothing is so scanty that it presents no problem. There is a certain amount of private property in connection with ornaments, implements of work, ceremonial currency, pigs and knowledge. Everyone lives in about the same style and there is no poverty. The private property that does exist in this community allows a man to make elaborate rites for his dead ancestors and so gain prestige for himself. Wealth is not hoarded, but is always being put in circulation by these frequent ritual feasts. Old people are well looked after by the community and have no need to save anything. Powdermaker describes the economic organization as well-integrated and as providing adequately for the needs of all the members of the community. The underlying social forces are the principle of reciprocity, the desire for prestige, respect for the old, and a closely-knit kinship system—these take the place of any individual competition for the necessities of life, and the result is security for all. In this system even the lazy man is not allowed to starve, but he has no importance in the community, no influence in discussion; it is difficult for him to secure a wife, he is unable to give big feasts and he lacks prestige. This is admitted to be a serious handicap, and it is a rare individual who will not do the work which is ordinarily required.

After a survey of the economic organization of a large number of primitive societies, Goldenweiser (*41*) concludes that complete communism is rare if not entirely absent, and that the theory which regards primitive communism as a prelude to the individual ownership of later history must as a consequence be rejected.

It contains, however, the germ of a truth, to this extent: in modern Western society, individual ownership has, as we know, acquired a significance and a role far beyond the importance of this institution among most primitives. . . . On the other hand, ownership of the essential articles needed for life or of the territories from which these are derived, in other words, just those things which in later times came to represent the most coveted of individual property, constitute among primitives the prerogative of the group: what is needed and used by all is held in common (pp. 148-149).

Even if complete communism, therefore, is never achieved, we may still say that many societies show a great deal more communism than our own, and it is clear that any insistence upon the psychological inevitability of economic competition to the extent that we know it is unwarranted. It should be added that the present Russian system, while its final form is as yet uncertain, at least indicates the possibility of a marked diminution in the acquisitive spirit common to the rest of the Western world.

For primitive man in general it has been suggested (46) that objects acquired or made by personal exertion are regarded as private property, whereas those acquired or made through the combined labor of a group are usually the common property of the individuals forming that group. There are, however, numerous exceptions. Among the Siberian tribes as well as among the Eskimo the seal or the whale killed by an individual was still divided with the other members of the community. The Eskimo had in addition the interesting rule that if one man borrowed something from another and failed to return it, nothing was done about it. The assumption was that the borrower needed it more and that the lender must have a surplus if he was able to part with it in the first place.

Among the Kaingang Indians of Brazil (50) when a hunter brings down a tapir he neither keeps the meat nor distributes it. He gives the whole animal to a close relative, who butchers it, giving some to the hunter, some to the other members of the camp, and keeping the greater part for his own use. The cleverest hunter has only slight economic advantages, since in the long run the product of the hunt is shared evenly.

Among the Arapesh also, it is not true that what a man acquires with his own hands belongs to him alone (*51*). The society has a system of exchanges and reciprocity, rather than one in which every man works for himself. An Arapesh man hunts only to send most of his kill to his mother's brother, cousin or father-in-law. "The lowest man in the community, the man who is believed to be so far outside the moral pale that there is no use reasoning with him, is the man who eats his own kill—even though the kill be a tiny bird, hardly a mouthful in all" (p. 29).

One other economic attitude of the Arapesh deserves a word of comment. They are very closely attached to their ancestral lands, but they do not conceive of themselves as owning the lands; rather they belong to the lands, and they feel none of the proud possessiveness of owners.

On a neighboring hilltop, the village of Alipinagle was sadly depleted. In the next generation there would not be enough people to occupy the land. The people of Alitoa sighed: "Alas, poor Alipinagle, after the present people are gone, who will care for the land, who will there be beneath the trees? We must give them some children to adopt, that the land and the trees may have people when we are gone." Such generosity had of course the practical consequences of placing a child or so in a more advantageous position, but it was never phrased in this way, nor did the people recognize any formulations based upon possessiveness about land (p. 18).

In this case, however, the difference between the Arapesh attitude and our own seems to be a matter of phrasing rather than a real difference in behavior.

Differing attitudes toward private property are illustrated in the experience of Rivers, who reports that after he had questioned his Melanesian subjects about their various customs, one of them put a question to him. He asked what Rivers would do if he found a sum of money which did not belong to him. Rivers answered that if he could not discover the rightful owner, he would naturally keep it for himself. When the Melanesians learned that he would not divide it equally with other members of his group, they were greatly disappointed at his evident greediness. It might be added that stinginess in any form is one of the greatest crimes among Melanesians, as it is among many other primitive peoples.

We noted above that in the case of animals the acquisition of property is usually subordinate to some other motive. The same holds for man, although of course the motives are quite different. The desire for prestige is undoubtedly one of the most significant in this connection. Among the Trobrianders, for example, food was collected not only for use as nourishment, but for purposes of display. This food was placed in large storehouses in such a way that through the openings others might see how much the owner had been able to acquire. Prestige rose and fell according to the amount. It was the greatest insult to say of someone that he was a "man with no food" (52). The possession of hunting trophies, of badges and ornaments testifying to the valor of the possessor, are all easily understood on the basis of the prestige motive. The most striking instance of the determination of property attitudes by the desire for prestige is undoubtedly found among the Indians of British Columbia and the Northwest Coast in general. Reference has already been made to the institution of the potlatch which centered upon the ability of the host to give away or to destroy a large amount of property. There was a tremendous, one might almost say an hypertrophied interest in property, but not in acquisition; property was merely a means to an end, that end being prestige. It is true that the property given away had to be returned later, often with about one hundred percent interest (38), but the primary consideration was clearly prestige, and was so understood by the Indians themselves. The fact that the most valuable property was so often destroyed or "thrown into the fire" without any possibility of concrete return, testifies to the correctness of this interpretation. Here, even more than in Melanesia, the greatest social sin was keeping all of one's property, and the man who gave no potlatches had no standing in the community. It is only fair to point out that in our own society as well some form of "conspicuous waste," as Veblen (53) long ago insisted, may have a definite prestige value, and may therefore constitute an important motive in the acquisition of property. With us it is secondary, however, whereas for the Kwakiutl and other Northwest tribes it represents the very core of the social and economic structure.

Among the herders of South Africa, the acquisition of large amounts of property may best be understood in terms of prestige. The man who owns great flocks usually puts them to no economic use whatsoever. He needs for his family only a fraction of what he possesses, and he might profitably dispose of the remainder in return for something else. This however he refuses to do, because his status depends on the size of his herd. "As a wealthy and successful herder, he is a great and admirable man, envied by those less fortunate. But this is where the matter ends. From the economic standpoint the whole business represents little but waste of energy and effort; but our standpoint is not that of the Africans" (41, p. 153).

The prestige motive played a similarly important part in certain of the economic practices of the Comanche (20). A leader of a war party could theoretically keep what he wanted, but he rarely kept more than a small share. It was generally believed that success in war was due to the leader's "medicine." If the leader kept the bulk of the spoils, this was confession that he felt his power was leaving him. The selfish leader thus lost prestige, and would have difficulty getting men for his next war party. If he gave freely, it was apparently because he knew that his medicine was strong, and his prestige rose accordingly. In this case if he had any marked acquisitive tendencies, they would have to be subordinated to his desire for status among his potential followers. It may be argued that the acquisitive drive is really primary here and that the leader is merely renouncing it temporarily for a later gain. It appears more likely, however, that the principal motive is the desire for prestige.

A recent analysis of acquisitive behavior in our own society regards it as motivated principally by some form of self-assertiveness.

Wherever acquisitiveness does appear it is not primary, as an instinct must by definition be, but secondary. . . . It is noteworthy that the fundamental, and therefore universal, human tendency of which it is but a particular expression, is the desire for pre-eminence, dominion, approbation, and the obverse of these, the eagerness to escape the contempt of one's fellows (54, p. 311).

Freeman believes that such apparently opposed forms of behavior as destruction of property on the one hand, and accumulation on the other, are both to be understood on the basis of a common psychological factor underlying them, namely, the desire for prestige or pre-eminence. Whether this desire for prestige is in its turn instinctive, he does not attempt to decide. "We may regard it as an instinct or not, just as we please, so long as we recognize that it is *prior* to and more fundamental than acquisitiveness. It is quite likely that it, too, is not an instinct. . . ." (p. 319) We shall return to this problem in a later section.

William James (55) also saw property in our society as an extension of the personality—as giving a sort of increase in psychic stature.

It is clear that between what a man calls *me* and what he simply calls *mine* the line is difficult to draw. . . . In the widest possible sense . . . a man's Self is the sum total of all that he can call his, not only his body, and his psychic powers, but his clothes and his house, his wife and children, his ancestors and friends, his reputation and works, his land and horses and yacht and bank account. All these things give him the same emotions. If they wax and prosper, he feels triumphant, if they dwindle and die away, he feels cast down—not necessarily in the same degree for each thing, but in much the same way for all (Vol. I, pp. 291-292).

It must be added, however, that this relationship between a man and his property is important only as a result of the folkways of the group. It is because a society attaches significance to property that a man feels his Self to increase and decrease with his possessions.

In the case of many primitive peoples this intimate connection between a man and what he owns is carried even further as a result of magical and religious ideas. It is stated that for the native Australian, property is so charged with the owner's personality that when changing camp a man may leave his valuable stone utensils lying about the ground, since he is absolutely sure of finding them whenever he returns. The other members of the group will regard these objects as bound to their owner so closely that they would not think of appropriating them. Similarly, land belonging to one Australian group was never taken by another, since it was the home not only of a people, but also of the spirits of their ancestors, and therefore could not possibly be used by anyone else. The Maori also recognized a similar identification with the land on which they lived (46).

It is sometimes argued on the basis of economic behavior in our society that some form of acquisitiveness in the shape of a profit motive is essential to a system of trade and economic exchange. From this point of view it is interesting to note the many cases in which trade occurs with the profit motive conspicuously absent. In the Marquesas, for example, trade was carried on by the exchange of objects of equivalent value, and was phrased in terms of the exchange of gifts. The initiator of the deal visited the other and made him a gift with expressions of good will and respect. In later conversation, he mentioned his own need very casually. After a polite interval, the other made a return visit presenting him with an object of exactly equivalent value. To give too much would be ostentation; too little would mean that he deprecated the value of the original gift. Both were social errors showing that the offender was unfamiliar with polite usage, and exposed him to ridicule (20).

On the island of Lesu similarly there seems to be no profit motive. The usual objects of trade are pigs, which are almost always purchased in connection with some ritual feast. The man buying a pig holds up a string of *tsera,* or ceremonial currency, and makes a short speech during which the tsera are in full view of all the bystanders. Payment is always made in this public manner for two reasons—first, everyone has witnessed the transaction; second, everyone knows what has been paid for the object, and should the owner ever wish to resell it, he must get for it exactly the same amount. There is no buying or selling for profit. There is of course a real purpose to the exchange, since each person presumably gets what he needs at the time, but apparently no permanent gain or loss is possible (49).

Many other non-economic motives may play a part in behavior that we usually term economic. It is reported of the Malagasy, for example, that they are shrewd traders, but count the amusement of bargaining an integral part of their commerce. Linton (20) tells of bargaining with a native at Tananarive for a piece of cloth and closing with the merchant for about a fourth above the regular price. He then offered to buy the whole stock at the same rate, but his offer was promptly refused. The merchant explained that if he sold out he would be left with nothing to do. A somewhat similar story is told of a Chinese merchant, although the motive was different. A European, satisfied with the knife he had purchased, offered to buy the merchant's whole stock at the same price. The Chinese demurred, asking a proportionately higher price if he disposed of all his knives, explaining that they were his specialty and that if other purchasers asked for them, he would lose face if he no longer had them to sell. Here again a prestige motive is stronger than any desire for profit (56).

Within our own society similar examples are not lacking. A salesman is reported to have remarked, when offered a position paying a hundred dollars a week on condition that he keep his salary a secret—"What's the use of having a swell job, if I can't talk about it?" An expert carpenter engaged in building target floats for the gun practice of battleships, after seeing the destruction of his work, quit his job for one paying only half as much but where his products had a chance to last (57).

These instances from primitive as well as from our own culture show that Adam Smith's (*58*) classical concept of the "economic man" who was apparently interested only in getting as much as possible and paying as little as possible for it, is far removed from the real man studied by the ethnologists and the psychologists. It seems fair to conclude that any economic theory which is in harmony with the facts will have to pay considerable attention to motives which are not primarily in the economic sphere.

A further significant fact about the economic life of primitive peoples is the frequency with which the concept of property is attached to incorporeal objects. In the Andaman Islands utensils, such as cooking vessels, are treated as communal property. No such latitude holds, however, with regard to the songs composed on the occasion of a tribal gathering. A song that has been received with applause may be repeated by request at later gatherings, but irrespective of its popularity no one dares sing it except the composer himself. Similarly, the concept of "property" applies to magical formulae and incantations among the Koryak of Siberia, local legends among the Torres Straits islanders, rituals among the Nootka Indians, the right to plant sacred tobacco among the Crow and membership in military organizations among the Hidatsa. All of these things may be bought and sold and are therefore property in a real sense, even though they are not embodied in any material object. It has been suggested (*30*) that there are many examples among ourselves of "incorporeal property," for example, patents on inventions, words of songs and stories, the "good will" of a business establishment, etc. It should be kept in mind, however, that these constitute property because they may be translated into goods of a more material kind. No such transformation is necessary in the case of primitive incorporeal property, although it may also occur; a Kwakiutl Indian may pawn his name if he has no other way of paying his debts.

This raises the interesting problem as to whether, granting for the sake of argument that there is an acquisitive drive, this might be sublimated in many different ways. There might, in other words, be some sort of "moral equivalent" of acquisitiveness, to paraphrase William James' phrase concerning war. The particular form that the drive takes would then be determined by the culture patterns, even if the drive itself has some more basic significance. We have seen, however, that there is ample justification for questioning the reality of the drive itself, although there can be no doubt that in our own society it has been erected into a value which may dominate the behavior of many individuals.

Acquisitiveness in Children. The nature of acquisitive behavior has also been investigated by a study of the collecting tendencies of children. It has been argued that if such tendencies occur with great frequency, this would constitute an important argument in favor of the innateness of the drive. In 1900 Caroline F. Burk (*59*), working under the direction of G. Stanley Hall, made a survey of 1214 children in California between the ages of three and fourteen, and found that about 90% of them were making some sort of collection at the time. In 1927, however, Lehman and Witty (*60*) studied 5000 children in the Middle West between the ages of eight and twenty and found hardly more than 10% so engaged. At no age level were as many as 15% of the boys making collections at the time of the study. They explain the discrepancy between their results and those of Burk as due to a change in social patterning in the meantime. With new interests and different types of leisure activity, collecting simply became less popular.

Two years later, however, Whitley (*61*) received four thousand replies to a questionnaire sent to children from the ages of seven to eighteen and found that the great majority had made some sort of collection during the preceding period. Below the age of twelve the motive was apparently play; after that age, girls said that they kept their collections in order to look at them, boys because they wanted to show them to others, or because they thought they might need them. In spite of the frequency of the collections, the investigator does

not ascribe them to any collecting instinct, but points out that
there is a whole web of complex influences in which the child's
age, intelligence, amount of leisure, economic status, stimulus
by playmates and a number of other factors participate. In
this same connection, Murphy, Murphy and Newcomb (62)
stress the specificity of the collecting activity, and the consequent impossibility of explaining it in terms of any general
"collecting instinct." "The collector of stamps need not collect
newspapers or Japanese prints, as would be the case if he
were simply a man with a 'strong collecting instinct' " (p. 104).
In other words, the collections are due to interest, previous
experience, perhaps also the desire for prestige as well as the
enjoyment of the objects, and many other possible motives.

As far as primitive children are concerned, Margaret Mead
(14) reports that the Manus children of New Guinea made no
collections and did not pass through any "collecting stage" of
the type regarded by G. Stanley Hall as a necessary aspect of
development. She found no child under thirteen or fourteen
with any possessions except his canoe or the bow and arrow
which were furnished him by adults. He might be interested
in a new toy for a very short while and then seemed to have
no further use for it. It would be worth while to extend this
type of investigation to other societies and to note specifically
how the acquisitive tendency develops, how it differs in "communistic" and "capitalistic" societies, and how the child ab-
sorbs the economic practices of his community. It is probable
that the tendency to collect and to hoard would by no means
be universal, and that when it occurred it could be explained
by the general structure of the society.

In conclusion a word should be said about the Freudian explanation of acquisitive behavior. The Freudians, particularly
Ernest Jones (63), regard this behavior as an outgrowth from
the interest in the products of one's own body. The child is
said to be naturally delighted with these products and to be
anxious to play with them and to possess them as long as possible. His education and training reverse this primitive attitude of delight into one of disgust; furthermore, his desire to

retain the products of his body is thwarted by both physiological and social factors. There is a consequent sublimation of the interest, which now becomes attached to the accumulation of money and other socially acceptable objects. One writer (42) even goes so far as to explain both our own acquisitive society and its socialistic counterpart on this basis.

Anal retentiveness will be credited with giving us misers, thrift, our banking systems and capitalist, co-operativist and collectivist ventures in cheap production and marketing. . . . It also underlies the interest in manipulation and construction which is of an importance in industry at least comparable with the love of gain and which interests people in such things as Five-Year Plans, and in reconstructing our whole industrial order (p. 136).

This omnibus application of the theory probably goes far beyond the opinions of other psychoanalysts.

The Freudians believe that those individuals who have received a particularly repressive toilet training in their childhood develop also certain character traits, for instance, obstinacy, procrastination and parsimony, which may similarly be regarded as sublimations. This interpretation does not seem to the writer to be particularly significant, since there are so many children for whom such a primary interest in their bodily products cannot be demonstrated. Even if there are anal character traits of the type described, it is not very likely that all acquisitiveness is to be explained on that basis. In any case, the theory is capable of verification or disproof through field work in different cultures. A beginning in this direction has been made by Roheim (64), who finds that the complete naturalness of the excretory processes among the Australian Arunta is accompanied by an indifference to private property and a generous attitude to one's fellows. Comparable material must be collected from other societies if we are to determine whether or not the alleged relationship among the Arunta is more than a coincidence.

We may summarize by saying that for acquisitiveness the criterion of continuity with animal forms is satisfied, but that the acquisitive behavior of animals may almost always be explained on the basis of other, more fundamental motives; the criterion of a visceral or physiological foundation for the drive is not satisfied; the criterion of universality is similarly not satisfied. The conclusion seems clear that acquisitive behavior is not to be regarded as innate or instinctive, and that important though it may be for certain societies, its nature and extent are culturally determined. It has a moderate degree of dependability because of the structure of certain types of society.

SELF-ASSERTIVENESS

One of the tendencies regarded by McDougall as instinctive is the desire to assert oneself, to obtain standing and position in one's community, to achieve superiority. In the system of psychology developed by Alfred Adler and his followers, this tendency is not merely an instinct, it is *the* instinct—that is to say, it is the principal motive of behavior, and the one most frequently used as a principle of explanation.

The question of the existence among animals of a self-assertive tendency similar to that which has been postulated for human beings, is difficult to answer. There is ample evidence that the stronger males in many mammalian communities fight for leadership. The recent studies of social relationships among monkeys and anthropoids by Zuckerman and Maslow, and among birds by Schjelderup-Ebbe and Murchison, referred to in Chapter II, point to an apparent striving for dominance among these animal forms. Since this type of self-assertiveness usually means that the dominant animal obtains for himself special privileges with regard to food and the possession of females, it may be that the behavior is to be interpreted as a means to these ends. In his earlier work Maslow regarded dominant behavior as an end in itself, but in his more recent statements, he adopts an interpretation more nearly in line with this one.

There is no known direct organic or physiological basis for self-assertive behavior. Adler, however, has indicated the possibility of an indirect basis, which in his opinion explains the universality of this tendency. Self-assertiveness is in his interpretation a reaction to, or a compensation for, a feeling of real or fancied inferiority. In cases of organic defect, for example, there may be a strong compensatory reaction which makes up for the defect, and in some cases leads to unusually successful achievement in the same direction. The classical example is that of Demosthenes, who conquered his stuttering to become one of the greatest orators of all time. Most people do not have such a striking inadequacy to overcome, but there is one type of inferiority which no one may escape, namely, that of once having been a child. This may seem too obvious to mention, but for the Adlerian it has a definite significance. The feeling of inferiority in the child is built up out of three related groups of experiences: first, the feeling of helplessness, second, the feeling of being weaker than adults, and third, the feeling of dependency upon adults. Every child wishes to be "grown-up" and strives for superiority in order to remove his feeling of inadequacy. This striving thus has a universal organic foundation, and the habits set up in this manner continue to play an important part in the life of the individual long after the inferiority has been removed by the natural process of growth. Self-assertiveness becomes in this manner a universal phenomenon.

This ingenious analysis has a certain amount of plausibility. In any case there is little doubt as to the strength and the prevalence of this particular motive for behavior. In the preceding account of aggressive and acquisitive behavior, it was necessary on many occasions to refer to the desire for prestige as the underlying drive. "Counting coup" among the Crow, giving potlatches among the Kwakiutl, displaying food among the Trobrianders, collecting cattle and even children among the Bantu, may all apparently be explained on this basis.

The prestige motive is almost but not completely universal. There are at least two known communities among whom it plays no important part. One is the Zuñi of New Mexico (65, 66) who do not welcome evidences of outstanding ability or originality among their members. The best thing to be said about any individual is that no one ever hears anything about him. So far do they carry their negative attitude against individual superiority that if a man wins a race in their annual athletic contest, they do not permit him to run again the next year. A modest amount of prestige may be obtained by buying one's way into certain secret societies, or by learning a great deal of ritual material, but even this confers no great honor or merit. Competition in general is reduced to a minimum. For the neighboring Hopi, Kennard (67) has reported that the children play no competitive games. Similarly, Asch (68) states that the Hopi school children will not compete against one another, and that all of the efforts of the teachers to make them do so are unavailing. One teacher once tried the new method of lining them up against a blackboard with instructions to complete their sums as quickly as possible and to turn to the front as soon as they had finished. She observed that as each child finished, he looked surreptitiously along the line to see how far the others had advanced, apparently unwilling to turn around until the others were also ready. These children grow up without any incentive to compete, and self-assertiveness, at least in our sense, seems to be almost completely lacking.

The other group for which a similar lack of self-assertiveness has been noted is the Arapesh tribe of New Guinea (51). There are leaders, but it is assumed that no one really wants to be one. Those who are in a position of authority "have to plan, have to initiate exchanges, have to strut and swagger and talk in loud voices, have to boast of what they have done in the past and are going to do in the future. All this the Arapesh regard as most uncongenial, difficult behavior, the kind of behavior in which no normal man would indulge if he could possibly avoid it. It is a role that the society forces upon a few men in certain recognized ways" (p. 27). When his eldest son reaches puberty, the "big man" can retire from the active competitive life which he has had to lead and which the society assumes, usually correctly, to be eminently uncongenial and distasteful to him.

These examples may seem rather extreme, and it is true that few societies, primitive or civilized, have limited self-assertiveness to this extent. The analysis of co-operative and competitive behavior in a large number of different societies has shown (69), however, that there may be almost any degree of this tendency, varying from the co-operative, submissive behavior of the Arapesh to the highly competitive, violently self-assertive attitudes of the Kwakiutl. These variations are not always easy to explain, but for our present purposes the fact that they occur is more important than the factors which are responsible.

Our own society is perhaps not the most self-assertive in the world (the Kwakiutl, for example, are probably more extreme in this respect), but it certainly ranks near the top in the emphasis which it places on this motive. It seems likely that Adlerian psychology owes some of its success to the fact that it fits so well the patterns of our own particular social structure. This is the point of view of Dollard (70), who writes:

It seems to the writer that Adler's psychology could be characterized as peculiarly bound by our culture and as emphasizing in psychology the motive which is most characteristic of it. This is certainly a value which will recommend it to many observers, but it also imposes a limitation on its use as a generalized social psychology which must be adapted to use in cultures which do not exhibit our powerful status and money competition and which do not put such a premium on fighting (pp. 70-71).

The Status of Children. From this point of view there is an important problem which requires study in the field, that is to say, by actual investigation of children in many communities different from our own. As we have seen, Adler bases the universality of the self-assertive drive on the weakness and dependence of children. This dependence, however, while probably always present to some degree, is not equally marked everywhere. It has frequently been pointed out that primitive children are usually given much more freedom and much fuller control of their own activities than is the case in our community. Among American Indians, for example, it was usual to regard the child as completely master over whatever property had been given to him. If a White man wished to buy something that belonged to a small child, the parents would regard it as entirely the child's affair whether it should be sold or not, and what price it should bring. If the child did not wish to sell, that ended the matter. Linton (20) makes a similar statement with reference to the Tanala tribe of Madagascar and reports that he had to strike a bargain with a child of five in order to buy some of his toys for a museum collection. It is highly probable that this complete control over property reduces the feeling of dependence in the child, and in line with Adler's theory, it might as a consequence reduce the later tendency toward self-assertiveness. It may be added that the total period of "childhood" is shorter among primitive peoples, largely because the things they must learn in order to become full-fledged members of the community are so much simpler, and their economic problems so much easier of solution.

There is also an allied phenomenon to be found in primitive societies, namely, that children are rarely punished. We have already referred to the horror with which groups like the Eskimos, the Tahitians and others react to the habits of the Whites in this regard. This, too, will mean that the physical inferiority of the child will not be felt so keenly, and will not constitute such a great handicap. Blackwood (22) points out that among the Melanesians of Buka Passage, children are subject to little or no discipline. A child will take or be given anything he wants, even if it is dangerous and likely to hurt him. If a father tells his daughter to do something and she refuses, he does nothing about it. The society does not grant him the right to punish her for her disobedience. In this setting it is not likely that a child would feel his inferiority nearly so much as where he is forced to do the bidding of his elders.

Given this wide variation in the treatment of children by adults, and in the control which children may exercise over their own destiny, it would be important to discover whether there is any relationship between the amount of dependence in early life and the degree of self-assertiveness in the adult. The organic inferiority of the child may still make it possible to understand the prevalence of this self-assertive tendency, but if Adler is right, the compensation for it will be much greater in some societies than in others. It is quite certain, however, that over and above any Adlerian mechanism there is the important influence of the folkways which makes itself felt throughout the lifetime of the individual. In some societies, asserting oneself is simply "the thing to do"; in others, it is condemned.

Additional evidence of the "learned" character of competition and self-assertiveness is to be found in the fact that this tendency is absent in very young children in our own society. One investigator (71) found that she could not use children below the age of five in a study of the effects of praise and competition on persistence or cite the performance of other children to motivate them. The five-year-olds, however, were good subjects for this type of experiment. In another study (72) no evidence was found for the existence of competition at the age of two years, whereas at five years 75.4%, and at six years 86.5%, of the children responded to competition. This suggests that the child must be well "socialized" before the prestige drive, at least in its competitive aspect, plays an important part. It would be interesting to conduct similar studies in other societies.

There is one other standpoint from which the self-assertive tendency may be viewed, and which in the opinion of the present writer makes it most clearly understandable. It is obvious that in every society it is to a man's interests to be well regarded, to have relations with others that will make it possible for him to carry out those activities with which he is most concerned. As Malinowski (73) has pointed out, a man acts in conformity with the customs of his community, not as a result of the mystical strength of custom, nor because he fears punishment, but mainly because otherwise he would be left out of all the social and economic exchanges which are necessary for well-adjusted behavior. If this is so, it is clear that a man would wish to stand well with his fellows, to have their respect and approbation. If he can best obtain this approbation by success in war, as among the Indians of the Plains, that will be the goal of his self-assertive behavior; similarly, he will give potlatches if he is a Kwakiutl, and collect herds if he is a Bantu. On the other hand, if he is a member of the Zuñi community, he will refrain from doing anything spectacular or outstanding, since such behavior would bring him condemnation. Stated differently, this means that there is no tendency toward self-assertiveness as such, but there is for very practical reasons the need to be approved by others. Self-assertiveness then becomes the means toward the acquisition of as large an amount of such approval as is possible. It is obvious that in many cases, too great concern with such approval defeats its own ends.

The interpretation of the prestige drive as a means to an end is in agreement with the view of Blatz (74), based on his observations of young children, and particularly of the Dionne quintuplets. Dominance (as well as submission) is sought when it serves as an efficient method for gratifying a need.

To summarize, we have seen that dominant behavior or self-assertiveness does occur in animals, but probably in the interests of more fundamental organic drives; it has no organic basis except possibly the indirect one postulated by Adler, namely, the universal organic inferiority of childhood; it is widespread, but not universal, and shows great variations in degree. It is probably to be explained as due mainly to a desire for social approbation for practical and utilitarian purposes.

SELF-PRESERVATION

The so-called instinct of self-preservation is in a quite different category from the others which we have so far discussed. It might better be regarded as the general goal which many of the drives have in common. In other words, the hunger motive, pugnacity, flight, the need for rest and elimination of waste products, all contribute to the preservation of the individual. On the basis of biological evolution it is pos-

sible to understand why all existing species should have patterns of behavior directed to this end; if these patterns worked
in the opposite direction, they would obviously result in the
destruction of the individual and therefore of the species.
The same considerations hold for those forms of behavior like
sex and maternal care, which are directed to the preservation
of the species rather than of the individual.

On this basis one would expect those tendencies responsible
for self-preservation to be found throughout the animal kingdom, as of course they are. We may therefore regard our
first criterion as satisfied. As for an organic basis, this is to
be found in connection with the individual motives which play
a part in self-preservation, rather than for self-preservation
in general. There is obviously a physiological foundation for
hunger, thirst, fatigue, elimination and so on.

The question of the universality of this motive presents
special problems. It is of course rare for a group deliberately
to destroy itself, or to act for any length of time in a direction
hostile to the continuity of its existence. It does happen that
a military group may sacrifice itself in the interests of patriotism, as in the case of the Spartans at Thermopylae, and the
"suicide squads" of recent military engagements. It has also
been observed (75) that many groups of South Sea Islanders,
both Melanesian and Polynesian, have as a result of the encroachment of the Whites on their territory and their culture,
no longer any desire to keep alive. Many of these groups have
disappeared not as the result of any specific disease or infec-
tion or because their livelihood has been interfered with, but
apparently because they feel they have nothing left to live
for. A similar explanation has been given for the disappearance of the Tasmanians, a number of whom were placed on a
sort of reservation after their disastrous defensive against the
British, and who, in spite of being given all the sustenance they
needed, died out in one generation. It seems therefore that
on certain abnormal but by no means rare occasions a whole
group may in this manner "commit suicide." It should be
pointed out, however, that this is not the type of suicide in

which an individual does away with himself. It seems rather to be due to a failure to marry or to have children, out of a more or less conscious conviction that future generations would be destined to a life of unhappiness. The individuals preserve themselves, but they allow their community to die. Something of this sort seems to be taking place among the Jews of Germany today, with a considerable amount of individual suicide as well.

As has already been mentioned, in a recent criticism of the concept of "human nature" as something common to all individuals, J. F. Brown (76) points out that even self-preservation is not to be regarded as common-human irrespective of the social field, since a man may be led to commit suicide as the result of certain social and cultural factors. There is no doubt that cultures differ widely in their attitude toward suicide, and that its frequency will vary markedly from group to group. Suicide, therefore, is not to be regarded as exclusively, perhaps not even mainly, an individual abnormal phenomenon, but as one which also is under the control of custom and convention. In a recent survey of the prevalence and causes of suicide among primitive peoples, Dublin and Bunzel (77) show clearly the wide variations in the attitudes which prevail; in some regions it is unknown, in others it is common and fits into the general cultural pattern. Among the groups for whom no cases of suicide have been reported are the Yahgans of Tierra del Fuego, the Andaman Islanders, the natives of western and central Australia, and the Zuñi of New Mexico. At the other extreme the Kamchadals of Siberia commit suicide at the least apprehension of danger, being convinced that the future life is much happier than this one; a Cherokee Indian committed suicide because his face had been disfigured by smallpox; the Ojibway often killed themselves after capture or disappointment, and the Navajos upon the death of a loved one or as the result of jealousy. Among the Melanesians of Buka Passage (21), the reasons given for real or attempted suicide include the following—(1) the wife was angry and insulted him, (2) the husband beat her, (3) his wife refused him intercourse on the grounds that it was too soon after childbirth, (4) his father would not get him a wife, (5) someone stole his ceremonial currency, (6) he was angry with another man. There seems in general to be a close correspondence between the frequency of suicide and the attitudes toward it held by the community in general.

It should be added that the fate of the suicide after death is viewed differently in various societies, and this, too, undoubtedly helps to determine the frequency of this type of behavior. The Catholic attitude on this point is well known; the body of the suicide may not be buried in consecrated ground and the soul is punished in the after-world. A similar stigma is attached to suicide in many other societies. The Ossetes of Siberia believed that punishment followed after death, and buried the body of the suicide apart. The Kayans of Borneo were taught that the spirits of suicides remained poor and wretched. The Paharis of India said that such souls could not be admitted to heaven and hovered eternally between heaven and earth. For the Omahas, the soul of a suicide ceased to exist. The Ashanti of Africa decapitated the body, and believed that the headless ghost would wander in search of his head until his destined time had run out, when he would return to the world as a cruel spirit who would also come to the same end (77). It is obvious that these beliefs would have a deterrent effect upon any individual contemplating such behavior.

In all probability the culture which most encouraged suicide was that of ancient Japan, and the attitudes which developed have persisted in somewhat slighter degree to the present day. A typical example from history is a case reported by Brinkley (78): "Nobunagu caused so much solicitude to his tutor and showed so much indifference to his remonstrances that finally the tutor committed suicide—the faithful vassal's last expedient" (p. 474). As for modern Japan, the newspaper accounts of the Sino-Japanese conflict (1939) give many instances of Japanese who have committed suicide because they would not face the dishonor of capture or because they disapproved of some of the Japanese war measures, and one case of a non-combatant who left his insurance money to the army. Only a short time ago it was reported that a Japanese tennis player committed suicide because he felt that he could not adequately represent his country in the forthcoming Davis Cup matches.

In ancient Japan the cult of Bushido, a code of moral conduct practiced particularly by the samurai, demanded suicide under certain well-established conditions (79). The type of suicide prescribed, known as *seppuku* or *kappuku* and more popularly as *hara-kiri,* consisted of self-immolation by disembowelment. The bowels were regarded as the seat of the soul, and this form of suicide meant: "I will open the seat of my soul and show you how it fares with it. See for yourself whether it is polluted or not." Death was considered the solution to many complex problems, particularly those involving a question of honor; to an ambitious samurai a natural departure from life seemed colorless. Seppuku was not mere suicide, but a legal and ceremonial institution, a process whereby warriors could expiate their crimes, apologize for their errors, escape disgrace, redeem their friends, or prove their sincerity. None could perform it without the utmost coolness of temper and composure of demeanor. For a variety of causes, often from our point of view entirely unreasonable, many young men thus ended their lives, and there were at various times in Japanese history veritable epidemics of hara-kiri. Life was unimportant compared to the conventionally accepted meaning of honor. It is clear that in this case a motive which has its root in the fundamental nature of biological processes, namely the preservation of the self, may give way completely to an attitude which has purely social and cultural definition.

Self-preservation, therefore, is not a single "fundamental drive," but a group of them. At the same time there is probably a desire to preserve the self, apart from the contributing motives. It has itself no organic basis but is the goal of many motives which do have such a basis. In that sense it is com-

mon to all species of animals. Among human beings it may
be absent in whole communities under special circumstances,
and in the case of individuals it may be subordinated to other
motivating forces. In spite of its biological nature, therefore,
it may within certain limits be controlled by the folkways of a
community.[5]

SUMMARY

In connection with the maternal drive, a distinction must
be made between the desire to have children (the pre-maternal
drive) and the urge to take care of them (the post-maternal
drive). The latter satisfies the criterion of continuity with
animals below man, and has a physiological basis; it is apparently found in all societies, though not in all individuals; the
phenomena of adoption and infanticide indicate the manner
and the extent of possible cultural patterning. In the case of
the pre-maternal drive, there is no evidence either for phylogenetic continuity or for a physiological basis; when children
are desired a variety of reasons, many of them practical in
character, may be operative. The attitude of the father appears to be determined mainly by the values which the culture
attaches to children, rather than by innate biological factors.

Aggressive behavior is found among many animal species.
It has an indirect physiological basis in terms of the "emergency theory" of emotional reactions. In the form of warfare, it is widespread, but by no means universal, and its occurrence may be explained as a means to an end rather than
as an end in itself. Aggressiveness between individuals may
be similarly explained, and is increased or decreased in amount
or altered in its expression under different social and cultural
conditions.

Acquisitive behavior shows some continuity with animals
below man, but has no definite physiological basis, and is far
from universal. It bears a close relation to the prestige drive,
as, for example, in the case of the potlatch and other culture

[5] The classical studies by Durkheim (*80*) and Halbwachs (*81*) discuss the
relation between suicide and the patterns of culture.

patterns. It occurs with some frequency not because of innate factors, but as a reflection of certain varieties of socio-economic structure.

Self-assertiveness, or the prestige drive, has certain parallels among animal groups, particularly in the establishment of a dominance hierarchy. On the physiological side, Adler has suggested with some plausibility that it may be due to a striving to overcome the inferiorities of early childhood, and it may therefore be regarded as having an indirect organic basis. It is found in the large majority of human societies, but shows marked variations in degree. It may be understood in large measure as an extension of the need for social approbation, which is required for the satisfaction of fundamental needs.

Self-preservation is really the end-result of a group of motives, such as hunger, thirst, the elimination of waste products, and so forth. These same motives are found throughout the animal kingdom. On the other hand, the phenomenon of suicide, occurring in most striking form among the Japanese, shows that in spite of the biological nature of the desire for self-preservation, it is still subject to variations under the influence of the folkways.

REFERENCES

1. Westermarck, E. A. *The History of Human Marriage.* 5th ed. 1921.
2. Warden, C. J., et al. *Animal Motivation.* 1931.
3. Young, P. T. *Motivation of Behavior.* 1936.
4. McQueen-Williams, M. "Maternal Behavior in Male Rats," *Science,* 1935, 82: pp. 67-68.
5. Rivers, W. H. R. *Report of the Cambridge Anthropological Expedition to Torres Straits.* 1904, vol. 5.
6. Man, E. H. "On the Aboriginal Inhabitants of the Andaman Islands," *J. Roy. Anthrop. Instit.,* 1882, 12: pp. 69-116, 327-434.
7. Hose, C., and McDougall, W. *The Pagan Tribes of Borneo.* 1912.
8. Thomas, W. I. *Primitive Behavior.* 1937.
9. Fortune, R. F. *Sorcerers of Dobu.* 1932.

10. Lowie, R. H. "Adoption, Primitive," *Encycl. Soc. Sci.*, 1930, 1: pp. 459-460.

11. Miller, N. *The Child in Primitive Society.* 1928.

12. Handy, E. S. C. "Polynesian Religion," *Bernice P. Bishop Mus. Bull.*, 1927, 34: pp. 1-342.

13. Bernard, L. L. *Instinct.* 1924.

14. Mead, M. *Growing Up in New Guinea.* 1930.

15. Hollingworth, L. S. "Social Devices for Impelling Women to Bear and Rear Children," *Amer. J. Sociol.*, 1916, 22: pp. 19-29.

16. Sumner, W. G. *Folkways.* 1907.

17. Stefansson, V. "Lessons in Living from the Stone Age," *Harper's*, 1939, 179: pp. 158-164.

18. Yerkes, R. M., and Yerkes, A. W. "Social Behavior in Infrahuman Primates," *Hdbk. Soc. Psychol.* (ed. by C. Murchison). 1935.

19. Malinowski, B. *Sex and Repression in Savage Society.* 1927.

20. Linton, R. *The Study of Man.* 1936.

21. Blackwood, B. *Both Sides of Buka Passage.* 1935.

22. Cannon, W. B. *Bodily Changes in Pain, Hunger, Fear, and Rage.* 1929.

23. Lafitau, J. F. *Moeurs des Sauvages Amériquains, Comparées aux Moeurs des Premiers Temps.* 2 vols. 1724.

24. Driberg, J. A. *The Lango.* 1923.

25. Hobhouse, L. T., et al. *The Material Culture and Social Institutions of the Simpler Peoples.* 1915.

26. Nansen, F. *Eskimo Life.* 1893.

27. Letourneau, C. *La Guerre dans les Diverses Races Humaines.* 1895.

28. Van der Bij, T. S. *Ontstaan en Eerste Ontwikkeling van den Oorlog.* 1929.

29. Smith, G. E. *Human History.* 1929.

30. Bunzel, R. L. "The Economic Organization of Primitive Peoples," *General Anthropology* (ed. by F. Boas). 1938.

31. Payne, E. J. *History of the New World Called America.* 1892-1899.

32. Spence, L. *The Mythologies of Ancient Mexico and Peru.* 1907.

33. Connelley, W. E. *The Wyandot Folk-lore.* 1899.

34. Parkinson, R. Notes on the Asaba People (Ibos), *J. Roy. Anthrop. Instit.*, 1906, 36: pp. 312-24.

35. Sumner, W. G., and Keller, A. G. *The Science of Society.* 4 vols. 1927.

36. Lowie, R. H. *Primitive Society.* 1920.

37. James, W. "The Moral Equivalent of War," *Pop. Sci. Mo.*, 1910, 77: pp. 400-412.

38. Boas, F. *Contributions to the Ethnology of the Kwakiutl.* 1925.

39. Jones, L. F. *A Study of the Thlingets of Alaska.* 1914.

40. Goldman, I. *The Alkatcho Carrier.* Unpublished MS.

41. Goldenweiser, A. A. *Anthropology.* 1937.

42. Hopkins, P. *The Psychology of Social Movements.* 1938.

43. Horney, K. *New Ways of Psychoanalysis.* 1939.

44. Kardiner, A. *The Individual and His Society.* 1939.

45. Rivers, W. H. R. "The Instinct of Acquisition," *Instinct and the Unconscious.* 1920.

46. Beaglehole, E. *Property: A Study in Social Psychology.* 1931.

47. Morgan, L. H. *Ancient Society.* 1907.

48. Haddon, A. C. *Report of the Cambridge Anthropological Expedition to Torres Straits.* 1904, vol. 5.

49. Powdermaker, H. *Life in Lesu.* 1933.

50. Henry, J. *The Kaingang of Brazil.* Unpublished MS.

51. Mead, M. *Sex and Temperament in Three Primitive Societies.* 1935.

52. Malinowski, B. *Argonauts of the Western Pacific.* 1922.

53. Veblen, T. *The Theory of the Leisure Class.* 1899.

54. Freeman, E. *Social Psychology.* 1936.

55. James, W. *The Principles of Psychology.* 2 vols. 1890.

56. Burgess, S. Personal communication.

57. Husband, R. W. *Applied Psychology.* 1934.

58. Smith, A. *An Inquiry into the Nature and Causes of the Wealth of Nations.* 2 vols. 1776.

59. Burk, C. F. "The Collecting Instinct," *Pedag. Sem.*, 1900, 7: pp. 179-207.

60. Lehman, H. C., and Witty, P. A. "The Present Status of the Tendency to Collect and Hoard," *Psychol. Rev.*, 1927, 34: pp. 48-56.

61. Whitley, M. T. "Children's Interest in Collecting," *J. Educ. Psychol.*, 1929, 20: pp. 249-261.

62. Murphy, G., Murphy, L. B., and Newcomb, T. M. *Experimental Social Psychology.* Rev. ed. 1937.

63. Jones, E. "Anal Erotic Character Traits," *J. Abn. & Soc. Psychol.*, 1919, 13: pp. 261-284.

64. Roheim, G. "Psychoanalysis of Primitive Cultural Types," *Internatl. J. Psychoanal.*, 1932, 13: pp. 2-224.

65. Bunzel, R. L. "Introduction to Zuñi Ceremonialism," *Bur. Amer. Ethnol.*, 1932, 47: pp. 467-544.

66. Benedict, R. F. *Patterns of Culture.* 1934.

67. Kennard, E. Personal communication.

68. Asch, S. E. Personal communication.

69. Mead, M., et al. *Cooperation and Competition Among Primitive Peoples.* 1937.

70. Dollard, J. *Criteria for the Life History.* 1935.

71. Wolf, T. H. "The Effect of Praise and Competition on the Persisting Behavior of Kindergarten Children," *Institute of Child Welfare Monograph,* University of Minnesota Press, 1938, No. 15.

72. Greenberg, P. J. "Competition in Children: An Experimental Study," *Amer. J. Psychol.,* 1932, 44: pp. 221-248.

73. Malinowski, B. *Crime and Custom in Savage Society.* 1926.

74. Blatz, W. E. "The Individual and the Group," *Amer. J. Sociol.,* 1939, 44: pp. 829-838.

75. Pitt-Rivers, G. H. L-F. *Clash of Cultures and Contact of Races.* 1927.

76. Brown, J. F. *Psychology and the Social Order.* 1936.

77. Dublin, L. I., and Bunzel, B. *To Be or Not To Be: a Study of Suicide.* 1933.

78. Brinkley, F. *A History of the Japanese People from the Earliest Times to the End of the Meiji Era.* 1915.

79. Nitobe, I. *Bushido: The Soul of Japan.* 1905.

80. Durkheim, E. *Le Suicide.* 1912.

81. Halbwachs, M. *Les Causes du Suicide.* 1930.

CHAPTER VI

THE DEPENDABLE MOTIVES (Continued)

SEX

THAT there is an innate or "instinctive" basis for sex behavior may probably be taken for granted. It is obviously a form of activity which is shared with all animal species above the very simplest forms. It has certainly an organic basis in the bodily changes which take place in the male and female organisms at the time of puberty and which prepare them for the act of reproduction. It is highly probable that even before adolescence, as the Freudians in particular have emphasized, there is a drive toward sexual manipulation and experimentation, presumably due to the special sensitivity of certain zones of the body, as well as to the stimulus of hormones active from early childhood. As Dollard (1) expresses it, it seems to be one of our cherished beliefs that the sex impulse emerges in adolescence; this is due in his opinion to the error of identifying sexual life with the capacity for reproduction. The frequency of pre-adolescent sexual play in many communities, the early development of interest in erotic books and pictures, as well as the sexual significance of Freudian mechanisms operating in early childhood testify to the appearance of the sex drive before it may be put to direct biological use.

Hooton (2) quotes Beaumarchais as saying, "That which distinguishes man from the beast is drinking without being thirsty and making love at all seasons" (p. 262). It is doubtful, however, whether there is a mating season among anthropoids; their sexual behavior is more or less continuous. As far as human beings are concerned, the organic basis is apparently the same in all groups. Crawley (3) expresses the opinion that the sex impulse is relatively weak among primitive as compared with civilized peoples, and cites as evidence for this view the difficulty in attaining sexual excitement among them without Saturnalian behavior. He believes also that there is a rutting season in the "lowest races" at the present time. This view may safely be dismissed on the basis of the mass of contrary information found in the ethnological literature.

As in the case of the motive of self-preservation, it may be said that the sex drive is universal in all cultures, but not in all individuals. Where it is absent, custom regards such individuals as abnormal, but as we shall see later, the concept of abnormality varies definitely from group to group, homosexuality, for example, being common in certain communities. The various religious orders which enforce chastity in their members testify to the possibility that the folkways may counteract this organic drive. That sex impulses often have considerable strength even under these circumstances is amply demonstrated by the stories of the temptations that beset the members of such groups. There are of course also individuals in whom the sex drive appears to be completely lacking, but this may usually be explained on the basis either of some organic defect or early negative conditioning. They represent exceptions which do not overthrow the rule that sex behavior has an organic foundation.

Even in the case of such an innate drive, however, the importance of cultural patterning may hardly be overestimated. Groups may differ, for example, in the importance which they attach to relations between the sexes. In our own society, it is usually regarded as the most important of all social relationships, and the source (even though the Freudians may exaggerate) of a great deal of our literature and art and other forms of creative activity. In other societies it may be taken rather more for granted, and relationships of a different order may receive greater emphasis. In China (4), for example, lyric poetry tended to celebrate the great and lasting friendships between men, rather than the romantic attachments between men and women; the latter relationship was by no means left out, but it was apparently less significant. Among the Comanche Indians, the most important social relationship was that of "brother-in-arms," a voluntary association with reciprocal rights and duties exactly defined, and with an emotional context deeper than all others. "It was to his brother-in-arms that a man turned first in any difficulty, and it was his brother-in-arms whom he saved first in time of danger" (5, p. 256).

The emotional attitude toward sexual matters varies widely. In the Western world, probably as the result of religious influences, the usual feeling about it, at least in public, is one of shame, although there has been a marked change in this connection in recent times. McDougall (6) believed that the feeling of shame was due to the proximity of the sexual and the excretory zones of the body, and that the disgust aroused by the latter was extended to include sexual matters as well. This explanation can have no universal significance, since there are many groups for whom neither sex nor excretion is associated with shame in any manner. The native Australians, for example, are completely "natural" about relieving themselves, and quite indifferent to the presence of others during the act. As for sex, although primitive cultures differ widely, the attitude is frequently one in which shame plays little or no part. In Buka (7), for instance, myths and stories with sexual incidents are told without any special comment, and are not made subjects of jest. Children's questions on these subjects are always answered directly, and there is no suggestion that such matters should not be discussed. There are taboos regarding sex, but there are taboos also regarding eating and conversing, and they are taken for granted in the same manner. In Lesu (8) children from about the age of four will imitate the sexual play of their parents. This is done openly, and the adults smile indulgently and regard it as natural. Children have full knowledge of almost everything pertaining to sex. There is only one rigid taboo in connection with it, namely, that there must be no sex play between children of the same moiety, that is, of the same subdivision of the tribe. "If this rule should be broken the children would be lectured, beaten, and thoroughly ashamed" (p. 85).

This attachment of shame to the tabooed relationships is paralleled by other variations in the situations giving rise to this emotion. In Buka, for example, the taboos regarding food appear to be much more serious than those concerned even indirectly with sex behavior. Two people who are "wagun" to each other, that is to say, in-laws of the same generation but of opposite sex, may not eat in each other's presence. If this cannot be avoided the woman must cover her face with a hood. A man may sleep in the same hut as his "wagun," but goes elsewhere for his meals, "thus precisely reversing the taboos observed among ourselves" (7, p. 65).

In Western society the emotion of shame is frequently associated with the exposure of the body, but it is easy to multiply examples from primitive peoples indicating their complete lack of concern on this point. There were many groups who went absolutely naked, or who wore clothing which did not cover those parts of the body which we regard it as modest to conceal (9). A feeling which with us is so strong as to appear "instinctive" may be entirely lacking in other communities. It is interesting in this connection to note the rapidity with which folkways may change, and the manner in which a former custom may come to be regarded with horror. In Buka, before the advent of the Whites, men wore no clothing of any kind, and women only a waist string of thin fiber, from which a bunch of leaves hung down in front, scarcely concealing anything. This is still true of certain of the mountain natives. When the ethnologist spoke to a woman in the village of Kurtatchi about it, the latter seemed quite horrified, and "hastened to explain that the Kanua people were only 'bush Kanakas' who did not know any better. Yet scarcely more than a few years ago they were following exactly the same fashion themselves" (7, p. 133).

The attitude toward pre-marital chastity in the woman shows similar variations. There were many groups among whom it was prized, others to whom it was a matter of indifference, still others to whom it was an actual drawback. Among the Bagesu, a Bantu people, "it is no disgrace to a young woman to become a mother before marriage, nor does it prevent her from obtaining a husband; indeed men like to know that a woman can bear children, and her fault thus rather adds to her value than detracts from it" (*10*, p. 171). Among the African Bushongo, the little girl remains with her parents until she is past puberty. "Then she is promiscuous until she has borne a child, when she goes to live with her husband, saying, 'Now I have passed my test and it will not be my fault if I do not give you children.' The child already born is left with her parents and regarded as theirs. No shame attaches to this" (*11*, p. 271). A Bontoc Igorot in the Philippines will not marry a girl until she is pregnant, because he wants proof that she is not sterile. If a girl should be deserted by the father of her child, her chances for a good marriage are better than if she had no child (*12*).

Throughout large parts of Melanesia and Polynesia promiscuity is permitted before marriage, and in many cases is accompanied by the rigid enforcement of chastity after marriage. In some groups, as for example the Trobrianders (*13*), unmarried girls are allowed as many affairs as they desire, but bearing an illegitimate child is a disgrace; Malinowski states that illegitimacy is rare, either because they have methods of birth control the nature of which he could not discover, or because the very fact of promiscuity is in itself a kind of contraceptive. In the island of Dobu, an affair may turn into marriage at the wish of the boy. The rule is for a boy at puberty to leave his parents' house at night and roam about until he finds a girl who will let him sleep with her. He prefers to sleep with a different girl every night to avoid permanent entanglement, but he must leave the girl's house before dawn. If he oversleeps and is caught publicly, he has to marry the girl, and so if and when he wishes to marry, he may deliberately stay later. It goes without saying that neither the boy nor the girl is condemned for this promiscuity. Here as elsewhere the line between right and wrong is culturally determined. On this point Lowie (*14*) makes an illuminating comment. "A Crow interpreter once twitted me with the indecency of the Caucasians who dare reproach the Indians with looseness of morals while themselves so shameless as to speak freely with their own sisters" (p. 99).

Closely related to the problem of sex behavior is the question of the standard of beauty, particularly with reference to women. It seems clear that what is sexually stimulating in one society may be a matter of indifference or even of disgust in another. There is, for example, a fatting-house for girls in Central Africa, where feminine beauty is all but identified with obesity. There at puberty a girl is segregated sometimes for years, fed with sweet and fatty foods, and her body is rubbed assiduously with oils. Her seclusion ends with a parade of her corpulence that is followed by her marriage to the proud bridegroom (*15*). The Batoka tribe in South Africa has the custom of knocking out the upper front teeth at the age of puberty. "This is done by both sexes; and though the under teeth, being relieved from the attrition of the upper, grow long and somewhat bent out, and thereby cause the underlip to protrude in a most unsightly way, no young woman thinks herself accomplished until she has got rid of the upper incisors" (*16*, p. 571). The people of Buka admire the effect produced by cicatrization; they say "that is a fine girl, she has marks all over her body" (*7*, p. 108). A servant of the king of Cochin China is reported to have spoken with contempt of the wife of the English ambassador because "she had white teeth like a dog, and a rosy color like that of potato flowers" (Waitz; see *17*, p. 31).

The phenomenon of romantic love, which with us represents the ideal if not the most frequent type of relation between the sexes, may in other societies be relatively unimportant. Even in Europe, as Linton (*5*) points out, it did not appear until the time of the thirteenth century troubadours, who though they glorified it, believed it to be impossible to married people. As late as the eighteenth century it played a small part in

European marriage. "All societies recognize that there are occasional violent emotional attachments between persons of the opposite sex, but our present American culture is practically the only one which has attempted to capitalize these and make them the basis for marriage" (p. 175). In most primitive societies such individuals are usually regarded as unfortunate, and the victims of these attachments are held up as bad examples. Linton goes on to say that their rarity in most societies suggests that they are psychological abnormalities to which our own culture has attached great value. It may appear strange to describe romantic love as an abnormality, but there is probably considerable truth in this notion. If, as George Bernard Shaw once said, the difference between one woman and another has been greatly exaggerated, our usual belief that one woman and that woman alone will be satisfactory as a marriage partner, must appear very odd to those groups who do not have the romantic tradition.

The prevalence of marriage by purchase among primitive communities illustrates the marked contrast between their attitude and our own. A girl in our society would feel forever ashamed if she were "bought and paid for"; where marriage by purchase is the prevailing form, she is proud of the price she brings. She would be despised if she cost nothing. It would mean that she or her parents regarded her as having so little value that she was willing to go to a man without a bride-price. There were many groups among whom this was the greatest degradation (18). An interesting example of a difference in attitude determined by the folkways is cited by Powdermaker (8). She states that when she described our own marriage customs to the natives of Lesu they were scandalized at the lack of payment for the bride, and asked how that could be a true marriage. They were almost equally shocked at the Continental custom of the bride's bringing a dowry. One native compared a Christian marriage without payment to the mating of pigs.

It should be made clear, however, that marriage by purchase does not permit a man to regard his wife as his own property in the same sense that inanimate objects are considered property. It is not the woman who is bought outright, but the privilege of using her body for the satisfaction of the husband and for the procreation of children by him. The woman still has rights of her own, and marriage by purchase is not in any way detrimental to her dignity. A man may not sell his wife to someone else, for example, nor may he treat her in any way he likes. Even where marriage is by purchase, the wife's family still retains a definite interest in her welfare and the right to insure that she will be treated properly. In Buka the regulations governing divorce of the wife, as well as the procedure to be followed on her death, show that the having of children is regarded as the most important aspect of wife-purchase. If a woman refuses to perform the duties of a wife, a man may divorce her and his money will be returned. If she has cause to divorce him, nothing is returned. If she dies without giving him a child, he will expect to be repaid unless he receives a sister in her place. If there is one child repayment is made in part. If she dies having borne more than one child no repayment is expected—"the husband has had his money's worth, so to speak" (7, p. 99).

Jealousy. The phenomenon of sexual jealousy has attracted considerable attention and opinions differ as to whether or not it is an inevitable concomitant of the sex relation (19, 5). Shand (20) defines jealousy as "that egoistic side of the system of love which has as its special end the exclusive possession of the loved object, whether this object be a woman, or other person, or power, reputation, or property" (p. 260). There is a great deal of evidence from primitive communities to show that such exclusive possession is by no means the rule, and apparently not even the goal of the relationship between the sexes. The wide prevalence of multiple marriage—in the form of group marriage, in which several husbands are married to several wives; or polygyny, in which one man has several wives; or polyandry, in which one woman has several husbands—is the best proof of this statement. Of these by far the most frequent is polygyny, and most reports agree that jealousy among the wives is a relatively rare occurrence. Driberg (21) states that among the Lango, a Nilotic African tribe, the women on the whole live in amity one with another. Jealousies are apt to occur if one wife thinks that the other receives undue favors or is preferentially treated in the matter of cultivation or gifts of food, and the husband may have to exercise considerable tact as a consequence. It is rare that any serious difference of opinion arises. "Indeed, instances are not wanting in which a woman, on growing old, of her own instances presses her husband to marry a younger and more attractive wife, and it is certainly true that the womenfolk would be the first to resent the institution of monogamy, as in a polygynous establishment, not only is the woman's work lessened, but in their husband's absence his wives avoid the solitude inherent in a monogamous union" (p. 155). In this community the women are treated with great courtesy and consideration, and they may if they wish prevent the husband from contracting a second marriage; it is said that this veto is rarely if ever exercised.

Among the Tanala tribe of Madagascar (5) the institution of polygyny is accompanied by a number of regulations which will appear strange to most of us. The first marriage is usually a love match. The second occurs three to four years later and in a large number of cases is instigated by the wife on the ground that there is too much work for her in looking after the fields and the children. The man and woman talk it over and decide on a second wife acceptable to both. When a man is detected in an affair with an unmarried woman his wives may insist upon his marrying her, on the principle that she should share in the labors if she has also a share in the privileges of marriage. When a man has three wives, each one has a separate house, and he spends one day with each wife in succession. If he spends one wife's day with another, it is adultery, and the slighted wife is entitled to divorce with alimony. If he really commits adultery in our sense, that is, with a woman to whom he is not married, it is the business only of the wife on whose day the offense was committed. In

other words, the issue is one of marital status rather than of
sexual jealousy.   There is always a tendency for the wives to
present a united front against the husband, and if one of them
is carrying on a love affair she can be certain that none of her
fellow wives will betray her.

In Lesu (8) marriage may be polygynous, polyandrous or
monogamous.   In the case of polyandry, the woman will sleep
alternately with her husbands and "there appears to be no
quarreling between the two men" (p. 227).   In this community also sexual life is not confined to marriage and it is the
socially accepted custom for a wife or a husband to have
affairs with a number of other people.   Either one if young
would be considered abnormal otherwise.   "A young married
woman without lovers would be in the same social position
as a young girl in our society who never has any beaux and
is never invited to parties" (p. 244).   In all cases of extra-
marital intercourse the man makes a payment of *tsera* or ceremonial currency to the woman, who hands it over to her husband.   The woman would consider it disgraceful if no money
were paid, since that would lower her prestige and position in
the community.   This is not a form of prostitution; a woman
does not sleep with her lover for the payment, but the payment is part of the relationship.   The husband accepts his
wife's children as his own and no disgrace is attached to illegitimacy.   Jealousy occurs, but it is exceptional.

Among the Kulus and other tribes in the Himalayas, polyandry occurs with some frequency, and is usually of the fraternal type, that is to say, a number of brothers have one wife
in common.   When all the brothers stay at home, the wife
usually bestows her favors on each of them equally in turn.
The house usually has two rooms, one for the wife, the other
for the husbands.   "When one brother goes into the wife's
room, he leaves his shoes or hat at the door, which is equivalent to the notice 'engaged'" (*Census of India;* see *17*, p.
119).   In the Jat tribe of the Punjab when women quarrel one
may say to the other, "You are one so careless of your duty

as not to admit your husband's brothers to your embraces"
(*22*, p. 86).

The phenomenon of wife-lending—the so-called "prostitution of hospitality"—is well known, and occurred in a large
number of widely scattered communities. Perhaps the most
familiar instance is that of the Eskimos, among whom it was the
custom for the host to lend his wife for the night and sometimes for longer periods to a guest toward whom he wished to
be gracious (*23*). It must be clearly understood that the wife
did not have the right to go to another man of her own initiative; this was adultery and was severely punished. This does
not mean, however, that the husband was jealous in our sense.
He apparently did not feel the need for exclusive possession
of his wife's favors. What he objected to was not any infringement on his sexual prerogatives, since he freely shared
these with others, but rather the infringement on his status
and property rights.

Linton (*5*) is of the opinion that sexual jealousy does have
some universal basis. He cites in support of this view cases
in which jealousy is theoretically outlawed but tends to crop
up on occasions in which the control by the folkways is temporarily in abeyance. In the Marquesan Islands, for example,
an unusual degree of sexual freedom is allowed both sexes before and after marriage. There appears to be little opportunity for the development of the notion of exclusive sexual
possession, since group marriage is the normal form and sexual
hospitality is commonly practiced. There are rarely any signs
of jealousy when the natives are sober. When they are drunk,
however, such jealousy frequently manifests itself and may
lead to numerous squabbles. These are considered breaches
of good manners and the participants are ashamed of themselves as soon as they recover. Among the Comanche an elder
brother would lend his wife freely to his unmarried younger
brother, and would expect the latter to return the compliment
after his marriage. This is interpreted by Linton as a voluntary restraint of jealousy, partly by the social approval of his
act, partly by his expectation of a return in kind. In both

these cases it is suggested that jealousy would develop if it were not for restraining influences.

The present writer is not prepared to accept this interpretation. The fact that jealousy does crop out on occasions even though it conflicts with the *mores* seems no proof of its innate universality. The prevalence of polygyny and polyandry, and the smoothness with which these institutions work in the large majority of instances, show that exclusive possession is not a necessary component of harmonious sex relations; the habit of wife-lending testifies in the same direction. It seems certain that only in some societies, notably our own, is the relation between the sexes regarded as ideally monogamous, and jealousy appears to develop principally in that context. Even in our own society there are many instances in which adultery would go unpunished and officially unnoticed, except that it has come to the attention of other people so that prestige and honor are also involved.

We may summarize the discussion of the sex drive up to this point. Sex has clearly an organic basis, and is also clearly common to animals and man. It is universal, with the exception that certain small groups and many individuals have voluntarily renounced sexual satisfaction in the interests of what they regard to be a greater value.[1] In spite of the innateness of the sex drive, the importance of cultural patterning may be seen in the varying emotional attitudes which it arouses; in the differing standards of beauty or perfection looked for in the sex partner; in the contrast between romantic love and a more matter-of-fact relationship; and in the many institutions which testify to the absence or at least to the relative unimportance of exclusive possessiveness or sexual jealousy. We turn now to another aspect of sex behavior which has sometimes been regarded as instinctive, namely the incest taboo.

The Incest Taboo. In every community known to us there are certain restrictions on the choice of the marriage partner. Usually, as we shall see, these restrictions apply par-

---

[1] The discussion of homosexuality, which is pertinent to this problem, has been reserved for a later chapter.

ticularly to other members of one's immediate family, and are accompanied by strong feelings opposed to any relaxation of the taboos. The term "incest" is ordinarily applied to such consanguineous matings, and the horror of incest appears to be so widespread that many ethnologists have suggested that it may have an innate or instinctive foundation.

There is no indication of any such "instinct" among animals other than man. Pliny (9) tells of a horse which on discovering that it had unwittingly been guilty of incest committed suicide by throwing itself over a cliff! This isolated anecdote is hardly convincing. On the contrary we know that inbreeding is common throughout the animal kingdom and is often the method used in order to develop certain desired characteristics in the offspring.

Lowie (24) states that in every part of the world there are restrictions on mating based upon propinquity of relationship. He cites Hobhouse's theory that this is instinctive and expresses his agreement with it. Wissler (25) also believes that all primitive peoples show a deep disgust over the marriage of brothers and sisters; it is also repugnant to them for a mother to marry her son and only slightly less so for a father to marry his daughter. The rules permit of certain exceptions, but these refer only to a few individuals in the community and are nowhere practiced by a whole tribe or nation. He believes this aversion to incest to be fundamental, since it is universally condemned in all types of culture. In his opinion it may be instinctive, but there is nothing impossible in the idea that it is only a convention. Linton (5), on the other hand, believes that the prohibition of marriage between mother and son is the only one universally present. Marriage between father and daughter is permitted in at least one society, the Azande, while several groups have recognized or even required marriage between brother and sister.

This last type of marriage, for example, has been reported for a number of scattered communities. In Egypt, particularly during the nineteenth and twentieth dynasties, every king married his own sister. Among the Incas of Peru, "so insistent was the feeling that the sovereign was raised far above every-one—nobleman or commoner—that he was compelled to marry into his immediate family" (26, p. 129). His official wife was either his sister or his half-sister. The ancient kings of Hawaii had a similar practice. In certain districts of Fin-land a tradition is preserved that in the old days a brother could marry a sister. Even within fairly recent times a story is told of a very pretty and hard-working girl who lived in the village of Dubensk. "Her parents were reluctant to part with her and give her in marriage to a stranger. So they sent her to pay a long visit to her relatives at a distance, and on her return they received her as a complete stranger. From that day they obliged her to consider her brother as her husband" (27, p. 183). The chiefs among the tribes of the Nilotic Sudan similarly object to their sisters and daughters going to commoners; they prefer to keep them for themselves, saying that they are more beautiful than the women in the remainder of the tribe. Marriage to a sister—more frequently a half-sister—is common (28). It is also stated that in former times the Veddas of Ceylon frequently married their younger sisters, although marriage with an elder sister seemed to them as hor-rible as it does to us (29).

The theory of the nature of the incest taboo which has re-ceived perhaps the most attention is that of Westermarck (30). In his opinion there are two reasons why this taboo has developed. In the first place, there is no innate aversion to marriage with near relatives, but there is an innate aver-sion to marriage between persons living very closely together from early childhood. Since such persons are in most cases members of the same family, the horror of incest manifests itself principally in connection with the marriage of near kin. It is not by degree of consanguinity, but by close living to-gether that the prohibitory laws against incest are determined. In the second place, says Westermarck, the incest taboo be-comes instinctive as the result of the harmful effects of in-breeding.

The first part of this theory was anticipated by Bentham

(*31*), who wrote: "It is very rare that the passion of love is developed within the circle of individuals to whom marriage ought to be forbidden. There needs to give birth to that sentiment a certain degree of surprise, a sudden effect of novelty. . . . Individuals accustomed to see each other and to know each other, from an age which is neither capable of conceiving the desire nor of inspiring it, will see each other with the same eyes to the end of life" (p. 220). There is some evidence in favor of this theory. Westermarck himself reports that he asked his Berber teacher from the Great Atlas whether marriages between cousins were frequent in his tribe, and the answer was: "How could you love a girl whom you have always seen?" (Vol. II, p. 194). In ancient Japan brothers and sisters might be permitted to marry provided they had not been brought up together.

On the other hand, among the Siberian Chuckchee a great many marriages between relatives are concluded at an early age, sometimes when the bridegroom and the bride are still infants. The marriage ritual is performed, and from that time on the children play together and spend as much time as possible in each other's company. Bogoras (*32*) here takes a view opposite to that of Westermarck and states that "Of course, the ties between them grow to be very strong, often stronger even than death; when one dies, the other also dies of grief, or commits suicide" (*17*, p. 183). Among the Arapesh also there were early betrothals, and the two people destined later to marry grew up together in terms of closest intimacy. Here again it is reported that affection developed rather than decreased as a result of this intimacy (*33*).

It should be added that incest is by no means so rare within our own society as is sometimes supposed. The reports from isolated mountain communities are to the effect that it occurs with considerable frequency, in spite of the intimacy of family life. Another argument against this portion of Westermarck's theory is to be found in the fact that there are many communities in which brother-sister incest is rigidly taboo, and where brothers and sisters do not grow up together. This is particularly true in many parts of Melanesia where there are special communal houses in which the boys live, and which make close intimacy with their sisters impossible. In general it is safe to conclude that the theory is not borne out by the facts and that on the contrary the intimacy within the family circle would lead to many more incestuous relationships if these were not restrained by the folkways of the group.[2]

The other aspect of Westermarck's theory, namely, that the incest taboo develops as a result of the dangers of inbreeding to the offspring, and that it consequently becomes instinctive, may also be rejected. The most common opinion among biologists at the present time is to the effect that inbreeding as such has no harmful effects, and it is only when there are latent defects in the parents that the marriage of close relatives will result in defective offspring. To cite one outstanding historical example, the pedigree of Cleopatra is remarkable from this point of view.

Not only had she nothing but royal blood in her veins . . . but over and over again, in the royal pedigree, she was derived from full brother and sister marriages. . . . Yet this woman, descended from a series of closely inbred ancestors, is not only handsome, vigorous, intellectual, but also prolific. Apart from her moral standard, which in any case was far removed from ours, or even from that of the great Greeks and Romans, she was as perfect a specimen of the human race as could be found in any age or class or society (Mahaffy; see 17, p. 195).

To take a more recent example, Leipoldt (35) tells of examining twin children, a boy and a girl of nine, whom he describes as about the most perfect specimens of juvenile humanity he had examined in a long series of 150,000 cases. He

---

[2] This is precisely the point made by Knight Dunlap (34), who argues that the lack of erotic attraction in housemates is not the cause, but the result of the incest prohibition. His own explanation is that the taboo is necessary in order to prevent sexual relations between persons in the same household. One wonders, however, why this need should ever have arisen. Dunlap's suggestion that otherwise sexual intercourse would begin early and be dangerously excessive is hardly convincing in view of the amount of sexual freedom permitted by many primitive communities. Unless incest can be shown to have some special danger, the origin of the taboo is still unexplained.

was told by the father with much embarrassment that his great-grandparents were brother and sister; that his father and mother were cousins, and that his wife was his own second-cousin. Leipoldt comments: "I know of no scientific reason why two persons, both physically and mentally sound, should not marry and breed equally sound progeny" (p. 78). It is stated also that certain Fijian stocks require first cousins to marry, and the ethnologist who studied them found no harmful effects of this practice (36). It is certainly difficult to imagine that any instinct should be based upon a biological principle so uncertain as that of the danger of inbreeding.

Perhaps the best argument against the instinctive nature of the incest taboo is to be found in the fact that although some form of marriage prohibition is universal, its exact character varies from group to group. In Dobu (37) mother-son incest is regarded as a great contamination, whereas father-daughter incest is not taken so seriously; biologically, of course, the two relationships are equally close. The greatest of all crimes is adultery between a man and his mother's brother's wife. In Buka the worst form of incest is between a man and his sister's daughter. Mother-son incest is rare; father-daughter incest more frequent. While disapproved of, it is not viewed with the same horror as intercourse between a man and his sister's daughter. From the point of view of this people, the father is a member of a different lineage from that of his daughter, but is of the same lineage as his sister and her daughter; this helps to explain the difference between their attitude and our own (7). In Lesu brother-sister incest is rigidly taboo, and there are a number of women whom a man calls "sister," even though from our point of view there is no biological relation between them. The taboo against these classificatory sisters is regarded just as strictly as the taboo against the real sister. It is clear that biological relationships can have little to do with the origin of the taboo in this case.

There are many instances of contrasting attitudes toward incest which show that social rather than biological factors are operative. The greater number of primitive groups are exoga-

mous, that is, they disapprove of marriage within the group
(or sib). Some sibs are endogamous, and require marriage
within the group. "The rightness of sib endogamy was expressed by the scorn of the Bella Bella of the Northwest Coast
of America who said, 'Who ever heard of a Raven marrying
an Eagle?' in contrasting their own custom with that of their
exogamous northern neighbors, the Tsimshian" (*38*, p. 417).
Mention was previously made of the brother-sister marriages
among the Egyptian and Peruvian rulers. On the other hand,
among the Loango of the Congo region (*39*) the king may not
marry any princess, because all princesses are considered his
sisters. There are a great many societies which forbid marriage with parallel cousins (that is, with children of the
mother's sister or father's brother) but permit, and on occasions prefer, marriage with cross cousins (children of the
mother's brother or the father's sister). Here a similar biological relationship assumes diametrically opposite forms, and
is associated with contrasting emotional attitudes because of
the folkways of the community.

In England until recently it was regarded as a very great
crime to marry the sister of one's deceased wife. This was
looked upon in the same manner as marriage with one's own
sister, and was spoken of as "psychic incest." A bill repealing
this law was adopted in 1850, but came into effect only in
1907. Before that time, this prohibition was spoken of as "a
law of God" and any breach of it was considered unnatural
(*17*).

This last illustration makes it clear that not only does the
nature of the incest prohibition vary from one group to another, but that even within the same group the passage of
time and the consequent alteration in the folkways may make
perfectly acceptable a union previously regarded as impossible. There seems to be no way of reconciling this variability
with the notion that the incest taboo is instinctive.

Another approach to the incest prohibition would regard it
as arising out of certain practical considerations. Tylor (*40*)
maintains that exogamy, or marrying outside of one's own

community, would enable a tribe to establish friendly relations with any number of other intermarrying groups, and would thereby give it an advantage in a struggle with an isolated community that lacked similar relationships with other groups. "Again and again in the world's history, savage tribes must have had plainly before their minds the simple practical alternative between marrying out and being killed out" (p. 267). Since exogamy would give the group this practical advantage, any incestuous marriage would be regarded as detrimental to the group's interests, and would be condemned. Fortune (*41*) develops this theory a little further on the basis of his experience in Melanesia. He states that in small communities social organization depends on the performance of obligations attached to family relationships. If the consanguineous relatives differ from the affinal relatives (the "inlaws") there is a wider recognition of social obligations, since the affinal relationship carries with it such duties as alliance in war and co-operation in hunting and in the mourning ceremonial. Marriage outside one's own family assures therefore a large group of allies in economic and other activities. "Any incestuous alliance between two persons within a single consanguineous group is in so far a withdrawal of their consanguineous group from the alliance and so endangers the group's survival" (p. 620). This theory has considerable plausibility. It may be objected, however, that it is not always true that such affinal relationships play a part in the economic and ceremonial life of the community, and that Fortune's account applies better to Melanesia than to groups in other parts of the world.

In the case of the Arapesh, a Melanesian tribe, there appears to be a conscious realization of the practical drawbacks to incest of the type which Fortune describes. In answer to a question regarding the possibility of marrying one's own sister, a native replied:

What, you would like to marry your sister? What is the matter with you anyway? Don't you want a brother-in-law? Don't you realize that if you marry another man's sister and another man marries your sister, you will have at least two brothers-in-law, while if you marry your own sister you will have none? With whom will you hunt, with whom will you garden, whom will you go to visit? (*33*, p. 84)

In this case, however, incest is regarded not with horror and repulsion, but as a stupid negation of the joys of increasing the number of people whom one can love and trust, and with whom one may co-operate.

Another native explanation of a somewhat different type is given by the African Chagga (*42*). An informant expressed it as follows:

At first people married their own sisters, but they noticed that they were beating their wives excessively, so they determined: We will not marry our own sisters but each will marry the sister of another, so that everyone will say: "If I beat my wife I shall be called to account by her brother and he will take my property away." If they had continued as they began they would have killed their wives, for they said: "If she dies what difference does it make, whose business is it?" (p. 38)

Malinowski (*13*) believes that the objection to incest arises from the fact that it would be a disruptive element within the family. The sensual approach of a son toward his mother would disturb the normal mother-son relationship, since it would be incompatible with the submission and reverence which a son would be expected to show his mother. It would also introduce an active hostile rivalry between father and son instead of the harmonious relationship otherwise to be expected. If incest were allowed, therefore, the family could not exist, and the aversion to incest is due to a complex scheme of cultural reactions dependent upon the interrelationships within the family. This point appears to be a sound one and is helpful as a principle of explanation. Even in the case of brother-sister incest, which Malinowski does not discuss in this connection, it is also applicable in certain instances. If a man married his sister, for example, his mother would also be his mother-in-law. Since in many communities there is the custom of mother-in-law avoidance (see below, p. 142), the intimate relationship with the mother would conflict with the expected attitude toward the mother of one's wife, and the normal family life would thereby be disrupted.

This whole approach to incest on the basis of its practical disadvantages is not always applicable. There are some cases in which brother-sister marriage in particular would be a real convenience. In our own society especially, the frequent difficulty of finding a husband for one's daughter could be met most easily by marriage with her brother. In justice to the theory, however, it must be added that this type of difficulty is a relatively new phenomenon due to the structure of our society and that it probably occurs rarely if at all in primitive communities. In general it may be concluded that the theory suggested by Tylor and developed by Malinowski and Fortune gives the best account of the probable origin of the incest taboo.

In his *Totem and Taboo* which represents the first important attempt to apply psychoanalytic principles to the interpretation of ethnological phenomena, Freud (43) suggests another explanation for the attitude toward incest. He starts from the Darwinian hypothesis of a primal horde, conceived after the analogy of gorilla society, in which a violent jealous father (the dominant male) keeps all the females for himself, and drives away the growing sons. These younger males would resent the power of the father and would of course desire possession of some of the females. One day, says Freud (although it is doubtful whether he thought this happened at a particular moment in history), the expelled brothers slew their father and thus put an end to the father horde. They had, however, as in the case of all sons, an ambivalent attitude toward their father; they hated him and resented his authority, but they also loved and admired him. They satisfied their hate by his removal, but then their suppressed tender impulses asserted themselves, and took the form of remorse and a sense of guilt. They tried therefore to undo their deed by declaring that the killing of the father substitute, the totem,[3] was not allowed, and they renounced the fruits of their act by denying themselves their father's women. This is the origin of the incest prohibition, as a result of which all men renounce the women of their own family group.

The urge toward incestuous relationships still remains, however; Freud approves Frazer's statement that the existence of a legal prohibition against it shows that many men have a propensity in that direction. "If the law represses it, it does so because civilized men have come to the conclusion that the satisfaction of these natural instincts is detrimental to the general interests of society" (p. 206). There is no innate aversion to incestuous relations; as a matter of fact the first sex impulses of the young are, according to Freud's theory, regularly of an incestuous nature. In this connection, the important part played by the Oedipus complex (see below) is well known. For Freud, therefore, it is not the dread of incest which is instinctive, but rather the desire for it, and this desire is kept in check by the folkways which have arisen as the result of the murder of the primal father by his sons.

It is difficult to criticize this theory of Freud's because the crime upon which it rests is so entirely hypothetical that any direct proof or disproof of it is unobtainable. It is possible to say, however, that there is no group of human beings among whom a primal horde such as Freud postulates has ever been known. In addition the theory may conceivably explain why a man should deny himself his mother or his sisters; it does not explain the extension of the incest prohibition to his daughters, a relationship which is forbidden as strictly as the others. Although undoubtedly there is some truth to the notion of an Oedipus complex and its derivatives, its extension backward into a particular point in time from which all incest prohibitions all over the world have originated is an assumption which

[3] The institution of totemism frequently, but not invariably, includes the prohibition against killing or eating the totem animal. For a full discussion of the characteristics of totemism see Goldenweiser (44).

ethnologists in general are not prepared to accept (*45, 46*). The theory as a whole must be regarded as unproven.

Another theory of the nature of the incest taboo is that of Briffault (*9*), according to whom it arose in two ways. For him the primitive family is matriarchal in character, with the principal authority vested in the oldest female. The mother is of course very much attached to the son, but as he matures he requires sex satisfaction and looks to his age-mates, that is, his sisters. The mother is jealous, however, and refuses her son access to his sister; from this refusal the incest taboo develops. This theory is something like that of Freud in reverse, with the jealous mother instead of the father, and without the primal crime. It is just as hypothetical, and has the additional defect of explaining only the brother-sister taboo, and none of the others. The second aspect of the theory is that males have an instinct to wander and this would result in the habit of obtaining mates outside one's own community. From this habit to the taboo against doing otherwise seems to Briffault an easy transition. Since no evidence is given for the existence of such an instinct, we need not take this theory too seriously.

In summary it may be said that of the various explanations suggested, the most probable is that the incest taboo arose from very practical considerations. Marrying out would have definite advantages, and incest definite disadvantages. It is natural therefore that the latter should be universally condemned. This theory does not adequately explain the nature of the prohibition in every case, but it is likely that it represents the principal consideration, with additions and alterations resulting from historical factors. There is no real evidence that the incest prohibition is instinctive.

Patterns of Avoidance. Allied to the problem of incest is the prevalence among primitive communities of certain patterns of avoidance. These are rules of relationship which may forbid any kind of social contact between certain individuals, and which are usually regarded as very important. Of these, by far the most widespread is the mother-in-law taboo.

Whereas among ourselves, the mother-in-law relationship has been the object of a considerable amount of ridicule and occasionally of unpleasantness, among a great many primitive communities it is characterized by an attitude of respect and avoidance. The taboo against speaking to one's mother-in-law is so strict among the native Australians that in former times the penalty for breaking it was death. Among the African Baganda a greater sanctity attached to the mother-in-law taboo than to the taboo against incest. A Navajo believed he would go blind if he saw his mother-in-law's face (9). In Buka it is the strictest of all taboos. The mother-in-law always carries with her a kind of pointed hood made of pandanus leaves; if she learns that her son-in-law is approaching she immediately covers her face. They must not eat together nor sleep in the same house nor speak to each other directly (7). A missionary in New Britain tells of trying to translate the passage in the Gospel of St. Mark in which Herod swears to give Salome whatever she asks, even to the half of his kingdom. When he investigated the natives' idea of what it meant to swear, he found that the most solemn oath a man could take was—"Sir, if I am not telling the truth, I hope I may shake hands with [touch the hand of] my mother-in-law" (47, p. 17). The taboo between father-in-law and daughter-in-law also exists but is not nearly so widespread nor so strict.

Several theories have been suggested in explanation of these avoidance patterns (3). Lubbock, for example, believes that in cases of marriage by capture the husband would fear the anger of the parents of his bride, and would consequently stay as far from them as possible. This theory is difficult to accept, first because marriage by capture occurs quite rarely, and second, because on this basis the husband would be expected to avoid his father-in-law at least as much as his mother-in-law, and this is not the case. A somewhat similar explanation is that of Tylor (40), who believes that the husband is regarded as an outsider and is "cut" by his wife's family. He cites in support of this the fact that often when a child is born the avoidance taboo no longer exists. This also fails to explain why the mother-in-law avoidance should be stricter than all the others.

Freud's theory is as follows: The mother-in-law is unwilling to give up possession of the daughter; she distrusts the stranger and wishes to retain her own dominant position. The man in his turn is determined not to subject himself to any foreign will, and is jealous of those who preceded him in his wife's affections. He is also averse to any disturbance in his "illusion of sexual over-evaluation," that is to say, the sight of his mother-in-law reminds him that his wife, too, will some day grow old, that she will not always possess the charm and the youth that he now sees in her. There are also unconscious factors at work. The mother-in-law lives again in the emotional experiences of her children and identifies herself with them; this may go so far that she also falls in love with the man her daughter has married. The avoidance would remove from her any possible temptation. In the case of the man, there may be identification of the mother-in-law with the mother, and since there is an ever-present incest temptation with regard to the latter, mother-in-law avoidance also develops as a protection against it.

This theory is part of the whole Freudian structure and cannot properly be criticized in isolation from it. It seems probable that in our own society difficulties do develop as the result of the unwillingness of the parents to surrender control over their children, and of the young husband to submit to such control. It should be noted, however, that in those primitive communities in which the avoidance is found, it is expressed not in terms of hostility, but in terms of respect. As far as one can tell from the reports of the ethnologists, the two parties to the avoidance may have the highest regard for each other. Lowie (14) tells of an incident among the Crow in which one man said to another, "What's the matter with your mother-in-law, Joe? She does not seem to have any respect for you at all!" (p. 88).

Another frequent type of avoidance pattern is that between

brother and sister. This may be regarded as an extension of the incest taboo, since the attitude toward it is determined by the fear that it may lead to incest. It is found in the most extreme form in Melanesia. So great is the objection to any degree of intimacy between brother and sister that there are parts of Melanesia where one of twin siblings may be put to death immediately on account of their objectionable contacts before birth (48). In the Trobriand Islands boys are separated from their sisters at a very early age and live in their own communal house. Malinowski (13) states that in this community by far the worst type of incest is that between brother and sister. This taboo relationship extends, however, to all other types of intimacy as well. Although complete sexual freedom is permitted before marriage, sex must not even be mentioned in the presence of a sister. Some of the consequences of this taboo will be discussed in greater detail below.

In Buka there is a feeling of "shame" between brother and sister which persists through life. They are ashamed to talk to each other unless other people are present. If a man's sister calls to him to come and take some food from her, he may do so, but more probably he will pretend not to hear her. Jokes on sexual subjects may not be told by anyone to a woman in the presence of her brother. It is not even permitted under such circumstances to use certain slightly improper words which otherwise are looked upon much as we consider slang (7). In Lesu, on the other hand, there is only semi-avoidance between brothers and sisters, and the most rigid taboos are reserved for the relationship between cross cousins of the opposite sex. Between these two, contacts are regulated by many ritual prohibitions. Personal names must never be mentioned between them; they must not go near each other; if they must speak, they do so briefly at a distance. Food may be exchanged, but only through the medium of a third person (8). These reports indicate that the avoidance relationships, like the incest taboos, may vary markedly from group to group and may apply to different members of the family. A relationship which is a familiar one in one group may be surrounded by the most rigid taboos in another. These variations appear to be due to cultural and historical factors and probably do not depend upon any fundamental or common human psychological attitudes. They may, however, have important implications for the personal relationships between members of a particular family.

The Oedipus Complex. This consideration leads to another problem within the general framework of sex relationships. Mention was previously made of the Oedipus complex, which Freud regards as one of the very foundations of our psychological structure. As is well known, this complex gets its name from the story of Oedipus, King of Thebes, of whom it was prophesied before his birth that he would kill his father Laius and marry his mother Jocasta. He was as a consequence exposed to die in the woods, but was saved and brought up in ignorance of his parentage. Eventually the prophecy was fulfilled. On his return to Thebes Oedipus killed Laius in a skirmish on a narrow road, and then married the widow. When the true relationship was discovered after many years, Jocasta killed herself and Oedipus put out his eyes. This tragic story moves us particularly, says Freud, because there is in every one of us the submerged desire to kill the father and possess the mother. In the development of the personality, the Oedipus stage is one through which all boys pass on their way to complete heterosexual maturity, but the incestuous wishes which form part of it are never completely lost. In dreams and in neuroses they may come to definite expression.[4] The hostility against the father may manifest itself in a host of ways, for example in the development of a general revolt against authority, and the consequent determination of one's economic and political attitudes. In general it may be said that these two aspects of the Oedipus complex, the hostility against the father (tempered by attitudes of love and respect as well) and the excessive love of the mother, are among the foundations of psychoanalytic interpretation.

[4] They have found their way into literature, as the writings of D. H. Lawrence, Sidney Howard, and Eugene O'Neill testify.

For Freud the Oedipus complex is regarded as a universal phenomenon. It is present in varying degree in all boys, and plays an important part throughout their psychological development. The ethnologists, however, have been skeptical of this universality and have thought it worth while to see whether it exists in similar form in all societies. There are, apparently, many groups besides our own in which it has been observed. Herskovits (49), for example, asked one of the Bush-Negroes of Suriname, or Dutch Guiana, the following question: "When a man dies, do they destroy his house?" The reply was: "Not unless he has done black magic. If he is an ordinary man, his widow lives there with his daughters." "What happens to his sons?" "They are sent away for a long time." "Why?" "Because the soul of a man loves his daughters but hates his sons, and if they remained in his house, his ghost would kill them." "And if a woman dies?" "Then the husband continues to live there with his sons, for if it is a woman's ghost, she will destroy her daughters. But her sons, she loves them and watches over them" (50, p. 139).

On the other hand, Malinowski's (13) observations indicate that there may be an intimate connection between the nature of the family and the social organization on the one hand and the characteristics of the Oedipus or "nuclear" complex on the other. He believes that this complex is to be understood as a reaction to the family in which the individual develops rather than as an inevitable stage through which every boy must pass. The Trobriand family, in which these observations were made, differs in certain fundamental respects from the family in our society. Fatherhood, for example, is a purely social relationship, which does not involve the presence of any authority over the children. It is the duty of the father "to receive the children into his arms"; he assists in looking after them and attending to their natural needs. He is much more active in caring for the child than is the father in our society. The attitude of the child to him is one of friendship and affection. There can be no fear of him, nor rebellion against him, since he never issues orders nor forces obedience from them. Authority is vested instead in the mother's eldest brother, who is idealized by his nephew and regarded as a model to be followed. He introduces into the life of the boy social ambition, glory, pride of lineage, promises of future wealth, power and social status. On his death he leaves to his nephew his most important possessions, including his most powerful magic. If there is any struggle against authority, therefore, it must be against the maternal uncle and not the father.

The relationship to the mother also differs from our own. Weaning, for instance, may be sudden and painful for a child in our society, and may constitute a very disturbing experience. The separation from the mother may leave a gap in the child's life and cause him to long for a return to her. Among the Trobrianders weaning takes place much later, when the child himself decides that he prefers other food. There is no great wrench from the mother, and since the desire for her is not repressed, it does not loom so large in his later life.

The important taboo, as was indicated above, is that between brother and sister, who are separated at an early age and are never together socially with any intimacy. Most important of all, neither one must ever show the slightest interest in the love affairs of the other. There is complete free play given to sexuality with the exception of this taboo. The sister is a mysterious being, therefore, with whom no intimacy is permitted. She is "the only spot in the sexual horizon permanently hidden," and any incipient tenderness toward her is immediately cut short. As the result of this family constellation, the nuclear complex is quite different from what it is in our society. "In the Oedipus complex, there is the repressed desire to kill the father and marry the mother, while in the matrilineal society of the Trobriands the wish is to marry the sister and to kill the maternal uncle" (p. 81).

Malinowski cites as additional evidence in favor of his interpretation the fact that the Trobrianders were unwilling to discuss with him the question of brother-sister incest, and showed considerable emotional disturbance when he questioned them about it.   They were amused rather than disturbed at any reference to incest between mother and son, referring to the difference in age as an adequate barrier to any such relationship.   No one admitted dreaming of incest with the sister, but many of them claimed to know that others had had such dreams.   In addition, Malinowski found that the mythology of the Trobrianders furnished evidence in the same direction.

This position has been subjected to considerable criticism on the part of orthodox psychoanalysts.   Roeheim (*51*), for example, questions Malinowski's competence in the application and interpretation of psychoanalytic method, characterizing him as little more than an amateur in this field.   It must certainly be admitted that the manifestations of the Oedipus complex in our society are not always obvious, and it requires considerable practice in the interpretation of dreams as well as of overt behavior to be certain of its existence.   There is always the possibility, therefore, that it does exist in the Trobriands in a form analogous to our own, but that Malinowski was simply not sufficiently well trained to observe it.   The probability remains that this complex does vary with the cultural setting, and that in the form in which we know it, it is not universal.   The analysis by Fromm (*52*) of the relation of various forms of parental authority to the family pattern points in the same direction.

This whole discussion of sex behavior has led into a number of bypaths not directly connected with the question of sex as a fundamental drive.   These additional considerations have been important, however, in showing the manner and the degree to which a drive which is clearly organic in nature may still be controlled by cultural factors.   Even those aspects of human nature which are universal and biologically determined are not understood unless they are seen in their social setting.

ORGANIC NEEDS

A number of the instincts included in McDougall's list refer to the satisfaction of definite organic needs, or "visceral drives.". In this category we find hunger and thirst, the need for rest or sleep, the elimination of waste products from the body, etc. These are primary urges which cannot be ignored if the organism is to continue in a healthy state. Their satisfaction is essential for life. When any one of them is unsatisfied a tension is set up in the organism which demands relief, and some kind of activity is undertaken until the relief is obtained. These needs have of course an organic basis. The most acceptable explanation of hunger is that it is experienced as a consequence of the rhythmic contractions of the stomach wall, resulting from the diminution of the sugar content in the blood. These contractions take place long before the organism is actually in a state of starvation, and constitute a sort of danger signal indicating that the energy requirements of the body are being depleted. The sensation of thirst is apparently set up by the drying of the tissues at the back of the throat and similarly indicates somewhat ahead of time that the tissues require more fluid. The need for sleep has been accounted for in various ways; one theory, for which there is experimental evidence, regards it as the result of the accumulation of certain chemical products in the cerebro-spinal fluid and the blood stream, these products being decreased after a period of sleep. The need for elimination of waste products is accompanied by a sensation of distension in the bladder or in the lower part of the large intestine. Although the exact mechanisms are in some cases debatable, these organic needs are obviously present also throughout the animal kingdom, except in the simplest species. We may speak of them therefore not only as "human nature," but more broadly still as "animal nature."

These organic needs have also, however, their social aspect. The elimination of waste products, for example, is in many societies subject to certain customs and conventions. In our case it must be carried out in strict privacy, but there are groups like the native Australians among whom no such taboo is observed. In the case of our children a long and sometimes painful period of training is necessary before the social requirements are properly satisfied. There are general rules also for the time and place for sleep, but these are not nearly so rigid nor so universally enforced.

In the case of hunger and thirst social factors play an exceedingly important part. The fact that we eat at least three meals a day at prescribed intervals is not due to any organic rhythm. In many primitive communities there are only two meals, and no one suffers particularly as the result of this different pattern. If we get hungry at meal-time, this is due at least in part to our previous socially determined habits of eating. As Malinowski (53) expresses it, "Appetite or even hunger is determined by the social milieu. Nowhere and never will man, however primitive, feed on the fruit of his environment. He always selects and rejects, produces and prepares. He does not depend on the physiological rhythm of hunger and satiety alone; his digestive processes are timed and trained by the daily routine of his tribe, nation, or class" (p. 943).

The kind of food we eat is also in large measure due to social factors. It may be that certain individuals, because of the chemical constituents of their tissues or their blood stream, have special food requirements which they try as far as possible to satisfy. One person may need more sugar, another more protein, and his diet may vary accordingly. Although individual differences in food preferences may partly be explained in this manner, this is not true of differences between groups. Wissler (25) states that there is probably no community which does not consistently refrain from eating certain available foods. This is not peculiar to primitive man; in our society there is a practical taboo against the eating of snakes, dogs, cats, rats and insects. These food aversions are held usually for no obvious reasons and are probably not based on practical considerations. As a rule there is no aversion to the most abundant and accessible foods in the habitat of a tribe; for example, many American Indian tribes which tabooed the eating of fish lived in regions which were not well watered and where the streams contained only small fish which were difficult to catch.

In an interesting article on "food prejudices" Townsend (*54*) gives many examples of the variations in food preference in different parts of the world. Clams and mussels, for example, are of the same family; in Europe mussels are eaten and clams are not, whereas in America the reverse holds true. Clams are actually shipped from England to Newfoundland to be used for bait; the English will not taste them. In England and the United States various species of flat fish—sole, plaice and flounder—are regarded as good and delicate eating; in Gaspé, Newfoundland and Labrador, they are used only as fertilizer. All along our coasts dogfish are thrown away as soon as caught, but in the Hebrides they are called "gray fish" and "rock salmon" and there is no prejudice against them. The Algonquin Indians were fond of skunk, which the Whites would not consider eating. Similar examples might be multiplied. It is important to keep in mind, however, that these food prejudices may be overcome as a result of necessity. It is said that the first Europeans and Americans to visit the Indians of British Columbia and the Northwest Coast found the food so saturated in fish oil that it was quite unpalatable. After a time they were able to eat it with relish. This means that biological necessity may counteract the force of socially determined food habits as well as of personal preference, but it is evidently only in an emergency situation that this takes place.

In this connection Katz (*55*) stresses the important distinction between hunger and appetite. In a series of interesting experiments he has shown how animals of different species can be made to eat even when they are not "hungry," that is to say, immediately after they have finished eating all they could of a certain food. The introduction of another food or of a hungry animal would stimulate the appetite and the apparently satiated animal would start eating again. Exactly the same observation has been made in the case of human beings. We may perhaps conclude that the hunger drive is organic and universal, but that appetite, which plays an exceedingly important part in our food habits, is socially determined. The same considerations apply to thirst, which therefore does not require a separate discussion. In general these organic needs are completely "dependable"; they must be satisfied at all costs.

GREGARIOUSNESS

The drive toward gregarious activity, sometimes called the herd instinct, has special significance in the field of social psychology. If there is such a drive, it makes it possible to understand why groups are formed and how a group behavior as distinct from individual behavior develops. In the psychological literature it has loomed largest in the writings of Trotter (56), for whom it is one of the four instincts which play the most important part in the life of man, the others being self-preservation, nutrition and sex.

Gregariousness, says Trotter, is a phenomenon of profound biological significance. "The only medium in which man's mind can function satisfactorily is the herd, which therefore is not only the source of his opinions, his credulities, his disbeliefs, and his weaknesses, but of his altruism, his charity, his enthusiasms and his power" (p. 47). The gregarious characteristics of man are shown by the fact that he is intolerant and fearful of solitude, physical and mental; that he is more sensitive to the voice of the herd than to any other influence; that he is subject to the passions of the pack in his mob violence and of the herd in his panics; that he is remarkably susceptible to leadership; that his relations with his fellows are dependent upon their recognition of him as a member of the herd. If this analysis of Trotter's is correct, the gregarious motive would stand in the very forefront of the mechanisms which we are here considering.

To return to the criteria which we have previously employed, we find first that there is continuity with the behavior of the lower animals, but that this continuity is difficult to interpret. It is well known that among certain of the insect species gregarious activity is carried to remarkable heights of complexity and thoroughness. Among higher species, however, particularly in mammalian groups, the gregarious behavior may be absent or reduced to a minimum. This is particularly true of the more ferocious animals like lions and tigers, who are almost invariably found singly or in pairs. Among the higher anthropoids, although accounts of their behavior in this respect differ, it is frequently reported that single individuals are encountered. On the whole we may conclude that the criterion of continuity with animals gives ambiguous results in this instance, since species may be found either with or without a "herd instinct."

The second criterion, namely that of a known physiological basis for the drive, is not satisfied in the case of gregariousness. It may be that further research will some day uncover such a foundation, but that is unlikely. In the light of our present knowledge of physiology it is difficult to conceive any neurological or endocrine pattern which would directly lead to gregarious activity. It is possible, however, that in the early experiences of the child the faces and persons of adults have a high stimulus value, partly because they actually constitute a large part of the environment and partly also because they are related to the satisfaction of fundamental needs. This might constitute a very indirect physiological basis, not in the form of a visceral or tissue need, but determined by the perceptual primacy of other human beings.

As far as the universality of this drive is concerned, it seems clear that a certain minimum amount of interaction between individuals would be necessary everywhere, although it is important to note that the extent of this association varies greatly. Certain groups have been described as "atomistic," in the sense that individuals or small family groups live in practical isolation. This is said to be true of many tribes in the Sahara and in Madagascar, as well as of the Jibaro Indians of Ecuador. The African pygmies are reported to be very anti-social even toward members of their own group, and in parts of Brazil each family lives by itself (57). Relatively small isolated groups, consisting at the most of a few families, have been reported for the Veddas of Ceylon, the Semang of the Malay Peninsula, several Australian tribes, and others

(58). There are apparently many groups among whom gregarious tendencies are limited to the members of one's own family, although there may be larger assemblages on special occasions.

This leads to a possible interpretation of gregarious behavior as an extension of the interrelationships within a family. Malinowski (59), for example, states that there is no herd instinct in man, but that common sociability develops by extension of the family bonds and from no other sources. The endurance of family ties is the pattern of all social organization, and the condition of co-operation. As an additional argument against the existence of a gregarious instinct as such, Malinowski points to the fact that as culture advances, individual activities, economic and otherwise, gradually disappear and are replaced by collective behavior. We should then have a case of an instinct increasing with the greater complexity of culture, which is a manifest impossibility. In other words, if we have a form of behavior which is relatively rare among more "primitive" groups and much more developed in complex societies, it is not very likely that it may be explained in biological terms. We may add here that Darwin (60) was also of the belief that "the feeling of pleasure from society is probably an extension of the parental or filial affection" (p. 80).

Hobhouse (58) makes the suggestion that groupings could have arisen out of the need to find mates outside of one's family. "The simplest social organization, therefore, postulates two or more families living together, but constantly united by cross ties of intermarriage" (p. 43). This would mean that a certain minimum amount of gregariousness would be necessary in order not to do violence to the incest taboo. The interpretation here given depends, however, upon the assumption that this taboo is primary, whereas in a previous section (see page 137) we have seen that in all probability the taboo develops as a result of practical considerations, included among which is the desirability of friendly co-operative relations with other people.

This suggests that gregariousness also may be understood in terms of practical advantages. Sumner and Keller (*57*) deny the existence of a herd instinct and state that association has become a characteristic habit of mankind because of its high survival value. Not only is it possible to carry on in the group certain economic and religious activities which would not be possible for an individual—for example, trade and exchange of goods at a common market, complicated ritual ceremonies, division of labor, united defense against an enemy, etc.—but it also makes life generally easier and more secure. In such associations the individual must inevitably give up a certain amount of his liberty, but the co-operation that results more than repays him for his loss. Life in society may consequently be regarded as a species of insurance, in which a small recurring calculable loss is substituted for a possible ruinous and incalculable one.

This theory makes it possible to understand gregarious activity as a means to a very practical end. The minimum amount of gregariousness found everywhere may be explained as the consequence of family life, which is in turn the effect of sex activity and the relationship between parents and children. Any extension beyond this family group is probably due originally to the mutual advantages resulting from this extension. Here as elsewhere, a mechanism may become a drive, to use an expression of Woodworth's (*61*); that is to say, a means to an end may become an end in itself. In this way it is easy to see why an individual may be unhappy when he is alone, or even why he may develop definite mental disturbance as a result. Even if the need for association is not a biological one, the fact that he has been accustomed to it all his life may make sudden and complete deprivation quite unbearable. The strength of a drive, as we have seen before, is no proof of its innateness.

It should be added that in a recent article Woodworth (*62*) discusses and rejects the theory that gregarious activity is the result of practical considerations. He believes that the individual derives great satisfaction from participation in selected external processes, both physical and social. "Social participation is not forced on the individual as a necessary means to satisfying other needs. It is, rather, a primary characteristic of his behavior" (p. 827). On the other hand, Blatz (63) has observed the manner in which the Dionne quintuplets as they grow older have gradually increased their social contacts with one another, and concludes that such contacts are not imperative to start with. "The social behavior and experience of individuals are wholly derived and cannot be said to be basic" (p. 829).

Our own conclusion with reference to gregariousness is that it has a possible though doubtful continuity with the behavior of animals; it has no known physiological or anatomical foundation; it is universal in a minimum form, but this minimum can probably be adequately explained on the basis of family relationships. The extensions beyond this are determined by practical considerations.

OTHER MOTIVES

There are a number of additional motives or "instincts" in the lists given by McDougall and others upon which we shall comment briefly. One of these is the form of behavior known as curiosity. In a previous section (see p. 91) it was noted that the acquisitive tendencies of certain birds were explained as due to their interest in strange and curious objects (18). It seems certain that the tendency to explore one's environment with some care is found among many animal species. As for a physiological basis, it is probable that exploratory behavior represents one of a group of activity drives, or "trends toward active motor response to the environment" (64, p. 94). There is apparently a good deal of activity for the sake of exercise, as is shown by the behavior of the rat in an activity cage, as well as in the apparently random muscular movements of the young child. When this activity is in response to some external stimulus which through its sensory qualities or novelty attracts "attention," there may be exploratory behavior in connection with it. At a more complex level, a great deal of exploratory activity is directed toward the mastery of the environment for practical or utilitarian purposes. In the satisfaction of a great many of the impulses common to animals and man, namely, sex, hunger, preservation from danger, it is clearly important to know the nature of one's environment. Exploration may lead to any one of these goals, and may best be understood on that basis. The study by Warden and others (65) of the strength of the various drives in the white rat showed curiosity to be much weaker than the other incentives measured. Although it is of course dangerous to apply this result to human beings, it seems probable that curiosity as such has no great power, unless it contributes in some way to the mastery of the environment.

Another group of motives has been labeled "esthetic drives," described as "the positive response of the little child to color and tone, to tactual stimulation, and to all those sensory attributes of the world which appeal to him, lead him to act, i.e., motivate him" (64, p. 94). In their elemental form, these drives seem to be direct responses to sensory stimuli, and are not always clearly distinguishable from activity drives, such as exploratory behavior. At a more complex level, however, they may be responsible for the vivid enjoyment of artistic creation, and for the positive pursuit of esthetic satisfactions.

The problem of the flight motive is very similar to that of aggressiveness, and many of the same considerations apply. There is of course throughout the animal world the tendency to escape as quickly and as effectively as possible from the menace of danger. On the physiological side, as far as we can tell at present, we have no direct flight mechanism; we have rather a general preparedness for activity in the face of an emergency situation. Whether this activity will be aggression or flight will be determined by the previous experience of the individual as well as by the conditions of the moment. There may also be organic differences between animal species in this respect, some like the lion showing more readiness for aggression, and others like the deer with a greater propensity to flight. This may also be connected, however, with the probabilities that aggression will be successful. Social factors will enter, both in the determination of what will cause flight and in the readiness with which it occurs. The fear of ghosts or of the dead will be great in one community and practically absent in another. Flight may be permitted to women and not to men under the same circumstances, and so on.

The so-called instinct of self-submission has been a special target for McDougall's critics, since it apparently exists side by side with its opposite, the instinct of self-assertiveness. It is argued that to explain two diametrically opposed types of behavior as due equally to instinct removes from this whole concept any claim to scientific validity. This criticism seems a sound one. On the other hand, we cannot deny the existence of a widely prevalent tendency for individuals to submit themselves to the will of someone else. At the present writing there is considerable following for a political philosophy known as the principle of leadership (Führerprinzip), which appears to depend upon such an attitude. It would be dangerous, however, to explain this on any instinctive basis. In the first place, there is still enough criticism of this principle and enough unwillingness to accept it, to cause us to doubt its universal validity; in the second place, it may better be understood on the basis of historical than on that of biological factors. In countries in which political stability has been threatened by factional strife, and in which serious difficulties have arisen as the result of a lack of agreement, it is possible to understand why so many people might be willing to sacrifice personal liberty to a leader who would make the decisions for them. Finally, it must be borne in mind that a very large number of individuals have been forced to subscribe to this principle of leadership against their will. It will probably never be known how many Italians and Germans remain quiet under a system of which they thoroughly disapprove, but which they have no means of combating. In any event it is a safe conclusion that the present political structure of these countries cannot be based upon any submissive instinct. Submissive behavior is to be understood as a means to an end.

THE DEPENDABLE MOTIVES IN GENERAL

As was pointed out in Chapter IV, the problem of dependable motives is not merely one of deciding which motives should appear on our list, but also of determining their degree of dependability. It is not sufficient to ask whether or not a certain drive is present in man, whether acquisitiveness or curiosity or self-submissiveness, for example, should or should not be included among the dependable motives; it is also important to know how dependable these motives are. There are undoubtedly some motives which are truly universal, others which permit of occasional exceptions, still others whose dependability is extremely limited.

In a recent discussion of this problem by Malinowski (53) it is stated:

Taking man as a biological entity it is clear that certain minima of conditions can be laid down which are indispensable to the personal welfare of the individual and to the continuation of the group. All human beings have to be nourished, they have to reproduce, and they require the maintenance of certain physical conditions. . . . (p. 940)

Actually, however, for each individual the need for nourishment has a degree of imperativeness much greater than the need for reproduction. The continuation of the group obviously depends upon sex activity, but many members of the group may under certain conditions dispense with this form of behavior, not without discomfort, perhaps, but probably without any fundamental injury to their "personal welfare." Hunger and sex have differing degrees of dependability; there is no possible "sublimation" of the hunger drive.

The following classification is tentatively presented:

1. Motives which are absolutely dependable, have a definite physiological basis and admit of no exceptions. Social factors play a part in their manifestations, but do not determine their existence. These include hunger, thirst, the need for rest and

sleep, the elimination of waste products from the body, and similar organic requirements; also activity drives and "esthetic" drives.

2. Motives which have a definite physiological basis, are found in all societies, but admit of exceptions in the case of individuals. Social factors not only determine the manner of their expression, but may also in certain circumstances cause them not to appear. These include sex, post-maternal behavior, and possibly also self-preservation.

3. Motives which have an indirect physiological basis and occur with great frequency, but admit of exceptions both in groups and in individuals. These include aggressiveness, flight and probably also self-assertiveness.

4. Motives which have no known physiological basis, but which occur with some frequency either because of social factors common to the majority of human communities, or as a means to the satisfaction of practical interests. They are primarily means to an end, but may come to function as ends in themselves. These include gregariousness, the paternal motive, the pre-maternal motive, the filial motive, acquisitiveness, and self-submission.

The list of possible motives is not complete, and many others might certainly be added. The extension of our knowledge in the fields of animal behavior, physiological mechanisms, and ethnological observation, may lead not only to a more adequate list, but also to a rearrangement of the individual motives in the hierarchy. It may also result in a finer discrimination between the motives now included within a single category of dependability. For these reasons the present classification is regarded as tentative, and subject to modification in the light of further analysis and more complete information.

This classification may in one sense be regarded as a compromise between those who have looked upon human nature as somewhat rigidly determined by a group of fundamental motives, and those at the other extreme who have seen it entirely as a by-product of social factors. The view here taken is that there are characteristics found among human beings all the world over, and others which though they loom large in our own society, have no such universality. It is of the utmost importance to stress the social and cultural influences entering into behavior, but we must not lose sight of the fact that these act upon a human being with essentially human (as well as animal) qualities.

It should be kept in mind that few instances of human behavior are to be explained on the basis of a single motive. A man may acquire property as a means of guarding himself against privation, or to gain prestige, or to obtain a suitable wife, or to make his children happy. Several of these motives may function simultaneously. A list of separate motives may therefore fail to do justice to the complexity of human activities.

SUMMARY

The sex drive satisfies the criteria of phylogenetic continuity and of physiological basis; it is found in the overwhelming majority of individuals, although direct sexual satisfaction may be renounced under certain conditions. Cultural influences determine varying attitudes toward the importance of the sex relation, the emotions associated with it, the values attached to chastity, standards of attractiveness in the sex partner, methods of acquiring a mate, desire for exclusive possession and other aspects of sexual behavior. The taboo against incest cannot be regarded as innately determined, since the exact nature of the prohibition varies from group to group. It is best explained on the basis of the practical advantages resulting from marriage with someone outside the immediate consanguineous family. The inevitability of the Œdipus complex, with its hostility against the father and incestuous attachment for the mother, is challenged by the material from the matrilineal Trobrianders, among whom the nuclear complex takes the form of hostility against the maternal uncle and desire for the sister. The complex, like other aspects of social and sexual relationships, varies with the cultural setting.

Visceral drives or organic needs belong in the category of complete dependability, since they satisfy the threefold criterion. They include hunger, thirst, the need for rest or sleep, the elimination of waste products, and probably the need for activity and exercise. Social factors in part determine the time, the place and the conditions for the satisfaction of these needs, but their existence is independent of society.

Gregarious behavior shows some continuity with the behavior of animals below man, but it has no known physiological foundation; some degree of social interaction is found among all human beings, but is probably to be explained on the basis of family groupings as well as of the practical advantages growing out of a larger range of social activities.

The classification of motives in a hierarchy of dependability has the advantage of indicating with what degree of assurance we may expect a given motive to appear in any given individual. Hunger, sex, aggressiveness and acquisitiveness, for example, belong in four different categories, arranged in a descending order of dependability. Further investigation may alter the exact nature of the classification.

REFERENCES

1. Dollard, J. *Criteria for the Life History.* 1935.
2. Hooton, E. A. *Up from the Ape.* 1931.
3. Crawley, E. *Studies of Savages and Sex* (ed. by T. Besterman). 1929.
4. Waley, A. *The Temple, and Other Poems.* 1923.
5. Linton, R. *The Study of Man.* 1936.
6. McDougall, W. *Introduction to Social Psychology.* 1908.
7. Blackwood, B. *Both Sides of Buka Passage.* 1935.
8. Powdermaker, H. *Life in Lesu.* 1933.
9. Briffault, R. *The Mothers.* 3 vols. 1927.
10. Roscoe, J. *The Northern Bantu.* 1915.
11. Torday, E., and Joyce, T. A. "Notes ethnographiques," *Ann. du Musée du Congo Belge* (quoted in Thomas (*17*)).
12. Jenks, A. E. *The Bontoc Igorot.* 1905.
13. Malinowski, B. *Sex and Repression in Savage Society.* 1927.
14. Lowie, R. H. *The Crow Indians.* 1935.

15. Van Gennep, A. *Les rites de passage.* 1909.
16. Livingstone, D. *Missionary Travels and Researches in South Africa.* 1858.
17. Thomas, W. I. *Primitive Behavior.* 1937.
18. Beaglehole, E. *Property.* 1932.
19. Mead, M. "Jealousy: Primitive and Civilized," *Woman's Coming of Age* (ed. by S. D. Schmalhausen and V. F. Calverton). 1931.
20. Shand, A. F. *The Foundations of Character.* 2d ed. 1920.
21. Driberg, J. A. *The Lango.* 1923.
22. Kirkpatrick, C. S. "Polyandry in the Panjab," *The Indian Antiquary,* 1878, 7: p. 86.
23. Boas, F. "The Central Eskimo," *Sixth Annual Report of the Bureau of Ethnology.* 1888.
24. Lowie, R. H. *Primitive Society.* 1925.
25. Wissler, C. *An Introduction to Social Anthropology.* 1929.
26. Radin, P. *The Story of the American Indian.* 1934.
27. Abercromby, J. *The Pre- and Proto-historic Finns.* 1898.
28. Seligman, C. G., and Seligman, B. Z. *Pagan Tribes of the Nilotic Sudan.* 1932.
29. Bailey, J. "An Account of the Wild Tribes of the Veddahs of Ceylon," *Ethnol. Soc. Trans.* N.S., 1863, 2: pp. 278-320.
30. Westermarck, E. A. *The History of Human Marriage.* 5th ed. 1921.
31. Bentham, J. *The Theory of Legislation* (ed. by C. K. Ogden). 1931.
32. Bogoras, W. "The Chuckchee," *Amer. Mus. Nat. Hist. Mem.,* 1904, 11: pp. 1-733.
33. Mead, M. *Sex and Temperament in Three Primitive Societies.* 1935.
34. Dunlap, K. *Civilized Life.* 1934.
35. Leipoldt, L. C. "The Wages of Sin," *Magazine Digest,* 1938, 16: pp. 77-78.
36. Thomson, B. H. "Concubitancy in the Classificatory System of Relationship," *J. Roy. Anthrop. Instit.,* 1894-95, 24: pp. 371-387.
37. Fortune, R. F. *Sorcerers of Dobu.* 1932.
38. Reichard, G. A. "Social Life," *General Anthropology* (ed. by F. Boas). 1938.
39. Bastian, P. W. A. *Die Deutsche Expedition an der Loango-Küste.* 1874.
40. Tylor, E. B. "On a Method of Investigating the Development of Institutions," *J. Roy. Anthrop. Instit.,* 1888-89, 18: pp 245-269.

41. Fortune, R. F. "Incest," *Encycl. Soc. Sci.*, 1932, 7: pp. 620-622.

42. Gutmann, B. "Die Frau bei den Wadschagga," *Globus*, 1907, 92: pp. 1-4.

43. Freud, S. *Totem and Taboo.* 1927.

44. Goldenweiser, A. A. *History, Psychology, and Culture.* 1933.

45. Kroeber, A. L. "Totem and Taboo: an Ethnologic Psychoanalysis," *Amer. Anthrop.*, 1920, 22: pp. 48-55.

46. Mead, M. "An Ethnologist's Footnote to 'Totem and Taboo,' " *Psychoanal. Rev.*, 1930, 17: pp. 297-304.

47. *Proc. Roy. Geo. Soc.* N.S. 9. (Quoted in Thomas (*17*).)

48. Goldenweiser, A. A. *Anthropology.* 1937.

49. Herskovits, M. J. "Freudian Mechanism in Negro Psychology," *Essays Presented to C. G. Seligman.* 1934.

50. Lincoln, J. S. *The Dream in Primitive Cultures.* 1935.

51. Roheim, G. "Psychoanalysis of Primitive Cultural Types," *Internatl. J. Psychoanal.*, 1932, 13: pp. 2-224.

52. Fromm, E. *Autorität und Familie.* 1936.

53. Malinowski, B. "The Group and the Individual in Functional Analysis," *Amer. J. Sociol.*, 1939, 44: pp. 938-964.

54. Townsend, C. W. "Food Prejudices," *Sci. Mo.*, 1928, 26: pp. 65-68.

55. Katz, D. *Hunger und Appetit.* 1932.

56. Trotter, W. D. *Instincts of the Herd in Peace and War.* 1919.

57. Sumner, W. G., and Keller, A. G. *The Science of Society.* 4 vols. 1927.

58. Hobhouse, L. T., et al. *The Material Culture and Social Institutions of the Simpler Peoples.* 1915.

59. Malinowski, B. *The Father in Primitive Psychology.* 1927.

60. Darwin, C. *The Expression of the Emotions in Man and Animals.* 1873.

61. Woodworth, R. S. *Dynamic Psychology.* 1918.

62. Woodworth, R. S. "Individual and Group Behavior," *Amer. J. Sociol.*, 1939, 44: pp. 823-828.

63. Blatz, W. E. "The Individual and the Group," *Amer. J. Sociol.*, 1939, 44: pp. 829-838.

64. Murphy, G., Murphy, L. B., and Newcomb, T. M. *Experimental Social Psychology.* Rev. ed. 1937.

65. Warden, C. J., et al. *Animal Motivation.* 1931.

CHAPTER VII

EMOTIONAL BEHAVIOR

THE PHYSIOLOGY OF EMOTION

IN the theory of McDougall which formed the starting point for our discussion of the dependable motives, there is postulated an intimate relationship between instinct and emotion. Each instinct is said to have a specific emotion which accompanies it, for example, the instinct of flight and the emotion of fear, the instinct of pugnacity and the emotion of anger, the sex instinct and the emotion of love, and so on. That the line between the two is difficult to draw is evident from the fact that in our preceding discussion there were several instances in which the physiological changes occurring in emotion were pertinent to an understanding of the drive itself. Murphy, Murphy and Newcomb (1) include the emotions in their classification of motives.

Since we are concerned primarily with social aspects of behavior, we may pass quickly over the physiological factors involved in the emotions. It is now well established, largely as the result of the experiments of Bard (2) on dogs, that the impulse to rage and probably also to other emotional activity comes from that region of the mid-brain known as the hypothalamus. Bard found that cutting through the brain above this region increased the amount of overt emotional behavior, evidently because the restraining influence of the cortex was thereby removed. On the other hand, section below the level of the hypothalamus caused a complete disappearance of the external bodily manifestations of emotion, thus clearly indicating that this was the region responsible. The hypothalamus initiates a series of internal changes which are more immediately under the control of the sympathetic nervous system and the adrenal glands. Cannon (3) has shown that in emotional excitement this sympathico-adrenal system brings on a number of reactions which prepare the organism to deal with an emergency. These include the flow of blood from the internal organs to the muscles of the arms and legs, which are enabled to exert additional strength; an increase in the coagulability of the blood so that wounds are less dangerous; a mobilization of the stored glycogen in the liver and its transformation into glucose which is a source of available energy; the chemical counteraction of the fatigue products in the blood, and other changes acting in the same direction. As was pointed out in a preceding section (see p. 79) the total group of emergency reactions is characteristic of emotional excitement, but does not distinguish one emotion from another. In spite of repeated experiments, Cannon and his collaborators have not found any difference between the glandular and visceral processes associated with fear, anger, and excitement, respectively. There may possibly be minute physiological differences which have not yet been discovered. As far as our present knowledge is concerned, however, we must depend upon social and situational factors in order to explain the differences in the manifestations of one emotion and another.[1]

An interesting example of the possible effects of these physiological changes is given by Collip (4). A diabetic taking insulin treatment found while walking on the street that he was being overcome by the physical and mental condition which follows the reduction of the amount of blood sugar. Having forgotten to provide himself with the sugar, he staggered into a drug store and incoherently demanded a bar of chocolate. The druggist thought he was drunk and threw him out. This of course enraged the man, and with his anger he suddenly recovered, and was then able to acquire the sugar which he needed to restore the equilibrium of his body fluids. Anger had so stimulated the output of the adrenals that there was a

---

[1] This brief discussion of the physiology of emotions should be supplemented by the account in any one of the standard psychological textbooks.

temporary increase in his blood sugar content sufficient to bring him through the crisis.

When we turn to the social aspects of emotional behavior, we find, as has been indicated elsewhere (5), that there are at least three distinct ways in which these are important. They may play a part first in determining the situations in which one emotion or another will be aroused; they may condition also the amount of overt emotional behavior occurring under these conditions; finally they may influence the manner in which the emotions manifest themselves. In this as in the preceding discussion, we depend largely on the findings of the ethnologists for pertinent material.

THE CAUSES OF EMOTIONAL BEHAVIOR

There are obvious differences between communities as to the situations which give rise to the various emotions. The same set of conditions may elicit diametrically opposite reactions. Thomas (6) has collected examples illustrating the varying emotional responses to the birth of twins. Among the Murngin of Australia (7) the mother kills one of the twins because it makes her feel like a dog to have a litter instead of one baby. With the Negroes of the Niger Delta the rule is that the mother and the twins are put to death. "In some cases the mother is allowed to live; but her life is little better than a living death, for she becomes an outcast and must live the remainder of her days in the forest" (8, p. 57). Less than a thousand miles away from this group live the Bankundo of the Congo valley, among whom at the other extreme the mother of twins is the object of honor and veneration throughout her life. "She is entitled to wear a special badge around her neck, and her name is changed to 'Mother-of-twins'" (9, p. 190).

In our society the failure to have children may be a source of great regret, but certainly anyone may mention the fact without conveying an insult. Among the African Lango (10) infecundity brings more shame and disrepute to a woman than the most riotous living. Many African tribes have a similar attitude, and life is said to become intolerable for a woman whose barrenness has been mentioned in public.

Death is a source of grief not only with ourselves, but probably in the majority of known cultures. There are cases, however, when it is an occasion for rejoicing. It has been reported of certain groups of Siberian natives and Eskimos as well as of the Fiji Islanders that people are actually anxious to die before they become too old. Their belief is that this life is merely a prelude to an everlasting life in which they will possess the bodily and mental powers with which they leave this one. If they live until they are decrepit they remain so forever. For this reason a dutiful son may kill his parents, secure in the conviction that he is doing them the greatest possible favor. A belief in immortality is present also among ourselves, but evidently we do not hold it with quite so much conviction.

The Bontoc Igorots of the Philippines (*11*) are reported not to take death very sorrowfully nor very passionately. A mother weeps one day for a dead child or husband. There is no self-mutilation, no somber colors, no earth nor ashes on the body. When a child or a young person dies, the women assemble and wail a melancholy dirge, and ask the departed why he went so early. For the aged there are neither tears nor wailing, but only a grim philosophy. "You were old," they say, "and old people die. You are dead and now we shall place you in the earth. We too are old and soon we shall follow you" (p. 74).

One further example of what to us would seem an unusual attitude toward death is reported for the Lango (*10*). On the death of a suicide there is very little mourning, and that is restricted to the closest relatives. This is due to their idea that "the self-sought death proves that the deceased wished to leave the world, and consequently an elaborate display of sorrow would be superfluous" (p. 169). Among ourselves the sorrow at the death of a suicide would probably not differ for this reason, although there would be added to it a sense of shame, especially where there is a religious proscription against it.

The discussion of jealousy in a preceding section may also be taken as illustrative of this variability in the causes of an emotion. The fact that a man takes a second wife may be welcomed in one society and unthinkable in another. The same variation holds for pre-marital chastity, wife-lending, illegitimacy, incestuous relationships, and the other aspects of sex activity; these may arouse quite different emotional reactions in different parts of the world, and even in the same society at different times.

It is possible that many of these differences are more superficial than real, and that a fundamental similarity underlies them. Shame, for example, may be the emotional reaction to the realization that one is condemned by his fellows; this may be universal, even though the specific condemned act may differ in each case. Jealousy may follow any failure to receive from one's marriage partner what the society regards as due, and this principle may be general in spite of the variations in detail. It is not always possible, however, to find such underlying similarities, although more intimate knowledge of the particular cultures might reveal them. In any case, in terms of overt behavior patterns, similar situations may provoke entirely different emotions according to the dictates of the folkways.

As an example of the manner in which these emotional reactions may be changed as a result of new habits, the case is reported of a missionary among the Carrier Indians, who have a strict taboo of the names of the dead. The missionary writes: "I, for instance, distinctly remember how, after many years spent in the closest intimacy with my Carriers, having gone to attend the funeral of my Bishop, I was indescribably shocked at the freedom with which his name was pronounced by the mourners and others, and felt prone to consider that sans-gêne as something little short of sacrilege" (*12*, p. 645).

THE AMOUNT OF EMOTIONAL BEHAVIOR

It is obviously difficult if not impossible to make any comparisons between groups as to the strength of subjectively felt emotions. Our comparisons must be restricted to the overt emotional behavior. In this respect we find that cultures differ widely from one another in the amount of emotional expression which is permitted. We speak, for example, of the imperturbability of the American Indian, the inscrutability of the Oriental, the reserve of the Englishman, and at the other extreme of the expressiveness of the Negro or the Sicilian. Although there is always some exaggeration in such clichés, it is probable that they do correspond to an accepted cultural pattern, at least to some degree.

In connection with the Oriental, the suggestion has been made that there may be an anatomical basis for the lesser degree of expression. Dr. Mêng (*13*), formerly connected with the Peking Union Medical College, and more recently with the Army hospital in Nanking, has shown the writer many of his dissections of the Chinese face. He has observed several peculiarities in the Chinese facial anatomy as distinct from that of the White European. The most important of these is the fact that one of the facial muscles, the quadratus labii superioris, is in the European face divided into three distinct parts, each of which may act semi-independently of the others, whereas in the Chinese face they are much more nearly fused together. In Dr. Mêng's opinion, this allows much freer play to the muscular contractions in the White face, and gives to the Chinese face an appearance of immobility. The other anatomical differences refer to the orbicularis oculi (the muscle surrounding the eye), which is larger and flatter in the Chinese; and the platysma muscle in the neck, which in the case of the Chinese extends much higher over the region of the lower jaw. These two muscles do not, however, play a very important part in facial expression.

These findings are of importance, but as yet they cannot be regarded as conclusive. Dr. Mêng's comparisons are between his own dissections of Chinese faces and the textbook descriptions of White facial musculature. In view of the great technical difficulty of making accurate anatomical dissections in a region of the body in which the muscles are so small and so numerous, a controlled study of White faces by the same investigator is essential.

Even if these anatomical characteristics of the Chinese face can be demonstrated, it is not probable that they compare in importance with the influence of cultural factors. Part of the education of the young Chinese consists of training in restraint. A Chinese girl is admonished—"do not show your unhappiness easily and do not smile easily," and "do not let your teeth be seen when you smile" (14). The boys are taught that it is unbecoming to the conduct of a gentleman to show anger or to be too boisterous. It may be, however, that the Chinese with whom we have had most contact, namely, residents of our large American cities, show an unusual amount of reserve because they are in an alien environment, and because they are not quite certain of their reception. Schrieke (15) has suggested that much of their apparent inscrutability is merely a precaution against embarrassment.

[The Chinese] do not want to go anywhere unless they are sure that no restrictions will be imposed. They are being forced to stay together as a group, separated from the American community. As a result of the rebuffs they have experienced, they have become more cautious, even suspicious, in their dealings with white Americans. They have learned the wisdom of keeping their thoughts to themselves and, consequently, seem cold and expressionless (p. 18).

This interpretation is borne out by the fact that when the Chinese are in an environment to which they are not alien, they give an impression of liveliness and vivacity in marked contrast to the usual stereotype. Somerset Maugham (16) writes: "You watch their faces as they pass you. They are good-natured faces and frank, you would have said, if it had not been drilled into you that the Oriental is inscrutable" (p. 83). Similarly, Gilbert (17) states that "the code of face often dictates that a Chinese should be restrained, calm and expressionless in the thick of trouble . . . but in the ordinary run of events his vivacity makes a Latin seem a restful companion" (p. 34). This is probably an exaggeration, since the precepts and admonitions to which we referred clearly encourage a certain degree of reserve in the Chinese which is not entirely due to his discomfort in a strange environment. The truth probably lies somewhere between the extremes which regard him on the one hand as "vivacious," and on the other as "inscrutable."

It is occasionally suggested that there may be racial factors responsible for differences in expressiveness. The whole question of race differences will be discussed in Chapter XI; at this point it may merely be pointed out that the probability is against this hypothesis, in spite of the anatomical features which have been described. The most important argument against a purely racial explanation is the fact that Chinese and Japanese vary so greatly in the degree of their "inscrutability" when they live in different social environments. Professor Romanzo Adams (18) of the University of Hawaii describes his observations in a rural district in Japan from which many of the Hawaiian Japanese had come. He met close relatives of those he had known in Hawaii, and had the opportunity of observing them and their children closely. He writes:

The mannerisms of the old country villagers seemed to an American to show a constraint not characteristic of the Hawaiian Japanese. There was less self-assertiveness, less expression of individuality. Their faces, especially those of girls, were less expressive. It seemed that the numerous little muscles about the eyes and the mouth that have to do with facial expression were relatively undeveloped from lack of use (p. 256).

In spite of its anecdotal character this observation is of great significance in this connection, since it indicates that inborn anatomical factors may not be nearly so important as Dr. Mêng has suggested.

Adams goes on to describe the marked difference in the behavior of the Oriental in Hawaii and on the mainland of the

United States.   Referring particularly to the Chinese, he makes an observation which tends to corroborate Schrieke's interpretation of Chinese inscrutability. He states that when a White man from Hawaii goes to California and meets the Chinese living there, he is impressed with a reserve on their part.   The normal attitude of a Chinese in San Francisco and elsewhere on the west coast toward a White stranger, even though he may have a friendly manner, is one of distrust. "The Hawaiian Chinese are, in the presence of Whites, more given to laughter and when in sorrow they may weep.   In an interracial group they act as if they have a sense of really belonging" (p. 319).   This difference is explained as due to the more satisfactory social status of the Chinese in Hawaii, and their consequent freedom from restraint.   In their tastes, mannerisms and loyalties, they are becoming Americanized or "acculturated" much more rapidly and more effectively than is the case in California.   This interpretation seems a highly plausible one, and indicates that the so-called Oriental reserve is dependent upon previous training and the social situation, rather than upon innate factors.

In connection with the amount of expression permitted in a culture, it is important to note that this may differ greatly according to the nature of the emotion involved.   In the two most "inscrutable" cultures we know, the American Indian of the Plains and the Chinese, overt expression of grief was not only permitted, but demanded.   The Chinese, who feel that a display of anger is never warranted and that affection should be shown only in strict privacy, insist upon a public manifestation of grief or sorrow.   One piece of advice to young girls reads: "If your father or mother is sick, do not be far from his or her bed.   Do not even take off your girdle.   Taste all the medicine yourself.   Pray your god for his or her health. If anything unfortunate happens cry bitterly" (14).   Not only is grief expressed, but there is an elaborate set of rules and regulations which ensure that it will be properly expressed. One of the Chinese classics is *The Book of Rites,* a considerable portion of which is devoted to the technique of the mourning ceremonial, with elaborate instructions as to just what procedure should be followed in order that the expression of the grief may be socially acceptable (*19*). The Plains Indians, in spite of their deserved reputation for imperturbability, expected a man literally to wail and howl for hours at a stretch at the death of his wife or child. It is reported of many African tribes that any public show of affection between husband and wife was regarded as disgraceful, although other emotions might be quite freely expressed. The same holds true for parts of Melanesia. It is clear that the repressive influence of a culture with regard to emotional behavior is not applied equally in all directions. It is perhaps unnecessary to add that the absence of the manifestation of an emotion does not prove that it is not experienced. It merely prevents our direct knowledge of its existence.

Even within our own society there are tremendous individual variations in the amount of expression. These may to some extent be due to organic factors, for example, to a relative stability or lability of the sympathico-adrenal system. There may be differences in the threshold for emotions generally, or for one or another emotion in particular, making one person angry and another frightened more easily than the average. Individual training and experience will also play a part. In addition, there are undoubtedly great variations in this respect between different social and economic classes, as well as between different regions of the same country. In the United States there are marked contrasts between New England and the South on the one hand and the Middle West on the other. Probably in all countries the urban population is much livelier and more expressive than the rural. As for socio-economic classes, it is usual to find more obvious emotional expression in the poorer than in the wealthier groups. In the latter, there frequently develops the ideal of the "gentleman" who does not wear his heart on his sleeve. The traditional reserve of the Englishman is apparently the product of the most exclusive schools, just as the self-control of the Chinese scholar was largely due to his education in the Confucian manner. In both cases other classes of the society were also affected, but not nearly to the same degree, so that a class distinction exists here as in other aspects of behavior.

A recent experiment (20) on the judgment of facial expression of emotions indicates the smaller amount of expression in the Chinese as compared with the American face. Chinese and American subjects posed for the illustration of different emotions, and these photographs were given to both Chinese and American students to judge. The results showed that both groups of judges were somewhat more successful with the American than with the Chinese pictures. The conclusion appears warranted that the American face is more expressive, at least in these artificial situations; the proof is not absolute, since the two groups of persons photographed could not be regarded as "equated" in every way. The result is in keeping, however, with general observations of the amount of expression normally permitted to Americans and to Chinese, respectively.

THE NATURE OF EMOTIONAL EXPRESSION

There are undoubtedly certain types of expressive behavior which are common to all human societies. Apparently all children cry considerably during the early years of life, when they are hungry or in pain, or when they require some attention. Apparently, also, at the outset the cry subserves a great many uses, expressing anger, for example, just as readily as it does physical pain; but with the passage of time it becomes associated with certain unpleasant emotions more than with others. The occurrence of the cry in grief or in "mental pain" is probably a still later extension from this origin. Laughter, too, is in all probability universal as a sign of joy or well-being, although the exact physiological mechanism involved is still in doubt (see below, p. 190). There are certainly other expressions which are universal, but in all of these, including the two which have been mentioned, social factors enter to a considerable degree.

The attempt was made by Darwin (21) to explain the origin

and nature of emotional expression in terms of the following three principles: (1) *The principle of serviceable associated habits* may be illustrated by the violent start which usually accompanies hearing a sudden noise. Originally this was due to the need to jump away as quickly as possible from danger, so that now even though the sound may not mean danger the same behavior ensues. The sneer which accompanies anger or contempt is similarly explained; it represents a survival from the time when teeth were bared as a preparation for their use in fighting. Darwin writes:

Certain complex actions are of direct or indirect service under certain states of the mind, in order to relieve or gratify certain sensations, desires, etc.; and whenever the same state of mind is induced, however feebly, there is a tendency through the force of habit and association for the same movements to be performed, though they may not then be of the least use (p. 28).

This principle is a significant one, but not so much may be said for (2) *the principle of antithesis*. According to this, when the opposite state of mind to the above is induced, there is a strong and involuntary tendency to the performance of movements of a directly opposed nature, though these may be of no possible use. A dog, for example, assumes the opposite attitude when at the feet of his master from that indicating an intention to fight. There appear to be few expressions to which this principle is applicable. Finally there is (3) *the principle of actions due to the constitution of the nervous system*. This would apply to the loss of pigmentation of the hair after extreme terror or grief, the trembling which accompanies various types of emotional excitement, perspiration, blushing, etc. These phenomena can now be explained on the basis of the physiological changes described by Cannon and others.

Emotional expression has been studied in a variety of ways. We are here not primarily concerned with the many investigations of the purely physiological changes accompanying the emotions. There have been measurements of changes in blood pressure, respiratory rate and the nature of the breathing curve, pulse rate, changes in volume in various parts of the body, electrical phenomena accompanying the psycho-galvanic reflex, etc. These studies, important though they are, concern themselves primarily with problems in individual psychology, and are not directly social except in regard to the causes of the emotions. More pertinent to the field of social psychology is the problem of the recognition of emotional expression by others. The observations of Bühler (22) have shown that recognition is not present at birth, but develops gradually through the first years of life. A very young child will not distinguish a friendly tone of voice or a scowling face from their opposites and must learn the difference. In the case of the adult a large number of investigations have been conducted on the recognizability of emotional expressions, particularly in the face. The pioneer work of Feleky (23) was followed by that of many others. Feleky showed that emotions differ widely in their recognizability, joy and fear being judged with ease, and sorrow, anger and surprise with greater difficulty. In the judgments of facial expression in general, although there are always a great many errors, the judgments are more frequently right than wrong. Dunlap (24) used the interesting technique of joining the upper portion of one facial expression to the lower portion of another in order to see which part of the face is of greater importance in determining the perception of the emotion. He found that the lower portion of the face was dominant. There was apparently a Gestalt or configurational effect, since the combination of the upper part of a "disgust" picture and the lower part of a "mirth" picture not only combined to give a judgment of mirth, but the eyes were actually seen to convey the same expression.

Studies have also been carried out on the recognizability of emotions as expressed in the voice. Gates (25) reports that when the letters of the alphabet are spoken with varying intonation, the voice may in a very large number of cases convey the meaning correctly. It is also possible to recognize emotions to some degree from posture (26), and from the position of the hands (27).

Pertinent to this whole problem is the question of the relationship between emotional expression in man and in the higher anthropoids. If expression is largely biological and innately determined, we should expect considerable similarity between these two closely related species. If, on the other hand, culture is largely responsible for expression, we should expect marked differences, since the anthropoids are presum· ably exposed to a culture only of the most rudimentary sort. Köhler (28), who had the opportunity of observing chimpanzees closely over a period of years on the island of Tene- riffe, states that he was able without too much difficulty to understand the emotions which these animals were expressing. Similarly, Mrs. Ladigina-Kohts (29) of the Laboratory for Zoo-psychology in Moscow regards the emotional expression of chimpanzees and of human beings as essentially the same.

This view has recently been subjected to an experimental approach by Foley (30), who made Ladigina-Kohts' pictures the basis for a study of the recognizability of chimpanzee ex- pression. The pictures allegedly represented the following emotional states—quietude, sadness, laughter, weeping, anger, excitement. They were presented to a group of students who judged each picture by choosing one out of a mimeographed list of sixteen emotions. The results showed great individual differences. The main finding of the investigation was that the number of correct judgments was just about what would be expected by pure chance. In other words, the judges failed to recognize the emotional expression in the face of the chim- panzee. In particular there was frequent confusion between the pictures representing physical pain, anger and joy. Foley points out that this type of confusion entered into a popular motion picture, "School Pals," depicting some curious antics of the chimpanzee.

At the conclusion of this picture, when the chimpanzee had just "played a trick" upon his adversary, it was desired to convey to the audience the impression that the chimpanzee was laughing. The animal's hand, hidden from direct view behind a board fence, was pinched or otherwise painfully stimulated. This immediately elicited the typical facial expression of rage or anger, which was interpreted by the audience as joy or laughter (p. 58).

Foley concludes that there are enormous differences in emotional expression between the chimpanzee and man, as well as a demonstrated inability of man to judge the expressive reactions of the chimpanzee.

The discrepancy between these results and the view of Köhler, referred to above, has a number of possible explanations. It may be that Köhler's rich experience has made possible for him a recognition of the emotions hardly to be expected from the untrained judges in Foley's experiment. It is also probable that if one sees the live active animal and knows the context of his behavior, one receives many cues not present in a photograph of the face alone. Finally it should be pointed out that Köhler's success may not necessarily be due to any essential similarity in the expressions of the chimpanzee and man; even if the expressions differ, continued observation of the animals in a variety of situations, as well as of the associations between these and their expression, might still make it possible that such recognition would occur. It is clear that further research on the emotional expression of the anthropoids is needed. Our tentative conclusion is that the weight of evidence is against any real similarity between anthropoid and man in this respect, and in favor therefore of the hypothesis of cultural or social determination of emotional expression.

The Language of Emotional Expression. Emotional expression is to be viewed not merely as a spontaneous result of inner physiological processes, but also as a means of social communication, a language. Among psychologists this has been most clearly recognized by Dumas (*31*), who believes that most expressions, whether they are explained in terms of psychology, physiology or physics, have become language in that we use them constantly in social life to convey information to others. It has frequently been noticed that if a little child hurts himself, he will usually cry very little or not at all if there is no one in his immediate environment. In the presence of a possibly sympathetic adult it is much more likely that the child will cry in order to be comforted. As adults we voluntarily put on an interested expression when we are taking part in conversation or listening to a lecture, we smile upon meeting an acquaintance we care nothing about, we put on a "long face" as we listen to bad news which does not concern us in the least. In all these cases the expression has exclusively the function of communication, and the signs are understood by others as clearly as if we had spoken. This of course does not mean that we never feel the particular emotion expressed, but it does mean that we do not need to feel it in order to express it. The ethnologist Tylor (32) correctly refers to physical expression as an important adjunct to spoken language.

There is another sense in which emotional expression is comparable to spoken language, namely, in the fact that it, too, must be learned. This may not be true to the same degree, but there can be no doubt that acquired as well as innate mechanisms play a part. Other societies besides our own have recognized this aspect of emotional expression. Rank (33) states that the first attempts to systematize human gestures are found among the Babylonians, who recorded their knowledge of the psychology of expression in the so-called "twitching books." The recognition of the conventional aspect of emotional expression is clearest among the Chinese. There is an interesting story in this connection included in *The Book of Rites*.

Yu-tze and Tze-yu (third to fourth century B.C.) saw a child weeping for the loss of his parents. The former observed, "I never could understand why mourners should necessarily jump about to show their grief, and would long ago have got rid of the custom. Now here you have an honest expression of feeling, and that is all there ever should be." "My friend," replied the other, "the mourning ceremonial, with all its material accompaniments, is at once a check upon undue emotion and a guarantee against any lack of proper respect. Simply to give vent to the feelings is the way of barbarians. That is not our way. The due regulation of the emotions is the function of a set ceremonial" (34, pp. 45-6).

There are certain expressions which are so obviously cultural that they present no special problem. This category includes, for example, thumbing the nose as a sign of contempt or defiance. It is not likely that an act of this kind has any biological meaning. The Maori have a sign of friendship made by doubling the forefinger of the right hand, and placing the projecting second joint to the tip of the nose, a somewhat similar act with exactly opposite significance. A Chinese mother pushes her child's head back with her forefinger to show that she is angry with him, or rubs her cheek with her finger instead of calling "shame." Acts like these will obviously vary from group to group.

The same holds true in all probability for the habit of kissing, although Crawley (*35*) speaks of it as "instinctive" in the higher societies and very rare among lower or semi-civilized races! It need hardly be pointed out that we know of no instinct present in some societies and not in others. The region of the lips is usually included among so-called erogenous zones which are capable of giving sensual satisfaction; in spite of this fact, the kiss is far from universal. In other societies it may be replaced by the rubbing of noses, touching the nose to the cheek, rubbing faces, touching the right nostril of the other person with the right index finger, and other forms of contact. In Japan, the kiss is (or was) restricted to the relationship between mother and child, and the Western habit of kissing between adults was regarded as disgusting. Crawley observes that not only is the kiss absent in many parts of the world, but that where it does occur, it has a wide variety of uses and applications. He refers to the early Christian habit of promiscuous kissing as a symbol of fellowship; the kiss of charity; kissing of knights after they were dubbed, and of persons elected to office; kissing the hands or breast or feet of superiors, kissing the feet of the monarch by his vassals; the kiss on the forehead conveying blessing or reverence; the kissing of sacred objects. It is of course still used, notably in France, in the ceremony of conferring special honors. It may be added that the religious significance of the kiss is by no means restricted to Christian and Jewish practice; Cicero observes that the lips and beard of the statue of Hercules at

Agrigentum were almost worn away by the kisses of the devout. It is clear that the kiss is not necessarily a sign of sexual affection, although the Freudians would undoubtedly contend that it is an extension from an erogenous origin. For our purposes it is sufficient to point out that it is not universally used with the same significance that it has among us. It may be added that when visitors to primitive communities remark on the lack of affection between husband and wife, this may be due to differences in the manner of expression. Here as elsewhere we must be familiar with the language of emotional expression in the group we are trying to understand.

In the case of other expressions, apparently more fundamental, the same variation may be noted. The occurrence of tears as a sign of grief is probably universal. Cultural factors enter, however, in the determination of the time, the place and even the amount of the crying which is expected. Mauss (36) has pointed out that among the native Australians the expression of grief upon the death of a relative was socially regulated in this manner. In China, as was mentioned above, there were elaborate ceremonial rules which made certain that the grief would be expressed in a manner acceptable to the society. As Granet (19) points out, there was the development of a true language of grief, with rules as exact as those of any grammar. A mourner was forbidden to have a grief which could not be expressed in terms of the required symbolism. There were certain rules associated with the ceremonial which seem strange to Western observers. For example, the severity of the mourning increased with the importance of the person mourned; a young woman should mourn more for the death of her mother-in-law than for her own mother; mourning may be discontinued if no visits of condolence are paid. The mourning required tears at certain stated times and under definite conditions. The same has been reported for Montenegro, where during mourning men weep at one time and women at another. At the funeral there is a period of wailing which is soon followed by tears, even in the case of those villagers who are not even related to the person whose

death they are bemoaning. Of one such occasion, Durham
(*37*) writes: "The Vrbica men mostly did not know the poor
boy's name and had to be coached in the details before beginning to wail, but within a minute or two of beginning they
were sobbing bitterly. Coming home people compared notes
as to who had cried best" (p. 298). This ability to cry at
stated times is by no means absent among ourselves, but it
is not common. In other societies there has apparently occurred a sort of conditioning process, which has associated
tears with specific situations, and the occurrence of such situations directly results in the appropriate shedding of tears.
It may be added that in China and Montenegro, and undoubtedly in many other countries as well, men weep as readily as
women on these occasions.

Apparently with the ability to weep at will under definite
conditions, there goes also the capacity of recovering quickly
from this display of emotion. Among the Huichol Indians of
Mexico the writer noted that when weeping occurred as part
of the religious ceremonial, it was possible for the man who
wept to stop at will, and as soon as it was over he returned to
his usual cheerfulness. A similar observation is made by
Blackwood (*38*) for the people of Buka, among whom there
is much weeping at funerals. She tells of a girl whose grief
seemed very profound and who had to be dragged away from
the coffin when it was finally taken to the burial ground, but
almost immediately after, she was talking and laughing with
the other girls of the village.

More striking still is the weeping which occurs in several
communities under conditions unconnected with either pain
or sorrow. For both the Andaman Islanders (*39*) and the
Maori (*40*) it has been reported that tears are shed when two
persons meet after a long absence, and when peace has been
declared between two warring parties. An early account of
this practice among the Andaman Islanders by Man (*41*) interprets it as follows:

Relatives, after an absence of a few weeks or months, testify their
joy at meeting by sitting down with their arms around each other's

necks and weeping and howling in a manner which would lead a stranger to suppose that some great sorrow had befallen them; and, in point of fact, there is no difference observable between their demonstrations of joy on these occasions and those of grief on the death of one of their number (pp. 147-8).

It is probably not correct, however, to regard weeping on these occasions as a sign of joy. The natives themselves say that it is weeping for the loss of those who have died during the time that the friends were separated. From our point of view it is important to note that even if no one has died in the interval, weeping still is the correct form of greeting.

Radcliffe Brown believes that this form of ritual weeping does have an emotional significance, even though it may not necessarily be an expression of sorrow. It represents the individual's emotional reaction to the notion of group solidarity, which has been threatened by absence or war and which has now again been restored. Even this degree of emotional response seems unnecessary, however, since Radcliffe Brown reports that when he asked the natives to show how it was done, two or three of them sat down and were immediately weeping real tears at his request. This means that we have here a complete divorce of weeping from true emotional expression, and its use as a conventional rite or ceremony. These natives do weep on painful and sorrowful occasions, as we do, but a process of conditioning has taken place which makes possible the association of the response of the tear glands to a secondary stimulus or situation. This phenomenon is of particular importance in the present discussion, since it indicates the possibility of cultural conditioning of a physiological response which is evidently universal, and which has a biological basis. For further discussion of this problem see (5).

In this connection an interesting observation was reported to the writer by Dr. Peter Buck, the director of the Bernice P. Bishop Museum in Honolulu. Dr. Buck is himself part Maori and has been able since his childhood to produce tears at will. He states, however, that the young Maori now growing up in New Zealand with a thoroughly Anglo-Saxon type of education, are rapidly losing this ability. They are finding it difficult to weep at the times indicated by the traditional ceremonials. This is an example of the manner in which a change in cultural pattern may affect deep-seated behavior tendencies. It shows incidentally that the relative facility in weeping is not a racial trait, since the Maori are losing it under changed conditions.

The emotion of anger and its manifestation have already been touched upon in connection with the discussion of aggressive behavior. It was pointed out that anger might be expressed by means of a potlatch, by the singing of satirical songs, by striking at a rock with a piece of wood, and so forth. We may mention here as an additional example the habit of the Melanesians of Buka, whose usual way of showing anger is to break up their own personal possessions. This occurs not in a fit of blind temper, but intentionally (*38*). It is similarly reported for the natives of Nicobar that in a serious quarrel a man may set fire to his own house (*42*). It seems evident that in anger there is a strong urge to do something, but that the outward expression of this urge will vary markedly according to one's previous training and experience.

The expression of anger among the Chinese shows interesting variations from our own behavior, and raises a number of important problems. A search through Chinese novels revealed many literary expressions of anger which might not readily be understood by a reader unfamiliar with them (*14*). We find, for example, "her eyes grew round and opened wide," or, "he made his two eyes round and stared at him." Although the Chinese condemn any outburst of anger, staring with fixed eyes seems to be an acceptable method of indicating one's attitude. Incidentally, the Chinese find that the faces of Europeans seem constantly to be expressing anger or irritation; this is probably due to the fact that the normally larger and rounder eyes of the European resemble the Chinese eyes in anger. Other expressions of anger are: "he laughed a great ho-ho"; "he smiled a chill smile"; "he looked at them and he smiled and cursed them." Both the laugh and the smile of contempt do occur in our own culture, but apparently not nearly so frequently as in China and in the Chinese literature. More striking still, one may read, "he was so angry that several times he fainted from his anger." When the writer expressed wonder at this, Chinese friends said that they in their turn could never understand why European ladies fainted so frequently in the mid-Victorian literature, and with so little cause. Certainly the delicately nurtured young lady of not so long ago did faint with astonishing ease and regularity; there were even rules of fainting which had to be followed. "Etiquette books taught them the correct way to faint elegantly. The emotions of women during the Victorian age were arranged and ordered for them, and they accepted these restrictions gracefully" (*43*, p. 202). This is certainly no less surprising than that the Chinese should faint in anger. The conclusion seems clear that fainting, like tears, may be conditioned by social custom to appear on entirely different occasions.

In connection with the Chinese expression of anger, undoubtedly the most striking phenomenon is the fact that death is alleged to be a possible consequence. We read in the literature: "his anger has risen so that he is ill of it and lies upon his bed, and his life cannot be long assured." " 'To-day am I killed by anger' . . . and when he had finished speaking he let his soul go free." This is reported as still occurring, and the writer saw a patient in a Peking hospital who stated in his family history that his father had died of anger after losing a lawsuit. It is important to note that this death cannot be explained as due to anything like an apoplectic stroke; it does not occur suddenly as a stroke would. When someone is very angry but forced to suppress his anger because there is nothing he can do about it, he may become ill, faint many times and take to his bed; death may follow after the lapse of some days or weeks. The only explanation is in terms of suggestion; the belief that people die of anger under these conditions may succeed in causing the death of an impressionable person. The case is similar to that of death in many primitive societies as a result of black magic or from the consciousness of having broken a serious taboo.

In connection with contempt, which is closely related to anger, Darwin suggested that spitting is an almost universal expression of it; it represents the rejection of anything offensive from the mouth, this sign then being extended figuratively to other types of rejection. There are, however, many cases which do not fit this theory. In a great many different communities spitting is a kind of blessing in critical situations and may be used to bring good luck and to ward off or cure disease. "Travellers report that in the ceremonial attending the birth of a child among the Arabians the priest, after invoking the blessing of God upon the child, whispers a few sentences in the child's ear and spits three times on its face" (*43*, p. 22). Even in Europe it was firmly held during the Middle Ages that spittle applied to the forehead or other parts of the body would ward off evil. It seems unlikely therefore that Darwin's explanation is the correct one.

Accounts of the expression of fear in different communities show a substantial degree of similarity. In the Chinese literature, for example, we find the following: "everyone trembled with a face the color of clay"; "every one of his hairs stood on end, and the pimples came out on the skin all over his body"; "a cold sweat broke forth upon him, and he trembled without ceasing"; "they stood like death with mouths ajar"; "they were so frightened that their waters and wastes burst out of them" (*14*). Allowing for the Chinese literary style, these expressions might just as easily have been used by Europeans. It is possible that in the case of fear the expressions are much more directly controlled by physiological processes, and that cultural patterning has played little or no part. Another possibility is that fear is an emotion which has an asocial character, and is thus less subject to control by social factors. Anger, love, surprise, interest, and most remaining emotional states are conveyed to others; they have at least in part the character of communication. Fear, however, is primarily a form of withdrawal, and as a consequence may have fewer social components.

Laughter. As far as joy and happiness are concerned, the smile and the laugh appear to be a universal expression. In no ethnological account familiar to the writer is there any indication of a people who fail to express their good spirits in this way. Although it is true that the infant passes through a short period before the smile appears, this indicates more probably a lack of muscular control than a need to be taught how to smile. It certainly is not long before the child laughs purely to express its happiness, and education appears to play only a small part in the process.

Before we turn to comparative material pertinent to this problem, some mention should be made of the various explanations and theories of laughter and a sense of humor. One of the most famous of these theories is that of Thomas Hobbes (44), who believed that laughter arises out of a feeling of sudden glory induced by the misfortunes of others and the consequent conviction of our own superiority. This would explain our laughter at all forms of slapstick comedy and similar occurrences in everyday life, as well as our amusement at the manners and customs of people different from ourselves. Apparently Hobbes' theory helped to spread the notion that it was somehow mean and rude to laugh, and one of Lord Shaftesbury's letters to his son urges him never to indulge in such ungentlemanly behavior. Another theory is that of Schopenhauer (45), who believed that laughter arises as a result of any perception of incongruity in a situation. We laugh when things are seen together which do not belong together, or when two lines of action are indulged in simultaneously in spite of being mutually incompatible. There is certainly a good deal of humor which would fit into this category, but it is possible also to see in the theory merely a more specific instance of the wider principle which Hobbes expressed. Incongruity may be regarded as one variety of defect or inferiority in the objects or situations which arouse our amusement. The same may be said of Bergson's theory

(*46*), which holds that we laugh whenever we see anything living acting like something mechanical or dead. This is the reason we laugh at the pompous gentleman who stubs his toe and falls. In all probability, however, this is also the perception of inferiority in someone else.

On the physiological side the important theory is that of Herbert Spencer (*47*), who regarded laughter, like play, as due to surplus energy. This arises principally in those cases in which we are all set for a difficult situation which suddenly and surprisingly turns out to be very simple, or when we are prepared for an emotional reaction which is no longer applicable. In such situations we have been prepared for a considerable expenditure of energy, and we find that this is no longer needed. The energy has been mobilized, however, and demands some kind of outlet. Since the muscles of the face and throat are among those most easily stimulated, the sounds and movements constituting laughter are the result. This theory explains in a similar manner laughter resulting from tickling; the outstretched finger or hand of another person originally signified danger, but in the case of tickling this danger becomes dissipated into nothing. The energy with which the danger would have been met is transformed into laughter.

Freud (*48*) has developed a theory of wit and humor which contains some of the elements of Spencer's view, and some more closely allied to Hobbes'. For Freud there are two kinds of wit. The first is "harmless wit," in which puns and plays on words, for example, are pleasing because of the economy which they effect in the expenditure of energy. Suppose, for example, we hear the Christmas vacation described as the 'alcoholidays.' In this case two words have been combined into one, and there is a consequent saving. This economy results in a surplus of energy which is released as laughter. This portion of Freud's theory does not carry very much conviction, since the amount of energy so saved is infinitesimal. The second type of wit is called *Tendenzwitz*, which might best be translated as tendentious wit, that is to say, wit which has some sort of barb or point and which serves as a means of expressing one's true opinions. In the form of a joke this type of hostility is socially permitted, but it none the less expresses the real (sometimes unconscious) hostile attitudes of the speaker.

We may give as an example of *Tendenzwitz* the famous story of the conversation between Whistler and Oscar Wilde. The former made some brilliant remark and Wilde said enthusiastically, "That's wonderful. I wish I had said that." "You will, Oscar, you will," was the reply. Presumably in this case Whistler meant what he said and the witticism gave him a chance, although in a friendly manner, to point out Wilde's tendency to repeat as his own the clever remarks made by his friends. The familiar expression "there's many a true word spoken in jest" illustrates this mechanism. In any case we see that this portion of Freud's theory of wit fits in perfectly with Hobbes' explanation of the nature of laughter, since the humor is clearly directed against somebody.

As Goldenweiser (*49*) has pointed out, it is very difficult for an ethnologist to become sufficiently well acquainted with the language and the customs of the group he is studying to understand the nature of their sense of humor. It seems clear, however, that although in many respects their humor may differ markedly from ours, laughter of the Hobbesian variety occurs everywhere. The specific examples from primitive societies are sufficiently rare to warrant a somewhat detailed description of some of them at this point. Blackwood (*38*) tells of the children in Buka that after the annual visit of the British governor they enacted the whole occasion, taking the salute and going through all the remaining official ceremonies. They ended by throwing to the other children bits of stick and pigs' teeth for which they scrambled just as the adults had scrambled for the governor's tobacco and sweets. It was all done very solemnly until the final scramble which ended with shrieks of laughter. Among the Ontong Java of the Solomon Islands, individuals are betrothed when very young. Hogbin (*50*) reports that on one occasion when assisting the medical officer to make an examination of the whole population, he called up a betrothed boy and girl at the same time to see what would happen. They seemed very shy and uncomfortable; the rest of the people were intensely amused at their embarrassment.

Among the Pueblo Indians of New Mexico there are a number of individuals who play the part of clowns or "delight-makers" (*54*). Their humor consists mainly of a mimicry or burlesque of the ceremonies as well as of forms of behavior which at other times are taken very seriously. Mimicry of the Whites, accompanied by considerable ridicule, occurs frequently. One of the Pueblo clowns once called out from the housetop that he had a message from the Indian agent that if any man or woman talked to another's husband or wife he would be brought up for trial. It seems clear that many of the agent's regulations must from the Indians' point of view have been just as ridiculous as this imaginary one, and their laughter indicated their attitude. In general, ridicule is used by primitive societies largely for purposes of social control. This use is of course present in our society also, as Bergson (*46*) pointed out, but in other groups it may take the place of more drastic forms of coercion. In Lesu, for example, it is the weapon employed by the wife to keep her husband at his appointed duties. If he should fail in these, she makes a speech before the villagers ridiculing him for not knowing how to work, for strolling about all the time, and for leaving it to her to mend the garden fence or to clear the ground where the taro is to be planted. The loud laughter with which this announcement is greeted is of course directed against the husband, who is shamed into doing what is required of him (*52*).

Wissler (*53*) states that in general primitive people are especially sensitive to the ridicule and the adverse opinions of their fellows, and that this more than anything else keeps the members of the community true to the principles of their elders. Particularly among the American Indians the rule was that most crimes were punished only by laughter and ridicule. Lowie (*54*) reports that among the Crow, when a man had committed a serious breach of morality, nothing would be done to him directly, but in the evening someone might call out to the whole group: "Did you hear about so-and-so?" Then amid great laughter his transgression would be commented upon in terms of the most scathing ridicule, and this might go on for a long time. The transgressor would be so shamed by the laughter of his fellows that he might even be driven to leave the community and not return until he had in some way redeemed himself.

There were some American Indian tribes which made use of ridicule as a means of social control through the institution of the "joking relatives." Although the exact relationship varied considerably, it conferred both the right and the duty of reciprocal ridicule and criticism. This served effectively to prevent any important deviations from the mores, since one's joking relatives always seized the occasion for merriment at the expense of the wrongdoer. The Pueblo clowns performed a similar function for the whole community. They would stand before the various houses in the pueblo, calling the inmates by name in song and twitting them for their stinginess, laziness, domestic infelicity, excessive fondness for American ways, and so forth (55).

On the basis of this and similar material, it seems safe to conclude that laughter is everywhere used with the meaning of ridicule and that this argues in favor of Hobbes' theory. It is also true, however, that laughter in young children, if not in adults, apparently expresses "pure joy" without any reference to the inferiorities and inadequacies of others. It is still "sudden glory," but it does not necessarily have the origin which Hobbes ascribed to it. If we broaden the theory to include all forms of joy or sudden glory no matter what their origin, we shall probably account for the majority of cases in which laughter is the means of expression. This would fit in also with Spencer's explanation in terms of surplus energy, since joy may exercise a dynamogenic effect, whether it is due to the feeling of well-being or to the consciousness of our own superiority over others.

There are cases, however, in which joy is not expressed in this manner. We have already mentioned the use of tears as a ceremony of greeting, on what would appear to us as a festive rather than a sad occasion. Wilson (56) reports the following experience in Tahiti:

In passing a few houses, an aged woman, mother to the young man who carried my linen, met us, and to express her joy at seeing her son, struck herself several times on the head with a shark's tooth, till the blood flowed plentifully down her breast and shoulders, whilst the son beheld it with entire insensibility (p. 70).

Williams (57) describes a festive ceremony among the Melanesian Orokaiva as follows:

The guests, arriving in their several parties, come striding single file into the village, each party headed by its man of first importance, befeathered club on shoulder. No smile adorns his face, but rather an expression of fierceness, which, however unsuited it may seem to the hospitable occasion, is nevertheless Orokaiva good form (p. 29).

Porteus (58) reports that the native Australians whom he studied inflict injuries upon themselves on both joyous and sorrowful occasions, and he saw no difference between the expressions of these two diametrically opposed emotions.

Not only may joy be expressed without a smile, but in addition the smile may be used in a variety of situations in a manner quite different from what appears to be its original significance. Even in our own society, we know that a smile may mean contempt, incredulity, affection, and serve also as part of a purely social greeting devoid of emotional significance. In China as we have noted, it accompanies anger much more frequently than among ourselves. In China also, as in Japan, the smile is the correct expression for a servant who is announcing to his superior some calamity that has befallen him. He smiles in order to minimize the importance of his misfortune, so that the other should not be troubled by it. The Chinese servant smiles also when he is being scolded, apparently so as to make the resulting unpleasantness less obvious.

Lafcadio Hearn (*59*), who spent many years among the Japanese, was perhaps the first to point out to Westerners the meaning of the Japanese smile. He gives many examples which illustrate principles similar to those which hold for the Chinese. In some instances, the misunderstanding of Japanese by Europeans on this account may even have tragic consequences, as in the case of the samurai whose smile when he was scolded by his employer so infuriated the latter that he struck him; in order to expiate this insult the samurai committed hara-kiri, or honorable suicide.

Hearn states that it was the Emperor Iyeyasu who first required that an inferior when reproved should not only not sulk, but should actually show pleasure. It gradually became a mark of disrespect to betray any feeling of grief or pain in the presence of a superior, and with it there arose an elaborate code of deportment which had to be followed.

It required not only that any sense of anger or pain should be denied all outward expression, but that the sufferer's face and manner should indicate the contrary feeling. Sullen submission was an offense; mere passive obedience inadequate; the proper degree of submission should manifest itself by a pleasant smile, and by a soft and happy tone of voice (*60*, p. 192).

Even the quality of the smile was regulated. It was a moral offense, for example, so to smile in addressing a superior that the back teeth could be seen. Among the samurai these rules of conduct were rigidly enforced. "Samurai women were required, like the women of Sparta, to show signs of joy on hearing that their husbands or sons had fallen in battle; to betray any natural feeling under the circumstances was a grave breach of decorum" (p. 193).

In these cases the smile obviously does not stand for sorrow, even though the occasions may be unhappy ones. It is rather that the sorrow may not be expressed, and that an appearance of joy must be maintained. In practice it does mean, however, that among the Chinese and Japanese the smile appears in circumstances which we would regard as quite foreign to it, and there is no doubt that serious misunderstandings arise as a consequence. In order to understand the behavior of a people we need to know not only their spoken language, but also their language of bodily expression.

Emotional Expression in General.   This survey has shown the wide variety of expressive behavior related to the emotions.   This does not mean that all emotional expression is to be regarded as artificial and flexible to the same degree as spoken language.   Apparently all degrees are possible.   At the one extreme we have the crying of the child in pain—an expression common to all individuals no matter what their culture.   At the other extreme we have the language of emotional expression on the Chinese stage, in which standing on one foot means surprise, and fanning the face with the sleeve means anger.   In this same category also we may put the custom of the Blackfoot Indians to express their mood by the color of the paint used on their faces.   "If we felt angry, peaceful, in love, religious, or whatever the mood was, we painted our faces accordingly, so that all who should come in contact with us would know at a glance how we felt" (*61,* p. 244).   Between these extremes we find every possible degree of cultural patterning.   In those cases in which culture has not interfered too greatly with physiological processes, or where such interference has proceeded along lines similar to our own, we can understand the emotional behavior of other peoples with some success.   Otherwise, we may be led far astray if we interpret their behavior patterns as necessarily having the same significance which they would have among ourselves.   It should be added that this type of misunderstanding may apply to linguistic as well as to bodily forms of expression.   This is illustrated by the comment of an aged Omaha Indian on the White people's custom of addressing one another by name, particularly if they were members of the same family.   "It sounds as though they do not love one another when they do not use terms of relationship" (*62,* p. 335), that is, when they do not express in their speech the exact relationship between them.   In this instance it is a member of another culture who is mistaken in his interpretation of us, but we are just as likely to err in a comparable manner.

Between any two groups of different culture it will probably be found that their patterns of emotional expressions show considerable overlapping as well as a definite amount of diversity. This was the result of the experiment referred to above (20), in which Chinese and American photographs were compared. Both groups of judges recognized a substantial proportion of the expressions in both groups of pictures, indicating that there must be many common factors. It was true, however, that the American judges recognized the American pictures better than did the Chinese, and that the Chinese in turn were better judges of the Chinese pictures than were the Americans. The factor of familiarity or acquaintance with the patterns of expression has an unmistakable effect. This is much more noticeable in certain emotions than in others. In surprise, for example, it is common for the Chinese to stick out the tongue; since this pattern is rare among Americans, the picture corresponding to it was more easily recognized by the Chinese. Allowing for all possible variations between the individual judges and the specific emotions, the experiment indicated clearly the existence of cultural patterning, as well as of aspects of expression common to the two cultures.

On the physiological side it is possible to understand the observed variations in emotional behavior on the basis of Cannon's (3) emergency theory. We know the physiological concomitants of emotion generally, but not of the specific emotions. The consequence may be that whereas in emotional excitement the organism is prepared to do something, the exact nature of the act will be influenced by social factors. This makes it possible to understand why, for example, a sudden death may be the cause of fighting among the members of the bereaved group, or why anger may be accompanied by such a variety of responses. The exact limits of the physiological as contrasted with the social factors have not as yet been exactly determined, and further research in this field is needed from both points of view. The study of expression in the case of subjects blind from birth should throw much light on this problem.

THE NATURE OF EMOTIONAL EXPERIENCES

There is still another possible way in which social factors may enter into the emotions, namely, in determining their subjective content and the meaning they have for the individual who is experiencing them. It may be that the very names and labels we give to the emotions have an entirely different connotation in one social setting and another. A few examples make this clear. Among the Kwakiutl Indians the death of a wife or a child is as among us an occasion for grief. They have the conviction, however, that this misfortune is not accidental, but is a kind of "insult" directed against them by the forces of nature. As with other insults, they feel shamed as a consequence, and seek some method of restoring their prestige by striking back (63). Grief in their case is accompanied by shame and anger, united in a configuration which would be extremely rare among ourselves. (With us also, grief may occasionally be associated with resentment, and under special circumstances with shame.) This certainly will alter the quality of the grief, which becomes a different emotion in the two cases. The emotion of love shows the same type of variation. In one society it is inevitably associated with the desire for exclusive possession of the loved one, so that jealousy becomes an important component of it; in other societies jealousy is apparently absent. The complex emotion known as "face" also shows the importance of social factors. Although the desire for prestige is present almost everywhere, in China and Japan it has become associated with a whole complex of relationships, in which prescribed forms of etiquette are of the greatest importance. The nature of "face" differs markedly in the East and in the West, so that it is doubtful whether the same term may appropriately be applied in the two cases.

In this direction, also, more research is needed. Ethnologists in the field would contribute to the further understanding of this problem by a careful description of the behavior accompanying every emotional situation, and of the manner in which the individuals concerned describe their experiences. A strictly behavioristic point of view in this field would lose sight of some of the most important implications of the response. Although the social setting must in every case be described in full, it must also be supplemented by information of a more personal kind. Linguistic research may turn out to be even more significant in this connection; that is, a detailed study of a people's emotional vocabulary, of the distinctions drawn between shades of emotion or between different kinds of grief or anger, of figurative expressions used in the descriptions of the emotions, and so on. This information would be of real value in clearing up the manner and the degree to which even the nature of an emotional experience is subject to social control. A genetic approach, revealing the gradual alterations both in the character of the emotional experience and the nature of emotional responses with increasing age, would also have great value, particularly if comparable data could be obtained from several different societies.

SUMMARY

Emotional behavior is accompanied by a series of physiological changes which presumably occur in all individuals. Social factors may, however, affect the emotions in various ways. There are, for example, differences in the situations which will arouse the various emotions in different societies; the contrasting reactions to the birth of twins, to death, to sex activity may be cited in this connection. There are differences also in the amount of overt emotional behavior, as well as in the specific emotions which are permitted expression. Although it has been suggested that anatomical characteristics may play a part, it is certain that cultural influences are much more important; the variations in the emotional behavior of the Chinese under different conditions are particularly striking.

Emotional expressions apparently common to all societies

are the occurrence of tears in pain or sorrow, of laughter as a sign of joy or well-being, of trembling and pallor in fear, and possibly others. On the other hand, the great difficulty experienced by untrained human observers in recognizing the emotions of chimpanzees from their facial expressions strengthens the hypothesis of cultural or social determination of the expression of the emotions in man. Emotional expression is analogous to language in that it functions as a means of communication, and that it must be learned, at least in part. Examples of cultural patterning are the variations in the means of expressing affection, the occurrence of tears in greeting among the Maori and others, of fainting in anger among the Chinese, of the smile of submission among the Japanese, and many others. For different emotions and in different situations there may be all possible degrees of cultural patterning. Even the content of a particular emotional experience requires analysis in terms of folkways and traditions.

REFERENCES

1. Murphy, G., Murphy, L. B., and Newcomb, T. M. *Experimental Social Psychology*. Rev. ed. 1937.

2. Bard, P. "Emotion: I. The Neuro-humoral Basis of Emotional Reactions," *Hdbk. Exper. Psychol.* (ed. by C. Murchison). 1934.

3. Cannon, W. B. *Bodily Changes in Pain, Hunger, Fear, and Rage.* 1929.

4. Collip, J. B. *Factors Determining Human Behavior.* 1937.

5. Klineberg, O. *Race Differences.* 1935.

6. Thomas, W. I. *Primitive Behavior.* 1937.

7. Warner, L. *A Black Civilization.* 1937.

8. Cardi, C. N. de. "Ju-ju Laws and Customs in the Niger Delta," *J. Roy. Anthrop. Instit.*, 1899, 29: pp. 51-61.

9. Faris, E. "Are Instincts Data or Hypotheses?" *Amer. J. Sociol.*, 1921, 27: pp. 184-196.

10. Driberg, J. A. *The Lango.* 1923.

11. Jenks, A. E. *The Bontoc Igorot.* 1905.

12. Morice, A. G. "Carrier Onomatology," *Amer. Anthrop.* N.S., 1933, 35: pp. 632-658.

13. Mêng, Dr. Personal communication.

14. Klineberg, O. "Emotional Expression in Chinese Litera-ture," *J. Abn. & Soc. Psychol.*, 1938, 33: pp. 517-520.
15. Schrieke, B. *Alien Americans*. 1936.
16. Maugham, W. S. *On A Chinese Screen.* 1922.
17. Gilbert, R. *What's Wrong with China.* 1926.
18. Adams, R. *Interracial Marriage in Hawaii.* 1937.
19. Granet, M. "Le langage de la douleur d'après le rituel funéraire de la Chine classique," *J. de Psychol.*, 1922, 19: pp. 97-118.
20. May, H. S. "A Study of Emotional Expression Among Chinese and Americans," *Unpublished Master's Essay*, Columbia University, 1938.
21. Darwin, C. *The Expression of the Emotions in Man and Animals.* 1873.
22. Bühler, C. "The Social Behavior of Children," *Hdbk. Child Psychol.* (ed. by C. Murchison). 1933.
23. Feleky, A. M. "The Expression of the Emotions," *Psychol. Rev.*, 1914, 21: pp. 33-41.
24. Dunlap, K. "The Role of Eye-Muscles and Mouth-Muscles in the Expression of the Emotions," *Genet. Psychol. Monog.*, 1927, 2: No. 3.
25. Gates, G. S. "The Role of the Auditory Element in the Interpretation of Emotion," *Psychol. Bull.*, 1927, 24: p. 175.
26. Blake, W. H. "A Preliminary Study of the Interpretation of Bodily Expression." *Teachers Coll. Contribs. to Educ.*, 1933: No. 574.
27. Carmichael, L., et al. "A Study of the Judgment of Manual Expression as Presented in Still and Motion Pictures," *J. Soc. Psychol.*, 1937, 8: pp. 115-142.
28. Köhler, W. *The Mentality of Apes.* 1925.
29. Kohts, N. *Infant Ape and Human Child* (*instincts, emotions, play, habits*). 2 vols. 1935.
30. Foley, J. P., Jr. "Judgment of Facial Expression of Emotion in the Chimpanzee," *J. Soc. Psychol.*, 1935, 6: pp. 31-67.
31. Dumas, G. *Traité de Psychologie.* 2 vols. 1923-1924.
32. Tylor, E. B. *Primitive Culture.* 1871.
33. Rank, O. *Art and Artist.* 1932.
34. Giles, H. A. *A History of Chinese Literature.* 1901.
35. Crawley, E. *Studies of Savages and Sex* (ed. by T. Bester-man). 1929.
36. Mauss, M. "L'Expression Obligatoire des Sentiments," *J. de Psychol.*, 1921, 18: pp. 425-434.
37. Durham, M. E. "Some Montenegrin Manners and Customs," *J. Roy. Anthrop. Instit.*, 1909, 39: pp. 85-96.

38. Blackwood, B. *Both Sides of Buka Passage.* 1935.
39. Brown, A. R. *The Andaman Islanders.* 1922.
40. Best, E. *The Maori.* 1924.
41. Man, E. H. "On the Aboriginal Inhabitants of the Andaman Islands," *J. Roy. Anthrop. Instit.*, 1882, 12: pp. 69-116, 327-434.
42. Westermarck, E. A. *The Origin and Development of the Moral Ideas.* 2 vols. 1908-12.
43. Bromberg, W. *The Mind of Man.* 1937.
44. Hobbes, T. *Human Nature* and *Leviathan, Works* (ed. by Molesworth). 11 vols. 1840.
45. Schopenhauer, A. *The World as Will and Idea.* 5th ed. 1906.
46. Bergson, H. *Laughter.* 1911.
47. Spencer, H. "The Physiology of Laughter," *Essays.* 2 vols. 1863.
48. Freud, S. *Wit and Its Relation to the Unconscious.* 1917.
49. Goldenweiser, A. A. *History, Psychology, and Culture.* 1933.
50. Hogbin, H. I. "The Sexual Life of the Natives of Ontong Java (Solomon Islands)," *J. Polynesian Soc.*, 1931, 40: pp. 23-34.
51. Parsons, E. C. "Notes on Zuñi," *Memoirs, Amer. Anthrop. Assn.*, 1917, 4: Pt. II.
52. Powdermaker, H. *Life in Lesu.* 1933.
53. Wissler, C. *An Introduction to Social Anthropology.* 1929.
54. Lowie, R. H. *The Crow Indians.* 1935.
55. Bunzel, R. L. "Introduction to Zuñi Ceremonialism," *47th Annual Report, Bur. Amer. Ethnol.*, 1932.
56. Wilson, J. *A Missionary Voyage to the Southern Pacific Ocean.* 1796.
57. Williams, F. E. *Orokaiva Society.* 1930.
58. Porteus, S. D. *The Psychology of a Primitive People.* 1931.
59. Hearn, L. "The Japanese Smile," *Glimpses of Unfamiliar Japan.* 2 vols. 1894.
60. Hearn, L. *Japan: An Attempt at Interpretation.* 1904.
61. Long Lance. *Long Lance.* 1928.
62. Fletcher, A. C., and La Flesche, F. "The Omaha Tribe," *Bur. Amer. Ethnol., Ann. Rep.*, 1905-1906, 27: pp. 15-655.
63. Benedict, R. F. *Patterns of Culture.* 1934.

CHAPTER VIII

SOCIAL FACTORS IN PERCEPTION AND MEMORY

SENSE PERCEPTION

IT is not usually recognized that sense perception constitutes in considerable measure a problem for social psychology. At first glance it would seem to be a purely individual phenomenon, the nature of which is determined by the pattern of neurones which bring impulses from the outside world to the central nervous system. If vision, for example, is due to the impingement of certain vibrations on the optic nerve, and the transmission of the impulse through the optic thalamus to the occipital part of the cortex, it may seem of little concern to the social psychologist as such. Considerable evidence has accumulated, however, which indicates that social factors must be considered if the phenomena of sense perception are properly to be understood.

Malinowski (*1*) gives an interesting example of the cultural patterning of visual experience. Among the Trobrianders, the idea of resemblance between parents and offspring, or between children of the same parents, is controlled by strict social norms. These may at times go counter to the evidence of one's senses. In the first place, resemblance to the father is regarded as natural and proper, and such similarity is always assumed and affirmed to exist. It is a great offense to hint that the child resembles his mother or any of his maternal relatives. "It is a phrase of serious bad language to say 'thy face is thy sister's,' which is the worst form of kinship similarity" (p. 88). In the second place it is taken for granted that brothers do not resemble each other. This is dogma; although both may resemble the father, everyone will deny that they look at all alike.   Malinowski once commented on the likeness of two brothers, and "there came such a hush over all the assembly, while the brother present withdrew abruptly and the company was half-embarrassed, half-offended at this breach of custom" (p. 92).   In this example it is difficult to know with certainty whether the sense perception has actually been interfered with, that is to say, whether the Trobrianders actually *see* the two brothers as different even though to us they would obviously resemble each other, or whether they are merely unwilling to acknowledge such a resemblance even when they do see it.   It is probable, however, on the basis of our knowledge of the degree to which we see what we are looking for, that the Trobrianders fail to note any resemblance because they do not want or expect to find it.   It may be added that the Trobriander belief in the resemblance between father and child is all the more surprising since according to Malinowski they are ignorant of the father's part in procreation; they assume that the father's function is the mechanical one of opening up the mother, and that any other mechanical means may be substituted for it.

To turn to a more specific visual phenomenon, the perception of color and of variations in hue may be shown to vary from group to group, largely under the influence of the color terminology.   The apparent inability of the members of certain groups like the Torres Straits Islanders and others to recognize certain colors, and their tendency to combine colors which seem to us unrelated, are probably linguistic in origin (2).   Wallis (3) writes:

Not infrequently the savage ignores distinctions observed by us or cross-sections our distinctions.   This frequently happens in color designations.   The Ashantis have distinct names for the colors black, red and white.   The term black is also used for any dark color, such as blue, purple, brown, etc., while the term red does duty for pink, orange and yellow (p. 421).

Of the New Guinea natives Margaret Mead (4) writes: "Their color classifications are so different that they saw yellow, olive-green, blue-green, gray and lavender as variations of one color" (p. 638). Strange as this confusion may seem to us, it is a perfectly natural response under the conditions imposed by their particular nomenclature. There can be little doubt that when the same name is used for two colors, they may be seen to resemble each other as a consequence.

This is not always the case, however, as the observations of Seligman in New Guinea (5) indicate. He gave to his native subjects the task of sorting colored wools, and there seemed to be little tendency to put together wools to which the same name would be applied. Members of the Takitaro tribe were especially quick and correct, in spite of their very incomplete color vocabulary. Color names do not necessarily affect perception, therefore, but it is highly probable that in many cases they would operate in that direction.

A significant experiment on the effect of social factors on visual experience has been carried out by Sherif (6). The study was undertaken in order to test the importance of social norms or "frames of reference," that is to say, standards which serve as means of judging the experience in question, or placing it in a proper framework. He was interested in seeing what would happen to a visual experience when there was no such frame of reference, and when the subject had therefore to create one. He experimented with the "auto-kinetic" phenomenon, produced by looking at a single point of light in a room which is otherwise completely dark; this point has no external frame of reference which determines its position in the visual field, and is consequently seen to move, probably as the result of physiological factors. The distance through which it moves varies considerably from one subject to another. Sherif found that when he placed three subjects together in the experimental situation, after having determined the average distance through which the point had previously moved for each one of them separately, there was a definite tendency for their reports to converge. The effect may in part be explained by suggestion, since the words first spoken by any one subject usually influenced the others, but in any case a social norm was set up under these conditions. More significant still, if the subjects who were together in the group situation were now tested separately, their reports continued to be about the same. In other words, the group norm is effective even when the subject is tested in isolation. This result parallels in certain respects the effect of cultural patterning on the sense perception of the individual, and is a significant attempt to bring such patterning within the field of laboratory experiment.

It is possible, however, to overestimate its implications. The experiment dealt after all with a form of sense experience in which there are no objective norms whatever, and the extension of the results to those cases in which the eye or the ear is actually stimulated by known wave lengths may be questioned. It seems certain nevertheless that even in these latter types of sense perception some degree of cultural patterning is possible, though it may not reach the extremes discovered by Sherif in connection with the auto-kinetic phenomenon.

On a more complex level, Zillig (7) was able to demonstrate the extent to which social attitudes may determine what one sees. In a preliminary survey of friendships within a classroom she discovered that certain children were almost universally liked, and others disliked to the same degree. In the experiment proper she took an equal number of pupils from these two extreme groups, and had them stand up in front of the class and perform calisthenic exercises under her direction. She had previously instructed the "liked" children to make mistakes, and had trained the "disliked" ones to follow her instructions exactly. At the end of the experiment, she asked the class to indicate which group had done the exercises correctly, and the majority of votes went to the popular group. It seems unlikely that the children designated the favored group as superior even though they saw them make the errors; Zillig believes on the basis of conversations with them that they actually "saw" the differences as they reported them. This experiment raises in a significant manner the whole problem of the relation of prejudice to sense perception. There is no doubt that a mental set of favor or prejudice toward a particular group may influence the observer in his perception of their behavior.

Among the interesting observations by E. L. and R. E. Horowitz (8) there is one which is particularly significant in this connection. They showed to southern children a picture of a fine home. Later the children were questioned about the picture, and many of them "saw" a Negro woman engaged in some sort of domestic occupation, although this was not in the original. Here the stereotype of the Negro and of his place in the socio-economic scale determined the perception, or at least the later report of it.

An essentially similar mechanism is apparent also in the experiment of Goring (9) who showed that because of the popular belief that intelligent people have high foreheads, those who were judged intelligent were also "seen" to have high brows; actual measurement showed the reverse relationship to hold true.

Another experiment dealing with social factors in perception is that of Ansbacher (10). Using ordinary postage stamps, the investigator found that those which were greater in value seemed larger than the others; Canadian stamps, with which the subjects had had less experience, seemed smaller than the American of the same denomination and actually of the same dimensions, apparently because they did not have the same value for the subject.

Sense perception, no matter which sense organ is involved, involves the question of selectivity. In other words, no one sees or hears everything in the environment, but makes a choice dependent upon previous training and acquired powers of observation. There are marked individual differences in this respect determined by occupational and other interests; it is obvious that a college professor, a dealer in antiques, and a prospective bride may "see" entirely different things in the same shop window. Selectivity enters also in other types of observation, as when a mother notices the cry of her child when no ones else hears it. There are cultural as well as individual differences in this respect. The reputedly greater sensory acuity of primitive peoples is undoubtedly due to training, and a White man may learn to make the same discriminations as do the natives. Conversely, a member of a primitive community would be confounded by the multiplicity of noises in any metropolitan center and would undoubtedly need some experience with automobile horns and the sounds made by street-cars and airplanes before these could stand out as recognizable stimuli.

The same considerations apply to auditory as to visual phenomena, although considerably more work has been done on the latter. We know that the combination of tones into various intervals may be regarded as consonant in one community and dissonant in another. Herzog [1] reports the occurrence of two-part singing in Melanesia one note apart, an interval which to us is the most dissonant imaginable. Even in the history of our own music the same discrepancy may be observed, and it is well known that Beethoven's harmonies were regarded as most unpleasant when they were first heard. Moore (11) has demonstrated experimentally that an interval which is heard as dissonant may become agreeable after it has been heard a number of times, and that conversely one which is at first pleasant may become disagreeable as the result of constant repetition. In this connection it is important to note that the theories of consonance like that of Helmholtz (12) which explain it on the basis of the physical relationships between the individual notes and their overtones, require at least to be modified so as to include the effect of previous training and experience.

The perception of intensity of sound may also, but probably to a lesser degree, show the effect of similar factors. Those who hear Chinese music for the first time, or who listen to the musical accompaniment to a Chinese play, are usually much disturbed by its intensity. They may even express their amazement that the Chinese can stand it. Lin Yu-t'ang (13)

---

[1] Personal communication.

in discussing this point makes a suggestion that the hearing of the Chinese may actually be different, and that loud noises may not affect them to the same degree as they affect us. This is highly improbable. It is much more likely that one's ear becomes accustomed to certain combinations of sounds so that they appear natural and satisfying. In support of this interpretation is the fact that Chinese find American jazz music as well as Wagnerian brasses much too loud for them at first hearing.

We have already referred to the variations in taste which make the same food palatable or disagreeable in two different communities. Similar considerations apparently apply to the phenomena of smell. It has been pointed out, for example, that the odor of valerian, which we regard as most unpleasant, has actually had a vogue as a sort of perfume. Junker (*14*) writes of the A-Barmbo tribe in Africa that they were "disgusted at the smell of some genuine old Edam (Dutch) cheese, of which I had eaten a few scraps, and gave out that the White people eat 'the foulest muck.' Many smells affect them differently from us, and they turn with loathing from eau de cologne, for example, and from scented soap" (p. 101). As far as the cheese is concerned, there are enough individual differences among ourselves to make this a doubtful example of cultural patterning, but the other cases clearly indicate the variations in the pleasantness and unpleasantness of odors.

The degree of adaptation to painful stimuli also shows wide variations between individuals and groups. There is undoubtedly a marked subjective component in the experience of pain, as hypnotic phenomena amply demonstrate. In our society, there is a sex difference in this respect (although with considerable overlapping), since it is regarded as more legitimate for a woman than for a man to give expression to pain. The training which the American Indians received seems to have resulted in an actual ignoring of the pain stimuli and the consequent diminution in the pain experience. Blackwood (*15*) gives an example of a similar effect among the people of Buka.

These people will put their hands into water that is only just off the boil, and take out a taro so hot that when they passed me my share I invariably dropped it. . . . Similarly they will plunge a hand into a potful of shellfish immediately it has been taken off the fire (p. 292).

These various instances combine to demonstrate the importance of social factors in perception. Not only as between different cultures, but also between sub-groups (occupational, national, class, etc.) in our own society and between individuals within the sub-groups, the whole pattern of previous experience, training and interest enter very definitely. As Freeman expresses it:

In a very literal sense, we tend to observe more after the manner of our own natures than photographically after the properties of the external world. This fact . . . explains not only why individuals from different classes of society with different common segments of apperceptive mass and response cannot think, feel, and believe alike, but why they cannot, in principle, even perceive alike (16, p. 49).

This does not mean that there are not certain aspects of perception which are common to all normal individuals, as a result of the nature of our neurological organism, but we must not neglect those social factors which create the differences to which we have referred.

A final example from the Maori is pertinent to this discussion, although it might be regarded as illustrating a conceptual difference, rather than one in sense perception properly so-called. An English painter while traveling through New Zealand made a number of portraits of the natives, including one of an old chieftain whose face was covered with the spiral tattooing typical of his rank. The artist showed the model his picture, expecting his hearty approval. The old man looked at the portrait, then declined it with the words, "That's not what I am." The artist then asked the chief to draw his own portrait. "When he handed the White man the result, with the words: 'That's what I am!' the latter could see nothing but the old chief's tattoo pattern which signified his tribal connection" (*17*, p. 44). Lips comments that this indicates that the world of Western thought with its emphasis on the individual is foreign to this Maori, for whom the concept of the community is paramount. This may be the correct explanation. For our purposes it is sufficient to point out that he apparently "saw" himself in a manner quite different from the White artist because of what he and his people regarded as important.

Perception of Time. There has been considerable discussion as to whether the perception of time is based upon organic or upon social factors. The fact that we get hungry at stated intervals, that we become sleepy at about the same time each evening, and awaken at about the same time each morning (some individuals acquire great precision in this latter respect), has suggested the possibility of internal organic rhythms serving as clues to the passage of time. Just what these rhythms are and where they are located it is not yet possible to say. Certainly they are notoriously defective for short intervals of time, although, as has been shown (*18*), they are rather more dependable in connection with the major physiological requirements of the organism. There can be no doubt, however, that social factors are also important. In the first place the importance of time will vary from one culture to another. Our own machine age has made speed a matter of utmost importance but this attitude is not shared by groups whose activities do not require to be done at any stated time. As Dollard (*19*) points out, time is a concept with social implications, and "especially in our culture it is one of the most vigorously felt and imposed basic concepts . . . and it has certainly 'social' as well as organic factors" (p. 103). One example of the relative indifference to time is that given by Kroeber (*20*) in the case of the California Indians. Among them no one knew his own age, nor how remote an event was that had happened more than half a dozen years ago; they kept no record of the passage of long intervals of time.

A second manner in which social factors enter into the perception of time is in connection with what has been called a "frame of reference." In this connection Sorokin and Merton (21) make use of the concept of "social time" to indicate the variations between one society and another.

The category of astronomical time is only one of several concepts of time. Social phenomena are frequently adopted as a frame of reference so that units of time are often fixed by the rhythm of collective life. The need for social collaboration is at the root of social systems of time. Social time is qualitatively differentiated according to the beliefs and customs common to the group (p. 629).

These writers give a number of examples to illustrate the variations in social time. In Madagascar the natives speak of doing something in a "rice-cooking," the equivalent of about half an hour; in the "frying of a locust," or a moment. The Cross River natives use an expression such as "the man died in less than the time in which maize is not yet completely roasted," that is, in less than fifteen minutes; or "the time in which one can cook a handful of vegetables." The Khasis name their months according to the activities which take place in each; there is a "month for weeding the ground," "a month when cultivators fry the produce of their fields," and so forth. Radcliffe Brown (22) states that in the Andaman Islands it is possible to recognize a distinct succession of odors throughout the year as the various trees and plants come into bloom. "The Andamanese have therefore adopted an original method of marking the different periods of the year by means of the odoriferous flowers that are in bloom at different times. Their calendar is a calendar of scents" (p. 311). That the subjective categories and subdivisions of time may be transformed is shown by the Russian experiment of changing the seven day week to one of five days. This makes the use of names for days of the week meaningless, and the Russians make their appointments always according to the days of the month. Ella Winter (23) observes that when Americans first come to Russia they find the system very awkward and insist upon knowing what day of the week is meant, but after a short time they completely lose track of the days of the week, and find themselves quite at home in the Russian system.

There are of course individual as well as group differences in time perception, and also in the attitude toward time generally. William Stern (24) speaks of a personal space and time, differing from one individual to another. Personal space refers to the region of possible movement and contact, and will obviously be different in the case of an international banker and in that of a farmer in the hills of Kentucky. Personal time refers to the tendency to see things in terms of their immediate or deferred consequences, differences in thought for the future and in the need for haste, etc. What causes these differences is difficult to decide, and need not conern us here. It is clear that the reaction to time, like other forms of sense perception, is by no means solely an organic matter. A clear example of the manner in which social factors may enter is given in the study by Lazarsfeld (25) of a little community outside of Vienna in which unemployment had affected the whole population. There were many consequences of this unemployment, among them the development of complete indifference to the passage of time and to the desirability of doing anything within a stated period. People would come hours late to an appointment as the result of this attitude.

Judgment. Allied to the question of sense perception is the problem of judgment. It is obvious that one's judgments of value will be determined by a wide variety of social and cultural conditions. Even one's judgment of matters of fact may be similarly conditioned. One of Zillig's (7) experiments, later corroborated by Sherif (6), brings this out clearly. She presented to a group of judges a number of pieces of poetry all by the same author. She had previously discovered, however, which poets the judges liked, and which they disliked. To the poetry samples she attached the names of these various poets, and asked the judges to rank the poems in order of merit. In spite of the fact that the same poet had written them all, the samples were ranked in accordance with the judges' preference for the alleged authors. The same sample would be judged good by some individuals and poor by others, depending upon the name which had been attached to it. Many similar instances could be given.

MEMORY

It is probable that a very large number of facts discovered by psychologists in connection with learning and memory are due to the nature of the nervous system, and are valid for human beings everywhere. We do not know yet to what extent the shape of the learning curve, the curve of forgetting, the principles of primacy, recency, intensity and so forth in learning, and the various methods used in the study of memory performance, are affected by the nature of the society in which the individual develops. Social factors clearly enter, however, in determining what one remembers. Here again an experiment of Zillig's is pertinent (7). She presented to a number of subjects, male and female, a list of statements that had been made at various times about the nature of women. Some of these were favorable, others, mostly from the writings of Schopenhauer and Oscar Wilde, were distinctly unfavorable. A week after this presentation, the subjects were asked to record from memory the statements that had been previously presented to them. The results showed a decided tendency for the women to remember more of those items which favored them, and for the men to remember relatively more of the unfavorable items. This simple but conclusive experiment demonstrates clearly that memory may be determined by other than neurological factors.

The same technique has recently been used in connection with a problem which belongs more directly in the field of social psychology. Margolies (26) gave to a number of students an attitude scale designed to measure the degree of their prejudice against the Negro. She then read to them a number of statements concerning the Negro, some of them favorable and others unfavorable. Some time later she asked her subjects to reproduce from memory the statements they had heard. While the results were not conclusive, they seemed to show on the whole a tendency for those with favorable attitudes to remember more of the favorable statements. This result is parallel to the common observation that when people read articles or books of a controversial nature, they show a definite tendency to remember those points which are in agreement with their own opinions, and conveniently to forget those that differ.

These facts are also in definite agreement with the Freudian theory of repression as the cause of forgetting. In general this theory holds that we forget those things the memory of which is unpleasant. This does not mean that the forgetting is pleasant or satisfactory, since it may result in considerable inconvenience; it does mean that in spite of such inconvenience, forgetting takes place because of the repression of the unpleasant memory into the unconscious. Prejudice in favor of one's own sex, or for or against the Negro, would then serve as the emotional basis of the repression.

The clearest recognition of the phenomenon of memory as a problem in social psychology is to be found in the work of William Stern (27), and more recently of Bartlett (28). Stern undertook a series of experiments on the psychology of rumor and testimony, one of the results of which was to demonstrate the frequency of errors in the reporting of what one has actually seen or read. Even when the subject was willing to take an oath upon his evidence, errors both of omission and of distortion still occurred. Social influences were studied by the method of chain reproduction, a story being transmitted through several subjects, each of whom attempted to repeat the account given him by his predecessor in the chain. The results show strikingly that even with a few transmissions (five, in one experiment) rumor becomes extraordinarily unreliable. There is, in general, a progressive abbreviation of the account, with the phrasing more general and less definite. Errors occurring most frequently include those of confusion, substitution, alteration of temporal and spatial setting, and of names and dates. In another experiment, a comparison was made between the reliability of testimony when the subject gave his own coherent report, and when he was subjected to cross-examination. The accuracy is much reduced in the latter case; when the witness does not have the correct answer in mind, he prefers to give an incorrect one rather than admit that he does not know. Here the social relationship between the "lawyer" and the "witness" plays a significant part.

In Bartlett's investigation, the subjects were asked to reproduce stories, usually of a mythological nature, which had previously been presented to them. Two principal methods were used. In the first, known as the Method of Repeated Reproduction, the subject is given a passage to study under prescribed conditions, attempts a first reproduction usually after an interval of fifteen minutes, and thereafter gives further reproductions at intervals of increasing length. In the second, the Method of Serial Reproduction, the reproduction by the first subject is presented to Subject B, and his version to C, and so on, as in the case of Stern's studies. The results of the second series are of greater interest to us as they carry Stern's analysis somewhat further. They show the substantial change which may take place in the nature of the original material, including the forgetting or distortion of proper names, a tendency to make the material concrete wherever possible, a loss of individual characteristics of style and content, an abbreviation of the length of the story, an attempt at rationalization or explanation, and frequently startling and radical alterations in the actual material. We have here an experimental verification of what happens in the case of rumor or gossip in which an original story is distorted far beyond recognition. As Bartlett points out, this is clearly a social process, the reproductions being influenced by the fact that individuals are communicating to one another.

In connection with cultural or group differences, Bartlett cites a number of interesting examples in the social psychology of memory, taken mainly from his observations among the Swazis of South Africa. He states that some years ago the Swazi chief and a number of his followers visited England in connection with a long-standing land dispute. On their return, they were asked what they remembered best among their

English impressions; and the one thing that remained most vividly fixed in their recollection was their picture of the English policeman regulating the traffic with uplifted hand. This may be explained by the fact that the Swazi greets his fellow or his visitor in a somewhat similar manner, and he was therefore impressed by the use of this gesture in a foreign country with such marked effect. It was one of the few things which fitted directly into the Swazi social framework, and so it was remembered.

The Swazi, in common with most Bantu-speaking tribes, are said to possess a remarkable memory. Bartlett subjected this to experiment, and found that their retentiveness as such was apparently not superior to that of the Whites. They did, however, remember certain things exceedingly well, for example the characteristics of the cattle which they owned or which they were tending, because of the importance which this had for their social and economic life and because of their previous training. We have here an example similar to that discussed in the case of the allegedly superior sensory acuity of many native peoples; it is not a matter of innate ability, but of socially determined powers and techniques.

Even the manner of remembering may be socially determined to a considerable degree. Bartlett reports that when he talked to a Zulu about the former military exploits of his people, the Zulu lived through his memories with the greatest vividness and emotional excitement. A Swazi would tell about similar incidents in a stolid and unmoved manner. It was not a matter of differences in temperament, since the Swazi also could be aroused to violent interest by other questions, particularly those dealing with cattle, women, marriage and children. The memories showed a marked difference in emotional tone in the two cases. One other characteristic of the Swazi manner of remembering may be mentioned. There is a definite tendency to recall in a recapitulatory or rote manner, with the introduction of a mass of apparently irrelevant detail. This may be particularly trying to all listeners in the case of a lawsuit, during which the Swazi witness will insist on telling the story in his own detailed way no matter how long it takes. He seems in fact often to be incapable of coming to the end of his account without going through all the intervening steps.

These observations indicate that social and cultural influences enter into the behavior of the individual even when he is not actually in the group situation. We may summarize this discussion in Bartlett's words:

This means that the group itself, as an organized unit, has to be treated as a veritable condition of human reaction. It means that, even if we said everything that theoretically could be said about experience and conduct from the point of view of its determination by external stimulation, or by internal factors of individual character and temperament, we should still leave wholly unexplained some— very likely a large number—of the most important human responses (p. 241).

SUMMARY

Although many of the phenomena of sense perception are undoubtedly due to the nature of the sense organs and of the nervous system, social and cultural influences also play an important part. Examples that may be mentioned in this connection are the socially determined resemblances between members of the Trobriand family, the relation of color perception to color nomenclature, the establishment of social norms in the experimental study of the auto-kinetic phenomenon, the variations in the perception of harmony in sound and of the affective qualities of tastes and odors, the degrees of adaptation to pain, the phenomenon of "social time," and many others.

The same considerations apply to the field of memory. Social factors may determine what one remembers, and the studies of testimony and of chain reproduction show the manner and the degree to which reproduction is influenced by the social situation. Observations among the Zulus and the Swazis indicate that even the manner of remembering may be at least in part socially determined. In the absence of re-

search on memory in a variety of cultures, it is not possible
to state whether the "laws" of learning and of forgetting would
be equally valid under all social conditions; it seems probable
that some of them are related to the nature of the nervous
system and would hold true universally.

REFERENCES

1. Malinowski, B. *Sex and Repression in Savage Society.* 1927.
2. Klineberg, O. *Race Differences.* 1935.
3. Wallis, W. D. *An Introduction to Anthropology.* 1926.
4. Mead, M. "The Primitive Child," *Hdbk. Child Psychol.* (ed.
by C. Murchison). 1933.
5. Seligman, C. G. "The Vision of the Natives of British
Guinea," *Report of the Cambridge Anthropological Expedition to
Torres Straits.* 1901, vol. 2.
6. Sherif, M. *The Psychology of Social Norms.* 1936.
7. Zillig, M. "Einstellung und Aussage," *Ztschr. f. Psychol.,*
1928, 106: pp. 58-106.
8. Horowitz, E. L., and Horowitz, R. E. "Development of Social Attitudes in Children," *Sociometry,* 1937-38, 1: pp. 301-338.
9. Goring, C. *The English Convict.* 1913.
10. Ansbacher, H. "Perception of number as affected by the
monetary value of the objects: A critical study of the method used
in extended constancy phenomena," *Arch. Psychol.,* 1937, No. 215.
11. Moore, H. T. *The Genetic Aspect of Consonance and Dis-
sonance.* 1914.
12. Helmholtz, H. v. *On the Sensations of Tone as a Physiological Basis for the Theory of Music.* 4th ed. 1912.
13. Lin Yu-t'ang. *My Country and My People.* 1935.
14. Junker, W. J. *Travels in Africa.* 3 vols. 1890-92.
15. Blackwood, B. *Both Sides of Buka Passage.* 1935.
16. Freeman, E. *Social Psychology.* 1936.
17. Lips, J. E. *The Savage Hits Back.* 1937.
18. MacLeod, R. B., and Roff, M. F. "An Experiment in Temporal Disorientation," *Acta Psychol.,* 1936, 1: pp. 381-423.
19. Dollard, J. *Criteria for the Life History.* 1935.
20. Kroeber, A. L. "Elements of Culture in Native California,"
Univ. Calif. Publ. Archaeol. & Ethnol., 1917-1923, 13: pp. 260-328.
21. Sorokin, P. A., and Merton, R. K. "Social Time," *Amer. J.
Sociol.,* 1937, 42: pp. 615-629.
22. Brown, A. R. *The Andaman Islanders.* 1922.

23. Winter, E. *Red Virtue.* 1933.

24. Stern, W. "Raum und Zeit als personale Dimensionen," *Acta Psychol.*, 1935, 1: pp. 220-232.

25. Lazarsfeld, P. F., Jahoda, M., and Zeisl, H. *Die Arbeitslosen von Marienthal.* 1933.

26. Margolies, H. "The Effect of Race Attitudes on Memory and Perception," *Unpublished Master's Essay,* Columbia University, 1938.

27. Stern, W. *Beiträge zur Psychologie der Aussage.* 2 vols. 1903-1906.

28. Bartlett, F. C. *Remembering.* 1932.

PART THREE

DIFFERENTIAL PSYCHOLOGY

CHAPTER IX

INDIVIDUAL AND CLASS DIFFERENCES

INTRODUCTION

WE turn now to a different branch of the field of social psychology. In the preceding chapters we have been discussing the problem of the "common human" and have reviewed the material pertinent to the discussion of what constitutes human nature. In the process of this review we have had to pay attention also to differences between groups and cultures, but mainly in order to distinguish between what is common and what is variable. Our concern in the succeeding chapters will be more directly with the problem of variations among human beings—a field which has received the name of Differential Psychology.

This field is relatively new. The concern of the earlier psychologists was with the establishment of laws in psychology which should hold good for all individuals. To the extent that individuals differ, their behavior and their introspections cannot easily be stated in terms of general principles, and consequently for a long time these differences were regarded as outside the scope of the science of psychology. They might be of practical interest to the social engineer or to the foreman of a factory, perhaps, but not of immediate concern to the psychologist.

It is usual to regard differential psychology as originating mainly in the work of Francis Galton (1). Although there were many precursors, Galton's study of individual differences in imagery as well as his examination of the genealogies of men of genius, may be regarded as the real starting point. The succeeding development of techniques and approaches in this field, notably the work of Binet (2) in testing intelligence, of Cattell (3) in the study of motor and sensory abilities, of Thorndike (4) in the development of statistical measures, and of William Stern (5) in his analysis of differential psychology as a whole, laid the foundation for further research. In recent years the interest in this field has grown enormously, and the careful surveys of the literature (6, 7) indicate its present scope and importance.

HEREDITY AND ENVIRONMENT

The problem of individual differences in psychology cannot be discussed apart from the general and apparently perennial question of heredity and environment. It is obviously outside the province of this book to attempt a complete analysis of this complicated matter, and we shall have to restrict our treatment to certain of the more essential aspects.

In the first place it is important to note that there has been a marked change in the formulation of this problem. It was formerly customary to ask concerning any specific trait or capacity whether it was caused by heredity *or* environment, by nature or nurture. There were many discussions, for example, as to whether musical ability was due to the one or the other. The individual was regarded as a sum total of characteristics and capacities, some of which he had inherited, whereas others had been acquired during the course of his lifetime. As an indication of the different point of view prevailing at the present time, we may take the treatment of this problem by Woodworth (8). He stresses the fact that both heredity and environment are effective. The influence of heredity may be demonstrated in the case of hybrids; though the mule and the colt both develop in the same prenatal environment, they have different characteristics which may be explained only in terms of a different genetic constitution. On the other hand, a change in the environment of the developing embryo may markedly affect characteristics normally under the control of heredity; for example, an alteration in the chemical content of the fluid in which young fish develop may cause the eyes to be formed closer together, and in some cases even to fuse into one central eye.

Every individual is the resultant of both of these factors. It is inaccurate, however, to say that he is so much heredity plus so much environment. He is not the sum, but the product. Since heredity and environment act upon each other, Woodworth suggests the analogy of a rectangle in which they represent the two dimensions. Individuals may differ from each other in either dimension or in both, and conversely, two individuals may show the same present capacity even though both their heredity and their environment are different.

The analogy of the rectangle must not be pressed too far. The relationship between nature and nurture is a phenomenon of interaction rather than of multiplication. It is probable, however, that no single characteristic is exclusively the result of the one or the other. Stature, for example, has usually been regarded as mainly genetic in origin, and yet we know that the nature of the living conditions may make a substantial difference in this respect. A recent study by Shapiro (9) has shown that Japanese born in Hawaii grow to be taller than their own relatives born in Japan. The field of botany is full of examples in which the same plant shows entirely different external characteristics if conditions of soil, light and moisture are made to vary. Conversely, the environment cannot act unless there is an organism which can respond to it and can be affected by it, and it is obvious that the nature of the response will differ from one organism to another. This constant interaction is much more complex than Woodworth's analogy would indicate.

Since both nature and nurture are always present, a proper formulation of the controversy would appear to be the one given by Murphy, Murphy and Newcomb (10). They state the problem to be essentially one of "variance," that is to say, the amount of variation between individuals that may be ascribed to nature, and the amount that may be ascribed to nurture. Every individual is the resultant of both, but the differences between individuals may be due more to variation in the one than to variation in the other. The same formulation applies also in the case of group differences; we do not ask whether, for example, the intelligence of Negroes and Whites is due to heredity or environment, but rather whether the apparent differences between the two groups are due to variations in one or the other. It is obvious, therefore, that the field of differential psychology depends in a very direct manner upon the correct answer to the nature-nurture question.

As for the exact nature of the hereditary mechanism, we can do no more than mention a few of the more important principles. The transmission of inherited characteristics takes place through the medium of the chromosomes—microscopic but observable bodies within the germ cells. To explain the manner in which a single chromosome may transmit a number of characters, there has developed the theory of genes, of which there are presumably a large number in each chromosome. It is important to bear in mind that genes are not actual bodies which may be seen under the microscope, although smaller particles have been observed within each chromosome. At the same time the theory of the gene (*11*) best fits the complicated facts of genetics. Human characteristics are each determined by a great number of genes—either as a result of their numerical combination, or of their pattern or arrangement within the chromosome. This multiplicity of determining factors makes it difficult to apply directly to human heredity the Mendelian principles.

Of these Mendelian principles, the distinction between dominant and recessive characters must be kept in mind. Dominant refers to those which will be present in the somatoplasm (or the observable organism) if they occur in the germ plasm (i.e., the germ cells); recessive characters are those for which the genes exist in the germ plasm without revealing themselves in characteristics of the body if the corresponding dominant genes are also present. These recessive genes may have an observable effect under certain conditions of mating. Their occurrence explains in part the distinction that has been drawn between phenotype and genotype; the latter refers to genetic constitution, the former to the observable character- istics of the organism. The Mendelian theory makes it pos- sible to see how two individuals might have the same pheno- type and still differ in their genetic make-up. As we shall see later, this imposes an important limitation in the inference from observable characteristics to the genes underlying them. One person with brown eyes, for example, may have genes which make it possible for him to have blue-eyed children; another brown-eyed individual may have no genes for blue eyes.

Inheritance of Acquired Characters. The chromosomes and the genes are located in the germ cells, and are not found elsewhere in the organism. This has led to the well-known theory of Weismann (*12*), which states that in hereditary transmission, the only influences which count are located in the germ cells, which are sharply separated from the other cells of the body. This leads directly to the consideration of the inheritance of acquired characters. On the basis of Weis- mann's theory, such inheritance is impossible since what hap- pens to the somatoplasm does not affect the germ cells, at least directly. Weismann did believe, however, that it might be possible for these modifications to have secondary or indirect effects, and so influence the offspring to some degree.

The problem is of vital importance. If acquired characters can be inherited, the results of education and training may be handed on not only through the social environment, but also in the genetic make-up of future generations. The whole process of evolution might be differently interpreted as a re- sult. As is well known, Lamarck (*13*) based his theory upon it, as in the famous example of the giraffe whose neck became so long as the result of continued stretching to reach the food at the tops of trees, the cumulative effects of this stretching being transmitted from one generation to another. The most direct expression of the opposite view is that of DeVries (*14*) who regarded sudden mutations, which happened to be adapted to the environment, as responsible for the changes which have taken place throughout the animal kingdom.

Research in this field has an interesting history. The earlier experimenters tried cutting off the tails of successive generations of rats, but each generation was born without any obvious change resulting from this method. More recently, the work of Kammerer (15), who believed he had proved the inheritance of characteristics induced in the parents by changes in the chemical composition of their environment, attracted great attention. Kammerer wrote and lectured on the basis of these results, and for a time there was a tendency to regard his theory as proven. It then developed that one of his assistants, perhaps in his zeal to prove his master correct, had introduced similar changes into the environment of each succeeding generation, so that no inheritance of this type was involved. Kammerer was so overcome at this revelation that he committed suicide. Pavlov (16) has reported the application of his conditioned reflex method to this problem. It is well known that after repeated association of food with the sound of a bell, the bell alone will elicit salivation in the animal. In this experiment the conditioned reflex was established in the rats, and these rats were then inbred; the next generation acquired the conditioned response after a smaller number of presentations, and so on with each succeeding generation. Pavlov believed it might be possible to breed rats which would salivate at the sound of the bell without any training whatever. This startling result is surrounded by a certain amount of mystery, since in his later publications Pavlov no longer referred to it, and he refused to answer any further questions about it. It is currently believed to be a repetition of what happened in the case of Kammerer, although fortunately without the same tragic consequences. At any rate, the result has not been verified.

A striking investigation in this field has been reported in a series of papers by McDougall (17). The procedure was similar to that used in Pavlov's study, except that the ability to solve a simple water maze was substituted for the formation of a conditioned response. Each generation of rats was taught to run the maze and then inbred, and for each succeeding generation the average number of trials, as well as the average time required to run the maze successfully, were substantially reduced. The results appear clear and incontrovertible. Serious criticisms of a methodological nature have, however, been leveled against McDougall's procedure. The principal objection has been that since in each generation it was obviously impossible to interbreed all the rats, McDougall chose from among them a limited number for this purpose; the question arises as to whether, quite unconsciously, he might have chosen in each generation those rats which had superior maze-running ability, so that the results might have been due not to the inheritance of acquired characters, but to selective breeding.

That this is at least a possibility is indicated by the work of Tryon (18), who used a more complex type of maze, and from each generation of rats chose those with very superior or inferior maze-running ability. These he bred separately, the superior with the superior and the inferior with the inferior. When this procedure had been repeated for several generations, he found that he had developed, by means of such selective breedings, two distinct "races" of rats, differing so clearly in maze-running ability that there was almost no overlapping between them. This study indicates that a result similar to McDougall's may be obtained without the intervention of any inheritance of acquired abilities. McDougall states, however, that in his experiments he was careful to choose the poorer rather than the better rats for purposes of inbreeding, and that the results which he obtained are not to be explained on the basis of selection.

Eugenics. The fact that improvement may be brought about in a stock by selective breeding, if not by the transmission of training, raises the important question of the applicability of a eugenics program to man. Such a program has attracted the attention and devotion of a number of biologists and geneticists, and in many parts of the world societies have been formed for the purpose of its advancement. It is customary to divide the eugenics platform into a positive and a negative aspect. The positive is the attempt to improve the quality of the stock by selective mating of its superior members. In connection with man, the valid objection has been raised that marriage has become associated with so many factors of an emotional and sentimental nature that the direct application of the same breeding principles used with other animals seems impossible. An attempt in this direction is being made by the present German government, but it appears to be based mainly upon the official racial theory and the effort to increase the population. In any case it is too early to say anything of its success, either in connection with its final aims or with the willingness of the Germans to be influenced by it. It seems safe to say that in general relatively few men and women would lend themselves to a breeding experiment of the type which some eugenists have advocated.

On the negative side the eugenics program stands mainly for the elimination of the unfit in a population by preventing their procreation. The method advocated is usually that of sterilization of those who are judged unfit in any serious manner, with the hope that in a generation or two such individuals may appear rarely or not at all. There are many countries and many states in this country which have sterilization laws of this type, although in the majority of cases it is a voluntary sterilization and takes place only with the approval of the persons most concerned. This form of eugenics has usually been received much more favorably than the other. It is important to point out, however, that the objections to it are in some ways at least as serious as those which apply to the more positive program. In the first place, the determination of what is fit or unfit is difficult to make with any objectivity; in one society the physically defective, in another those who criticize their government, might seem to be the ones who should be eliminated. In any eugenics program, positive or negative, the community is at the mercy of those who establish the standards of fitness. It is obvious that this possibility leads into such serious danger that the greatest caution is necessary in its application. This danger becomes a real one when we think of the number of outstanding men of genius in our history who have had defects which would lead to their inclusion among the unfit from certain points of view. In the second place, such individuals might not only have defects themselves, but come of families similarly defective. A eugenics program would have prevented their birth, and the loss would have been incalculably greater than any conceivable gain. Third and most important, the reduction in the amount of defect by this method is so small that it would take many generations to effect a perceptible improvement. As Jennings (*19*) and others have pointed out, although there may be rather more defective offspring proportionately among defective than among normal parents, the large majority of defectives come from parents who are perfectly normal as far as all our tests make it possible to determine. The distinction between phenotype and genotype is pertinent at this point. A great many persons who appear healthy may still be capable of breeding defective children, and since there is no way of determining this in advance, negative eugenics would be of little help in improving the population. Hogben (*20*) has made a statistical study of the possibility of reducing defects in this manner, and he shows clearly that it is remote.

As a summary standpoint of the views of careful biologists on the questions of eugenics, we may cite the conclusion of Pearl (*21*):

In absolute numbers the vast majority of the most superior people in the world's history have in fact been produced by mediocre people or inferior forebears; and, furthermore, the admittedly most superior folk have in the main been singularly unfortunate in their progeny, again in absolute numbers. . . . In human society as it exists under present conditions of civilization, many a gaudy and imposing phenotype makes a very mediocre or worse genotype . . . and most eugenic selection of human beings is, and in the nature of the case, must be based solely upon phenotypic manifestations (p. 266).

We may add that even in connection with negative eugenics, the recent report of Myerson and his associates (22) indicates that sterilization must not be expected to effect any substantial reduction in the amount of mental defect and abnormality in the general population.

This problem is on the borderline between biology and social psychology. It is obviously not the province of the psychologist to determine directly the facts or the mechanism of heredity. It is, however, his very serious concern to devise measures of population quality in connection with mental abilities, and to use these as far as possible to indicate the presence or absence of genetic relationships. The work of Galton (23) on hereditary genius may be regarded as a first step in this direction. His results show that there is a definite tendency for ability to run in families, so that eminent men have eminent relatives in a proportion far greater than would be expected by chance. This study inspired the family histories of the Kallikak family by Goddard (24) and of the Jukes family by Dugdale (25) and Estabrook (26); both of these showed the frequency with which defects of a mental and physical nature occurred among the descendants of individuals who were themselves defective. At the other extreme the detailed study of the Edwards family by Winship (27) apparently showed a similar tendency for superior ability and mental adjustment to be found consistently in the same family. All of these studies, however, suffer from a fatal methodological defect, namely, that these families were relatively homogeneous not only in their heredity, but also in their environment. Family histories of this type fail to separate the two factors and are of little help in this problem. More pertinent is the study by Voss (28) of a musician whose first wife was musical, and the second, not; his children by the first wife showed more than the average interest and ability in a musical direction, and those by the second, nothing outstanding in this respect. It is to be noted that both groups of children lived under the same socio-economic conditions. Even in this case, since the mother constitutes an important part of the environment of the child, we cannot be certain that the effect is due solely or even primarily to heredity.

STUDIES OF TWINS

In the attempts to devise a technique for the separation of hereditary and environmental factors, the greatest attention has been directed to the question of twins. A distinction is made between identical twins who originate from the division of a single fertilized ovum, and non-identical, or fraternal twins, who develop from two separate fertilized ova. In the case of the former, the heredity is presumed to be identical; in the latter, it is as much alike as in the case of ordinary siblings (i.e., brothers and sisters). Obviously, identical twins must be of the same sex, whereas the non-identical may be of the same or of opposite sexes. It is the sex ratio which constitutes the greatest argument in favor of the existence of identity in twins. If there were no identity, one would expect by chance that there should be just as many like-sex as unlike-sex twins. Actually there are about 63% of like-sex twins, which is due to the fact that 25% of all twins, or 40% of like-sex twins, are identical (29).

Even in the case of identical twins slight differences may be observed, due either to certain asymmetries or to late division of the ovum. The rare cases of Siamese twins and of monsters of various kinds are due to very late and incomplete division. The diagnosis of identity is made on the basis of the general close resemblance, as well as by specific similarities in the prints of the fingers, the palms of the hands and the soles of the feet. Identical twins may in addition look like mirror images of each other, so that the left side of the one resembles the right side of the other, and vice versa. In some cases there may be only one placenta, which makes the diagnosis of identity certain. There are a great many instances in which the diagnosis of identity is exceedingly doubtful, since the similarity may be very close and yet not close enough to result in any confusion of the two individuals. It is important to keep in mind, therefore, that the distinctions be-

tween identical and fraternal twins upon which so much research has been based, must be used with considerable caution. If we accept the distinction, as most investigators have
done, the issue may be put in this way—if variations in heredity are more important than variations in environment, identical twins should resemble each other more closely than do
the non-identical in any psychological measures which we use
for purposes of comparison; if variations in the environment
are more important, the results should be the same for the
two groups, since the environments in both cases are presumably identical.

This last point requires a word of comment. The assumption that the environment of twins is necessarily identical has
not gone unchallenged. Certainly in the case of unlike-sex
twins, the cultural pattern of treatment of boys and girls
may play an important part from infancy on. In the case of
like-sex twins, the chances for an essential similarity in the
environment are much greater, but the very fact of great
similarity in appearance may also be responsible for a greater
similarity in treatment than would be the case for non-identical
twins. With these sources of error in mind, it may still be of
interest to summarize a few of the more important studies in
this field.

Tallman (30) gave the Stanford-Binet to 162 pairs of twins
and to 199 siblings. She found an average difference in I.Q.
of 13.14 in the case of siblings, and 7.07 in the case of the
twins. This might be regarded as an argument in favor of
heredity except for the fact that the environment of siblings,
due to the difference in age and to possible changes in the
domestic situation or in the family fortunes, may differ much
more than in the cases of twins. In order to answer this question, Tallman reports that siblings less than two years apart
had an average difference of 11.96, slightly less therefore than
that for all siblings, but still substantially greater than the
difference in the case of twins. When the group of twins was
further subdivided, the following results were obtained:

Opposite-sex twins, 84 pairs, average difference		8.48
Like-sex	78	6.42
Identical	63	5.08
boys	29	5.82
girls	34	4.22
Non-identical	39	7.37
boys	17	7.56
girls	22	7.14

Tallman concludes that among the like-sex twins those who look alike (identical twins) resemble one another more closely in their I.Q. than those who look distinctly different. She regards her results therefore as indicating the greater significance of hereditary factors.

There is, however, the significant fact that the non-identical twins, whether of the same or of opposite sex, resemble each other much more closely in their test scores than do ordinary siblings, in spite of the fact that the hereditary resemblance is the same in the two cases. This in turn seems to point to the significance of environmental factors, although it must be borne in mind that the results of an intelligence test given at different age levels are not strictly comparable.[1] There appears to be only the small difference between 5.08 (for the identical twins) and 7.37 (for the non-identical), i.e., a little more than two points in I.Q., which may safely be ascribed to the greater similarity in heredity. This study may therefore be interpreted as having indicated that heredity does have an effect upon the intelligence test scores, but not as having demonstrated that this effect is a marked one.

The degree of relationship between twins as compared with siblings can be expressed also in terms of the correlation coefficient. The following table from Viteles (31) is based upon results obtained by Thorndike (32), Merriman (33), Lauterbach (34), and others. The correlations refer to intelligence test scores.

[1] This is due to the tendency for the I.Q. to decrease slightly with age, particularly in the case of the brighter children, because of the manner in which the Binet is constructed.

Identical twins	.90
All twins	.75
Fraternal twins	.70
Siblings	.50
Cousins	.20
Unrelated	.00

These results apparently demonstrate the effect of both hereditary and environmental factors. The difference in the correlation coefficients for identical twins and fraternal twins argues in favor of hereditary factors; the difference between the latter and siblings, in favor of environment.

The relationship between twins has also been studied in connection with other psychological characteristics. McNemar (35) gave five tests of motor skill to 93 pairs of male twins, including 46 non-identical and 47 identical twins in a junior high school. The correlations ranged from .39 to .56 for the non-identical, and from .71 to .95 for the identical twins. The investigator concludes that hereditary factors play a major part in twin resemblance in motor abilities. It seems probable that heredity would be more important in these than in more intellectual activities, because of the closer dependence upon sensory and muscular development.

A study of the handwriting of a pair of male identical twins and of female Siamese twins has been made by Seeman and Saudek (36). A detailed examination showed a marked degree of similarity in both cases. It is interesting to note that Newman (37), who examined the same pair of Siamese twins, found them to differ rather markedly in their personalities. This seems to be at the same time an argument against graphology as a means of personality diagnosis and in favor of the possibility that identical twins may develop in different ways.

One of the most striking studies in this field is that by Lange (38), who in the Bavarian prisons found thirty men with twin brothers. There were 13 who were identical twins, and of these, ten had twin brothers also in prison. Of the 17 fraternal pairs, only 2 men had twin brothers also in prison.

Lange states that even in the detailed nature of their criminal careers there was a close resemblance within each pair of identical twins. He concludes that crime is due primarily to destiny, which in turn has its basis in the germ plasm and not in the environment. These results have recently received a certain degree of confirmation in the study by Rosanoff (39) of twin resemblances in psychosis. The only questions which we must ask are whether the environment of the identical twins was any more similar than that of the non-identical, and whether on the average they were separated at about the same time of life. If the results cannot be explained on the basis of this environmental difference, Lange's study must be regarded as an important argument in favor of the hereditary basis of similarities in personality. This does not mean, however, that criminality as such is inherited. There remains the possibility that certain personality tendencies are inherited, and that under certain social conditions these will readily lead to crime.

In the cases so far discussed (with the possible exception of some of Lange's subjects), the identical twins were raised together, and as has been mentioned, some of the striking similarities between them may be explained on that basis. For that reason the interest of investigators in this field has been aroused particularly by the cases of identical twins reared apart. There are not many of these that have so far been studied; altogether there are ten such pairs, one of them examined by Muller (40), the other nine by Newman (41). They had all been separated early in life and saw little or nothing of each other until they had become adults. When they were tested the average difference in I.Q. was 7.7 points, with a range from 0 to 17. This means that twins reared apart may resemble each other very closely, but that there may also in some cases be marked differences between them, and the results are therefore difficult to interpret in connection with the nature-nurture controversy. Reinhardt (42) summarizes his review of this material as follows:

There are marked similarities in mental qualities between the individuals of three pairs. The individuals of five pairs showed almost equally marked differences in these qualities, while the differences were present but less distinct in two other pairs. In five pairs striking dissimilarities existed in non-intellectual traits, and noteworthy differences existed in two others. There is, furthermore, no apparent tendency for so-called intellectual and non-intellectual traits to run concurrently in pairs. In other words, one set of twins may be very similar in one kind of qualities and very unlike in another (p. 141-142).

One of the reasons for the difficulty in interpretation is the fact that the environments to which the separated twins went were in some cases similar, and in others dissimilar. If the twins grow up in separate but more or less equivalent environments, the similarities between them may be due to that fact in addition to the similar heredity. Differences in age at the time of separation may also have had an effect. The problem is further complicated by the fact that in the case of identical twins reared together, whereas the average difference between the individuals in each pair is only 5.3 I.Q. points, the range of the differences is from 0 to 20. Why there should ever be a difference of 20 points in I.Q. between two individuals whose heredity and environment are both presumably identical (or nearly so) is difficult to explain. The Dionne quintuplets are also reported (43) to show definite individual variations, in spite of their biological and environmental "identity." It is of course probable that the social environment does differ to some degree for each individual even in this closed group. What is needed in this whole field is a much more careful analysis of the nature of the environment in each case and of the manner in which the individual and his environment interact.

Newman and his collaborators (41) maintain a middle-of-the-road position in their interpretation of the data. They feel rightly that any dogmatic conclusion is at the present time premature. In the writer's opinion the studies of twins indicate the presence of both hereditary and environmental influences in the causation of individual differences, with the latter playing the larger part.

Before leaving the field of family resemblances in mental test performance, mention should be made of an approach by Thorndike (44) to this problem. He gave intelligence tests to 1800 pairs of siblings and found a positive correlation between them of .60. It happens, however, that in a previous study by Pearson (45) of family resemblances in physical traits the correlations obtained were .52 for eye color, .55 for hair color, and .49 for cephalic index. Thorndike argues that since the relationship in intelligence is approximately the same as for physical traits known to be determined by heredity, it is reasonable to assume that intelligence is similarly determined. This inference appears on the surface to be reasonable, but it is not really justified. There are many possible reasons why two similar correlations, even in the case of the same individuals, may be due to entirely different factors. The similarity between them may be largely a matter of chance.

This does not mean that there is no genetically determined family relationship in intelligence; it merely means that this argument cannot be accepted as it stands. In all probability intelligence is to a certain degree inherited along family lines, although there is no doubt that social and environmental factors exercise a constant and important influence.

OCCUPATIONAL DIFFERENCES

A great many investigations agree in their demonstration that occupational groups differ markedly from one another in their mental test performance (10). The individual studies differ in the details of their procedure and in the tests used, but show substantial agreement in their results. The investigation by Collins (46) may be taken as representative and his results are presented in the following table.

Occupation	No. of Families	Range of Middle 50%	Median I.Q.
Professional	90	106-126	116
Clerical	131	105-122	113
Managerial	165	104-123	112
Trade	413	100-120	110
Foreman	106	98-118	109
Skilled labor	569	94-114	104
Unskilled labor	377	85-108	95

It may be added that results of this type are found not only in the case of school children (as in Collins' study and many others), but also among adults (47) and among pre-school children (48). They were not demonstrated to exist in the case of children below one year of age (49), but in view of the difficulty of equating these tests of infants with those used in the case of older children, the interpretation of this study is doubtful. In general we may say that the evidence conclusively demonstrates a relationship between socio-economic status as indicated by occupation and the scores obtained on the standard intelligence tests.

In the study of gifted children by Terman and his associates (50), it was also revealed that extraordinary ability was found much more frequently in the upper than in the lower economic groups. The following table shows the distribution of occupations of the fathers of the gifted children, compared with the proportion of these occupations in the whole population of Los Angeles and San Francisco, where the study was conducted.

Occupation	Percentage of Gifted Children	Occupations in General Population
Professional	29.1%	2.9%
Public Service	4.5	3.3
Commercial	46.2	36.1
Labor	20.2	57.7

A study among Negro college freshmen at West Virginia State College showed a similar hierarchy (51). The results follow:

Occupation	Number	%	Median	Interquartile Range
Professional	49	11.1	98.15	72-150
Commercial	18	4.1	94.99	68-157
Artisan	28	6.4	93.50	80-135
Skilled labor	182	41.3	87.50	60-126
Unskilled labor	164	37.1	73.10	52-103

The test used was the American Council Psychological Examination, and the results are not directly comparable with those reported above. The occupational hierarchy, however, is similar.

The results are clear, but the interpretation is very difficult. There are at least two ways of explaining the data. One may argue that these differences point to variations in the hereditary intelligence of the occupational groups, that those in the upper socio-economic levels are there because of their superior intelligence, which is transmitted to their children. This is the explanation preferred by the majority of those who have reported results of this type. On the other hand it might be argued that the difference in "intelligence" as measured by the tests is not the cause, but the effect of the socio-economic variations, and that the superior home and school environment of the more favored groups is responsible for their better performance. It is of course also possible that both factors are operative. As the results stand, they lend themselves equally well to either of these interpretations. It is important to see what additional light may be thrown upon them by other pertinent material.

THE EFFECT OF SCHOOL TRAINING

A direct approach to this problem is the investigation of the degree to which a change in the environment will effect a change in the test scores. If we can study the same children in both favorable and unfavorable environments, we may hope to determine to what extent the environment is responsible. Obviously the environment is a complex of a great many factors and requires the most careful analysis, but we shall be most concerned here with the effect of a change in education, and a change in the economic status of the home.

In connection with the former the most significant study is that of Wellman (52), who studied the effect of nursery school training on the intelligence test scores of children. She had of course a control group, matched with the experimental group in every way except that it did not receive this training. The results showed significant and marked gains in I.Q. in the case of the experimental group—gains which were maintained over a period of four to eight years during which the children were studied. Wellman concludes: "A permanent change in intellectual standing can be effected in one to one-and-one-half years that will last four to eight years." Since there can be no doubt that in general the schooling of children in the higher occupational levels is of a superior type, this may certainly account for part of the obtained differences. Wellman's study was carried on long enough to show that the effect of superior training was maintained over a long period. Since the superior schooling in the case of the higher economic groups continues for a longer period of time than in the case of Wellman's investigation, we might expect the results to be even more marked. In any case this study may be regarded as constituting a strong argument in favor of the environmental interpretation. We may add that in the case of Negro children, Foreman's (53) demonstration of a close relationship between the achievement of the school children and the amount of money expended upon their education points in the same direction.

THE INTELLIGENCE OF FOSTER CHILDREN

As for the second approach, namely, by a study of changes in the home environment, the most satisfactory technique has been developed in the study of foster children. If children are taken from poor to good or at least better home environments, a direct indication of the extent of the environmental effect should be obtainable. There are at least three important investigations in this field, differing in their approach and, as we shall see, in their interpretation, but all of sufficient importance to warrant somewhat detailed consideration.

The first of these to be described is the well-known study by Freeman, Holzinger and Mitchell (*54*) on foster children in and near the city of Chicago. One part of the study dealt with 130 pairs of siblings who had been separated four years or more. The homes to which these children went were rated by field workers, and were found to differ considerably. The investigation showed that the average test score for siblings in poorer homes was 85.7, and for those in better homes, 95.0—a difference of 9.3 points. Various factors make a correction necessary, and the investigators estimate that the real difference is about six points. If we could assume that on the average the intelligence of siblings is about the same, this difference would be attributable to the nature of the home environment.

A more direct method was applicable in the case of 74 children who were retested after they had lived four years in their foster homes. On the first test their average score was 91.2, and on the second, 93.7—a gain of 2.5 points, which in this case is statistically significant. This result appears much more striking when it is further analyzed. It was found, for example, that those children who went to better homes gained 5.3, and those in poorer ones, 0.1. Those who were adopted at an early age gained more; children who were under twelve at the age of re-test gained on the average 5.2, and those over twelve showed an insignificant loss of 0.4.

Correlations were calculated for the degree of resemblance between siblings. It was found that when they had been separated before either one was six years old, the correlation coefficient was .25; when the foster homes were of different grade, it was .19. As was indicated above (see p. 236), there is a correlation of at least .50 for siblings brought up together, and the results of Freeman and his collaborators show the extent to which this resemblance may be decreased when the home environments differ.

Finally, the test scores of the foster children were compared according to the occupations of the foster fathers, with the following results.

Occupation	Average I.Q.	No. of Cases
Professional	106.8	61
Semi-professional and business	101.1	160
Skilled labor	91.6	149
Semi- and slightly-skilled	84.9	19

There were no unskilled laborers among the foster parents. The table shows a hierarchy similar to that reported for occupational groups in general, although the figures are somewhat lower for foster children than for those born into homes of corresponding quality. This discrepancy in the scores argues in favor of native factors, if it were certain that the treatment accorded the two groups of children was the same in every particular, and that their social environments were identical. That this may be questioned is indicated in the analysis of these results by Anastasi (7), who believes that the very early training of the children before they were placed in the foster homes, as well as the unrealized but undoubted differences in the attitudes of the parents, may be responsible for these results. It is difficult to ascertain with any definiteness the force of this argument, but it is probable that it has considerable significance.

The fact that the hierarchy of occupational groups exists among foster children would seem to be a strong argument in favor of the environmental hypothesis. It seems difficult otherwise to understand why children going into professional homes should differ so markedly (on the average by more than twenty points in I.Q.) from those going to homes of semi- and slightly-skilled laborers. It may be added that since there were no really "poor" homes among the foster parents, even this large difference may still not represent the whole possible environmental effect. The significance of this argument is weakened, however, by the possibility that another factor is operative, namely, a selective effect upon the placement of children. It has been suggested that professional people will either demand or be given the brighter children; they may ask for some indication of the mental level of the children they propose to adopt, or the placement bureau of the orphanage may attempt to "match" the children with their prospective parents. That this procedure is followed in many institutions is certain. Freeman and his associates are of course aware of this possibility and discuss it at considerable length, but point out that from their knowledge of the conditions of placement in the institutions from which they obtained their children, there seems little possibility that selection entered to any important degree. If that can be regarded as certain, the strength of the environmental explanation of the results is greatly increased. It would undoubtedly aid the final evaluation of results of this kind, however, if more direct information could be obtained as to the degree to which selective factors related to intelligence may enter into the placement of children in one foster home or another—whether, for example, similarity of appearance is more or less important than mental level, whether foster parents ask for I.Q.'s and whether the institution furnishes such information, whether they are content to know that the child is "intelligent" or insist upon knowing just how intelligent he is, and so on.

In summary it may be stated that this investigation constitutes an important argument in favor of an environmental explanation of occupational differences in intelligence. The improvement in the scores of the children after re-test, the fact that children in superior homes rank considerably higher than their siblings in poorer ones, and the occupational hierarchy found among the foster children, all point in that direction. On the other hand, the fact that the foster children do not do so well as children born into similar homes argues in favor of hereditary factors. The investigators themselves interpret their results as indicating that the environment is much more important than is usually realized.

Another important study in this field was made by Burks (55). The approach in this case was to compare the degree of resemblance between parents and their children on the one hand, and foster parents and their foster children on the other. The subjects were homogeneous as to race and educational opportunity, and the study was conducted in three California cities, San Francisco, Los Angeles and San Diego. The children were all placed in the foster homes before the age of twelve months, with three months as the average age of placement. The experimental group consisted of 214 children and 342 foster parents, and the control group, of 105 children and 205 parents. The environments of the two groups were carefully matched by field workers. The correlation of test scores of parents and children gave the following results: foster father and foster child, .07; foster mother and foster child, .19; own father and child, .45; own mother and child, .46. There is obviously a much greater resemblance in intelligence when there is also a greater similarity in heredity, with the environment presumably held constant. The results are interpreted therefore as arguing definitely for the operation of hereditary factors. The question arises here again, however, as to whether the environment of a foster child is really identical with that of an own child. The very fact that parents will look for resemblances to themselves in their own children has been regarded as helping to create such resemblance. It is difficult to know how much force there is in this criticism, and it is possible that only the most detailed analysis of the environments in question would provide the necessary information.

In a second portion of the study correlations were calculated between the I.Q.'s of the foster children and the quality of their environment, measured by a rating scale which took into account a large number of the characteristics of the home. The correlation coefficient was .42; since this figure is squared in order to indicate the factors common to the two variables, it was concluded that the total contribution of the measurable home environment to the intelligence of the child is about 17%. The remaining 83% presumably represents the contribution of heredity. This conclusion of Burks has attracted considerable attention and has been subjected to criticism from various quarters. Apart from the doubtful procedure of attaching definite statistical figures to the relative importance of nature and nurture, there is the more important objection that the home does not constitute the totality of the child's environment. There may be many other factors—the school, the neighborhood, friends, recreations, etc.—which may also play a significant part and account for a portion of the 83% ascribed to heredity. There is the additional fact that *measurable* home environment is not the same as total home environment, and that an error consequently enters into the result which makes the use of actual percentages a still more doubtful procedure. Burks recognizes that the measures she uses do not exhaust the scope of environmental influence, and it is all the more surprising therefore to find her giving so much weight to this one correlation.

In this connection, it is important to keep in mind Freeman's conclusion that the environment may raise or depress the mental level of a child by ten points or more in the I.Q. Since, however, the occupational differences referred to above show a difference of about twenty points in the I.Q. of the best and the poorest groups, the addition of the ten points to those of low economic status, and the subtraction of an equal amount from those most favorably situated, would result in the complete disappearance of the difference between them. If this analysis is correct, and it seems a logical one, the conclusion is justified that there is nothing in the occupational hierarchy that cannot be explained on the basis of the environmental hypothesis.

There is an important point which must be borne in mind. The conclusion that occupational differences in intelligence may be explained on an environmental basis does not mean that there are no inherited differences in intelligence as regards individuals. Within each occupational group there is still a wide variation. The son of one lawyer may have a very much higher I.Q. than the son of another. Although we are not suggesting that one professional home is necessarily the equal of another, the great range of differences within the professional group in all probability requires at least in part an explanation in terms of heredity. Adlerian psychologists may point to position in the family and to compensatory mechanisms as explaining these differences, but it is much more likely that they have also a biological basis.

The importance of the distinction between individual and group differences in the nature-nurture problem comes out clearly in connection with an important third study in this field. Leahy (56) approaches the problem somewhat as Burks did, through the comparison of two groups of children living in approximately identical environments. One group consisted of adopted children, unrelated to the persons who shaped the environment; the other consisted of children living with their own parents. Both heredity and environment operate to produce resemblances in the latter group, only environment in the former. It is argued that with measurable environment identical for both groups of children, differences in the relationship of the child's intelligence to that of the parents must be the result of the presence of a common heredity in the case of true parents and offspring, and the result of the absence of hereditary likeness in the case of adopted parents and children. The problem of selective placement does not enter into this study, since the two groups of subjects were not compared with each other, but were deliberately matched for a number of factors—sex, race and nationality, size of community, mental age, paternal occupation, and fathers' and mothers' schooling. The adopted children had all been in the foster homes from the age of six months or younger. At the time of the study the age range was from five to fourteen, with the average 9:3 for the adopted group and 9:4 for the controls. There were 194 subjects in each group.

The main results of this study refer to the degree of relationship between the child's I.Q., as measured by the Otis Self-Administering Test, Intermediate Form, and various aspects of the environment, including the characteristics of the parents. They are presented in the following table.

Correlated Factor	Adopted Children	Control Children
Father's Otis score	.15	.51
Mother's Otis score	.20	.51
Mid-parent Otis score	.18	.60
Father's vocabulary	.22	.47
Mother's vocabulary	.20	.49
Mid-parent vocabulary	.24	.56
Environmental status	.19	.53
Cultural index of home	.21	.51
Child training index	.18	.52
Economic index	.12	.37
Sociality index	.11	.42
Father's education	.16	.48
Mother's education	.21	.50
Mid-parent education	.20	.54
Father's occupational status	.12	.45

The differences between the degree of relationship for the two groups are impressive, and appear to point to a much greater resemblance between children and parents when there is an hereditary as well as an environmental factor at work. The only possible question that arises is the one referred to in the case of Burks' study, namely, the possibility that true parents look for greater resemblances in the case of their own children, and that this may play a part in determining such resemblance. It is doubtful, however, whether it should be regarded as affecting the findings to any great extent. Leahy's contention that the results of this study show the hereditary component in intelligence tests to have a greater significance than the environmental component would seem justified, with the important limitation that it has been shown to apply in the case of a group with relatively homogeneous background, and that the results are not to be extended beyond these limitations without further proof.

This restriction in the validity of Leahy's results is not merely the one commonly expressed in psychological research, namely, that the conclusion must not be extended beyond the scope of the actual data. In this particular case it has a different meaning. The environments included in this study were all of a superior type, and we find none of the marked discrepancies in home background and educational opportunity characterizing the occupational groups previously discussed. Children are rarely adopted into homes comparable to those of the day laborer or farmer group in the occupational hierarchy. It is highly probable therefore that whereas the average differences between occupations are best explained in terms of environmental factors, the individual or family differences within the occupation, or within any relatively homogeneous background, may be strongly influenced by heredity. That parents and children should resemble each other is to be expected; that day laborers as such are inferior and have inferior children has never been proven, and cannot be until the economic system gives them exactly the same opportunities for advancement as it does to the sons and daughters of professional and business men.

In connection with this occupational hierarchy, eugenists have frequently expressed concern over the existence of a differential birth rate, with a tendency for wealthier and more successful families to have comparatively fewer children than those at lower economic levels (57, 58, 59). There is talk of race suicide, of degeneration, of a gradual decrease in the level of intelligence and ability, etc. In their concern for the future of the race, the eugenists have urged that steps be taken to bring about a change in the differential birth rate, either through a process of education, or by subsidies for children, or by a combination of these and other methods. If our analysis of the occupational differences in intelligence is correct, these fears are unfounded. The apparent inferiority of those in poor economic classes will in all probability disappear as soon as their cultural and educational environment is raised to a satisfactory level. A wise eugenics program in that case would focus attention upon such an environmental improvement rather than upon the hypothetical dangers arising from differences in the birth rate. An improvement of this type would have also the direct eugenic effect of improving the community by increasing the chances of bodily as well as of mental health.

Even if the occupational hierarchy does correspond to a real difference, it must be kept in mind that there is a tremendous amount of overlapping between the groups. In other words, in spite of the difference in averages between the children of professional men and laborers, there is a substantial number in the latter group superior to the professional average. A consistent eugenics program would concern itself therefore not merely with occupational groups as such, but would be obliged to choose from within each group those most capable of producing superior offspring. It becomes again a matter of superiority of families or of individuals rather than of groups. A further correction would have to be made by the addition to the scores of those in a poor environment of an amount corresponding to their handicaps, and by a corresponding subtraction from the scores of the superior groups. That this is hardly feasible goes without saying. In the light of these various considerations, it is not difficult to understand why some eugenics societies have altered their original program substantially in the direction of working toward an improved environment instead of attempting first to improve heredity, and why they are laying more and more stress on individual rather than on group differences.

Even if we use economic success as a direct indication of superior ability, there is ample evidence of what Sorokin (60) calls "social mobility," or a tendency for considerable movement up and down the economic scale. This means that many individuals from poorer groups become successful in spite of the alleged relationship between intellectual ability and the economic status of the parents. Sorokin points out that among captains of industry and finance in the United States, 38.8% in the past and 19.6% in the present generation started poor; 31.5% among deceased and 27.7% among living multi-millionaires started neither rich nor poor; among the first 29 presidents of the United States, 14, or 48.3%, came from poor and humble families. These results do not prove complete equality of opportunity, but they do indicate that there is no necessary relation between economic status of the parents and the ability of the children.

Further data compiled by Sorokin show that of 885 leading men of science in the United States, 21.2% were sons of farmers; of 1000 men of letters, 13.9% were sons of farmers, and 4.8% of skilled and unskilled laborers; of 45 State Governors in 1909, 41 were sons of farmers or of parents in equally humble circumstances; of 56 cabinet officers between 1869 and 1903, 47 were farmers' sons; of those listed in *Who's Who in America* (1922-1923), 23.4% were sons of farmers and 6.7% of skilled and unskilled laborers.

Throughout this account of occupational differences, the criterion used for the measurement of intelligence (apart from Sorokin's data) is the intelligence test. The use of this measure raises a number of important questions, only a few of which may be touched upon here.[2] It is, however, important to mention at this point that many psychologists do not now regard the intelligence test as a measure of native intelligence independent of environmental factors, but rather as a measure of achievement into which both native and acquired factors enter. If the test is given to a group of children all of whom have had approximately equal environmental opportunities, the differences in test scores will probably correspond roughly to differences in native ability. If, on the other hand, the background differs markedly, the test scores may be affected by the background to such a degree that any conclusion as to variations in native intelligence would be unwarranted. Tests may still be of use in vocational guidance or in school placement, but they will have to be interpreted with caution until the necessary corrections have been made for the element of nurture. It is safe to conclude that the occupational differences depend certainly to some degree, and probably entirely,

[2] For further discussion of the uses and abuses of intelligence tests see *61, 62, 63, 64.*

on the relative opportunities created by the background for the acquisition of the information and the techniques which aid in the solution of the problems presented by the tests.

REGIONAL DIFFERENCES IN INTELLIGENCE

Similar considerations apply to differences in mental test performance among children in different regions, and particularly in the case of rural and urban communities. Extensive studies by Book (65), Pressey (66), and others find definite evidence for the superiority of urban groups in this respect. As in the case of the occupational hierarchy, there is the difficulty of knowing what is the cause and what the effect in the explanation of the findings. It is possible to argue that the city environment, with its better schools and more varied opportunities for education, creates the difference between the two groups; it may also be urged on the other hand that there has been a selective migration of the superior individuals from the country to the city, resulting in the better showing of the urban group.

That environmental factors undoubtedly play a part has been pointed out by Shimberg (67), whose investigation showed the important influence of previous information in certain types of intelligence tests. The study indicated that for the usual test the questions asked were such as to give to city children a definite advantage. It was possible to devise an information test based upon the experience of rural children in which urban children were at a definite disadvantage and showed themselves to be inferior. Shimberg's opinion is that one procedure is as reasonable as the other, and that neither one warrants any conclusion as to superior or inferior native intelligence. As an extreme example of the manner in which background factors may enter into test performance, Pressey (68) cites the experience of an investigator among the Kentucky "poor whites." He presented the familiar Binet problem: "If you went to the store and bought 6 cents' worth of candy and gave the clerk 10 cents, what change would you receive?" One youngster replied, "I never had 10 cents and if I had I wouldn't spend it for candy, and anyway candy is what your mother makes." The examiner made a second attempt and reformulated the problem as follows: "If you had taken 10 cows to pasture for your father and 6 of them strayed away, how many would you have left to drive home?" The child replied: "We don't have 10 cows, but if we did and I lost 6, I wouldn't dare go home." The examiner made one last attempt: "If there were 10 children in a school and 6 of them were out with measles, how many would there be in school?" The answer came even more promptly, "None, because the rest would be afraid of catching it too" (p. 237).

This example is of course not conclusive in itself, but it raises the whole question as to the familiarity of rural children not only with the content of the test, but with the very procedure of testing. If they are unaccustomed to the need for imagining these hypothetical situations and answering questions concerning them, their whole attitude may be completely negative. It goes without saying that such unfamiliarity is not equally marked in all rural communities, and that the Kentucky mountaineers represent an extreme case of isolation.

The theory of selective migration has attracted considerable support. Probably its first clear formulation occurred in the work of Otto Ammon (69), who tried to establish the thesis that the superior individuals, who are also dolichocephalic, migrate to the cities, whereas the relatively inferior brachycephals remain on the land. He based his conclusion mainly upon measurements made in and near Karlsruhe, where he found the urban population had longer heads than their rural neighbors. This theory was checked by Livi (70) in Italy and by Beddoe (71) in England, and no such anthropometric difference between city and country was noticed. It is not usually realized that certain of Ammon's own results argue against the theory of a selective migration with reference to intelligence. Among other things, he compared the occupational distribution of immigrants to Karlsruhe with that of their own descendants and obtained the following results.

Generation	Lowest Economic Group	Middle Group	Professional Group
Immigrants	82%	14%	4%
Their sons	41	49	10
Their grandsons	40	35	25

This would seem to show that the immigrants themselves are not a superior group to start with, but that with the passage of time they improve their economic status and become much like the average city population. It seems more likely that this is to be explained on the basis of a gradual assimilation to the environment than through the innate superiority of the migrants.

In more recent discussions of this problem, Ammon's anthropometric linkage plays little part, but the theory of selective migration is still appealed to in order to explain observed differences in population quality. Pintner (72), for example, summarizes the results of the testing of rural children and concludes that "in general . . . it would appear as if the urban districts rate higher in intelligence than rural districts and that this is due to the migration of superior intelligence to the cities" (p. 253). In connection with the mountaineers of Kentucky, Hirsch (73) concludes that close inbreeding in conjunction with selective migration is responsible in large part for the low general intelligence of the East Kentucky mountaineers today. Plant (74) expresses the opinion that "the stream coming from rural areas into our metropolitan districts represents a group highly selected as to ability and general stability. There are, it is true, other factors at work but a persistent tendency for the more venturesome, the more able, to move towards city life is an outstanding characteristic of this movement" (p. 147). Finally, Doob (75), writing of the poor Whites in the South, states that "moving from a known area into an unknown one requires courage, intelligence, and initiative in meeting new economic conditions and in establishing new social ties" (p. 457). Although he has no data applicable to his particular community, he feels that the presumption is in favor of this generalization, since it has been found to be true for other communities in the past.

In spite of the prevalence of the belief in selective migration, there is little direct evidence in its favor. In the case of the writers mentioned in the preceding paragraph, the argument appears to be based on logic rather than on objective data. It is believed that certain qualities are necessary for migration and that therefore the migrants must be in possession of such qualities. Neither half of this proposition has so far been proved. On a priori grounds one can make as good a case for the inferiority as for the superiority of the migrants. During an investigation of Negro migration in the South (see below, Chapter XI) the present writer found many southerners, both Negro and White, who did point out that it requires energy and initiative to start over again in a new community, as well as intelligence to see the advantage of the new environment over the old. There were just as many, however, who argued that those who are more successful in the old environment, who have achieved a certain social and economic position, who possess property and friends, are less likely to wander off in search of fresh opportunities than those who are shiftless and unsuccessful and have nothing to lose by leaving. It was rare to hear the opinion that those who left were neither better nor worse than those who stayed behind. It is clear that in this whole field there is need for objective information, and that the argument from logic is not to be relied upon.

On the basis of his analysis of migration from the tidewater region of Virginia, Gee (76) concludes that those who migrate are slightly better educated than those who remain, but that there is some tendency for those who own their own farms, and who therefore are presumably more successful, to stay where they are. The results are therefore inconclusive as far as selective migration is concerned. Zimmerman (77) has studied migration in Iowa and is of the opinion that the very successful and the unsuccessful groups migrate, and that those in an intermediate position remain in their original homes.

An investigation has recently been completed of White

migrants from rural New Jersey to urban centers in the vicinity (78). There were several New Jersey counties in which intelligence tests had been given in the rural schools during the past years, and it was possible to find a considerable number of migrating children for whom test records were available. It was felt that a comparison of their scores with those of the non-migrating population would yield direct information as to which group was superior. The scores of 597 migrants were studied and they were found to be slightly below those of the general non-migrating group. These scores were made by children who were taken to the city by their parents, and who did not themselves initiate the migration, but since we are interested in the quality of the stock rather than of any particular individual, the use of the children's test scores would seem justified. A second study was, however, made of adult migrants in South Germany, although in their case it was necessary to use school records rather than intelligence test scores. The total number of cases in this study is very small (66), but their average school standing was slightly above that of the non-migrant group, and therefore appears to represent a moderate degree of selection.

In the present state of our knowledge it is impossible to make a definite statement as to whether or not the migrants as a whole are superior to the non-migrants as a whole. In the German group the migrants were slightly superior; in the New Jersey study they were average or slightly inferior. Any blanket concept of "selective migration" with respect to intelligence is not justified by the evidence.

The problem is much too complicated to be stated in terms of intelligence alone. There must be some selection, since not everyone migrates, but this selection may be determined by a number of different causes. Economic factors undoubtedly play an important part, and bad conditions at home and good conditions elsewhere will certainly provide a definite spur to migration. A recent study by Raper (79) has shown how the boll weevil caused an exodus of Negroes from one county in Georgia, whereas there was little or no migration from a neighboring county which had not been similarly affected. It is probable that economic factors operate usually in a much more complicated manner; it may be that differing economic conditions will cause an exodus of a different type of migrant in each case. Careful study is required of the manner in which such factors may operate. A second group of factors relates not so much to the intelligence as to the personality of the migrants. Such characteristics as a desire for novelty or adventure, adaptability to the speed and noise of the city, lack of emotional attachment to the home—these and allied qualities may determine migration quite apart from intelligence. A third group of factors may be regarded as accidental. The inducements held out by friends or relatives in the city, misdemeanors committed at home, failure in social adjustment, may all play a part. Migration is by no means always the result of a spontaneous decision to move. This complexity in the factors involved, as well as the objective data to which reference has been made, indicates that we have no right to interpret the apparent superiority of urban over rural groups as due to selective migration. It seems much more probable that it is the city environment which is responsible.

Further evidence in this direction is furnished by the results of a study of rural Negroes who migrated to the city of New Orleans (*80*). It was found that those children who had lived longer in the city were superior in their intelligence test scores to those who had been there a shorter time; there was in fact a close correspondence between length of residence and average test score. This would seem to indicate that the environment is clearly responsible, and that when favorable conditions are introduced into the life of the rural child, there is a notable improvement in his mental level.

The problem of selective migration will come in for further consideration in connection with the studies of Negro intelligence, and particularly with reference to the differences between southern and northern Negroes (see Chapter XI). At this point it will suffice to state that migrants may apparently be superior, inferior, or equal to the non-migrants in intelligence, and that we have no right to use selective migration as an explanation of the observed differences unless we have direct evidence that it is at work in the specific situation under discussion.[3]

SUMMARY

The field of differential psychology is closely related to the nature-nurture problem. The present position is that both nature and nurture are responsible for the characteristics of all individuals; the question is rather as to the amount of variation between individuals that may be ascribed to nature and nurture, respectively. The number and complexity of genes within the human germ-plasm make the direct application of Mendelian principles difficult, but the distinction between dominant and recessive characters is especially important.

The experimental studies of the inheritance of acquired characteristics have not succeeded in demonstrating such a possibility. The apparent success of McDougall is probably due to selective breeding, as Tryon's studies suggest. This does not mean, however, that artificial control of breeding, in the form of either positive or negative eugenics, is capable of producing any marked improvement in the human stock. Positive eugenics is not feasible, and negative eugenics not especially promising. The lack of any acceptable standard of population quality adds danger to a eugenics program.

Research on identical and non-identical twins has demonstrated that the former resemble each other somewhat more closely; this points to a demonstrable, though not a very marked, effect of heredity on intelligence test scores. Identical twins reared apart usually continue to have approximately equal scores, but substantial differences have been found in certain cases. Both hereditary and environmental factors must therefore play a part.

An occupational hierarchy in test scores has frequently been demonstrated. That this is at least in part due to environ-

---

[3] For a recent critical review of the literature on several of the problems discussed in this chapter, see *81*.

mental influences is indicated by the marked effect of school training, as well as by the gains reported for foster children placed in homes of good economic level. In view of the known effects of variations in the environment, the occupational hierarchy may be explained adequately without the assumption of inherited differences. On the other hand, individual variations within a particular occupational group clearly point to the importance of heredity, partly because the range of variations is too great to be ascribed to nurture, and partly because of the much greater resemblance between true parents and children than between foster parents and children in comparable environments. Variations between groups, therefore, are almost certainly environmental in origin; variations between individuals within a homogeneous group are due to a combination of hereditary and environmental factors. In this latter connection, the demonstrated effects of nature and nurture are of about the same magnitude.

The same considerations apply to the differences between urban and rural groups. The explanation in terms of selective migration has not been substantiated. In some cases it is a superior group which migrates to the city; in others, an inferior group. There are other factors—economic, personal, accidental—which determine the nature of the migration. The superiority of the city groups is much more probably due to the nature of the urban environment.

REFERENCES

1. Galton, F. *Inquiries into Human Faculty and Its Development.* 1883.
2. Binet, A., and Henri, V. "La Psychologie Individuelle," *Année Psychol.,* 1895, 2: pp. 411-463. See also subsequent volumes of the *Année Psychologique.*
3. Cattell, J. McK. "Mental Tests and Measurements," *Mind,* 1890, 15: pp. 373-380.
4. Thorndike, E. L. *An Introduction to the Theory of Mental and Social Measurements.* 1904.
5. Stern, W. *Die Differentielle Psychologie in Ihren Methodischen Grundlagen.* 1921.

6. Freeman, F. S. *Individual Differences.* 1934.

7. Anastasi, A. *Differential Psychology.* 1937.

8. Woodworth, R. S. *Psychology.* 3d ed. 1934.

9. Shapiro, H. L. *Migration and Environment.* 1939.

10. Murphy, G., Murphy, L. B., and Newcomb, T. M. *Experimental Social Psychology.* Rev. ed. 1937.

11. Morgan, T. H. *The Theory of the Gene.* 1926.

12. Weismann, A. *The Evolution Theory.* 2 vols. 1904.

13. Lamarck, J. B. *Philosophie Zoölogique.* 2 vols. 1809.

14. De Vries, H. *Species and Varieties, Their Origin by Mutation.* 1905.

15. Kammerer, P. *The Inheritance of Acquired Characteristics.* 1924.

16. Pavlov, I. P. "New Researches on Conditioned Reflexes." *Science,* n.s. 1923, 58: pp. 359-361.

17. McDougall, W. "An Experiment for the Testing of the Hypothesis of Lamarck." *Brit. J. Psychol.,* 1927, 17: pp. 267-304.

18. Tryon, R. C. "The Genetics of Learning Ability in Rats"— a preliminary report. *Univ. Calif. Publ. in Psychol.,* 1929, 4: pp. 71-89; "Studies in Individual Differences in Maze Ability: I. The Measurements of the Reality of Individual Differences," *J. Comp. Psychol.,* 1930, 11: pp. 145-170.

19. Jennings, H. S. *The Biological Basis of Human Nature.* 1930.

20. Hogben, L. T. *Nature and Nurture.* 1933.

21. Pearl, R. "Biology and Human Trends," *J. Wash. Acad. Sci.,* 1935, 25, No. 6: pp. 265-266.

22. Myerson, A., et al. *Eugenical Sterilization.* 1936.

23. Galton, F. *Hereditary Genius.* 1869.

24. Goddard, H. H. *The Kallikak Family: a Study in the Heredity of Feeblemindedness.* 1912.

25. Dugdale, R. L. *The Jukes: a Study in Crime, Pauperism, Disease, and Heredity.* 1877.

26. Estabrook, A. H. *The Jukes in 1915.* 1916.

27. Winship, A. E. *Jukes-Edwards: a Study in Education and Heredity.* 1900.

28. Voss, G. See Reference *31.*

29. Schwesinger, G. C. *Heredity and Environment.* 1933.

30. Tallman, G. G. "A Comparative Study of Identical and Non-Identical Twins with Respect to Intelligence Resemblances," *Twenty-Seventh Yearbook Nat. Soc. Stud. Educ.,* 1928, Part I: pp. 83-86.

31. Viteles, M. S. *Industrial Psychology.* 1932.

32. Thorndike, E. L. "Measurement of Twins," *Arch. Psychol.*, 1905, No. 1.

33. Merriman, C. "The Intellectual Resemblance of Twins," *Psychol. Monog.*, 1924, No. 5.

34. Lauterbach, C. E. "Studies in Twin Resemblance," *Genetics*, 1925, 10: pp. 525-568.

35. McNemar, Q. "Twin Resemblances in Motor Skills, and the Effect of Practice Thereon," *J. Genet. Psychol.*, 1933, 42: pp. 70-99.

36. Seeman, E., and Saudek, R. "Self-Expression in Twins' Handwriting and Drawing," *Char. & Pers.*, 1933, 1: pp. 91-128.

37. Newman, H. H. "Differences Between Conjoined Twins," *J. Hered.*, 1931, 22: pp. 201-216.

38. Lange, J. *Crime and Destiny.* 1929.

39. Rosanoff, A. J., et al. "The Etiology of So-called Schizophrenic Psychoses," *Amer. J. Psychiat.*, 1934, 91: pp. 247-286.

40. Muller, H. J. "Mental Traits and Heredity," *J. Hered.*, 1925, 16: pp. 433-448.

41. Newman, H. H., et al. *Twins: A Study of Heredity and Environment.* 1937.

42. Reinhardt, J. *Social Psychology.* 1938.

43. Blatz, W. E. *The Five Sisters.* 1938.

44. Thorndike, E. L., et al. "The Resemblance of Siblings in Intelligence," *Twenty-Seventh Yearbook Nat. Soc. Stud. Educ.*, 1928, Part I: pp. 41-53.

45. Pearson, K., and Lee, A. "On the Laws of Inheritance in Man: Inheritance of Physical Characters," *Biom.*, 1903, 2: pp. 357-462.

46. Collins, J. E. "The Intelligence of School Children and Paternal Occupation," *J. Educ. Res.*, 1928, 17: pp. 156-169.

47. Yerkes, R. M. "Psychological Examining in the U. S. Army," *Memoirs Nat. Acad. Sci.*, 1921, 15.

48. Goodenough, F. L. "The Relation of the Intelligence of Pre-school Children to the Occupation of their Fathers," *Amer. J. Psychol.*, 1928, 40: pp. 284-294.

49. Furfey, P. H. "The Relation Between Socio-economic Status and Intelligence of Young Infants as Measured by the Linfert-Hierholzer Scale," *J. Genet. Psychol.*, 1928, 35: pp. 478-480.

50. Terman, L. M. *Genetic Studies of Genius.* Vol. I: *Mental and Physical Traits of a Thousand Gifted Children.* 1925.

51. Canady, H. G. "The Intelligence of Negro College Students and Parental Occupation," *Amer. J. Sociol.*, 1936, 42: pp. 388-389.

52. Wellman, B. L. "Growth in Intelligence under Differing School Environments," *J. Exper. Educ.*, 1934, 3: pp. 59-83.

53. Foreman, C. *Environmental Factors in Negro Elementary Education.* 1932.

54. Freeman, F. N., Holzinger, K. J., and Mitchell, B. C. "The Influence of Environment on the Intelligence, School Achievement, and Conduct of Foster Children," *Twenty-Seventh Yearbook Nat. Soc. Stud. Educ.*, 1928, Part I: pp. 103-217.

55. Burks, B. S. "The Relative Influence of Nature and Nurture upon Mental Development, etc." *Twenty-Seventh Yearbook Nat. Soc. Stud. Educ.*, 1928, Part I: pp. 219-316.

56. Leahy, A. M. "Nature-nurture and Intelligence," *Genet. Psychol. Monog.*, 1935, 17: pp. 235-308.

57. McDougall, W. *Is America Safe for Democracy.* 1921.

58. Wiggam, A. E. *The Fruit of the Family Tree.* 1924.

59. Holmes, S. J. *The Trend of the Race.* 1921.

60. Sorokin, P. A. *Social Mobility.* 1927.

61. Garrett, H. E., and Schneck, M. R. *Psychological Tests, Methods and Results.* 1933.

62. Freeman, F. N. *Mental Tests, Their History, Principles and Applications.* Rev. ed. 1939.

63. Peatman, J. G. "Hazards and Fallacies of Statistical Method in Psychological Measurement," *Psychol. Rec.*, 1937, 1: pp. 365-390.

64. Klineberg, O. *Race Differences.* 1935.

65. Book, W. F. "Variations in Mental Ability and its Distribution among the School Population of an Indiana County," *Bull., Ext. Div., Indiana Univ.*, 1918, 4, No. 4: pp. 100-131.

66. Pressey, L. W. "The Influence of Inadequate Schooling and Poor Environment upon Results with Tests of Intelligence," *J. Appl. Psychol.*, 1920, 4: pp. 91-96.

67. Shimberg, M. E. "An Investigation into the Validity of Norms with Special Reference to Urban and Rural Groups," *Arch. Psychol.*, 1929, No. 104.

68. Pressey, S. L. *Psychology and the Newer Education.* 1933.

69. Ammon, O. *Zur Anthropologie der Badener.* 1899.

70. Livi, R. *Anthropometria Militare.* 1896.

71. Beddoe, J. *The Races of Britain: a Contribution to the Anthropology of Western Europe.* 1885.

72. Pintner, R. *Intelligence Testing; Methods and Results.* 1923.

73. Hirsch, N. D. M. "An Experimental Study of the East Kentucky Mountaineers," *Genet. Psychol. Monog.*, 1928, 3: pp. 183-244.

74. Plant, J. S. *Personality and the Cultural Pattern.* 1937.

75. Doob, L. W. "Appendix I" in J. Dollard's *Caste and Class in a Southern Town.* 1937.

76. Gee, W., and Corson, J. J. "Rural Depopulation in Certain Tidewater and Piedmont Areas of Virginia," Univ. of Va., *Soc. Sci. Monog.,* 1929, No. 3.

77. Zimmerman, C. C. "The Migration to Towns and Cities," *Amer. J. Sociol.,* 1926, 32: pp. 450-455; 1927, 33: pp. 105-109.

78. Klineberg, O. "The Intelligence of Migrants," *Amer. Sociol. Rev.,* 1938, 3: pp. 218-224.

79. Raper, A. F. *Preface to Peasantry.* 1936.

80. Klineberg, O. *Negro Intelligence and Selective Migration.* 1935.

81. Neff, W. S. "Socio-economic Status and Intelligence: a Critical Survey." *Psychol. Bull.,* 1938, 35: pp. 727-757.

CHAPTER X

SEX DIFFERENCES

INTRODUCTION

THE subject of sex differences is one of the most controversial in the whole field of social psychology, and at the same time one of the most interesting. The obvious physical differences between the sexes and their varying roles in society have been responsible for almost endless discussion of their possible psychological significance. Not so long ago the assumption was usually made that the psychological differences between the sexes were fundamental and biologically determined; it is only in recent times that women have been regarded as having brains capable of coping with higher education and that they have been admitted to colleges and universities on terms of equality with men. That the belief in intellectual differences between men and women still prevails among some observers is indicated in the following quotation from a recent book by Alexis Carrel (1).

The same intellectual and physical training, and the same ambitions should not be given to young girls as to boys. Educators should pay very close attention to the organic and mental pecularities of the male and the female, and to their natural functions. Between the two sexes there are irrevocable differences. And it is imperative to take them into account in constructing the civilized world (p. 92).

Huxley and Haddon (2) believe that the apparent differences between the sexes are probably due mainly to upbringing, and they cite as an instance of changed habits in this respect the exclamation of the third century Greek gossip writer, Athenaeus, "Whoever heard of a woman cook?" (p. 69).

In this connection Margaret Mead (3) points out that although most societies assume some psychological difference between the sexes, the exact nature of this assumption varies from group to group.

With the paucity of material for elaboration, no culture has failed to seize upon the conspicuous facts of age and sex in some way, whether it be the convention of one Philippine tribe that no man can keep a secret, the Manus assumption that only men enjoy playing with babies, the Toda prescription of almost all domestic work as too sacred for women, or the Arapesh insistence that women's heads are stronger than men's (p. xix).

As we shall see later, her own study of the relation between sex and temperament in several primitive societies has indicated some of the patterns of sex differences for which culture may be responsible.

In deciding upon the relative importance of nature and nurture in the determination of sex differences, several lines of evidence require examination. These include the material collected by means of actual physical and psychological measurement of the two sexes in our own society, the comparative data collected by the anthropologists, and the related material from biology.

QUANTITATIVE STUDIES

Between men and women in our own society and probably in most other groups as well, there are certain physical differences apart from those relating to the primary or secondary sex characters. Men are taller and heavier than women, the average height of English males being 67.5 inches and of females 62.7 inches. Men weigh on the average twenty percent more than women, although women usually have relatively more fat on their bodies; Dunlap (4) cites the observation that their "bodies are said to burn more readily on funeral pyres." Both in absolute and relative brain weight women are inferior to men, although the overlapping is considerable, as it is with all of the measures cited. The basal metabolism of women is usually somewhat lower. Girls mature more rapidly than boys, and as a result may exceed boys of the same age in stature and weight until after puberty. Of these various differences, the only ones which may have psychological significance are those referring to brain size, metabolism and rate of maturation, but the experimental work relating to these three characteristics has so far shown little direct relationship to psychological functions.

More direct psychological measurements have revealed the presence of a number of points of difference. For the youngest period of childhood the summary of the available material by C. C. Miles (5) indicates that in general sex differences are very slight and do not usually pass the test of statistical significance. There are, however, certain trends which appear definite enough to warrant further study.

Boys seem to be more curious, more interested in origins, more successful in puzzle problems, more active, independent, and self-expressing. Girls are more successful in assigned tasks, further developed in speech, and in memory ability, probably also in motor coordination and in bodily nervous habits (p. 708).

Wellman (6) points out that in the early years girls are clearly ahead in language development—in the age at which they begin to talk, in the size of their vocabulary, in sentence structure, in the number of speech sounds used, etc. There appears to be some indication that this superiority in language ability may persist in later life. There have been some studies, however, which have failed to demonstrate such a superiority. In children of the third and fourth grades in New York City schools, Schiller (7) found no reliable sex differences in the ability to handle verbal concepts. Bryan (8) obtained a slight, though insignificant, superiority of five- and six-year-old boys in a vocabulary test.

In connection with language ability the interesting observation has been made that stuttering is much more frequent among boys than girls, the ratios reported varying from 2:1 to 10:1. The reason for this clear-cut difference is not entirely certain, but Dunlap (9) has suggested a possible explanation. He believes that one of the important causes of stuttering is the fear on the part of the child that he may say something bad, or use tabooed and naughty expressions for which he may be punished. Boys, playing on the streets more frequently, are much more likely to pick up such expressions than are girls, and the fear will consequently be greater in their case. This theory is in need of further verification before it can be accepted; it is possible that the discrepancy between the sexes in knowledge of naughty words is not so great as Dunlap imagines. Even if there is such a discrepancy, it has not been proven that this is responsible for the difference in the frequency of stuttering.

Studies of sensory capacities have shown women to be slightly superior in color discrimination, and to have a much smaller incidence of color blindness. Men are superior in motor and mechanical abilities, and on the average obtain much higher scores on spatial tests, mazes, construction tests, the Stenquist mechanical aptitude test, etc. In tests involving number ability, men do somewhat better, but the difference is not consistent. In most tests of general intelligence, girls are slightly superior until about the age of fourteen, beyond which there is substantial equality. This equality may be to some degree an artificial consequence of the construction of the tests, which are usually standardized on both boys and girls, and which would not be regarded as satisfactory if there were a marked sex difference in the results. At the same time the test scores indicate an apparent female superiority in linguistic ability, and a male superiority in numerical, spatial and mechanical abilities. In spite of the similarity in average scores for the two sexes, however, it was noted in the study of gifted children by Terman and his collaborators (10) that there were 116 boys to 100 girls with I.Q.'s in the "genius" class; at the high school age the proportion of boys is even greater. In scholastic achievement, in tests of memory, and in the Social Intelligence test girls are somewhat superior. In the Allport-Vernon (11) Study of Values, girls more frequently obtained high scores in esthetic, social and religious values, and men, in economic, political and theoretic values. (See 12 for a summary of these various studies.)

The most careful and elaborate experimental study of sex differences in personality is that of Terman and Miles *(13)*, who devised a "masculinity-femininity" index based upon their examination of many hundreds of subjects, including elementary and high school children, college and graduate students, unselected adults, members of several occupational groups, athletes, juvenile delinquents and homosexuals.

The sexes were compared in terms of (1) a word association test, (2) ink-blot association, (3) information, (4) emotional and ethical responses, (5) interests, (6) opinions, and (7) introversion-extraversion. The investigators are careful to state that their conclusions apply to men and women in our culture only; they may be true for other societies as well, but that remains to be demonstrated. With that limitation clearly understood, the results indicate that the males, in the main group studied, showed a distinctive interest in exploit and adventure, in outdoor and physically strenuous occupations, in machinery and tools, in science, physical phenomena, and inventions; usually also in business and commerce. The females showed more interest in domestic affairs and in esthetic objects and occupations; they preferred more sedentary and indoor occupations, and those more directly ministrative, particularly to the young, the helpless, the distressed.

The males directly or indirectly manifest the greater self-assertion and aggressiveness; they express more hardihood and fearlessness, and more roughness of manners, language, and sentiments. The females express themselves as more compassionate and sympathetic, more timid, more fastidious and esthetically sensitive, more emotional in general (or at least more expressive of the four emotions considered), severer moralists, yet admit in themselves weaknesses in emotional control and (less noticeably) in physique (pp. 447-8).

The extent of the differences found is sometimes very marked, and indicates the reality of a relationship between sex and temperament, although it leaves open the question as to the factors determining this relationship. The comparative material collected by the anthropologists throws considerable doubt, as we shall see, on the universality of many of these differences.

A survey of the available ethnological data indicates that at least one sex difference in behavior is widely prevalent, namely, that power is usually in the hands of the males. There is a theory in anthropology developed by Bachofen (*14*) and followed by Briffault (*15*), that society was originally a matriarchate, with the authority vested in a woman. The opinion of most modern anthropologists is, however, against this view. Lowie (*16*) states that a genuine matriarchate is nowhere to be found, though in a few places feminine prerogatives have evolved to a marked degree in certain directions. The Iroquois Indians probably furnished the closest approximation to the matriarchal condition. Women arranged marriage, owned houses and land, managed some of the most important ceremonial organizations, furnished three out of six of the ceremonial officials of each sib, nominated the candidate for a vacancy in the council of chiefs, and had the right to impeach or admonish an unworthy chief-elect. Even among the Iroquois, however, no woman had a place on the supreme council of the League, and it may not be said that more power was in the hands of women than of men. In other alleged matriarchates, their power was considerably less. In societies like those of Melanesia, where matrilineal descent prevailed, and where authority over the children was vested in the mother's family, it was the men and not the women of the family who had this authority. It was the maternal uncle rather than the father whom the boy was obliged to obey; the mother had considerably less authority over him. As far as economic prerogatives are concerned, there are instances in which those of women were on a par with men (for example, the Iroquois, the Zuñi, the Khasi of Assam, etc.), but these are exceptions. In general the lesser power of women shows itself also in certain disabilities in property rights (*17*).

It has been suggested that the reason for the greater power

of men is to be found in their physical superiority (*18*). Since man was strong enough to force woman to obey him, it may seem natural that he should have kept the greater authority in his own hands. There are, however, a few communities in which women are reputedly stronger and physically more capable than men.

Work is to the Mkamba nothing short of a misfortune; when he does take to it a very little discomfort, such as he would otherwise not notice, will completely incapacitate him, while he has then the appearance of undergoing the deepest misery. . . . But if the men are unfit for hard work, the women are exceedingly tough and hardy, and whereas a man can rarely carry more than a 45-lb. load, most women will easily shoulder 60 lbs. I have seen women carrying as much as 140 lbs. At an early age the men become useless for work, while the women will continue to labour up to a great age (*19*, pp. 490-1).

This instance is not entirely convincing, since it may have been unwillingness rather than incapacity for work which prompted the men to behave as they did. It is reported that Arapesh women regularly carry heavier loads than men because their heads are regarded as much harder and stronger. These exceptions to the general rule are so rare, however, that it seems highly probable that men are usually stronger than women, and that to a certain extent the relation between the sexes is determined by male superiority in this direction.

In this same connection Sumner (*20*) believes that the physiological differences between the sexes place the woman at a definite disadvantage. "No amount of reasoning, complaining, or protesting can alter the fact that woman bears children and man does not" (p. 112). This apparently obvious remark also points, however, to the disabilities of maternity and menstruation, which result in a periodical weakness on the part of women and handicap them in any struggle with the other sex. That these disabilities exist is undoubted, but it is certain that they have been greatly exaggerated by the mode of life imposed upon women by our folkways. There can be no doubt that child-bearing has become for women in our society a much more troublesome and complicated undertaking than it is in most primitive groups and peasant communities. The accounts of the way in which women in such groups continue working in the fields until the last possible moment, and resume their work almost immediately after childbirth, indicate that the disability need not be nearly so great as is usually supposed. The literary accounts by Knut Hamsun and Pearl Buck about Norwegian and Chinese peasants, respectively, have received ample corroboration from the observations of ethnologists among primitive peoples.

This raises the whole question of sex differences in occupation, and the degree to which they are to be explained by the biological nature of the two sexes. A survey of the available material by Goldenweiser (21) reveals few if any occupations which are exclusively practiced by either one sex or the other. It is commonly, but not uniformly true, that agriculture was formerly in the hands of women and that it became the work of man only after the introduction of domesticated animals. The allotment of agriculture to women in primitive societies may in many cases be due to the notion of their greater fertility. It is reported that an Indian in Orinoco said to a missionary, "You must remember that our women know how to bring forth, and we do not. If they sow the seed . . . everything is increased. Why is this? Because women are able to bring forth, and are able to command the seed they sow to be productive" (22, p. 318). At any rate, there are exceptions even among primitive groups to the rule that agriculture is woman's work, so that even its indirect relation to the biology of woman is by no means a necessary one. In general, there is no obvious division of labor among pastoral and agricultural peoples.

In other arts and handicrafts there seems to be little consistency in this respect. In British Columbia and southern Alaska, men are responsible for the elaborate wood industry— totem poles, memorial columns, boxes, canoes, etc.—and women make the blankets. The California baskets and Pueblo pots are made entirely by women, although in many other parts of North America this is the work of men. The rule that men do the more difficult manual labor and that women engage in domestic occupations has a great many exceptions. In the Marquesas, for example, even cooking, housekeeping and baby-tending are proper male occupations. Among the Tasmanians, the difficult work of seal-hunting was done by women. "They swam out to the seal rocks, stalked the animals, and clubbed them. Tasmanian women also hunted opossums, which required the climbing of large trees" (*18*, p. 117). It is probable, however, that the physical differences between the sexes do play a definite part in the division of labor in some communities.

Among people who hunt large roving animals with spear or bow and arrow women's physical disabilities are most conspicuous. A woman who is carrying a child or nursing an infant cannot pursue animals hour after hour. To women fall the more sedentary occupations, frequently just as difficult and arduous, but requiring less muscular strength, and fleetness of foot (*23*, p. 369).

Even warfare is not exclusively practiced by men. In certain of the complex societies of Africa regiments of women were occasionally formed, as for example, the famous bodyguard of the King of Dahomey. These women were especially trained for the warrior profession and acquired sufficient expertness in it to enjoy a high reputation both for their proficiency in the art and for their ferocity (*24*). Similarly the Iroquois women showed considerable ingenuity as torturers and apparently enjoyed it.

One of the most amusing examples of a difference in attitude toward what should be woman's occupation comes from British Central Africa. Among these natives sewing was man's work, upon which no woman ever thought of encroaching; there was therefore considerable feeling against the missionaries who instructed the women in an art which "ought" not to be feminine (*25*). Similarly in Samoa, men did all the cooking, even the chiefs taking part in the preparation of meals for the community (*26*).

The most thoroughgoing ethnological study of sex differences is that by Margaret Mead (*3*) in her analysis of the relation between sex and temperament in three Melanesian societies. She was interested in discovering whether the differences in temperament popularly supposed to hold true for men and women generally would also be found in societies with an entirely different cultural background. More particularly she wished to test the assumption that men were naturally more aggressive, and women more passive and submissive in their usual social reactions. She summarizes her conclusions as follows:

We found the Arapesh—both men and women—displaying a personality, that, out of our historically-limited preoccupations, we would call maternal in its parental aspects, and feminine in its sexual aspects. We found men, as well as women, trained to be cooperative, unaggressive, responsive to the needs and demands of others. We found no idea that sex was a powerful driving force either for men or for women. In marked contrast to these attitudes, we found among the Mundugumor that both men and women developed as ruthless, aggressive, positively sexed individuals, with the maternal cherishing aspects of personality at a minimum. Both men and women approximated to a personality type that we in our culture would find only in an undisciplined and very violent male. Neither the Arapesh nor the Mundugumor profit by a contrast between the sexes; the Arapesh ideal is the mild, responsive man married to the mild, responsive woman; the Mundugumor ideal is the violent aggressive man married to the violent aggressive woman. In the third tribe, the Tchambuli, we found a genuine reversal of the sex-attitudes of our own culture, with the woman the dominant, impersonal, managing partner, the man the less responsible and the emotionally dependent person (p. 279).

There are of course many deviants from this pattern, and Miss Mead describes these in some detail, but she regards her descriptions as true of the large majority of the men and women in these three communities. With the inclusion of our own society her data indicate that man's aggressiveness may be equal to, greater or less than that of woman, and that both sexes may resemble either the "masculine" or "feminine" types to which we are accustomed in our own community. There appears to be little left in temperament that may safely be ascribed to the direct biological or physiological influence of sex.

Several specific examples from Miss Mead's study may be mentioned as illustrative of this general thesis. The "maternal" attitude of Arapesh men is associated with the belief that a father "bears" children just as the mother does. After children are conceived, the father must "work" sexually in order to build them; the semen is regarded as food for the developing embryo and as essential for its proper growth. Later on the father takes care of the children in the same way as the mother. ". . . if one comments upon a middle-aged man as good-looking, the people answer: 'Good-looking? Ye-e-s! But you should have seen him before he bore all those children'" (p. 39). Among the Tchambuli there was a widow who indulged in a series of sexual affairs during the period pending her remarriage; she was excused on the grounds that women are so highly sexed that any other type of behavior would be difficult for them. "Are women passive sexless creatures who can be expected to wait upon the dilly-dallying of formal considerations of bride-price? Men, not so urgently sexed, may be expected to submit themselves to the discipline of a due order and precedence" (p. 259).

As far as the contrast between the active and the passive role in sex behavior is concerned, the ethnological material shows that variations in this respect may occur. Powder-maker (27) reports that in Lesu when the man desires his wife he goes to her bed, and when he has finished returns to his own bed almost immediately. "The woman never takes the initiative in going to her husband's bed, and when asked the question my women friends regarded such a procedure with horror, and asked if the woman should be a man" (p. 240). It is probable that in most societies the man does take the lead in sex relationships. In Buka on the other hand (28), it appears that the reverse may be true. The Whites who have lived there express the view that the woman was more frequently the instigating partner in love affairs. The folk tales commonly contain incidents in which a woman pretends to be ill in order to persuade the attending medicine-man to have sex relations with her. It is difficult to be certain of the facts in matters of this kind, and in any case this may be an exception to the general rule.

PHYSIOLOGICAL FACTORS

In connection with the whole question of sex differences in behavior, the problem of homosexuality requires some consideration. There is still much controversy as to the degree to which organic factors determine deviations of this type. There is no doubt that in a large number of cases such deviations are the result of social factors. It is difficult otherwise to explain the prevalence of homosexual activity in certain occupations which require the members of one sex to spend a great deal of time completely separated from the other; it is probable that homosexual behavior also occurs with some frequency in prisons and in schools restricted to the members of one sex. These facts would fit Miss Mead's hypothesis that the nature of sexual attitudes and behavior is culturally determined. On the other hand, it seems more than likely that there are many men and women so constituted organically that they can find sexual satisfaction only from members of their own sex. In their case it is usual to assume the presence of the hormones of the opposite sex. Kahn (29) in his discussion of psychopathic personalities suggests that it is important to distinguish between active and passive homosexuals. An active female homosexual may be the result of male hormones, and a passive male of female hormones. The passive female and the active male may contain respectively the hormones of their own sex, although they have been conditioned to prefer homo- to hetero-sexual relationships. If this analysis is correct, it becomes necessary to explain at least in some cases the female or male attitude toward sex activity in terms of organic factors. It is even possible that many more persons would be homosexual if it were not for the disgrace and often the actual punishment which may follow such behavior.

These facts are somewhat difficult to reconcile with Miss Mead's thesis. It must certainly be granted that she is correct in emphasizing the wide range of temperamental characteristics found among men and women, respectively, and that a good deal of the difference which holds for the sexes in our community is by no means universal. Whatever the organic basis of sex differences in behavior, these are undoubtedly subject also to the influence of the folkways. Even within our own society, marked changes have occurred in what are regarded as the typical characteristics of women. The delicate fragile lady of the 1800's is almost extinct. We know that many forms of behavior which at that time were regarded as "unnatural" to women have since then been practiced by them with conspicuous success. There has clearly been a growth in self-reliance and independence, and with these a willingness to engage in the kinds of work which used to be regarded as exclusively masculine in character. Particularly in Russia have occupational and social differences between the sexes largely been wiped out by the theory and practice of sex equality. With all that, however, the known organic differences due to the effect of the male and female hormones respectively, and the fact that these determine not only morphological but also physiological and functional characteristics, must cast considerable doubt upon the theory that sex differences in behavior are entirely due to culture. The evidence from zoology and experimental biology is especially pertinent in this connection.

SEX DIFFERENCES AMONG ANIMALS

The experimental work on animals by means of the removal of the sex glands or the implantation of those of the opposite sex have shown that the animal is altered not only with reference to its anatomical development, but also in its behavior. If the sex glands of a young stag are removed, the horns do not develop, and in addition the animal shows none of the typical combative tendencies in the presence of the female, but remains quiet and peaceable. The capon does not crow like a cock, nor will he fight with other male birds. Examples of this type could easily be multiplied. On the other hand, when male glands are implanted into a castrated female guinea pig, there develops not only a hyper-masculinization in external appearance, but the animal also pursues females in heat, calls like a male, and fights with normal males (30). Experiments of this type indicate that not only the direct sexual behavior but the general nature of the social responses of the animal, including combativeness and self-assertion, have a definite organic basis in the nature of the particular sex hormone which is operative. Although there is always some danger in applying the results of animal experimentation to man, it is unlikely that such behavior could be entirely cultural among human beings in the light of this clear indication that among other animals it is organically determined.

An additional argument in this direction is the indication that among animals close to man, but without human culture, masculinity and femininity are well developed. This has been reported by Carpenter (31) in the case of the howling monkeys. He describes the male as more aggressive, protective and defensive than the female. On the other hand, Carpenter indicates that some at least of the sex differences ascribed to human beings do not hold for the howling monkeys. When in the sexually receptive state, for example, the female may either approach or be approached by a mature male; either sex may initiate the sexual advances preparatory to copulation. There is no indication that in this particular respect the male is necessarily more active. Apparently there are organically determined sex differences in aggressiveness, but these do not necessarily apply to the actual sex relationship.

WOMEN OF GENIUS

There is one final problem in this field which requires mention. The intelligence tests have revealed no dependable difference in the level of intellectual performance of the two sexes, and it is now customary among psychologists to assume that there is no sex difference in this respect. It has frequently been pointed out, however, that among persons possessing the outstanding ability and achievement which we term "genius," women are relatively rare. Goncourt (*32*) wrote, "There are no women of genius; all the women of genius are men" (p. 138). He meant by this that even when there are women who are in the genius class, they have probably within them a definite masculine component; cases like those of Rosa Bonheur, George Sand and George Eliot come to mind in this connection. An alternative explanation is possible. We know that it is only in very recent times that women have been given opportunities comparable to those of men; even in our own generation they suffer from definite handicaps with regard to appointments and promotion in positions of importance. It is exceedingly likely that this discrimination may explain their relatively rare appearance among outstanding personalities. As for Goncourt's dictum, there are of course many cases of distinctly feminine women, like Marie Curie or Elizabeth Barrett Browning, with undoubted standing in their own field; it is also probable that some at least of the masculine characteristics of women of genius were deliberately cultivated in order to improve their chances in a man's world. One other possible explanation of the difference in the frequency of genius in the two sexes in spite of the similarity in average intelligence is that men are more variable, with a larger number of deviations at both ends of the scale of intelligence. There is some evidence in this direction but it is not conclusive (*6*). There may also be personality factors affecting genius which occur more frequently in men than in women. The most probable explanation of the observed differences is, however, that they are due to the relative opportunities for advancement that have been open to the two sexes.

SUMMARY

In addition to the primary and secondary sex characters, there are differences between the sexes in rate of growth and development which appear to have implications for behavior; the earlier maturation of girls is especially significant. Other observed differences, as for example in the metabolic rate, have not been shown to affect behavior to any marked degree. In these as in other comparisons there is great overlapping between the sexes. The fundamental biological difference in connection with child-bearing results in a periodical incapacitation of woman which may have an effect on other social and occupational relationships, but undoubtedly this has been exaggerated in our culture.

The ethnological material shows the wide variations in the behavior of the sexes under the influence of social and cultural factors, even with regard to aggressive and submissive attitudes. It seems probable, however, on the basis of the data furnished by zoology and experimental biology, that in spite of these variations, temperamental characteristics are to some degree dependent upon the respective sex hormones.

The results of psychological studies showing sex differences in interests, linguistic and mechanical ability, memory and information, etc., may best be explained in terms of the social environment of boys and girls in our society. The discrepancy in the frequency of occurrence of "genius" in the two sexes may also be ascribed to differences in training and opportunity.

REFERENCES

1. Carrel, A. *Man, the Unknown.* 1935.
2. Huxley, J. S., and Haddon, A. C. *We Europeans.* 1935.
3. Mead, M. *Sex and Temperament in Three Primitive Societies.* 1935.
4. Dunlap, K. *Civilized Life.* 1934.
5. Miles, C. C. "Sex in Social Psychology," *Hdbk. Soc. Psychol.* (ed. by C. Murchison). 1935.
6. Wellman, B. L. "Sex Differences," *Hdbk. Child Psychol.* (ed. by C. Murchison). 1935.
7. Schiller, B. "Verbal, Numerical and Spatial Abilities of Young Children," *Arch. Psychol.* 1934, No. 161.
8. Bryan, A. I. "Organization of Memory in Young Children," *Arch. Psychol.* 1934, No. 162.
9. Dunlap, K. "The Stuttering Boy," *J. Abn. Soc. Psychol* 1917, 12: pp. 44-48.

10. Terman, L. M. *Genetic Studies of Genius.* 1925, 1926 and 1930. 3 vols.

11. Allport, G. W., and Vernon, P. E. "A Test for Personal Values," *J. Abn. Soc. Psychol.* 1931, 26: pp. 231-248.

12. Anastasi, A. *Differential Psychology; Individual and Group Differences in Behavior.* 1937.

13. Terman, L. M., and Miles, C. C. *Sex and Personality; Studies in Masculinity and Femininity.* 1936.

14. Bachofen, J. J. *Das Mutterrecht.* 1861.

15. Briffault, R. *The Mothers.* 3 vols. 1927.

16. Lowie, R. H. *Primitive Society.* 1925.

17. Goldenweiser, A. A. *Early Civilization.* 1926.

18. Linton, R. *The Study of Man.* 1936.

19. Dundas, C. "History of Kitui," *J. Roy. Anthropol. Inst.* 1913, 43: pp. 490-491.

20. Sumner, W. G., and Keller, A. G. *The Science of Society.* Vol. I. 1927.

21. Goldenweiser, A. A. *Anthropology.* 1937.

22. Lévy-Bruhl, L. *Primitive Mentality.* 1923.

23. Bunzel, R. L. "The Economic Organization of Primitive Peoples," *General Anthropology* (ed. by Franz Boas). 1938.

24. Seligman, C. G. *Races of Africa.* 1930.

25. Werner, A. *The Natives of British Central Africa.* 1906.

26. Turner, G. *Samoa: A Hundred Years Ago and Long Before.* 1884.

27. Powdermaker, H. *Life in Lesu.* 1933.

28. Blackwood, B. *Both Sides of Buka Passage.* 1935.

29. Kahn, E. *Psychopathic Personalities.* 1931.

30. Scharpey-Schafer, E. *The Endocrine Organs.* Parts I and II. 1924.

31. Carpenter, C. R. "A Field Study of the Behavior and Social Relations of Howling Monkeys." *Comp. Psychol. Monogr.*, No. 10, 1934.

32. See Lombroso, C. *The Man of Genius.* 1891.

CHAPTER XI

RACIAL DIFFERENCES

INTRODUCTION

THE problem of psychological differences between racial and national groups has always been of interest to the social psychologist. In recent years, however, it has received a practical application and a political significance which have made it far more than an academic question. Since these practical applications have been justified in the name of science, it is especially important to know with some precision the findings of scientists who have worked in this field. It is a field in which objectivity is rare, but for that reason all the more important, and it has become the real duty of the student of social science to inform himself as to what may legitimately be said on so controversial a topic.

THE ANTHROPOLOGICAL APPROACH

To the anthropologist the popular use of the concept of race is seen to be accompanied by an almost hopeless confusion of terms. Anthropologists themselves might not agree upon the exact definition, but the following statement would probably be accepted by most of them, namely, that race is a large subdivision of mankind, "the members of which are distinguished by possession of similar combinations of anatomical features due to common heredity" (1). A similar idea is expressed more briefly by Boas (2), who regards a race as "a group of common origin and of stable type." The application of racial terms to groups not so characterized is anthropologically unsound.

In actual practice the most frequent confusion is found between the concepts of race and nation, and race and language.

There is no nation which is physically sufficiently homogeneous in physical type so that it may be described as "racially pure." As Retzius (3) pointed out long ago, even the Swedes, who are regarded as unmixed representatives of the Nordic or North European racial type, show such marked divergences among themselves that only a minority actually possesses the combination of physical features usually regarded as Nordic. This is of course even more marked in other European nations, and Dixon (4) refers to the fact that anthropometric research in Germany was once stopped because it revealed so many individuals who did not conform to the alleged German type.

This means that the attempts by the Germans and the Italians at the present time to keep the nation "pure" in the anthropological sense have no meaning. Many German writers have seen the impossibility of reconciling their political aims with accepted anthropological doctrine, and have had as a consequence to create an anthropology of their own. The identification in the popular mind between "German" and "tall, blond and blue-eyed" has been officially condemned because of the tremendous number of obvious exceptions. One writer (5) has insisted that many people who look like Nordics do not have Nordic souls, and that conversely there may be a Nordic soul within a non-Nordic body. This serves as a political expedient, but it is scientifically meaningless. The recent insistence of a group of Italian professors on the homogeneity of the Italian "race" because of its isolation during the last thousand years is also untenable. The North Italian is blonder and taller and has a rounder head than the Italians farther south, and resembles the Frenchman of Auvergne much more than he does the Sicilian. Anthropologists of other nations have not been so blind to the facts, and British and French writers have frequently stressed the heterogeneity in the physical characteristics of their respective peoples.

The confusion between race and language is even more frequent. To the anthropologist, for example, there is no "Latin race," but a group of languages of Latin origin; these languages may be spoken by people differing greatly from one

another in their physical appearance. The term "Semitic" also
has a linguistic significance; the fact that Semitic languages
include not only Hebrew and Arabic, but also Amharic, the
official language of Ethiopia, indicates clearly the variations
in the racial constitution of the Semites. Even these sub-
groups cannot be spoken of as racially pure; the Jews, for example, show physical variations almost as great as those found
in all Europeans taken together. Huxley and Haddon (6)
point out that in the Caucasus, for example, the large majority
of Jews are roundheaded or brachycephalic, whereas among
the Yemenite Jews dolichocephaly is the rule. In parts of
Poland and Lithuania the average stature of Jews is 5′ 4″, and
in certain districts of London it is 5′ 8″. Similar variations
have been reported for color of the skin and of the eyes and
hair. There is no Jewish race. This statement represents the
opinion of the majority of American and British anthropologists who have written on this question. The work of Huxley
and Haddon (6), Dixon (4), and Boas (7) may be mentioned
as representative. In a recent pamphlet on "Race," a similar
statement is approved by Fay Cooper-Cole of the University
of Chicago, Ralph Linton of Columbia University, and H. L.
Shapiro of the American Museum of Natural History. On the
other hand, Hooton (8) and Coon (9) at Harvard believe that
inbreeding among the Jews has created a distinctively Jewish
physical type, even though one may not legitimately speak of
a Jewish race.

By far the most striking misuse of the term "race" occurs
in connection with the "Aryans." This term more than any
other has recently been given political significance and has
been made a basis of legislation in Germany. The word
"Aryan" was probably first introduced to the West by Sir
William Jones, a British philologist who lived for some time in
India and made a special study of Sanskrit and other Asiatic
languages (6). He used the word "Aryan" to apply to these
languages. Later the problems of linguistic relationship were
taken up in Germany by the Schlegels, Bunsen, and others,
and in England by a young philologist of German origin, Max

Müller. Research showed that there were certain similarities
in vocabulary between these Asiatic languages and the overwhelming majority of languages spoken in Europe, and they
were together referred to as the Aryan or Indo-European or
Indo-Germanic family of languages. It was probably Max
Müller who first spoke of an "Aryan race" to refer to that
group of people who originated the Aryan language; he thought
of them as a superior people because of their discovery of such
an efficient and flexible means of linguistic expression. In the
years which followed, speculation as to the homeland of the
Aryans occupied the attention of many anthropologists and his-
torians, and a large number of different hypotheses were defended. The origin of the Aryans was variously ascribed to the
Baltic region, Germany, Russia, central Asia, India, Persia and
even North Africa. This uncertainty as to the place of the
origin of the Aryans was paralleled by the uncertainty as to
their physical appearance. For these reasons Max Müller came
to realize that the term "Aryan" could legitimately be used
only in a linguistic sense, and that any racial implications were
entirely unwarranted. In a famous passage in a later book (10),
which appeared in 1888, he stated that when he used the word
"Aryan" he posited nothing about the physical appearance of
the Aryans, about their status as conquerors or conquered, or
about their place of origin; the word "Aryan" was used in a
linguistic sense alone. "To me an ethnologist who speaks of
Aryan race, Aryan blood, Aryan eyes or hair, is as great a
sinner as a linguist who speaks of a dolichocephalic dictionary
or a brachycephalic grammar" (p. 120).

This complete recantation of an earlier position came too
late. In the meantime the concept of a superior Aryan race
had been seized upon by a number of writers, and had received its most complete development in Gobineau's *Essay on
the Inequality of Human Races*. Gobineau was not the first
to speak of superior and inferior races; as Barzun (11) points
out, this type of thinking goes back as far as Tacitus, who for
political reasons glorified the Germanic tribes at the expense
of the Romans. In its modern form, however, the race theory

owes most to Gobineau and his followers, although his *Essay* depends upon a concept which its originator correctly repudiated.

The Classification of Races. Even if we are careful to restrict the term "race" to hereditary physical characteristics, we still find considerable difficulty in discovering an acceptable criterion for racial classification. In the past many criteria have been used—skin color, shape of the head, stature, color of the eyes and hair, shape of the hair in cross section, and many others. The difficulty arises from the fact that the use of different criteria gives mutually contradictory classifications. Blumenbach (*12*), for example, is responsible for the familiar classification into five races according to skin color— the White or Caucasian, the Yellow or Mongolian, the Black or Ethiopian, the Red or American and the Brown or Malayan. Sergi (*13*), on the other hand, prefers to employ head shape, and speaks of two main species or races, the Eurasiatic, or roundheaded, found in Asia and Central Europe, and the Eurafrican, or long-headed, originating in Africa, but found also in Northern and Southern Europe. This classification unites in one category the blondest Scandinavian and the darkest Negro, because both are long-headed, and it ignores all the differences between them. Since there seems to be no way of deciding whether skin color or head shape is the more significant criterion, and since the two divisions are mutually incompatible, considerable doubt is thrown on the whole process of racial classification among human beings. The difficulty is not removed if we use a number of criteria in combination. This was attempted by Deniker (*14*), who arrived at 17 main races and 29 sub-races by this method; the process could be carried on indefinitely, depending upon the aim and interest of the classifier.

The notion that racial classifications may be artificial and arbitrary is not a new one. In 1843 Pritchard (*15*) expresses the opinion "that all mankind constitute but one race, or proceed from a single family." The French naturalist Buffon (*16*) wrote "species, orders, and classes exist only in our imagination. They are merely conventions. Nothing really exists but the individual. Nature does not recognize our definitions: she has never classified her work by group or kind." The German philosopher Herder (*17*) also protests against the use of the term "race" in connection with man, since there are always transitional forms between one alleged race and another. Even Blumenbach insists that "the various types of men differ from each other in degree and not in kind and are connected with each other by innumerable gradations" (*6*, p. 27).

The discrepancies in the racial classifications, the fact that transitional forms may always be discovered, and the marked degree of overlapping in physical characteristics between one group and another, appear to justify the conclusion that human races, in any strict sense of the term, exist only in the mind of the classifier. It may be that at some future date new methods in the field of physical anthropology may make it possible to arrive at a more accurate differentiation, but the techniques at present available hold little hope in this direction. When the method of blood groupings was first applied to race by the Hirszfelds (*18*) it was thought that it might eliminate the difficulties inherent in other approaches and make it possible to arrive at an objective and scientifically acceptable classification. This hope has now been shown to be unfounded, and the complications in the use of the blood groups are at least as great as those found with the more usual physical criteria. Although many anthropologists insist upon retaining the concept of human races, and many new classifications still appear, by far the most reasonable position seems to be that there is only one human race, and that the distinctions found within it are relatively unimportant.

Even if this position is accepted, however, the problem of the meaning of physical differences still exists, and requires more direct consideration. Although the usual distinction between the Negro and the Caucasian may have little significance in terms of a scientifically valid classification, it is certainly taken seriously by the large majority of people. On the basis of the customary racial classification, a great deal of research has been carried on, and there is now a voluminous literature on the question of the psychological and cultural implications of race differences. Most of this has centered upon the problem of racial differences in ability, and we turn now to an appraisal of the arguments which have been used in this connection.

THE BIOLOGICAL ARGUMENT FOR RACIAL SUPERIORITY

One type of argument heard with some frequency is to the effect that races differ in their degree of "primitiveness"— more specifically that one race, for example the Negro, may have developed earlier from the ancestral anthropoid stock and represents therefore a species inferior to the later evolved Caucasian or Mongolian. This assumption determines the nature of the developmental or genealogical trees found in books by Osborn (19), Warden (20) and others. It rests upon the observation that in certain physical characteristics, for instance, the wide flat nose, the long arms, etc., the Negro resembles the anthropoid more than do either of the other two racial stocks. This argument has been examined in detail by Boas (21), Kroeber (22), and others. As they have pointed out, this hierarchy of races depends upon the nature of the criteria used. There are many characteristics in which the Negro resembles the anthropoid less than do either of the other races. In hairiness of the body, for example, the Caucasian is most like the anthropoid; the thin lips of the Mongolian represent much less of a departure from the anthropoid type than the thick everted lips of the Negro, which are most "human." As Kroeber points out, there is an approximately equal number of ape-like characteristics in the three races, and no decision is possible as to which is the most primitive.

It is frequently argued that the physical differences between races create a presumption in favor of psychological differences. Kroeber (23) states that "there is . . . no sound reason to expect anything else but that races which differ anatomically also differ in some degree physiologically and psychologically" (p. 352). On the contrary, there is no sound reason to expect any such relationship. Races differ anatomically by definition; if they did not differ anatomically, they would not be different races. Before we may assume that this has any psychological significance, however, we must have independent evidence of some genetic or other relationship between psychological characteristics and those anatomical features used in racial classification. Differences in skin color, for example, may have arisen in response to the direct or indirect effect of the physical environment. It is possible, as Linton (24) suggests, that the different skin color in tropical and in cold regions may be related not to differences of heat, but of light intensity. The actinic rays of the sun are beneficial in small quantities, but harmful in large ones. The skin pigment seems to act as a ray filter, its efficiency being related to the depth of color. In the tropics a dark skin color is an advantage since it prevents the absorption of too great a quantity of actinic rays; in cold regions a light skin color aids in the absorption of the necessary amount. Under these conditions a process of natural selection may help to fix one or the other skin color as a racial trait. If this interpretation is correct, there is no reason to suppose that psychological factors are in any way involved in the process of selection. The dark skin would simply be more advantageous in one physical environment and would therefore survive. Unless there is some other reason to assume an original relationship between skin color and psychology, the probabilities are that this form of natural selection would have no psychological significance whatsoever.

In the second place, Kroeber's argument assumes that there is in general some necessary connection between physical and psychological characteristics. This is a problem which has interested psychologists and physiologists throughout the history of their research, and a large amount of material has been accumulated. There have been studies of the possible psychological significance of various physiognomic features, including skin color, shape of the head, size of the nose, height of forehead, convexity and concavity of facial profile, glandular make-up and general bodily constitution. Some of these attempts, for example the last, have for a time held out promise of the establishment of a positive relationship, and in particular Kretschmer's (25) theory of the relation between constitution and temperament has received considerable attention. More recently, however, the theory has been challenged on a number of grounds, and a series of careful investigations have thrown considerable doubt on the connection between constitution and normal personality (26, 27). The glandular approach has similarly been questioned and appears to be helpful mainly in cases of marked deviation from the norm. As for the other approaches, the careful examination of the research data by Paterson (28) justifies the conclusion that not a single one of them has proved any positive relationship between physique and mentality. This means that we have no right to assume a relation between physical and psychological differences, and to treat the problem of race differences as if this assumption had been verified. (The problem of sex differences is, of course, in a different category.)

There is one physical feature which requires somewhat more detailed consideration—namely, the size and shape of the brain. As far as size is concerned, the earlier studies apparently demonstrated racial differences in average, that of the Negro being somewhat smaller, for example, than the brain of the White. Some significance has been attached to this difference. It must be borne in mind, however, that the overlapping is very great, so that there are a great many Negro brains larger than that of the average White. In addition, the fact that the brains of certain Negro groups like the Kaffirs and the Amaxosa are on the average larger than those of certain White groups like the Scotch, makes it difficult to assume any significant race difference in this respect. It is probable that general body contours as well as physical well-being also play a part in determining brain size. Most important of all, a very careful study of Negro and White brains from similar (low) socio-economic status made by Todd and Lindala (*29*) revealed "no significant stock differences." Finally, the fact that studies of brain size within the White group have failed to show any close correspondence with level of mentality and the further fact that the brain size of women is both relatively and absolutely inferior to that of men, throw further doubt on the psychological significance of possible racial differences in this respect.

In connection with the qualitative characteristics of the brain, the early investigations of Bean (*30*) have focused attention upon possible Negro-White differences. In a series of studies Bean arrived at the conclusion that the frontal area of the brain was less well-developed in the Negro than in the White, and the posterior area better developed. He believed that this difference paralleled the "known fact" that the Negro is inferior in the higher intellectual functions and superior in those concerned with rhythm and sense perception. Another important difference was in the depth of the convolutions of the cortex, those of the Negro being much shallower and more "childlike" than those of the White. There were also differences in the shape of the corpus callosum, which connects the two hemispheres of the cerebrum, and in the temporal lobe, but these were not regarded as having any direct psychological significance. It happened that these studies were carried out at Johns Hopkins University under the direction of Professor Mall, head of the Department of Anatomy. Mall was for some reason uncertain of Bean's results, and he repeated the whole study (*31*) on the same collection of brains on which Bean had worked; he took the precaution, however, of comparing the brains without knowing in advance which were Negro and which were White. When he and his associates placed in one group those brains which had rich convolutions, and in another those with convolutions which were shallow, they found exactly the same proportions of Negro and White brains in the two groups. When further they measured the size of the frontal and posterior lobes in the two groups of brains, they found no difference in their relative extent in the two races. Mall came to the conclusion that Bean's findings had no basis in fact, and that it had not been demonstrated that Negro brains differed in any essential manner from those of Whites. Incidentally, these two studies taken together illustrate in a very significant manner the importance of stereotypes and "mental set" in determining what one will see in any given situation. There can be no doubt that Bean was sincere in his belief that he had observed these differences between the two groups of brains. It seems clear, however, that because of the expectation of finding signs of inferiority in the Negro, and because of his knowledge of the racial origin of the brains he was examining, he actually "saw" differences which did not exist. In any case Mall's more carefully controlled study testifies to the fallacy of the popular assumption that one can recognize a Negro brain by the presence of certain definite inferiorities.

THE CULTURAL ARGUMENT

A second group of arguments in favor of the superiority of certain races over others centers upon the question of their relative contributions to culture or civilization. This is the type of argument made popular by Gobineau and used by many writers who more or less followed his example. Gobineau spoke of the superior race as the Aryans; Houston Stewart Chamberlain (32) glorified the Teutons; Madison Grant (33) and Lothrop Stoddard (34) and many others have spoken of the supremacy of the Nordics. Throughout the variations in terminology there is the common tendency among these writers to regard as superior the North European, usually conceived as tall, blond and blue-eyed; the other European groups are regarded as having made relatively inferior contributions, but they are still superior to the Mongolians, and even more markedly to the African Negroes. This point of view has been developed so frequently in the last few decades that it is customary to think of the problem mainly in terms of the alleged superiority of the Nordics.

The first important consideration in connection with this

type of racial evaluation is the need to place it in proper historical perspective. Even if one were willing to grant that at the present time certain of the North European nations appear to stand in a position of political, military and possibly also artistic superiority over those in other parts of the world (and this is a large assumption), it is necessary to keep in mind that we have no right to argue from a temporary to a biological and permanent superiority. It is illuminating in this connection to examine some of the judgments of racial ability found in the earlier literature. We know that Aristotle (35), for example, basing his argument mainly upon the effects of climate, regarded the North Europeans as barbarians incapable of a creative culture, particularly in the field of politics. The Roman Vitruvius (36) took a similar position. At the time these men wrote, no one could possibly have made a reasonable case for the superiority of the Nordics. Even in very recent times there is by no means unanimity in connection with this judgment. Writers like Huntington (37) and Dixon (4) regard the contributions of the Alpines as superior. Sergi (38), Elliott Smith (39), and Huxley and Haddon (6) believe that the Mediterraneans had laid the foundations of European civilization long before the Nordics came upon the scene, and that the contribution of the latter is relatively insignificant. Elliott Smith in particular thinks of civilization as having originated among the Mediterranean Babylonians, Sumerians and Egyptians, and having later traveled through the world from that source. W. I. Thomas (40) points out that our Western European civilization is a composite containing contributions from peoples all over the world, including those of Asia and Africa, and that to think of it as exclusively or predominantly Nordic in origin indicates merely regional or national chauvinism. We see that even within the framework of our own type of Western civilization there is by no means unanimity of judgment as to which group has made the most important contribution.

In the second place, however, the argument becomes even more tenuous when we remember that other groups may legitimately protest against our judging them in terms of our own criteria. We tend to think of the Chinese or the Africans as inferior because they have failed to develop our type of civilization. There is, however, no universal criterion which enables us to determine the superiority of one culture or civilization over another. Marco Polo may have ridiculed the Chinese for wasting their discovery of gunpowder on firecrackers, but they with at least equal right might have questioned the intelligence of using it for the destruction of human beings. Rivers (41) in an amusing passage imagines the effect of our civilization upon a Melanesian; he suggests that to the Melanesian our failure to keep clearly in mind the degrees of consanguinity of all our relatives would certainly indicate our incapacity, since to them nothing is more important than social and family relationships. Lips (42) has collected many illuminating examples of the manner in which members of primitive groups have reacted to the presence of Whites among them. There are cases in which the Whites are admired, but more frequently they are despised and hated as criminals and oppressors. LaPiere and Farnsworth (43) quote from a letter written by a Chinese of the 17th century, following upon the first visits of Jesuits to his country, in which doubt is expressed that these "Ocean Men" are human in the same sense as are the Chinese. Nansen's example of the Eskimo who wished to send medicine men as missionaries to the Whites in order to teach them the advantages of peace, may again be cited in this connection (see p. 80). As has been pointed out many times, Western man has shown the greatest skill and ingenuity in his mechanical inventions and in his conquest of physical nature generally, but he has so far not succeeded in devising a satisfactory formula for living. The one fact that we live in constant fear of the destruction by war of everything we have created makes it impossible in any objective sense to regard our civilization as superior.

A third reason for questioning any intimate relation between race and culture is the great amount of variability found within any one race in this respect. The most cultivated Chinese and the simplest tribes of Siberia are of the same race or physical type; the same is true of the Incas of Peru and the Mayas of Yucatan on the one hand, and the rude communities of the California Indians on the other. These wide divergences within a single race make it impossible to assume that race is in any direct way the cause of culture. They indicate rather that we must take into account a whole host of geographical and historical factors which are relatively independent of race, and which make it possible for one community to reach the height of complexity in its cultural and social life, and which keep another at a relatively simple level. Individuals within various groups may differ in their biological make-up, but in the examples cited above they are racially homogeneous.

This last consideration applies equally well to the problem of the *nature*, as distinguished from the *level*, of the cultural contribution of different races. There have been many attempts to characterize races from this point of view—one group is described as warlike, another as adventurous, a third as artistic, and so on. Here again the historical point of view is an essential corrective to hasty judgment. In a book by Kruse (*44*) dealing with the anthropology of the Germans and of neighboring European peoples, and written at a time when Fascism had been introduced into Italy but not yet into Germany, these two nations are described as possessing very different political characteristics. The Italians are Fascists, according to the explanation given, because they are by nature willing to be subjected to authority; the Germans on the other hand are by nature democratic and individualistic, so that an authoritarian regime is fundamentally uncongenial to them, and can never be put into practice in Germany. It was only a few years after the appearance of this book that the Nazi regime came into power in Germany. This is the clearest example, but by no means the only one, of the way in which judgments of national culture have been upset by history. The present-day picture of the reserved, unemotional Englishman contrasts markedly with the "merrie England" of

Elizabethan times; English leadership in music at the time of Purcell was not a permanent, but a temporary one. The characteristics of the Japanese and of their culture were fundamentally altered by contact with the West since 1842, even though their "race" remained the same.

The frequent contrast between different sub-groups of the same race also argues in this direction. McDougall (45) believed that suicide occurs with great frequency among peoples of the Nordic race because of their tendency toward introversion, which causes action to be directed to oneself in any crisis situation. He cited figures to prove that this was an essential Nordic characteristic. More complete statistics showed, however, that this was by no means necessarily true; the figures for Norway, to take only one example, were among the lowest, in spite of the marked predominance of the Nordic racial component among Norwegians; France and Switzerland, with the Alpine the most frequent physical type, had very high rates of suicide (46). The alleged frequency of homicide among Mediterranean peoples is also linked to their racial constitution, but recent studies have shown (47) that the homicidal tendencies of Italians in America are markedly reduced after the passage of one generation, and that American-born sons of Italian parents have a homicide rate closely approaching that of the American population in general.

The same variability within each racial group holds for other characteristics of culture and of personality. The American Indians of the Plains were warlike, and their whole social structure depended upon war as an institution; the Pueblos of the Southwest were a peaceful group, at least in recent times, who fought only in self-defense. The American Negroes are said to be musical, but there are many tribes in Africa for whom ethnologists have reported little or no music. The plastic art of Benin and Dahomey is famous the world over, but there are large areas in Africa where this type of art is unknown. It is difficult to understand this great variability on the assumption that these aspects of culture are directly associated with the genetic constitution of the race.

This discussion of the relation between race and culture has been somewhat "subjective," in the sense that the judgments which have been discussed and described depend to a considerable degree upon personal bias and point of view. One writer may be impressed by the similarities between the Plains Indians and the Pueblos, and another by the differences; one person may judge the civilization of the Chinese to be inferior to that of the Germans, and another may regard it as superior. It is obviously desirable to make use of more objective criteria whenever they are available, and among these the intelligence test has received the most attention in this field.

TESTING RACIAL INTELLIGENCE

There have been many reviews of the literature dealing with the application of mental tests to the study of racial and national differences in intelligence. The reader will find extensive discussion of the techniques and results in the books by Garth (48), Anastasi (27), and Klineberg (49). At this point we shall attempt only a brief summary of what seem to be the more important considerations.

There have been marked changes in viewpoint among investigators in this field since the work of testing racial intelligence on a large scale was begun during the World War. The analysis of the results of this study by C. C. Brigham (50) came to the conclusion that there was clear evidence for the innate intellectual superiority of Whites over Negroes, and of North Europeans or Nordics over Alpines and Mediterraneans. These conclusions were widely quoted and generally accepted by psychologists at the time of their appearance, although criticism, especially at the hands of anthropologists, was by no means lacking. As the result of further critical analysis, doubt was thrown not only upon the racial distinctions used in the study, but also on the capacity of the tests themselves to measure native intelligence apart from the effect of environment. More refined statistical analysis of the nature of the Army Alpha tests supported the growing conviction that these conclusions were invalid. Brigham himself in a later publication (51) carried certain of these criticisms to their logical conclusion, and with fine scientific and objective candor withdrew completely from his earlier position, stating that all the studies which had appeared to demonstrate racial differences by means of intelligence tests, including his own, fell completely to the ground. In Brigham's own change of attitude may be seen the reflection of a change typical of a great many psychologists. It is unfortunate that so many people have been influenced by the original study, whereas relatively few know of the recantation.

Even apart from the question of race, the conviction has grown that so many environmental factors enter into the use of the intelligence test that any conclusions with regard to innate ability must be drawn with caution. As between Terman's (52) earlier position that the tests were a measure of native intelligence and the insistence of Garrett and Schneck (53) that "the examiner must always remember that comparisons are permissible only when environmental differences are absent, or at least negligible" (p. 24), there can be no doubt that at present most psychologists would accept the latter position. As was pointed out in an earlier chapter, there are sufficient indications of a change in mental test performance resulting from a changed environment to make it absolutely essential to keep the environmental effect constantly in mind.

In the field of racial comparisons, a number of environmental considerations have been regarded as important. The relationship of the subjects to the tester, or the degree of rapport between them, may obviously differ in the case of two racial groups. Their motivation, or their anxiety to do well on the test, cannot always be presumed to be similar. The discussion of occupational differences in intelligence in Chapter IX has shown that even within one race, socio-economic and educational factors are of importance; their weight is all the greater in any comparison, for example, of Negroes and Whites, who differ so greatly in economic opportunities and in the nature of schooling and other education available. The frequent reliance in the intelligence test upon speed as a measure of capacity has also been shown to be unfair to those groups outside of our own culture who place no premium upon getting things done in a hurry. There may also be, as Porteus has pointed out (54), an actual misunderstanding of the purpose of the test on the part of those who are not accustomed to being tested. There are varying attitudes and points of view which we collectively call "culture," which may produce such different reactions as to make direct comparison of two racial or cultural groups scientifically valueless.

It is not suggested that there are many studies of racial differences in which all of these environmental factors enter. It is hard to imagine an investigator so naive that he would compare two groups differing in all of the above respects. It is more probable that some of these factors operate in one investigation, but not in another; one group may be handicapped by linguistic disability, a second by poor schooling, a third by lack of adequate motivation, a fourth by a combination of any of these, and so on. Taken all together, these environmental factors may account for a good part if not all of the differences found in the mental test performance of racial and national groups.

Even if the two groups are adequately equated in these respects, there still remains an important source of error—namely, the factor of sampling or selection. Obviously an investigator or a group of investigators cannot test all the members of any two groups which are being compared, and only a relatively small sample of each group may possibly be examined. This raises the question as to the degree to which this sample is truly representative. To take a specific instance, the comparison of Scotch and Italian children in New York City, even if all of the environmental factors have been adequately considered, may still not hold for Scotch and Italians generally, since the migrants to this country may not represent similar samples of the total Scotch and Italian populations. This makes it necessary to restrict the conclusions to the particular samples studied. An investigation by Franzblau (55) indicates that the superiority of Danish over Italian children in this country does not extend to Danish children in Copenhagen as compared with Italian children in Rome. In spite of statistical and other checks on the validity of a sample, this remains a constant problem and a possible source of error in all group comparisons.

This question of the nature of the migrants within any given population has already been discussed in Chapter IX in connection with rural-urban comparisons. It has special significance with reference to the Negro. The investigation by the Army testers showed the superiority of White recruits over Negroes in general, but they also indicated that the Negroes of certain of the northern states, especially Pennsylvania, Ohio, New York and Illinois, were superior to the White recruits from the southern states. This raised the question as to whether the superiority of the northern Negroes was due to the better educational and economic opportunities available to them in the North, particularly in the large cities, or whether there had been a selective migration of superior Negroes from South to North. The Army testers did not commit themselves to either of these alternatives. A study by Peterson and Lanier (56) of twelve-year-old Negro and White boys, found the Whites superior in Nashville, slightly superior in Chicago and equal to the Negroes in New York. The investigators decided that selective migration to New York was responsible, although their evidence does not seem to support this conclusion. In a recent more direct attack upon this problem in a series of studies (57) there appeared to be no indication of a selective migration to the North, since the school records of the migrants were not in any way superior to those of the non-migrants; on the other hand there was definite indication of an improvement in the intelligence test scores of southern Negro children living in New York City, which was clearly related to the length of time during which they had lived in the superior environment. There was direct evidence of an environmental effect, but no indication of selective migration. Since the average test scores of the Negroes even in New York City were slightly inferior to the White norms, this study cannot be regarded as disposing of the question of race differences. It must be borne in mind, however, that even in New York City the environment of Negroes cannot be regarded as completely equal to that of Whites. The study does at least indicate that as the environment of the Negro improves, his test scores rise correspondingly. It seems to the writer highly probable, if not certain, that with complete environmental equality, the present difference between Negroes and Whites would entirely disappear.

It is important to remember that when it is alleged that Whites are superior to Negroes, it is a superiority *on the average* which is being defended. In other words, even if there is a race difference of this type, it is still true that a great many Negroes are superior to a great many Whites. Any restrictions therefore upon the education or occupation of Negroes on the basis of the results of psychological studies is unwarranted. In this connection it is interesting to consider some of the cases of gifted Negro children recently described by Witty and Jenkins (*58*). One of these, a young girl of nine, of almost unmixed African ancestry, had a Binet I.Q. of 200 with correspondingly high scores in a number of other intelligence tests. This score has been matched by very few indeed of the thousands of White children tested. It goes without saying that any restrictions placed upon this girl on grounds of race have no foundation in the science of psychology.

A new and interesting approach in this field is to be found in Garth's (*59*) study of American Indian children who have been placed in White foster homes. Most investigations of the mental test performance of American Indians have yielded results definitely inferior to those of Whites. These foster children, however, obtained scores equal to and in many cases superior to the White norms. We have here again the problem of selection, since these children may have been superior to the average among American Indians, but Garth reports that the adopted children obtain much higher scores than their own siblings, who have approximately the same heredity, but who have remained in an American Indian environment.

Garth regards this finding as corroborative of his general conclusion that the apparent intellectual inferiority of the American Indian is merely a function of his different background
and training.

Among psychologists engaged in the experimental investigation of race differences, one of the very few who apparently
still believe in their existence is Porteus. In a series of studies
he has reported the results of testing a number of racial and
national groups in Hawaii, as well as native Australians, Africans and Malays (54). He finds differences between these
groups which in his opinion cannot be explained by the operation of environmental factors, and which he therefore ascribes
to innate racial characteristics. Even if we grant, however,
that the environment is not responsible for the findings,
Porteus' results still do not lend themselves to a racial interpretation. Many of the differences which he reports are much
more significant between two different sub-groups in the same
race, for example two tribes of Australians, than between two
distinct races. The differences may be genetically determined,
but they are not racial. Similarly in the Hawaiian material
there is a greater contrast between the Portuguese and other
Whites than between either of these and the other racial
groups in the community. There is therefore no indication
of any genetic relationship between race or physical type and
level of intelligence.

As far as nations within the White race are concerned, there
is almost complete unanimity among psychologists that biologically determined differences between them have never been
proven. As we have seen above, the most extensive investigation in this field has been repudiated by its author. It may
be added that an attempt to compare groups of Nordic, Alpine
and Mediterranean children, selected in Europe according to
the most rigid anthropological criteria, failed to reveal any
significant differences between them (60). To speak of national instead of racial differences really begs the question,
since nations are political and not biological entities.

As an indication of the change in attitude among social

scientists on this question, we may cite in conclusion a recent statement by Odum (*61*) that among "the errors of sociology" is "the assumption that races are inherently different rather than group products of differentials due to the cumulative power of folk-regional and cultural environment" (p. 338). This statement is all the more significant in view of the fact that Odum himself in an earlier work on the social and mental traits of the Negro (*62*) expressed the very definite conviction that Negroes are constitutionally inferior to Whites.

The conclusion of this discussion is that there has as yet appeared no adequate proof of inherent racial differences in ability. The various arguments used in support of such differences are not scientifically valid. This does not mean that we rule out heredity as an explanation of certain individual and possibly even group differences. As was pointed out in Chapter IX, it is perfectly consistent to regard the differences between large groups, socio-economic or racial, as due to environmental factors, while insisting that within each of these groups the individual differences may at least in part be determined by heredity. In connection with race, the differences between Whites and Negroes in present achievement may be explained in terms of the background of the two races, but the tremendous variations within the Negro and within the White group may still reveal the influence of hereditary factors. Expressed differently, a White superiority of ten or twenty points in average I.Q. may be explained by the environment, but a range of at least 100 points between the best and the poorest members of each group may hardly be accounted for in the same manner. This does not mean that the environment plays no part in the causation of these individual differences, but it is certainly not entirely responsible for them.

THE MEASUREMENT OF NON-INTELLECTUAL TRAITS

The study of differences between racial and national groups in the field of personality, as distinct from intelligence, has attracted considerable attention. The various objective meth-

ods used in the study of personality will be discussed in greater
detail in Chapter XVI. At this point it may suffice to state
that there is still so much doubt as to the validity of personality tests that the results of their application to the problem
of racial differences may hardly be regarded as significant.
In addition, the results conflict to such a degree that any conclusion from them is unwarranted. This is true, for example,
of tests of musical ability, in which even the alleged rhythmic
superiority of the Negro is by no means a consistent finding.
There are, however, a few studies in this field which raise
problems of special interest in this connection.

One of the most significant of these is the study by Efron
and Foley (63), which deals with the gestural patterns sometimes regarded as being racial or national characteristics. By
means of very careful sketches and motion picture recordings
it was possible to compare in great detail the gestures used
by Jews and Italians in a large variety of social conditions.
There were marked differences between the two groups, the
Italian gestures being much more frequently symbolic and
conveying a definite meaning, whereas those of the Jews were
rather a running accompaniment to speech, but without significance when taken by themselves; there were differences
also in the nature of the movements employed, those of the
Italians tending to extend laterally away from the body, and
those of the Jews forward toward the person addressed. The
interesting finding was, however, that in spite of these marked
differences between the immigrant Jews and Italians, the gestures almost entirely disappeared with the passage of one generation. There was clear indication therefore of the temporary and cultural rather than of the native character of the
gestures.

The problem of speed is also of interest in this connection.
Not only is it of significance in relation to intelligence test
scores, but it has also some direct bearing on the general question of personality differences. It has been suggested that
races may differ in this respect because of the direct effect of
physiological factors. In connection with the apparently more

easy-going tempo of the Chinese, for example, Earle (*64*) has suggested that a difference in basal metabolic rate between the Orientals and the Whites may be responsible. This seems unlikely for several reasons—first, because the basal metabolism is affected by factors of diet, climate, occupation and other environmental circumstances; second, because the metabolism of members of the same race living in different environments may vary greatly; and third, because experimental methods have failed to reveal any direct relation between basal metabolism and speed of behavior in normal subjects.

The more direct approach to the question of differences in speed by means of reaction-time experiments as well as measurement of rate of movement have revealed marked variations between groups, but apparently not determined by racial factors. Indians on the Yakima reservation, for example, moved very slowly in the test situation and showed a corresponding decrease in the number of errors during the solution of a performance test; this qualitative difference between Indians and Whites did not obtain in the case of pupils at the Haskell Institute, where the Indian children are brought up in a manner comparable to Whites generally (*65*). The conclusion that differences in speed are cultural, not racial, is supported by the careful study by Foley (*66*), who showed a relationship between type of occupation and speed of movement in a variety of test situations. It is true, however, that this study did not entirely control the factor of selection, and there is the possibility that those who prefer a quicker tempo find their way into certain occupations. Foley prefers the conclusion that tempo is determined by habits acquired by the individual.

The use of personality tests of the usual type, including those of the paper-and-pencil and of the performance variety, have failed to reveal any significant race differences. A recent study (*67*) involved the application of the Bernreuter inventory, the Allport-Vernon Study of Values, a persistence test, a test of suggestibility, and Maller's honesty test to students in a number of academic institutions in New York City and vicinity. These were divided according to their "racial" characteristics into Nordic, Alpine and Mediterranean groups, as well as into Jews and non-Jews. The results showed these "racial" differences to be insignificant, although there were rather marked variations among sub-groups of the same "race" in different academic institutions and different socio-economic classes. This result finds support in an earlier observation by Hartshorne and May (*68*) who in their *Studies in Deceit* noted that Jewish children in a poor neighborhood cheated more frequently than the average, and those in a good neighborhood less frequently. Their conclusion is that honesty in these situations appears to be a function of intelligence and background and not of racial or ethnic origin.

In this whole field the unsatisfactory nature of the tests must impose caution as to any conclusions drawn from them. What we can say is that with the methods at present available personality differences between races have not been demonstrated. Here as in the case of the intelligence test studies, there is ample room for heredity to exert a significant effect upon the range of variations among individuals within any community and in all probability these variations do have in part a biological origin. Our negative conclusion with regard to hereditary factors applies again therefore not to individual, but to group differences.

THE PROBLEM OF RACE MIXTURE

In the whole field of race there is probably no question that has attracted more attention and aroused more acrimonious discussion than that of race mixture. It is a problem which has direct practical significance since it has been advocated as the best solution of racial conflict, as for example that aroused by the presence of a distinctive Negro population in America; and it has recently achieved political importance in the official attempts of certain European nations to keep their race "pure" and prevent mixture with what they regard as undesirable elements in the population. As far as this last point is concerned, the earlier discussion of the relation between race and nation should have made it clear that racial purity in any strict anthropological sense is impossible of attainment by any nation today. Huxley and Haddon (6) go so far as to suggest that there may never have been any such thing as racial purity, since the earliest prehistoric evidence already indicates the concomitance in one geographical area of many different physical types.

The attitude toward race mixture may to a considerable extent depend upon one's attitude toward one's own race. If we regard our own group as superior, we shall probably consider any mixture with an "inferior" group as a mongrelization destined to bring about the degeneration of the race. Our survey of the material pertinent to the question of race differences has indicated the lack of evidence for the superiority of any one race over any other, and we may therefore dismiss this as an argument based upon sentiment rather than upon science.

If the notion of racial equality is accepted, there are still two possible points of view toward race mixture. On the one hand it may be regarded as desirable because of the phenomenon which has been termed "hybrid vigor." It is argued that since inbreeding is bad, the maximum of outbreeding is clearly desirable, and this is most easily attained in marriages between members of different races. There is some direct evidence in favor of hybrid vigor, as for example in Boas' (69) finding that American Indian and French Canadian hybrids had larger families and seemed physically more robust than either of the two parent groups. Against the theory of hybrid vigor it is urged that inbreeding is not necessarily bad except when there are defects in the parents, and that in any case it is possible to find sufficient disparity in genetic constitution between two members of the same race without resorting to race mixture.

Those who argue against race mixture have usually stressed the possibility of disharmonies arising in the offspring. Davenport (70) and his associates have been most active in support of this point of view. He points, for example, to the fact that since Negroes have on the average longer arms and legs than

the Whites, the hybrid may inherit the disharmonious combination of the long legs of the Negro and the short arms of
the White. This may have the practical disadvantage to the
hybrid of making him unfit for occupations which require
picking things off the ground. Similar disharmonies are regarded as occurring in other aspects of the body. There is
the possibility, for example, that if one parent is a robust, well-
built Nordic, and the other a short, slender Mediterranean,
the offspring may inherit the large bony structure of the former
and the small internal organs of the latter; this might result
in his having a heart or a stomach too small to do the work for
a large organism, or there might be a visceroptosis or a dropping of the organs of the body because of insufficient support.
Conversely, the inheritance of a small frame and large internal
organs would cause congestion and consequent internal dam-
age. Another possible disharmony is a discrepancy between
the size of the teeth and of the jaw, and Davenport believes
that excessive race mixture is responsible for much of the
dental trouble in America.

This argument depends entirely upon the theory that size
is inherited separately for different organs in the body, so that
the genetic basis for length of leg would be entirely distinct
from that determining length of arm. This theory has been
effectively disproved in a series of experiments by Castle (71),
who showed among other things that in the crossing of two
breeds of rabbits of markedly different size, the hybrids were
harmonious in every respect. There is an apparent confirmation of Davenport's point of view in the experiments by
Stockard (72) which showed that the crossing of dogs might
result in very unsatisfactory combinations, as, for example, a
large body upon legs too short to support it adequately. It
must be kept in mind, however, that the differences between
these dogs are immeasurably greater than those found between
any two human physical types, and that therefore the argument from one to the other is not tenable. The direct observation and measurement of human hybrids shows only an
occasional disharmony probably of no more frequent occur-

rence than among members of a single unmixed race. The mulattoes in America are certainly not conspicuous for any excessive frequency of disharmonies in their physical constitution.

On the biological side therefore we may conclude that neither the arguments for nor against race mixture have any special cogency. It is not necessary to go outside of one's race in order to marry someone whose genes are sufficiently different to avoid any possibly harmful effects of inbreeding. On the other hand, the disharmonies alleged to follow miscegenation seem to be for the most part imaginary, and constitute no valid argument in favor of racial purity. Race mixture in itself is neither good nor bad; its results depend upon the nature of the individuals who enter into the crossing.

From the sociological point of view, however, the problem is a much more serious one. If there is general objection to race mixture, and if as a consequence the hybrids find it difficult to fit into the social and economic life of either of the parent groups, the effect upon them as individuals may be very unfavorable. As Castle points out in this connection, the real problem of race mixture is not one of biology, but of personal and social relationships. This becomes clear if we contrast the descriptions of Chinese-White crosses in Shanghai and in Hawaii; the former are described by Lamson (73) as maladjusted, unfortunate individuals who are found mainly in the less savory occupations of the city, whereas Romanzo Adams (74) speaks of the healthy integration of this group with every aspect of life in Hawaii. It is clearly the attitude toward the hybrids, not their biological make-up, which determines their place in the community. For this reason many valid objections may be raised against race mixture within any society in which the half-caste is looked upon with contempt or finds adjustment difficult. It must be kept clearly in mind, however, that in these cases it is not race mixture which is harmful, but the treatment accorded to the hybrids.

The problem of race mixture has also been studied by means of the application of intelligence tests to the hybrids. It has been urged by Herskovits (75), Witty and Jenkins (76), and others that this approach might help to settle the problem of race differences; if, for example, Whites are superior to Negroes, then among the mulatto group there should be a direct correspondence between level of intelligence and degree of White admixture. This argument depends, however, upon the assumption that the mixture is made up of comparable samples of both races. This has not so far been demonstrated. As a matter of fact Reuter (77) has suggested the possibility that the mixture is composed of an average White but a superior Negro component, owing to the fact that within the social framework of slavery White men would choose the best Negro girls for their mistresses. This also has not been proved, especially since there is no known relation between beauty and intelligence, but it does raise the problem of selection or sampling in this whole connection. Until we know more of the nature of this sampling, we cannot argue from the characteristics of the mulatto to the nature of the component races.

The actual results in this field were formerly regarded as indicating clearly the relationship between degree of White blood and standing on the intelligence tests. The early study by Ferguson (78) came to this conclusion, but made use of relatively crude measures both of mental level and of racial constitution. The more recent studies by Herskovits (75), Peterson and Lanier (56), and Klineberg (65) used more careful measurements of Negroid characteristics such as skin color, nose width and lip thickness, and found that within relatively homogeneous socio-economic groups of Negroes the correlations of these measures with intelligence test scores were negligible. Garth's (48) studies on American Indian crosses were also formerly interpreted as indicating the importance of degree of White mixture, but his latest conclusion is that there is no proof of such a relationship.

It is true, however, that among the American Negroes there has in the past been a definite tendency for leadership in the fields of art, science and business to be largely in the hands of the lighter-colored mulattoes. There was a general belief to

the effect that this was due to the admixture of White blood.
It is much more likely, however, that the true cause is to be
found in the fact that in the past mulattoes have had much
better opportunities for education and advancement than full-
blooded Negroes. There have been many reasons for this.
In the first place, at the time when Negroes were prohibited
by law from acquiring an education, this did not apply to the
mulatto children of White men, and they thus secured a definite advantage; in the second place these lighter-colored Negroes were given the preference in those jobs which brought
them into contact with Whites; and finally Negroes themselves,
accepting to a large extent the notion of White superiority,
regarded the mulattoes as an intermediate group and treated
them accordingly. This last point is particularly significant,
since it has led to a tendency among Negroes to rate high those
physical characteristics which are least Negroid, and the success of cosmetic establishments emphasizing preparations for
bleaching the skin and straightening the hair is indicative of
this trend. This attitude is prevalent even at the present time,
and as Herskovits has shown (79), it expresses itself also in
the preference of successful Negroes for light-colored wives.
As far as leadership among the Negroes is concerned, however, it is not nearly so true now as it was in former days that
the mulattoes preponderate. In the Negro universities, for
example, there has been a progressive "darkening" in the complexion of the average student. It seems clear that the superiority of the mulatto is a temporary one and that it also is
rooted in social and educational rather than in biological
factors.

SUMMARY

The word *race* refers to a group of people of similar physical
type and common heredity. In popular usage it is frequently
confused with nation, which is a political grouping consisting
of individuals heterogeneous in origin and in physical characteristics; there is no German or Italian or American race.
Another type of confusion is with language; the terms "Latin,"

"Semitic," "Aryan," all refer to families of languages, and not to race. Similarly, there is no Jewish race.

The very concept of race as applied to man has been challenged because of lack of agreement as to the criteria of classification. Subdivisions based on skin color are in conflict with those based on cephalic index, and there appears to be no means of deciding which is to be preferred. This supports the notion that "all mankind constitute but one race."

The physical differences which do exist have often been regarded as having psychological implications. It has been urged, for example, that the characteristics of the Negro are more primitive than those of other races, but ape-like features occur with equal frequency in all groups. The brains of Negroes and Whites appear to be approximately equal in size, and to have the same conformation. In general, there has been no demonstration that psychological differences of any significance are associated with the physical features used in race classification.

The cultural argument for racial superiority is unsatisfactory because of the great variations in the cultural level of the same racial group at different times in history, as well as of different sub-groups within the same race, and also because there is no acceptable criterion which may be used in judging all cultures. As far as intelligence tests are concerned, it was formerly believed by many psychologists that racial differences had been demonstrated, but the present consensus is to the effect that so many environmental factors enter into the comparisons that no conclusion as to innate ability is justified. The superiority of northern over southern Negroes argues in favor of the environmental determination of the test scores, since there is no definite evidence for the selective migration of a superior group. The discovery of individual Negro children with Intelligence Quotients at the extreme upper end of the distribution, as well as the excellent showing made by American Indian children adopted into superior White homes, also testify to the absence of innate racial differences in intelligence.

The measurement of traits of personality has yielded mainly negative results in this field, partly because of the nature of the tests used, and partly because of the inconsistency of the findings. In this respect also, sub-groups within the same ethnic population differ markedly according to variations in the socio-economic and cultural environment.

The mixture of races has been on the one hand opposed because of the physical disharmonies which are alleged to result, and on the other hand advocated because of the phenomenon of hybrid vigor. Neither argument appears to be particularly significant. The results of race mixture depend upon the nature of the individuals who participate in the crossing, and upon the attitude which society adopts toward the hybrid.

REFERENCES

1. Hooton, E. A. *Apes, Men and Morons.* 1937.
2. Boas, F. *General Anthropology.* 1938.
3. Retzius, G., and Fürst, C. M. *Anthropologia Suecica.* 1902.
4. Dixon, R. B. *The Racial History of Man.* 1923.
5. Kossinna, G. *Ursprung der Germanen.* 1928.
6. Huxley, J. S., and Haddon, A. C. *We Europeans.* 1936.
7. Boas, F. "Aryans and Non-Aryans," *American Mercury,* 1934, 32: pp. 219-223.
8. Hooton, E. A. *The Twilight of Man.* 1939.
9. Coon, C. S. *The Races of Europe.* 1939.
10. Müller, F. M. *Biographies of Words and the Home of the Aryas.* 1888.
11. Barzun, J. *Race: A Study in Modern Superstition.* 1937.
12. Blumenbach, J. F. *Anthropological Treatises.* 1865.
13. Sergi, G. *L'Uomo, secondo le origini, l'antichità, le variazioni e la distribuzione geografica.* 1911.
14. Deniker, J. *The Races of Man.* 1900.
15. Pritchard, A. *The Natural History of Man.* 1843.
16. Buffon, G. L. *Histoire Naturelle.* 36 vols. 1749-1788.
17. Herder, J. G. *Ideen zur Philosophie der Geschichte der Menschheit.* 1784-1791.
18. Hirszfeld, L., and Hirszfeld, H. "Serologic Differences Between the Blood of Different Races," *Lancet,* 1919, 2, No. 5016: pp. 675-678.
19. Osborn, H. F. *Men of the Old Stone Age.* 1918.

20. Warden, C. J. *The Evolution of Human Behavior.* 1932.
21. Boas, F. *Anthropology and Modern Life.* 1928.
22. Kroeber, A. L. *Anthropology.* 1923.
23. Kroeber, A. L. "Cultural Anthropology," *The Problem of Mental Disorder* (ed. by M. Bentley and E. V. Cowdry). 1934.
24. Linton, R. *The Study of Man.* 1936.
25. Kretschmer, E. *Physique and Character.* 1925.
26. Klineberg, O., Asch, S. E., and Block, H. "An Experimental Study of Constitutional Types," *Genet. Psychol. Monog.*, 1934, 16, No. 3.
27. Anastasi, A. *Differential Psychology.* 1937.
28. Paterson, D. G. *Physique and Intellect.* 1930.
29. Todd, T. W., and Lindala, A. "Dimensions of the Body; Whites and Negroes of Both Sexes," *Amer. J. Phys. Anthrop.*, 1928, 12: pp. 35-119.
30. Bean, R. B. "Some Racial Peculiarities of the Negro Brain," *Amer. J. Anat.*, 1906, 5: pp. 353-432.
31. Mall, F. P. "On Several Anatomical Characters of the Human Brain," *Amer. J. Anat.*, 1909, 9: pp. 1-32.
32. Chamberlain, H. S. *The Foundations of the Nineteenth Century.* 2 vols. 1911.
33. Grant, M. *The Passing of the Great Race.* 1916.
34. Stoddard, T. L. *The Rising Tide of Color Against White World Supremacy.* 1920.
35. Aristotle. *The Politics of Aristotle.* 1885.
36. Vitruvius, P. *The Ten Books on Architecture.* 1914.
37. Huntington, E. *The Character of Races.* 1924.
38. Sergi, G. *The Mediterranean Race.* 1895.
39. Smith, G. E. *Human History.* 1929.
40. Thomas, W. I. *Primitive Behavior.* 1937.
41. Rivers, W. H. R. *Psychology and Ethnology.* 1926.
42. Lips, J. *The Savage Hits Back.* 1937.
43. LaPiere, R. T., and Farnsworth, P. R. *Social Psychology.* 1936.
44. Kruse, W. *Die Deutschen und ihre Nachbarvölker.* 1929.
45. McDougall, W. *Is America Safe for Democracy?* 1921.
46. Hankins, F. H. *The Racial Basis of Civilization.* 1926.
47. Stofflet, E. H. "A Study of National and Cultural Differences in Criminal Tendency," *Arch. Psychol.*, 1935, No. 185.
48. Garth, T. R. *Race Psychology.* 1931.
49. Klineberg, O. *Race Differences.* 1935.
50. Brigham, C. C. *A Study of American Intelligence.* 1923.
51. Brigham, C. C. "Intelligence Tests of Immigrant Groups," *Psychol. Rev.*, 1930, 137: pp. 158-165.

52. Terman, L. M. *The Measurement of Intelligence.* 1916.

53. Garret, H. E., and Schneck, M. R. *Psychological Tests, Methods and Results.* 1933.

54. Porteus, S. D. *Primitive Intelligence and Environment.* 1937.

55. Franzblau, R. N. "Race Differences in Mental and Physical Traits: Studied in Different Environments," *Arch. Psychol.,* 1935, No. 177.

56. Peterson, J., and Lanier, L. H. "Studies in the Comparative Abilities of Whites and Negroes," *Ment. Meas. Monog.,* 1929, 5.

57. Klineberg, O. *Negro Intelligence and Selective Migration.* 1935.

58. Witty, P. A., and Jenkins, M. D. "The Case of 'B,' a Gifted Negro Girl," *J. Soc. Psychol.,* 1935, 6: pp. 117-124.

59. Garth, T. R. "A Study of the Foster Indian Child in the White Home," *Psychol. Bull.,* 1935, 32: pp. 708-709.

60. Klineberg, O. "A Study of Psychological Differences Between 'Racial' and National Groups in Europe," *Arch. Psychol.,* 1931, No. 132.

61. Odum, H. W. "The Errors of Sociology," *Soc. Forces,* 1936-37, 15: pp. 327-342.

62. Odum, H. W. *Social and Mental Traits of the Negro.* 1910.

63. Efron, D., and Foley, J. P., Jr. "A Comparative Investigation of Gestural Behavior Patterns in Italian and Jewish Groups Living under Different as Well as Similar Environmental Conditions," *Zscht. f. Sozialforschung,* 1937, 6: pp. 151-159.

64. Earle, H. G. "Basal Metabolism," *The Caduceus,* 1922, 1: pp. 81-85.

65. Klineberg, O. "An Experimental Study of Speed and Other Factors in 'Racial' Differences," *Arch. Psychol.,* 1928, No. 93.

66. Foley, J. P. "Factors Conditioning Motor Speed and Tempo." *Psychol. Bull.,* 1937, 34: pp. 351-397; "An Experimental Study of the Effect of Occupational Experience upon Motor Speed and Preferential Tempo." *Arch. Psychol.,* 1937, No. 219.

67. Klineberg, O., Fjeld, H., and Foley, J. P. Unpublished study.

68. Hartshorne, H., and May, M. A. *Studies in Deceit.* 1928.

69. Boas, F. "The Half-Blood Indian," *Pop. Sci. Monthly,* 1894, 14: pp. 761-770.

70. Davenport, C. B., and Steggerda, M. *Race Crossing in Jamaica.* 1929.

71. Castle, W. E. "Race Mixture and Physical Disharmonies," *Sci.,* 1930, 71: pp. 603-606.

72. Stockard, C. R. *The Physical Basis of Personality.* 1931.

73. Lamson, H. D. "The Eurasian in Shanghai," *Amer. J. Sociol.,* 1936, 41: pp. 642-648.

74. Adams, R. *Interracial Marriage in Hawaii.* 1937.

75. Herskovits, M. J. "On the Relation between Negro-White Mixture and Standing in Intelligence Tests," *Ped. Sem. and J. Genet. Psychol.,* 1926, 33: pp. 30-42.

76. Witty, P. A., and Jenkins, M. D. "Intra-Race Testing and Negro Intelligence," *J. Psychol.,* 1936, 1: pp. 179-192.

77. Reuter, E. B. *Race Mixture.* 1931.

78. Ferguson, G. O. "The Psychology of the Negro," *Arch. Psychol.,* 1916, No. 36.

79. Herskovits, M. J. "Color Line," *American Mercury,* 1925, 6: pp. 204-208.

PART FOUR

SOCIAL INTERACTION

CHAPTER XII

THE INDIVIDUAL IN THE GROUP

INTRODUCTION

IN this chapter we deal with the question of the manner and the degree in which the behavior of an individual is altered by the actual presence of others. In terms of our definition of social psychology as the study of the individual in the group situation, this may be regarded as one of our central problems. It represents one of the oldest and at the same time one of the newest approaches in this field, involving on the one hand the time-honored problem of crowd mentality, and on the other a series of important studies which have laid the foundation for an experimental social psychology. There are many different directions from which the effect upon the individual of other individuals or of a group has been approached.

IMITATION

The most obvious manner in which one person may be affected by another is through imitation, or through the direct and usually immediate reproduction of behavior occurring in his environment. There has been considerable discussion in the literature as to the true nature of this process. William James and Baldwin regarded it as instinctive. McDougall believed that it should not be regarded as instinctive, since there are no specific forms of behavior characteristic of it and the mode of expression varies according to the external situation. The consensus among psychologists at the present time, for reasons to be discussed below, is against the explanation in terms of instinct.

Historically the most important use of imitation in the field of social psychology is that of Gabriel Tarde (1) who built upon it a theory of the nature of society. Himself a criminologist, Tarde rejected the current theory of Lombroso that crime is based upon the biological nature of the individual, and looked rather for a social explanation of this and allied phenomena. He was influenced by the psychiatry of his day, particularly by the growing knowledge of hypnotism, and of the suggestible and imitative behavior characteristic of the hypnotic state. He studied the nature of "crime waves" and "crime epidemics" from this point of view, and extended the theory to other forms of social behavior. Imitation was for him the fundamental social fact, and there were laws which described its nature and its effect. Social change is possible because people imitate the novel and the striking. Society without imitation is unthinkable.

It is doubtful, however, whether imitation can ever be used as a principle of explanation. Even among animals, imitation apparently occurs only under specific conditions and in response to definite goals; that is to say, the animal imitates when something is to be gained by it, when it enables him to reach food, and so on. Similarly, among human beings, there seems always to be a selection from a great many possibilities, and imitation occurs only when it brings some kind of additional satisfaction. As Brown (2) expresses it:

Humans imitate when this type of behavior enables them to arrive at certain goals in the psychological field. The underlying dynamic situation creates the imitation, rather than a force called imitation creating these goals. Whenever a shopgirl cuts her hair in a Garbo bob, she does this, not because imitation as a force causes her to do it, but rather because she perceives it as means towards arriving at the type of life that either Garbo or one of the heroines she portrays lives (p. 92).

Freeman (3) also insists that imitation can occur only in so far as the imitated act already possesses meaning and functional significance to the mimic, and only to the extent that one desires to imitate. Behavior may be imitated because it appears to have brought success to others, or because we approve of it, as in the familiar saying that "imitation is the sincerest form of flattery." As a result, we follow the customs of the "best people," of our hero or heroine, and children repeat the words and actions of their elders, particularly of their own parents. F. H. Allport (4) adopts a similar position. It seems clear that imitation is not in itself a sufficient explanation of uniformities of behavior, since such uniformities appear to develop only under certain conditions and not under others.

We did, however, make use of the concept of imitation in the account of the development of language in young children (Chapter III). The child repeats the sounds which he himself has made, as well as those which he hears from others. The explanation of this form of behavior is to be found, however, not in a tendency to imitate, but in a conditioned response of the circular type (see p. 47). Hearing a sound, for example, then becomes the stimulus to producing it, and the result may look like a direct imitative process. Actually, it is merely one of a large variety of phenomena explained by the conditioned response, which is applicable to many instances of animal as well as human imitation.

The point has also been made that what appears to be imitative behavior may be due to the similarity in the conditions affecting different individuals at the same time. The fact, for example, that when one guest leaves the others follow, does not necessarily indicate imitation, since they may all feel that it is about time to go. When a theater audience laughs at a humorous situation on the stage, the individuals are all responding to the same external stimulus rather than imitating one another; at the same time, there is the additional phenomenon of interaction between individuals which contributes to the final result.

We may conclude that the behavior described as imitative can be explained in a variety of ways, and represents a variety of different phenomena. At one time it is a form of conditioned response; at another it merely represents similar reactions of several individuals to the same external situation. When imitation of a direct character does take place, it is to be understood as a means to an end, and occurs because value is ascribed to the act which is imitated or to the person who has performed the act.   There is no drive to imitate.

SUGGESTION

It is difficult to draw a sharp line between suggestion and imitation, and as we have seen, Tarde's laws of imitation were based upon the facts of suggestion and hypnosis described by the psychiatrists.   William Stern (5) has attempted to distinguish between the two concepts on the ground that suggestion is a higher and more complicated stage of behavior which includes some degree of interpretation.   If someone claps his hands, for example, and a child repeats the action, it is imitation; if someone weeps, and the child realizes that this person is unhappy and therefore himself begins to cry, it is suggestion. It is doubtful, however, whether the distinction can be validly drawn in terms of the interpretation involved.   In the case in which the subject is told, under conditions of waking suggestion, that he is falling forward, he may accept this idea and react accordingly, without interpreting it in any way.   It is precisely the *unreasoned* acceptance, to use F. H. Allport's (4) phrase, which is essential to the phenomenon of suggestion.

Murphy, Murphy, and Newcomb (6) indicate that the term "suggestion" has been used for three quite distinct human tendencies which have been confused.

1. The tendency to make a response which has been previously made in a similar situation, whether appropriate or inappropriate at the time.   This includes habit and the response by analogy (the "transferred conditioned response").

2. The tendency to go on doing what one has started doing. This is said to be due to suggestion if the experimenter believes that the tendency to go on with the act involves gross failure to realize its inappropriateness.

3. The tendency to believe or to do what one is told because of social motives such as dependence upon, or fear of, or fondness for, some person.   This includes hypnosis.

The first two of these are not always distinct, however, and there are many cases in which both operate at the same time. In the well-known test of progressive lines devised by Binet (7), the fact that successive lines presented to the subject regularly increase in size for a time, appears to produce a set in the subject so that he continues to report the increase even when the size of the lines is kept constant. In this case there is habit and the response by analogy, but also the tendency to go on doing what one has started doing. There is still an important distinction between these first two types which together constitute what Aveling and Hargreaves (8) call ideo-motor suggestion, and "the tendency to believe what one is told" which they call prestige suggestion. In the former case the suggestion or idea comes from the nature of the material or of the act previously performed, whereas in the latter it depends upon the relation to some other individual or group of individuals.

There are many experiments which illustrate the effect of ideo-motor suggestion. Binet's illusion of progressive lines belongs in this category, as well as the similar illusion of progressive weights. In the field of social psychology, however, prestige suggestion is by far the more important. Experiments in this field range from simple conjuring tricks in which the experimenter tells a group of children that he is about to throw a ball into the air (and finds that about fifty percent of them see him do it) to the complicated relationships found in hypnosis and in the mechanisms underlying propaganda and public opinion. This is a phenomenon which differs in important respects from ideo-motor suggestion, since it is affected by a host of social and emotional attitudes. The marked difference between the two types of suggestion probably accounts to a considerable degree for the low correlations reported between the different tests of suggestibility, and makes it impossible to speak of suggestibility as a trait of character or personality (see p. 447).

The use of "leading questions" in connection with testimony is frequently also an example of prestige suggestion. When a picture is shown and the subject asked what kind of hat the man in the picture was wearing, it is difficult to resist the suggestion that he was wearing one, even though actually he was not. There have been so many experiments which have demonstrated this tendency that one can certainly understand the insistence of the judge in a law court upon eliminating such questions as far as possible.

In connection with the prestige phenomenon, there are many tests of waking suggestion such as the instruction to a subject that he is about to fall forward, used with considerable effect by Hull (*9*) in selecting suitable subjects for hypnosis. Aveling and Hargreaves (*8*) suggested to their subjects that their hand would remain rigid, and found that about 46 percent of them responded positively; in the case of hand levitation ("Your hand is getting lighter. It is rising in the air."), 42 percent accepted the suggestion. In these experiments the interesting phenomenon of "negative" or "contrary" suggestion enters, some of the subjects responding in a manner opposite to that suggested by the experimenter. On the statistical side this is shown by the fact that in the ideo-motor type of test there is an approximately normal distribution of responses, whereas in prestige suggestion the curve is U-shaped, indicating that subjects tend to fall into two distinct groups, the suggestible and the negatively suggestible. This has obvious significance in the social field; as we shall see later, in the experiments on propaganda there are always some subjects who react in a manner opposite to that anticipated by the propagandist. We are dealing here with personality characteristics of a complicated and obscure type, and further research is needed upon the factors operative in situations of this kind.

The phenomenon of hypnosis is one of the most striking in this whole field. As is well known, the use of hypnotism received its greatest impetus through Anton Mesmer's theory and practice of animal magnetism. His notion of animal magnetism as a kind of impalpable gas or fluid which could be manipulated and transported has been entirely discredited, but his work led to the discovery of the artificial somnambulism which we call the hypnotic state, and which includes phenomena of great scientific interest. Although the French psychiatrist Charcot in part revived the notion of animal magnetism, it was proved beyond any possible doubt by Liébeault and Bernheim of the Nancy school that the hypnotic trance state could be explained as an extreme form of suggestion. It is important for social psychology precisely because it represents in marked form phenomena similar to those found under normal conditions. As in ordinary prestige suggestion, the subject in an hypnotic trance is willing to accept the ideas presented to him; in both cases, however, there appears to be some control and criticism left, so that for example the subject in a trance will commit an imaginary murder with a paper knife, but will not actually do harm to anyone.

This commonly accepted view has recently been challenged in an investigation by Rowland (*10*). There were some subjects who under deep hypnosis reached out toward a coiled rattlesnake when told it was a rubber rope, and who after some urging threw sulphuric acid at the experimenter, protected by an invisible sheet of glass. Most of the subjects were, however, frightened at the appearance of the snake and would not come close to the box.

A serious danger in connection with prestige suggestion lies in the assumption that a person of outstanding ability in one field is also to be taken seriously in another. In connection with advertising and propaganda, this becomes especially dangerous; an important baseball player endorses a candidate for the Presidency, a physicist expresses his belief in spiritualism or in one particular type of economic system, a movie star endorses a new automobile, an aviator analyzes the international situation. The legitimate acceptance of a man's preeminence in one field leads to an unwarranted assumption that he also has authority elsewhere. The prestige effect of large numbers is a similar one. Since the classical experiment of Moore (*11*) on the effect of knowledge of popular opinion upon the attitudes of the individual, many investigators have demonstrated a similar influence in a variety of situations.

It is important to keep in mind, however, that the nature of the group may make a real difference, and Lewis (*12*) has recently shown that majority opinion does not always have the same prestige effect. In one experiment she presented to a group of students a list of ten political slogans, chiefly of contemporary political interest, and asked them to rank these for their "social significance," "author's intelligence," and so forth. The slogans included: "Give me liberty or give me death," "Balance the Budget," "Workers of the world, unite," and seven other expressions used by conservative and radical leaders. Another group of students was then given the same task, but this time with the knowledge of the rank order for "author's intelligence" presumably obtained from 500 college students. The results showed for the various rankings a definite shift in the direction of the "prestige suggestion" for those subjects who were political liberals but not for those who were political radicals (there were no conservatives in this group). It seems probable that for the radical subjects the opinions of the majority have little or no prestige, since the radicals know that their own views differ from those generally accepted.

In a further study a similar procedure was followed, but the ratings for "author's intelligence" were presumably made by Franklin D. Roosevelt, Herbert Hoover, and Earl Browder respectively. It was felt by the experimenter that the views of the General Secretary of the Communist Party in the United States might have true prestige for the radical students. The rankings ascribed to Browder were inversely related to those which the radical students had previously given. The results still showed little shift in the direction of the new ratings, in spite of the prestige with which they were presumably associated for the radical students. This suggests that prestige works very differently under different conditions. Interviews with the subjects showed, for example, that most of the radicals refused to believe that the given rankings correctly presented Mr. Browder's opinions. The author concludes that:

Radicals do not shift their judgments markedly under the influence of a most authoritative, but conflicting standard. . . . The authoritativeness of a standard, i.e., its effectiveness, requires as a minimum condition the presence of some point of integration between it and the subject's opinions. . . . The operation of prestige suggestion is confined to ambiguous, ill-defined situations.

These are important suggestions for further study in connection with prestige suggestion, especially as related to propaganda and the influencing of public opinion.

Suggestion has been used as an explanation of many phenomena of an otherwise mysterious nature, examples of which have been reported with some frequency, particularly in the ethnological literature. Suggestion is certainly responsible for the case of the Polynesian native who died when he discovered that he had eaten food touched by the chief; belief in the potency of the taboo is apparently sufficient, at least in some cases, to bring about this extreme result. The fact that a Crow Indian sees a vision after four days of prayer and fasting, or that natives all over the world are reported to succumb to witchcraft, may be similarly explained. It is probable that suggestion also operates to ensure a reasonable amount of success in the use of oaths and ordeals as part of the legal procedure of the Africans; the belief, for example, that the guilty man will be destroyed by the "poison" which he is given, is often strong enough to cause the death of the man who knows he is guilty. Not all the ordeals lend themselves to this interpretation, and it is certain that they do not always result in freeing the innocent, but in many instances the effect of suggestion will be in the "right" direction. Similar examples might be multiplied. It is important, however, not to go too far in using this mode of explanation. There is some tendency to account for everything from seasickness to paralysis in these terms, and although suggestion may play an important part in many cases, we must not assume that it is always responsible. The exact manner in which suggestion works to influence organic functions is not always clear, but it seems probable that beliefs and emotions may have a direct effect upon the autonomic nervous system, which in turn acts upon the viscera. In spite of the wide variations in their specific character, these examples all belong in the category of prestige suggestion, the prestige being located in an individual (as in the case of the hypnotist) or less tangibly in the folk beliefs of a community (as in the ethnological examples cited).

The usual assumption that one of the essential characteristics of suggestion is that an idea or stimulus comes to the individual from the outside, seems to conflict with the existence of the phenomenon of auto-suggestion. This form of suggestion, popularized by Coué, appears to demonstrate that the idea may also come from within, and in that case the process would seem to be an unreasoned and uncritical acceptance of one's own ideas. This is probably an incorrect way of looking at the matter, however, since it is certain that in a great many of the cases of auto-suggestion the idea actually comes from outside. Coué taught his patients certain formulae which they could use in his absence, but actually it was his ideas and suggestions which were operative. Phenomena of this type do not necessitate any restatement of the essential nature of suggestion.

THE CROWD AND THE GROUP

The problem of the relation of the individual to the group comes into clear focus in connection with the study of crowds and crowd behavior. This field of social psychology is usually regarded as having its principal origin in the work of Gustave LeBon (13), who insisted upon the unique nature of the crowd and its distinctness from the individuals of which it is composed.

Whoever be the individuals that compose it, however like or unlike be their mode of life, their occupations, their character, or their intelligence, the fact that they have been transformed into a crowd puts them in possession of a sort of collective mind which makes them feel, think, and act in a manner quite different from that in which each individual of them would feel, think, and act were he in a state of isolation. There are certain ideas and feelings which do not come into being, or do not transform themselves into acts except in the case of individuals forming a crowd (pp. 29-30).

The crowd therefore is not a mere sum or average of its component individuals, but a different entity.

According to LeBon there are three causes which predispose to the phenomena of crowd behavior. First there is the feeling of invincible power, which makes the crowd more primitive and less subject to control by conscience or by fear of punishment; second, the fact of contagion or imitation; and third, allied to this, heightened suggestibility. These factors help to make of the crowd a single being, less civilized, less intelligent, and more dangerous, though potentially also more heroic, than individuals in isolation.

There have been other attempts to define the characteristics of the crowd. Scott (14) thinks of the crowd as highly emotional and suggestible with complete absence of any feeling of individual responsibility, without ability to reason or to be critical of the ideas suggested to it, and at a more primitive level than that of its component individuals. Everett Dean Martin (15) has attempted a description of the crowd in terms of psychopathic behavior. As in psychopathic cases there may be a release of repressed impulses, delusions of grandeur and of persecution, lack of awareness of the true motives for the behavior, and a regression to a more primitive level. These descriptions do not differ markedly from those of LeBon; they are merely expressed in a somewhat more modern terminology.

At the other extreme F. H. Allport (4) has insisted that there is no real difference in the nature of the individuals when they are in a crowd and when in isolation. "The individual in the crowd behaves just as he would behave alone, *only more so*" (p. 295). This means that there may be at the most a facilitation in the crowd of certain activities, but not the creation of any that are really foreign to the nature of the individuals. Allport admits, however, that emotional reactions in the crowd are increased by the expressive behavior of others, and also that there is prestige suggestion resulting from the presence of a large group of persons, and an attitude of compliance in the individual as a consequence. He agrees also that acts may be performed in a crowd because the individuals in it go unperceived, or at least unpunished. In spite of these points of agreement with LeBon, there is a real distinction between the two positions. Allport would admit that individuals are affected by others in the vicinity, but this would not constitute the formation of a new entity called the "crowd mind." Two crowds composed of entirely different individuals would differ because of the nature of their components.

The problem of whether a new psychological entity arises whenever individuals constitute a group has been given a practical turn as the result of recent political occurrences in Europe. In an excellent critique of this concept by Freeman (3) it is pointed out that the notion of a "group mind" was elevated by Hegel into the philosophical idea of a *Volksgeist,* or folk-soul. In the writings of Hegel as in those of his Italian followers Croce and Gentile, there developed a romantic and mystical concept of the nation as having a reality and an importance distinct from the individuals who compose it. This has led to a false distinction between the welfare of individuals and the good of the group or nation, and in recent fascist literature there is a definite expression of the idea that the national good is paramount.

Freeman ascribes to Herbert Spencer the responsibility for the development of the concept of the group mind and of the social good as distinct from that of the individual. It is true that Spencer was impressed with the analogy between the individual and the group, and believed that social phenomena such as the division of labor, for example, closely parallel a similar division in the functions of the various cells and organs within the individual. Spencer himself was fully aware, however, that there were important distinctions between the group and the individual and that the concept of organism could be applied to the former only with certain definite limitations. In an article on "The Social Organism," he wrote:

. . . while in individual bodies the welfare of all other parts is rightly subservient to the welfare of the nervous system, whose pleasurable or painful activities make up the good or evil of life; in bodies politic the same thing does not hold good, or holds good to but a very slight extent. It is well that the lives of all parts of an animal should be merged in the life of the whole, because the whole has a corporate consciousness capable of happiness or misery. But it is not so with a society; since its living units do not and cannot lose individual consciousness; and since the community as a whole has no general or corporate consciousness distinct from those of its components. And this is an everlasting reason why the welfare of citizens cannot rightly be sacrificed to some supposed benefit of the State; but why, on the other hand, the State must be regarded as existing solely for the benefit of citizens (*16*, pp. 98-99).

Although Herbert Spencer did speak of a social organism, he did not make the mistake of assuming the existence of a group mind or corporate consciousness. In any case the concept of a "mind" without any definite organic basis, without any specific brain or nervous system connected with it, is impossible to accept.

ᐟ It remains true, however, that in certain respects the individual is altered by his presence in the group situation. As we have seen, there appears to be a greater degree of emotional reactivity, and a lessening of the inhibitions due to the fear of discovery or of punishment. There is the tendency to accept the notions current in the crowd or group—the familiar phenomenon of prestige suggestion. There is further the fact of interaction between individuals, so that they mutually affect one another. As Lewin (*17*) has correctly pointed out we must not look upon the individual as a static entity, but rather as a dynamic being whose characteristics and actions change under the varying influence of external situations, or "the social field." ᐟ The crowd constitutes one such social field and we would expect the behavior of the individual to be modified as a consequence. We may even go one step further with the Gestalt psychologists and agree that the whole is always different from the sum of its parts, that it even determines the nature of the parts, and that a group therefore has a reality different from that of the sum of its individual members. At the same time, just as the Gestalt psychologists would admit the importance of the elements which constitute the totality, we must not lose sight of the nature of the individuals who constitute a group. As individuals they have a background and a set of folkways and traditions which they retain even in the crowd situation. There are some people, for example, who probably never under any conditions would become members of a lynching mob.

Our compromise position is therefore in agreement with Allport that the crowd is not entirely distinct from the individuals, and that these latter do not entirely lose their identity within it; on the other hand, the phenomena of increased emotionality, heightened suggestibility and the effect of certain individuals upon others lend support at least to that part of LeBon's theory which insists that the group is more than the sum of its parts and that the individual is altered by his presence in it. The notion of a group mind or a corporate consciousness must, however, be definitely rejected.

In connection with the wider problem of the relation of the individual to his group or society, the important question arises as to why the individual is almost always willing to accept uncritically the customary behavior of his community. There are of course dissenters, but they are on the whole rare. The sociologist Bagehot (18) speaks of the "cake of custom" in this connection, and seems to regard it as literally difficult, if not impossible, for the individual to break through. There are probably four main reasons for this customary conformity. There is first the phenomenon of prestige suggestion to which we have already referred, and which in this case is associated with the fact that the group has power and importance, and ideas coming from it will therefore tend to be accepted. There is in the second place the fact that the individual often knows no other customs than those of his own community; this is of course true only of relatively small isolated groups, but among them it is highly probable that they act as they do because they are unfamiliar with any alternative. A third important factor is that the individual who does not practice the customary behavior related to the social and economic life of the group will soon be regarded as outside the system of reciprocal rights and duties upon which life in the community may depend; if there is a system of gift exchange, for example, and he fails to return an equivalent value, he will simply not be included in the next round of gifts, and will not be able to obtain what he wishes in exchange. Finally, and allied to this last, there may be punishment for transgression. This punishment may be violent and coercive in nature, but much more frequently in small communities it takes the form of ridicule. These four factors together make it possible to understand why individuals conform, without the necessity of assuming that custom in itself has power and authority.

In this connection F. H. Allport (*19*) has indicated some of the special features of conformity behavior. The reactions of individuals to the social institutions of their community show a different distribution from that characteristic of most psychological phenomena. Instead of fitting into the pattern of the normal probability curve, with the frequencies gradually tapering off in either direction from the mode or other measure of central tendency, conformity behavior tends to take the form of the J-curve. This means that there is an asymmetrical piling up of most cases at one end—the conformity end—of the distribution, with a small number of cases showing the opposite type of behavior. Most individuals conform more or less closely, and there are only a few deviants. Allport's examples include the reactions of automobile drivers to a red light, the time of arrival of employees at their work, and the performance of ritualistic acts upon entering a place of worship. It is still uncertain whether this finding holds for all social institutions, but it is important to realize that at least in some cases the customary "normal distribution" does not operate.

The phenomena of "crowd behavior" may not be confined to the actual crowd situation in the narrower sense, in which a number of individuals congregate in one place at the same time and in a more or less unorganized manner. The various so-called "mental epidemics" belong in the same general category. There have been many historical instances in which the factors of suggestion and interaction have resulted in the

widespread occurrence of striking and bizarre forms of behavior over an area much larger than a single locality or a
single group. Kimball Young (20) mentions among these the
various crusades and pilgrimages between the years 1000 and
1270 which became a universal mania and even caused children in many cases to claim to be prophets and to join in the
crusades despite the protests of their parents; the spread of
the practice of flagellation from Italy in 1260 as an expression
of remorse for real or fancied transgressions; the demonopho-
bia or fear of the devil which took the form of persecution of
alleged witches, lasting a century and a half, and causing the
torture and death of an untold number of innocent persons;
the tulipomania in Holland in the seventeenth century resulting from the mad scramble for tulips in the belief that fortunes could be made by their cultivation; the many religious
revivals throughout history and lasting up to the present time,
etc. These all indicate the manner and the degree of "crowd
behavior" on the widest possible scale. In this general category also we may put the phenomenon of fashion, not only in
dress but in other forms of activity as well; there is the same
spread from a center of origin or a leader, the contagion or
imitation determined by the prestige of certain individuals or
of the group as a whole, and usually an uncritical acceptance
of the new form of behavior. There is even the same lack of
individual responsibility, since a new fashion, no matter how
bizarre or irrational, may be accepted without fear of ridicule
as long as it is common to a great many individuals.

In the behavior of crowds, as well as in group phenomena
generally, the function of the leader has been variously interpreted. It has been argued on the one hand that leadership
exercises a creative influence upon the activities of the group,
and on the other hand that the leader can do no more than express and exemplify what the group has already accepted. In
this latter connection there is a story of the uprising in Paris
in 1848, during which the police had made a number of arrests.
One of those who had been halted cried out, "Let me go. I
must follow that crowd over there. I am their leader." At

the same time we cannot escape the conviction that the present shape of the world would be markedly altered without the presence of men like Hitler and Mussolini in positions of leadership. Once again we may adopt a compromise position; the leader has great influence, but only on certain groups under certain conditions. Change these, or change him, and the resulting behavior is markedly altered. There have been several studies of the psychological characteristics of leaders among school and college groups, but the results cannot yet be applied to the wider aspects of social behavior.

SOCIAL FACILITATION

A more direct attack upon the problem of the individual in the group situation and the manner in which the group affects the behavior of the individual, has been made by means of a series of ingenious experimental techniques. This approach originated in the work of Mayer (21) and Schmidt (22), who were interested in the difference between work done by school children in the classroom situation and when they were alone in their own homes; the procedure was crude, but it suggested the presence in the former situation of a "social increment" which has been made the basis of many further studies. The most important of the early investigations in this field is that by Moede (23), who showed the effect of the group on the individual in a variety of situations. He found in the first place that in an experiment involving the ability to bear pain, the boys who were his subjects always accepted a great deal more pain without complaining when they were in the presence of others. This was all the more marked when two boys who were rivals were tested together. This result is not so difficult to understand since the pain sensation is to a considerable degree subjective; as we know from the phenomena of hypnotic anaesthesia as well as from the reputed ability of certain groups like the Plains Indians to bear pain without complaining, the majority of us can probably stand a great deal more pain than we willingly accept under normal conditions. A second experiment of Moede's raises a more interesting problem. His subjects pressed upon a dynamometer, which measures the strength of grip in the hand, presumably as hard as they possibly could. This "maximum" was, however, exceeded in the group situation, the improvement being most marked again when rivalry was introduced. We have here apparently some form of dynamogenesis, or the liberation of additional energy, as a result of the changed conditions. This effect is probably analogous to that which occurs in conditions of emotional excitement, in which certain physiological changes occur which enable the organism to put forward more energy than under normal circumstances.

Other experiments by Moede included the use of cancellation tests in the individual and in the group situation, the results indicating that work in the presence of others tended on the whole to be quicker but less acurate than when it was done individually; the benefit of the group situation appeared to be greater for the poorer subjects whose work was stimulated as a consequence, whereas the efficiency of the best workers was lowered.

One of the most significant experiments in this whole field was conducted by F. H. Allport (4). In a series of simple motor tasks there was noted a social increment of the type reported by Moede, most marked in the case of the slowest subjects. In judgments of an esthetic nature, in connection with the pleasantness and unpleasantness of odors, there was the important finding that there were more extreme judgments in the individual situation, and that the presence of others tended to bring the extremes somewhat closer together. We have here therefore an experimental indication of the process of conformity resulting from the group situation. In another part of the experiment Allport had his subjects produce as many word associations as possible within a given period of time, and found a definite facilitation under group conditions. Finally, the subjects were asked to write arguments for and against excerpts from Marcus Aurelius which were presented to them for discussion, and Allport states that whereas more arguments were produced in the group than in the individual situation, they were on the average not of such good quality. In other words, there appears to be a social increment for quantity, but a social decrement for quality of production in this complicated intellectual activity. This final result, if verified, has undoubted practical significance, since it points to the necessity of varying the nature of the conditions, whether group or individual, depending upon the kind of work which is being performed. Unfortunately, judgments of quality under these conditions are somewhat subjective, and it would be valuable to have this experiment repeated under more rigid experimental conditions.

In most of the experiments of Moede and Allport the effect of the group situation may be twofold, that is to say, there may be a direct social facilitation and there may also be the factor of competition. If, for example, there is an increase in speed in a cancellation test when others are present, it is not clear whether this is due to seeing others work, or to the fact that one is competing with others, or to both. The attempt was made by Dashiell (24) to separate these two factors by having one experimental situation in which each individual worked separately but knew that he was competing with others, and another situation in which he worked with others but at slightly different tasks so that the competitive factor could not enter. There were in addition the usual "group" and "individual" conditions of the former experiments. The results showed that the competitive effect alone was greater than the social or ideo-motor effect. In other words, working by oneself becomes a special situation when it is known that others are competing at the same time. It would seem that much of Allport's "social facilitation" effect is really due to the facilitating factor of competition.

It should be clear from the discussion of motivation and particularly of the prestige drive in Chapter V that any generalization from these results to what might be expected in other cultures is quite impossible. In our own society the drive to excel others is so great and so intimately bound up with many aspects of our social and economic organization that it seems safe to assume its operation in any experimental situation of the type we have been reviewing. The careful analysis of competitive and co-operative habits in a number of different communities by Margaret Mead (25) and her associates, reveals very wide variations between cultures in this respect. There is reason to believe that in certain American Indian communities we would be much more likely to obtain a social decrement in many situations of this kind; these same communities might, however, show social facilitation in the ability to bear pain, since this is an important value in the group and there is a tradition of competition in this respect. This means that we would have to revise our inferences as to the effect of social and competitive factors in other cultures from two points of view, first with reference to the amount of facilitation present, and second as related to the specific situations in which the facilitative effect might be expected to occur. There is need here for a series of experiments, the results of which would undoubtedly be of great interest in this whole field, particularly if they could be carried out in a number of widely different communities. It is probable that the Zuñi at the one extreme and a Melanesian tribe like the Mundugumor at the other, would make particularly interesting subjects for these experiments. Failing these, it would still be worth while to repeat them upon any other non-Western groups available.

Another series of experiments has dealt with the effect of the group on the individual in the situation in which only one person is working at a time, so that the rest of those present constitute an audience rather than a co-working group. In one such experiment by Gates (26) the tasks consisted of the three-hole steadiness test, color naming, analogies, and the number of nouns named in one minute. There was no clear influence of the audience except a general leveling tendency, so that the variations between the individuals were reduced under these conditions. A well-known experiment in this field is by Laird (27), who had a number of fraternity men razz their pledgees while the latter were engaged in the performance of a number of tasks, including speed of tapping, the three-hole steadiness test, steadiness in sitting and steadiness in standing. In the last two of these tests almost all the subjects performed more poorly when they were being razzed than in the "alone" situation; in the other two tests a few of them actually improved under the razzing. There are interesting individual differences, therefore, in the effect of a difficult social situation of this kind.

Still another approach in this field has concerned itself with the study of groups as groups. This has consisted of a series of experimental investigations in which the attempt was made to note the characteristics of group judgments and group behavior as contrasted with those of the individual. These studies are distinguished from those previously described, in which attention remained focused upon the individual, alone or in the group situation, rather than upon the group as such. The general conclusion from these studies appears to be that the group is far superior to the average of the individuals of which it is composed; to put it another way, most individuals are poorer than the group in the capacities measured, but there are usually some few individuals who are superior. In one study (28), forty-six subjects judged the effectiveness of fifteen advertisements, and the judgments were correlated with the actual sales records. For the individuals the correlations ranged from —.71 to +.87, with an average of +.19. For the group as a whole, the correlation was +.63. The greater success of the group is clearest in those cases in which the situation is additive, as for example in a word-building experiment, or in those permitting much interstimulation between individuals. There is no close correspondence between the size of the group and its efficiency.[1]

POLITICAL SYSTEMS

Recent studies of the manner in which an individual may be affected by his group have had important implications for

[1] See Murphy, Murphy, and Newcomb (6) for a review of experimental work in this field.

the psychology of political systems. One of the most strik-ing investigations is that by Lewin, Lippitt and White (*29*), who studied the patterns of aggressive behavior in experi-mentally created "social climates." These climates were of three main types, authoritarian, democratic and laissez-faire. Clubs were formed of boys who, to begin with, were carefully equated, and who were then placed in one of the three ex-perimental groups. In the authoritarian group, for example, all policies were determined by the leader, techniques and activities being indicated by him one at a time so that future steps were always uncertain, and the "dictator" remained aloof from active group participation except when demonstrating to the others what they were to do. In the democratic group all policies were determined by group discussion, the members were free to work with whomever they chose, and the division of tasks was determined by the group. In the third situation there was complete freedom for group or individual decision, and the leader supplied the information, but took no other part in group discussions. The factor of personality differences in the boys was controlled by having each group pass through au-tocracy and then democracy, or vice versa. The factor of the leader's personality was controlled by having each of four leaders play the role of autocrat and the role of democratic leader at least once.

In one experiment hostility was thirty times as frequent in the autocratic as in the democratic group. Much of the aggres-sion was directed toward two successive scapegoats within the group; none was directed against the autocrat. In a second experiment, the boys in the autocratic groups showed less aggressiveness, but their behavior was of an apathetic type. This lack of aggression is interpreted as due to the repressive influence of the autocrat. Among the boys in these groups there were outbursts of aggression on the days of transition to a freer atmosphere, and a sharp rise of aggression when the autocrat left the room. Nineteen out of twenty boys liked their democratic leader better than their autocratic leader, and seven out of ten also preferred their laissez-faire leader.

This study is of great interest because it submits to experimentally controlled procedures many of the hypotheses which have been suggested as to the effect of various political structures on individual personality. Students of politics, for example, have observed that fascist dictatorships are frequently characterized by the appearance of a scapegoat upon whom all ills may be blamed (see Chapter XIV). This study has revealed that even in an artificial dictatorship of this type such a scapegoat mechanism may easily be elicited. Although value judgments are not usually regarded as within the province of a social psychologist, the apparent superiority of the democratic over the autocratic form of society may be mentioned as one of the important findings of this study.

Political institutions have been subjected to a psychological analysis of a different type by other social scientists. Schuman (30), for instance, in his historical study of the Nazi dictatorship has applied psychoanalytic concepts to the understanding of the trend of events in Germany. He has attempted to describe the frustrations of the lower middle class and their reactions to this frustration. He has seen in the personality of the leaders, particularly of Hitler, indications of abnormal psychological manifestations, especially of the paranoid type. Although it is obviously impossible to make a satisfactory psychiatric study of an individual at a distance, Schuman's suggestions are fruitful and stimulating. Abel (31), on the other hand, has looked for an explanation of the Nazi rise to power in the life histories of individual members of the Nazi party. Since such persons would, however, be largely ignorant of the motives operating within them, their own conscious account of what happened would probably be superficial to a marked degree. Abel criticizes Schuman's approach on the basis of its speculative character, but his own type of interpretation seems less likely to give a real insight into the political changes which occurred.

Another significant attempt to analyze the psychological implications of democracy, fascism and communism has been made by Dollard, Doob and others (32) from the standpoint of the relation between frustration and aggression. The general hypothesis underlying this approach is that aggression is always a consequence of frustration. From this point of view the frustrations encountered in these three political systems are described, together with the forms of aggression to which they lead. Although a democracy like ours may contain many sources of frustration, particularly for those who have failed to reach satisfying economic and social levels, the authors feel that these are much more marked in totalitarian states. The aggressions on the other hand are much more heterogeneous in a democracy, whereas in the other systems they are released in a more or less uniform fashion against the reputed enemies of the regime. This appears to be more marked in the case of fascism than communism, and the alleged fact that the majority of criminal offenses in the Soviets appears to be of a trivial nature "can be interpreted as showing either a significant diminution of frustration or the effects of the advanced system of penology or both" (p. 166). This hypothesis is an interesting one, and seems particularly applicable to the phenomenon of race prejudice which is characteristic of fascist dictatorships (see Chapter XIV).

PUBLIC OPINION

The controversy to which we referred in connection with the crowd or the group mind reappears in the case of public opinion. Here again we have contrasting definitions such as that by Ellwood (*33*), that public opinion is "a rational, collective judgment formed by a group regarding a situation," and at the other extreme that of F. H. Allport (*4*), who speaks of it as "merely the collection of individual opinions" (p. 396). It seems clear that an opinion must be held by an individual; it is a psychological phenomenon demanding conscious activity of a type which we are not prepared to ascribe to a group as such. Public opinion, then, would have to be defined as the opinion of the majority of the individuals within any large group; it is rarely if ever the unanimous opinion of the group as a whole, since trends and cross currents still exist which represent the opinions of minority groups. As in the case of the crowd, however, factors of prestige suggestion and mutual interaction play an important part. We may say therefore that although public opinion is the opinion of a number of individuals and not of a group as such, there are group factors which determine the origin and spread of the opinions as well as the limits of their modifiability. This whole problem of the formation of opinions and attitudes and of their control by the so-called "organs of public opinion" has in recent years been the object of important theoretical analyses, as well as of significant and varied experimental attacks. These will occupy us in the following chapter.

SUMMARY

Imitation is not a force or an instinct, but occurs when the action or the person imitated has value for the subject. In some cases it is a form of conditioned response. It is closely related to suggestion, which consists essentially of the unreasoned acceptance of an idea presented to the subject from an outside source. Of the various types of suggestion, the most important for social psychology is "prestige suggestion," in which the relation to some other individual or group of individuals determines the response. The phenomenon of hypnosis belongs in this category, as does also the prestige effect of large numbers and of folk-beliefs and superstitions.

The crowd has been regarded by LeBon and others as an entity different from that of the individuals of which it is composed, and with a specific mentality. Although F. H. Allport correctly attacks this position, it remains true that the phenomenon of social interaction (the social field) does have a marked effect upon behavior. The notion of a group mind, however, must be definitely rejected, and with it the false distinction between the welfare of individuals and of the group as such.

The behavior of the individual conforms to custom for four main reasons—(1) the effect of prestige suggestion; (2) lack

THE INDIVIDUAL IN THE GROUP

of knowledge of contrasting customs; (3) the practical need to participate in the social and economic exchanges of the community; (4) punishment for transgression. Even the leader must in a sense "follow" the group, though he is not without influence upon its future course.

Experimental studies of the effect of the group on the individual have demonstrated social facilitation in the ability to bear pain, in the output of energy and in speed of response in a variety of situations. These effects are evidently due more to the phenomenon of competition than to the mere presence of others. There is some evidence also that the group situation increases the amount of conformity among individuals, and produces a "social decrement" in the quality of intellectual activity. Comparative studies in other cultures are needed in order to check the universality of these phenomena.

The experimental investigations of "social climates" have shown the possibility of subjecting certain political systems to controlled study. The aggression against a scapegoat under the authoritarian system is a particularly striking phenomenon.

REFERENCES

1. Tarde, G. *Les lois de l'imitation.* 1890.
2. Brown, J. F. *Psychology and the Social Order.* 1936.
3. Freeman, E. *Social Psychology.* 1936.
4. Allport, F. H. *Social Psychology.* 1924.
5. Stern, W. *Psychology of Early Childhood.* 2d ed. 1930.
6. Murphy, G., Murphy, L. B., and Newcomb, T. M. *Experimental Social Psychology.* Rev. ed. 1937.
7. Binet, A. *La suggestibilité.* 1900.
8. Aveling, F., and Hargreaves, H. L. "Suggestibility with and without Prestige in Children," *Brit. J. Psychol.,* 1921, 18: pp. 362-388.
9. Hull, C. L. *Hypnosis and Suggestibility.* 1933.
10. Rowland, L. W. "Will Hypnotized Persons Try to Harm Themselves or Others?" *J. Abn. and Soc. Psychol.,* 1939, 34: pp. 114-117.
11. Moore, H. T. "The Comparative Influence of Majority and Expert Opinion," *Amer. J. Psychol.,* 1921, 32: pp. 16-20.

12. Lewis, H. B. "An Approach to Attitude Measurement," *Psychol. League J.*, 1938, 2: pp. 64-67.

13. LeBon, G. *The Crowd.* 1896.

14. Scott, W. D. *The Psychology of Public Speaking.* 1907.

15. Martin, E. D. *The Behavior of Crowds.* 1920.

16. Spencer, H. "The Social Organism," *Westminster Rev.*, 1860, 73: pp. 90-121.

17. Lewin, K. A. *A Dynamic Theory of Personality.* 1935.

18. Bagehot, W. *The Works of Walter Bagehot* (ed. by F. Morgan). 5 vols. 1889.

19. Allport, F. H. "The J-Curve Hypothesis of Conforming Behavior," *J. Soc. Psychol.*, 1934, 5: pp. 141-183.

20. Young, K. *Social Psychology.* 1930.

21. Mayer, A. "Über Einzel- und Gesamtleistung des Schulkindes," *Arch. f. d. ges. Psychol.*, 1903, 1: pp. 276-416.

22. Schmidt, F. "Experimentelle Untersuchungen über die Hausaufgaben des Schulkindes," *Arch. f. d. ges. Psychol.*, 1904, 3: pp. 33-152.

23. Moede, W. *Experimentelle Massenpsychologie.* 1920.

24. Dashiell, J. F. "An Experimental Analysis of Some Group Effects," *J. Abn. and Soc. Psychol.*, 1930, 25: pp. 190-199.

25. Mead, M., et al. *Cooperation and Competition Among Primitive Peoples.* 1937.

26. Gates, G. S. "The Effect of an Audience upon Performance," *J. Abn. and Soc. Psychol.*, 1924, 18: pp. 334-342.

27. Laird, D. A. "Changes in Motor Control and Individual Variations under the Influence of 'Razzing,'" *J. Exper. Psychol.*, 1923, 6: pp. 236-246.

28. Knight, H. C. "A Comparison of the Reliability of Group and Individual Judgments," *Unpublished Master's Essay,* Columbia University, 1921.

29. Lewin, K. A., Lippitt, R., and White, R. K. "Patterns of Aggressive Behavior in Experimentally Created 'Social Climates,'" *J. Soc. Psychol.*, 1939, 10: pp. 271-299.

30. Schuman, F. *The Nazi Dictatorship.* 2d ed. 1936.

31. Abel, T. F. *Why Hitler Came into Power.* 1938.

32. Dollard, J., et al. *Frustration and Aggression.* 1939.

33. Ellwood, C. A. *An Introduction to Social Psychology.* 1918.

CHAPTER XIII

ATTITUDES

INTRODUCTION

IN a significant article by Gordon Allport (*1*) it is stated that the concept of attitude "is probably the most distinctive and indispensable concept in contemporary American social psychology." Several writers have in fact defined social psychology as the scientific study of attitudes. The first important use of the concept as a central characteristic of sociological problems was made by Thomas and Znaniecki (*2*), who in their study of the Polish peasant in America in 1918 concerned themselves largely with the question of his adjustment to the changed social environment in America. They saw the problem in terms of the substitution of new values for old, and its main feature was therefore the question of attitude, which they defined as a state of mind of the individual toward a value. More recently Bogardus (*3*) and Folsom (*4*) have also described social psychology as concerned mainly with the question of attitudes.

Allport suggests that one reason for the popularity of the concept of attitude in social psychology is that it escapes the ancient controversy concerning the relative influence of heredity and environment. Attitudes can be and have been studied without any direct reference to their possible biological origins. There have been investigations, however, which have concerned themselves with this question of origins. Moore (*5*), for example, made an attempt to discover some relationship between radical and conservative attitudes on the one hand, and the supposed hereditary temperamental make-up of the individual on the other. The problem of race prejudice is sometimes stated in terms of a direct, biologically determined hostility or aggressiveness between different racial groups. In these cases we have not escaped the nature-nurture problem, and it would seem therefore that Allport's explanation of the popularity of the concept is only relatively, and not absolutely, correct. It seems more probable that the concept has come into such wide use in recent years because within its confines are included fundamental relationships to the problems of public opinion, propaganda, hostility between groups, economic rivalries, religious beliefs, and other issues of practical as well as theoretical importance in the field of social relationships.

Allport gives the following definition: "An attitude is a mental and neural state of readiness, organized through experience, exerting a directive or dynamic influence upon the individual's response to all objects and situations with which it is related" (p. 810). It connotes "a neuropsychic state of readiness for mental and physical activity"; that is to say, the presence of an attitude prepares the individual for a certain response. An attitude of hostility against the Negro, for example, predisposes the individual to participate in activities in which such hostility is expressed, whether it be merely the perception and recollection of unfavorable news items in the newspapers, the expression of arguments against the Negro, or actual participation in some violent overt act. Even when this person is engaged in some perfectly harmless activity which does not concern the Negro in any way, we still speak of him as having an anti-Negro attitude because of his readiness to respond in a hostile manner.

In connection with the formation of attitudes, Allport mentions four common conditions. There is first the accretion of experience, that is, the integration of numerous specific responses of a similar type. Our hypothetical anti-Negro, for example, may have had so much experience with Negroes as servants that he cannot accustom himself to seeing them in any other relationship. This is supplemented, in the second place, by individuation, differentiation, and segregation; further experiences make the attitude more specific, and distinguish it from other allied attitudes. A third possible cause of the formation of an attitude is a trauma or a dramatic experience. Again to take our hypothetical case, a particular crime committed by a Negro against a member of one's family may determine a hostile attitude; conversely, being saved from danger by a Negro may be responsible for a favorable attitude toward all members of the race. Finally, an attitude may be adopted ready-made by imitation of parents, teachers, playmates, etc. Allport does not decide the order of importance or of the frequency of these four conditions in the formation of attitudes. It is probable, however, that the last one named far exceeds the others in significance; as we shall see more clearly later, attitudes appear to depend much less upon individual experience than upon the ready acceptance of viewpoints already current in the community. It has been shown by Horowitz (6), for example, that some degree of discrimination against the Negro may be found in very young children under the influence of this mechanism. The problem then becomes one of understanding the origin and spread of these opinions in the community, in addition to the manner in which the individual integrates these with his own personality.

Another possible source of attitude formation should be considered in addition to those mentioned by Allport. The psychoanalysts have suggested that certain attitudes may be a direct or indirect reflection of family relationships; to take a specific example, anarchism or any other form of radicalism may be due to a revolt against authority in general, resulting from the revolt against the father in particular. Lasswell (7) has made use of this method of interpretation in his analysis of the life histories of radical leaders, and Fromm (8) has shown how the pattern of family authority may shape the reactions to political movements. There have been attempts to check this hypothesis in a quantitative manner. Klein (9) gave to seventy students a questionnaire scored for the frequency of extremely radical replies in connection with public issues, and another questionnaire dealing with antagonism against the father—fantasies of revenge, degree of suffering under parental discipline, feelings of fear, and so on. There was a correlation of +.60 between extreme radicalism and father antagonism. On the other hand Newcomb (*10*) found no clear relationship between parental antagonism and attitudes toward the Church and toward communism. More work in this field is therefore needed, although it should be kept in mind that the parental antagonisms may not be clearly verbalized by the subject, and as a consequence may not be brought out by the questionnaire. It seems certain that although the mechanism operates occasionally, it is not responsible for all cases of economic and political radicalism.

Allport indicates that it is possible to classify attitudes in various ways. A distinction may be made, for example, between positive and negative attitudes—those for and those against something. The definition of attitude by Bogardus (*3*) refers to it as "a tendency to act toward or against some environmental factor which becomes thereby a positive or negative value." It is probable, however, that there are many attitudes which cannot be classified in this manner. A second distinction is between specific and general attitudes. There has been some controversy as to the existence of the latter, some writers believing that attitudes are as numerous as the objects to which a person responds, but general attitudes may certainly be found as well. Still another distinction is that between common and individual attitudes, the former being roughly common to all persons "because they are based upon similar underlying conditions of inheritance, natural environment, and social influence. These are so fundamental that they are sometimes confused with instincts" (*1*, p. 826). This last confusion, incidentally, indicates that Allport is not quite correct in his assertion that the nature-nurture controversy does not enter into the study of attitudes. Common attitudes are not universal, however, and complete certainty of prediction is virtually impossible in social psychology because no one of these attitudes is free from many exceptions.

STEREOTYPES

In connection with the study of attitudes, the nature and the content of stereotypes are of the greatest importance. In his book on *Public Opinion,* Walter Lippmann (*11*) refers to the influence upon our behavior of these stereotypes or "pictures in our heads." Only part of our concept of an object consists of immediate or stored sense impressions. The rest is "filled out" with ideas about the class to which the object, perhaps on insufficient evidence, has been referred. Our concept becomes therefore a composite of the real and the imputed character of the object. As expressed by Stuart Rice (*12*), the "element in the composite which is pre-existent or stored—which does not consist of immediate sense impressions—may be regarded as a stereotype" (p. 54). It is clear that to certain groups or individuals the mention of a word like "Bolshevik" immediately brings up a certain fairly definite picture modeled largely upon cartoons current in our newspapers not so long ago, and corresponding little if at all to the truth. Similarly, the words "capitalist," "senator," "cowboy," "gigolo," as well as all terms referring to racial and national groups, elicit stereotypes the correctness of which has never been demonstrated.

In connection with the stereotype of the "criminal," there were several classical experiments performed by Sir Charles Goring (*13*), the British criminologist who led the opposition to the theories of Lombroso (*14*). The latter, as is well-known, believed that a criminal could be recognized by the presence of certain definite physical characteristics, spoken of as "stigmata of degeneration" (see Chapter XX). Without using the term "stereotype," Goring believed that some such mechanism was responsible for the belief in the criminal type. He had an artist draw from memory the portraits of a great many inmates of a penal institution in London. He made a composite photograph of these drawings, and found that this did look very much like the usual conception of the criminal. Then he took actual photographs of these same criminals and

made another composite photograph out of these. This
showed no trace of the familiar "criminal type," and was quite
unlike the one based upon the drawings. The effect of the
stereotype on the artist is clear. In another experiment he
asked a warden and a prison physician to rate the intelligence
of 300 convicts, and also to estimate roughly the height of
their foreheads. The results showed that those who were regarded as highly intelligent were also "seen" as having high
foreheads, and conversely, the unintelligent as having low
brows. The foreheads were then actually measured, and it
was found that as a matter of fact those who were judged to
be "unintelligent," "weak-minded" and "imbeciles" had on the
average higher foreheads than those who were judged "intelligent." Here the stereotype of the "high brow" as a concomitant of superior intellectual ability determined the judgments.
It may be added that a recent study by Sherman under the
direction of Clark Hull (15) showed a slight *negative* correlation between height of forehead and scholastic achievement.

A careful experimental study of stereotypes was made by
Stuart Rice (12), who used as his material nine portraits
which appeared in the *Boston Herald* for December 15, 1924.
These portraits were of Edouard Herriot, the French political
leader; James Duncan, then Vice-President of the A. F. of L.;
Leonid Krassin, the first Soviet Ambassador to Paris; Joseph
W. McIntosh, then Deputy-Comptroller of Currency; Martin
H. Glynn, a former Governor of New York State; Max Agel,
a bootlegger; Charles M. Schwab, the industrialist; Howard
Heinz of the 57 varieties; and Senator Pepper of Pennsylvania. In the first portion of the experiment, the subjects
were 141 students who were told which occupations were represented among the men whose photographs were shown to
them. If the photographs were identified entirely by chance,
there would be 168 correct identifications out of a possible
total of 1224. Actually, 337 identifications were correct, or
about twice as many as the chance expectation. The photograph of the Bolshevik Krassin yielded a result far below

chance, as his well-groomed appearance and short Van Dyke beard gave him an aristocratic air, quite different from the usual Bolshevik stereotype. The photographs of McIntosh and Pepper were also judged below chance, whereas all the others were judged better than chance. In the second portion of the experiment the subjects were Grange members and they gave similar stereotypes. The only important difference was that they showed a higher concentration of results, that is, greater agreement among the subjects and therefore greater strength of the stereotypes. The experiment as a whole has two interesting results, first, that stereotypes may and do distort judgments to a considerable degree, but second, that they are not mere chance products and that they do contain at least a germ of truth. The danger, of course, lies in the undue generalization and extension to all cases within a given category.

A study of racial stereotypes has been made by Katz and Braly (16). The ethnic groups were first ranked for preference by 60 students, with results somewhat similar to those obtained in earlier studies by Bogardus (17) and others. In a second part of the experiment one group of students listed what they regarded as the typical psychological characteristics of each race or nationality, a total of 84 traits being named in this manner. Another group of 100 students chose from this list the five traits which they regarded as the "most typical" of each of the ten racial groups. The investigators were interested in the definiteness of the stereotype as measured by the degree of agreement between the judges; they used as their measure the smallest number of traits of the five checked which had to be included to find 50% of the 500 checks made by the subjects. The possible range is therefore from 2.5 at the one extreme, indicating that every one of the subjects chose the same five traits for the same ethnic group, to 42 at the other, which means that all the 84 traits were used in the characterization of the group. The results were as follows:

Negroes	4.6
Germans	5.0
Jews	5.5
Italians	6.9
English	7.0
Irish	8.5
Americans	8.8
Japanese	10.9
Chinese	12.0
Turks	15.9

The first interesting result is that there appears to be little direct relation between the definiteness of the stereotype and the amount of prejudice against any group. The Negroes, with the most definite stereotype, and the Turks with the least, were both responded to unfavorably in the first portion of the experiment. The results cannot be explained in terms of familiarity either, since presumably the subjects were most familiar with Americans, who occupy an intermediate position. It is possible, however, as Murphy, Murphy, and Newcomb (*18*) suggest, that stereotypes are most definite toward nationalities with whom one's own group is or has recently been in conflict; least definite for distant and unfamiliar peoples; and intermediate for one's own and related groups. The investigators conclude that racial prejudice is a generalized set of stereotypes of a high degree of consistency which includes emotional responses to race names, a belief in typical characteristics associated with race names, and an evaluation of such typical traits.

Stereotypes may apply to individuals as well as to groups; we may have a "picture in our heads" of the essential characteristics of an individual which will affect our judgment of what he says and does. The experiment of Zillig referred to above (see p. 206) indicated that a favorable attitude toward certain children in a classroom situation determined the observers to "see" them as performing their tasks correctly when this was not the case. A similar investigation was carried out by Saadi and Farnsworth (*19*), who first submitted to their students a long list of names of well-known persons; from these, ten names were chosen as uniformly liked and ten others as uniformly disliked. The former group included Lindbergh, Aristotle, Einstein and Mark Twain; the latter, Al Capone, Aimee Semple McPherson and William Randolph Hearst. Thirty controversial statements were then presented to three other groups of students, each statement attributed to a liked name for one group, and to a disliked name for the second, and given to the third with no names whatsoever. The results showed, as we would expect, that the statements were most readily accepted when associated with a liked name, and least readily when associated with a disliked name. There were certain limits to the suggestibility of the students in this respect, so that a statement on military affairs coming from Einstein did not carry any special conviction, but in general the favorable and unfavorable stereotypes held. We have here again the phenomenon of prestige suggestion, working both in a positive and in a negative direction, on the basis of a preexistent stereotype.

It is hard to overestimate the strength and the importance of stereotypes. In the chapter on racial differences, for example, reference was made to the "discovery" by Bean (see p. 291) of certain characteristics of the Negro brain indicating its inferiority. It seems clear in the light of the negative results obtained in the more careful study by Mall that Bean was influenced by the "picture in his head" or stereotype of the Negro. The study by E. L. and R. E. Horowitz (see p. 207) (20) points in the same direction. When they presented pictures to White children and asked for an interpretation, the stereotype of the Negro entered to a considerable extent. For instance, when the children were shown an attractive house and grounds and asked what the colored woman was doing, many of them said she was cleaning up the place, although there was actually no colored woman in the picture. Given the stereotype of the Negro as a domestic servant, it was difficult for the children to imagine her in such a fine house in any other capacity. As we shall see later, the presence of an attitude of this type may play an important part in preventing any improvement in race relations on the basis of increased contact between two conflicting groups. It may result in a literal inability to see those things which conflict with the stereotype.

The part which words play in the formation of stereotypes is illustrated by an interesting experiment of Stagner's (*21*) on fascist attitudes. Stagner found that 73% of his subjects disapproved strongly of fascist Germany and its policies. At the same time many of the subjects made very favorable scores on a questionnaire which had been carefully prepared to include the actual components of fascism. Such word stereotypes may have an important influence upon the success or failure of various types of propaganda.

THE MEASUREMENT OF ATTITUDES

Thorndike's dictum (*22*) that "everything that exists, exists in some amount and can be measured," has been applied also to the question of attitudes. There have been many criticisms, particularly by sociologists, of the notion that something so intangible and at the same time so variable as an attitude can be measured. It is true that there are serious difficulties which must be faced, but several methods have been suggested and used which deserve careful consideration.

Allport (*1*) groups these methods into three main categories. There is first the simple census of opinions. Two groups may be compared in terms of the percentages favoring one alternative view or another. This method can be used only if the issue is stated in definite form and usually in terms of a simple choice between two alternatives. Comparisons may be made, for example, between two different sections of the country or two different student populations as to their attitude for or against collective security, increased immigration, a higher tariff, and other issues which permit a definite answer. The survey of student opinions on a variety of topics by Katz and F. H. Allport (*23*) and also the political polls by the American Institute of Public Opinion under the direction of George Gallup belong in this category.

A second method is by means of the construction of an a priori scale, that is to say, a scale ranging between two extremes, but constructed on a logical rather than an empirical basis. In this method the scoring is arbitrary and depends upon the investigator's judgment of what steps or intervals should be included. The best known example of this type is the Bogardus Social Distance Scale (17), which was constructed in order to measure racial attitudes. The subjects were asked to indicate on a scale at what "distance" they wished to keep members of various racial and national groups. At one end of the scale the groups were to be kept out of the country altogether, at the other, they would be permitted to intermarry with members of one's own family. The intervening steps included admission to the country, but not to citizenship; to citizenship, but not to one's own vocation, and so on. This type of scale involves the assumption that the acceptance of any one point automatically includes the other points below it.

A third type of scale is described as the psycho-physical or rational scale, and is mainly the result of the work of L. L. Thurstone (24). The usual procedure is to have all the statements in a scale arranged by a number of judges according to discriminable differences between the items. The psychophysical method of "equal-appearing intervals" has been made the model for the construction of this type of scale. Thurstone himself is responsible for a large number of different attitude scales, designed to measure attitudes on race, on socio-economic questions, on internationalism, on prohibition, etc.

The objections that have been raised against the measurement of attitudes are similar to those directed against the use of questionnaires in general. The problems of the reliability of the scale can usually be handled successfully, since care in the selection and phrasing of the items usually gives high reliabilities, by both the split-half and the repeat methods. The problem of validity is a much more serious one. We mean by validity the success with which the attitude scale measures what it purports to measure. This is usually taken to refer to the correspondence between what the subject describes as his attitude, and the actual overt activities in which he participates. To be more specific, a valid scale of attitudes toward the Negro would indicate from this point of view, not only how the subject *talks* about the Negro but also how he *acts* in the same connection. This approach would regard verbal behavior as significant only to the extent that it gives information about overt behavior. An alternative and more correct view would regard verbal behavior as important in its own right, since the attitudes of a person as expressed in his speech and in his writings may also have direct practical consequences for himself and for his social relationships. In that case the attitude scale would be valid if the subject told the truth as well as he could, and understood the questions correctly. Incidentally, the subject can falsify his actions just as he can his words.

It is important to know, however, whether the verbal and overt behavior are consistent, and many investigations have been directed to this end. The usual method has been to validate the scale against ratings by teachers and associates, and although this may often be the only method available, it has all the drawbacks inherent in the rating method. By far the better procedure is to validate against the actual stand taken by the subjects, or by the behavior which they have already exhibited. In some instances this can be done successfully. The validity of a scale for the measurement of economic radicalism, for example, may be indicated by its ability to differentiate between members of the Communist and the Republican parties. It may be possible also to validate a scale of attitudes toward the Negro by comparing the results with actual behavior in a mixed racial situation.

Stouffer (*25*) has attempted validation through a comparison of the results of a questionnaire on attitudes toward prohibition with corresponding items in the case histories of his subjects. The relationship was close; the validity coefficient, i.e., the correlation between the score on the attitude test and the composite ratings of the case histories by four judges, was +.81. Stouffer concludes:

Unless spurious factors entered to account for the agreement between the findings of the statistical and case history method, one would seem justified in concluding that, whatever it may be that the two methods were measuring, each measured substantially the same thing (quoted in Murphy, Murphy, and Newcomb, *18*, p. 909).

In this case, however, since the subjects wrote their own case histories, the validation is really of one form of verbal behavior against another. It seems fair to say that the correspondence between verbal and overt behavior has not been demonstrated for the attitude scales in common use, and the degree of this correspondence remains an important problem for further investigation.

Katz (*26*) makes an interesting suggestion for a possible use of attitude measurement as "the accurate and reliable recording of the ideologies or attributes of people." He regards this as the best method of arriving at the content of a culture, and believes it may be used as an adjunct to anthropological research. It has in his opinion many advantages over the usual approach, since anthropologists bring back a description of a culture as a whole, and tell very little of the range and frequency of the attitudes held by the individuals in the community. When any particular belief is mentioned as current among the members of a primitive culture, little is said about its extent, or about the number and variety of deviations from it. Katz is correct in his suggestion that a knowledge of the range of attitudes would add valuable material to the reports of the anthropologists. In actual practice, however, it is probable that the measurement of attitudes within a primitive culture will be beset by many more difficulties than a similar study in our own society. There will be not only the customary problems, but the additional one of stating the questions in terms sufficiently devoid of ambiguity so that they will have the same meaning to the subjects and to the investigator. The difficulty of placing oneself at the standpoint of another culture becomes intensified with the necessity of asking questions of all informants in exactly the same form. Some knowledge of the variations within a community would be gained, however, and would to some extent make up a definite deficiency in much anthropological writing.

Within our own society, attitude measurement may be used to indicate some of the phenomena of culture and cultural change. In an extensive investigation by Murphy and Likert (27) it was possible to give the same attitude scales to a group of college students at Columbia and Michigan in 1929 and again in 1934. The retest showed a general drift in the radical direction, more impressive in the case of the Columbia than the Michigan students. The change is, of course, important from many points of view, and the demonstration of its existence and its extent is made possible by the quantitative approach to attitudes and their distribution. It may be of interest to note also that there was a correlation of +.40 to +.50 between total scores for "internationalism" and "radicalism" on the one hand and college grades on the other. This is in agreement with the results reported in a number of previous investigations; for example, Moore and Garrison (28) found a very much higher proportion of the good students in the "radical" than in the "reactionary" group.

PROPAGANDA

In the field of the scientific study of attitudes the question of propaganda, which is essentially the technique of controlling attitudes, has taken a central place. In recent years it has played such an important part in political change and in governmental control over the individual in many countries, and especially in Germany, Soviet Russia and Italy, that it has acquired a significance far greater than ever before. In the United States it has also played an important part, probably more in the relatively harmless field of advertising than in the more dangerous one of political control, although there are signs of its increasing influence in the shaping of opinions over a wider area.

Lumley (29) points out that the term "propaganda" is related to the Latin "propagare," meaning to fasten down layers, shoots or slips of plants for the purpose of reproduction, hence to generate, reproduce, and generally to extend or increase. Etymologically, therefore, "propaganda is not a breeding that would take place of itself; it is a forced generation" (p. 186). Kimball Young (30) defines it as "the propagation of ideas, opinions and attitudes, the real purpose of which is not made clear to the hearer or reader" (p. 653). In the recent book by Doob (31), propaganda is described as "a systematic attempt by an interested individual (or individuals) to control the attitudes of groups of individuals through the use of suggestion and, consequently, to control their actions" (pp. 75-76).

In spite of its respectable etymological origin, the term "propaganda" is in bad odor. It suggests a manipulation of opinions for ulterior purposes. There is in many quarters, however, a frank recognition of its importance, and as is well known it has achieved a position of respectability in Germany where one of the most important members of the Government is titled "Minister of Propaganda and Enlightenment." In America it is customary to distinguish it from education, on the general ground that education is concerned with truth, whereas propaganda is indifferent to truth. Doob states that the essence of education is its objectivity in the light of the scientific truths prevalent at the time, whereas propaganda intentionally or unintentionally is an attempt to control the attitudes of the people. In this sense propaganda should receive a stigma only when its social effects are harmful. Whether propaganda is good or bad depends not upon the fact that it is propaganda, but on the uses to which it is put.

In practice, the distinction between propaganda and education is difficult to maintain. Freeman (32), in an interesting discussion of "impartiality," shows how in a text as harmless in appearance and as far removed from the social scene (apparently) as a book on arithmetic there may still be an unintentional manipulation of attitudes. He takes as an example Thorndike's *Arithmetic,* Book II, which appeared in 1917. In less than 200 pages, says Freeman, there are 643 problems which not only deal with, but accept and stress the concepts of capitalism and of our familiar commercial practices. These problems in one obvious way or another lay stress on commercial transactions depending upon the profit motive. There is selling, buying and re-selling, rent, working for wages, employing others for wages and interest on loans. As an indication of what he means by arithmetic problems which do not stress the profit motive and which therefore do not contribute to the perpetuation of attitudes favoring the present economic system, Freeman suggests the following. If a family needs fifteen dollars a week for food, but receives five dollars on the dole, what is the percentage of undernourishment? If in a southern cotton mill, one out of every hundred has pellagra, how many new cases will appear when the mill expands by one thousand employees? If in a modern war there were ten million combatants and two million casualties annually, what are the probabilities of remaining unscathed during four years of participation? "Books containing such problems, although they taught the abstract relationship of numbers as well as any others, would be dismissed as propagandistic and unworthy of the dignity of pure arithmetic" (p. 265). It goes without saying that Thorndike is here not accused of deliberate propaganda, but merely of taking for granted existing economic practices and unwittingly helping to keep them alive by the examples he uses. In this connection it is interesting to note that Russian educators have recently been disturbed by the frequency with which the profit motive has persisted in their arithmetic books, and have taken steps to make the necessary alterations in the direction of their own economic ideology.

This raises the general question as to whether the term "propaganda" is legitimately used in those cases in which there is no intention to control the opinions or attitudes of anyone. Is there any meaning, in other words, to "unintentional prop-

aganda"?   There is a legitimate difference of opinion on this
point, some writers contending that propaganda is defined by
its effect, and others by its motive.   In the interests of a satisfactory terminology it would seem advisable to use the word
in those cases in which there is a deliberate attempt to control
opinions and attitudes.   When this control is unwittingly
exercised the results may be the same, but the effect is accidental.

The Principles of Propaganda.   For this reason we are
not inclined to lay much stress upon the first among the "principles of propaganda," which Doob develops. This is termed
the Principle of the Intention of the Propagandist; Doob
states that "in intentional propaganda, the propagandist is
aware of his interested aim; in unintentional propaganda he
does not appreciate the social effect of his own actions" (p.
90).   This is as a matter of fact in conflict with Doob's own
definition of propaganda as a "systematic attempt" to control
attitudes.

The second principle is that of Perception.   "The propagandist makes his stimulus-situation stand out from its competing ground," that is to say, he wishes his message to be perceived and tries to give it some stimulus value which sets it off
from the general background of sense impressions in the environment of the individual at the time.   Various methods may
be used to accomplish this end.   Auxiliary attitudes may be
called in which have nothing to do with the final act, as when
an advertiser of tomato juice shows it being drunk by a pretty
girl; or the stimulus may be repeated many times to increase
the probability that it will be perceived, as when a radio an-
nouncer brings in the name of his product continually; or use
may be made of the principle of simplification, in which the
stimulus situation is simplified so as to bring it within the
range of the average individual, as when scientific statements
about the nature of vitamins are reduced to their simplest
terms in order to help sell a particular product.   These various
methods serve just as well in political as in advertising propaganda; the techniques of repetition and oversimplification are

being used by the German government to persuade the people
of the identity of their enemies.

The third principle is that of the Type of Propaganda.
"The propagandist employs any one or all of the following
types of propaganda, revealed, delayed revealed, and concealed propaganda." In the first of these, use is made of direct
suggestion, and the aim of the propagandist is clear from the
beginning. In delayed-revealed propaganda an interval of
time elapses which is presumably long enough to enable related and auxiliary attitudes to be aroused; for example, during a war the attempt may first be made to arouse patriotic
motives in general, and only later will young men be directly
induced to enlist. Although this was the aim in the first place,
it is not brought out into the open until the ground has been
properly prepared. In the concealed type, the propaganda is
indirect, and the propagandist refrains from stating his aim at
any time. This may be illustrated by the celebrations in honor
of Edison conducted by certain electric power companies, in
which the primary aim of persuading people to use electric
power was left to indirect suggestion.

There is fourth the Principle of Related Attitudes. "In the
process of suggestion, the propagandist arouses related attitudes that are instrumental in bringing about the desired integration." There are many ways in which this is done. Very
recently opponents of the Roosevelt administration, for example, have attempted to make use of the general attitude of
"fear of dictatorships" in order to win support for candidates
and a platform quite irrelevant to this issue. Similarly a
politician may try to win the favor of a group of lawyers by
telling them that their profession contributes to civilization,
or an automobile company may provide beautiful symphonic
music in order to attract favorable response to their product.
The propagandist may also vary the content of his stimulus-
situation to appeal to people of many different interests, as
when a hotel simultaneously advertises accessibility to the
downtown shopping district, a radio in every room, garage
facilities, etc.

A fifth principle is that of the Desired Integration. "The propagandist secures a desired integration that predisposes people toward his aim." This should really be expressed as a hope rather than as a method, since of course the desired integration or activity does not always follow. In this connection Doob discusses the theory of Biddle (33) to the effect that the desired action may be brought about by a process of emotional conditioning. If, for example, the florists wish to increase their sales they develop Mother's Day and relate the thought of purchasing flowers to existing emotions attached to the mother. Biddle believes that "theoretically any emotion can be drained off into any activity by skillful manipulation." It is Doob's contention, on the other hand, that it is only when the two emotions are related that any conditioning occurs; in other cases, the secondary stimulus-situation has value only in attracting attention. In the familiar example of the pretty girl drinking tomato juice, Biddle would expect the favorable attitude towards the attractiveness of the girl to determine a favorable attitude to the tomato juice; Doob would regard her function as that of making certain that the tomato-juice advertisement is perceived. Both points of view appear to be correct in part. Biddle's idea that any emotion can be drained off into any activity is undoubtedly extreme; on the other hand, if the tomato-juice advertisement were presented in a particularly unattractive or even repulsive setting, it would probably be perceived without any difficulty, but the desired integration would certainly not follow. The girl undoubtedly functions both as a method of attracting attention and of arousing a favorable attitude. In summary and criticism it may be said that this principle of the Desired Integration should really not be listed with the others, which refer to methods, whereas Integration or action is rather the goal. Several of the other principles describe the means used to achieve the Desired Integration.

The sixth principle is that of the Sphere of Unpredictability.

Before the desired integration is achieved between the related attitudes and, except in the case of concealed propaganda, the comprehension of the propagandist's aim and before it leads to action, there is a sphere of unpredictability due to the temporal character of the propaganda, the presence of competing propagandists, and the complexity of the person in the group with which the propagandist must deal.

Various methods are suggested for reducing this unpredictability and for making it more probable that action in the desired direction will take place. The phenomenon of prestige suggestion, for example, is very important in this connection, and may enter through the use of slogans or objects of positive social value, such as the American flag, "100% American," etc., or by creating the impression of universality—"everybody's doing it." In the case of groups which have complete control of all the organs of propaganda the sphere of unpredictability may be reduced by limitation of the kind of material available to the individual, as in the German censorship not only of their own newspapers and radios but also of foreign sources of information. Unpredictability may also be reduced by means of primacy, that is to say, by reaching children at a very early age before conflicting integrations can possibly be formed; early education by the Catholic Church or by the Nazi and Communist parties are instances of this technique. There can be little doubt that the earliest impressions are the most stable and the most difficult to eradicate, and any system of propaganda which achieves such an early start is difficult to combat.

Doob's seventh principle is that of Counter-propaganda. "The propagandist uses counter-propaganda when conflicting attitudes tend to prevent the desired integration from emerging." It is not enough for the German propaganda to be pro-Nazi; it is also anti-communist, anti-Jew, anti-democratic, and these negative suggestions with reference to outside groups and organizations help to solidify the more positive ones toward the Germans. It is reported that leaders of Nazi meetings have been instructed to let no occasion pass without attacking something, the idea apparently being that the in-group is strengthened by clear and definite denunciation of the enemy. This principle is used in a somewhat different manner in advertising; cigarette manufacturers, for example, employ counter-propaganda against the notion that smoking is harmful, shortening the wind, etc. Here the advertising in many cases stresses as virtues those effects which contrast directly with the arguments usually directed against smoking.

Finally Doob mentions the Principle of Persuasion. "The propagandist uses persuasion as a supplementary method." Persuasion here refers to the process of getting some prominent person to endorse a particular program or product in the expectation that the prestige suggestion will attract very many followers. In the case of advertising, the prominent movie actress who endorses a cosmetic preparation is usually "persuaded" to do so by some direct material gain; in other cases a program of propaganda may be required to persuade the individual before his name in turn may be used to propagandize others.

We have discussed these principles at some length, because they represent the most logical and systematic attempt so far made to reduce propaganda to its essentials. They are equally applicable to many different fields, and in spite of the criticisms which may be leveled against the details, the principles are of help in the understanding of what happens when attempts are made to mold and modify the opinions of others.

There arises the important problem of the limitations which are to be placed on the possible effects of propaganda. Many who have witnessed the occurrences in Germany have come away with the feeling that propaganda is all-powerful. There can be no doubt that its use there has been directed with a thorough efficiency which it would be difficult to overestimate. As Freeman (32) expresses it:

As far as the technique of procedure goes, the psychologists can have nothing but admiration for the attempt to create a mystical communion of racial, political, religious, and industrial elements. Whatever one may think of the uses to which this enthusiastic communion is put, the procedure is psychologically sound so far as it goes (p. 335).

The fact remains, however, that the efficient propaganda campaign of the Nazis in Germany is only part of the reason for their success. The historian who wishes to understand the factors which were responsible for the Third Reich will have to take into consideration the whole political and socio-economic condition of Germany in 1933. The defeat in the World War, the humiliating conditions of the Versailles Treaty, the multiplicity of political parties and the consequent frequency of elections, the gradually lowered standard of living, the tragic effects of inflation—all prepared the way. Without them, and without the actual use of force, it is not probable that the propaganda would have achieved its goal. In the absence of efficient propaganda, on the other hand, the exact nature of the "solution" to these problems might have been quite different, and Hitler would probably not have had the support which finally persuaded Hindenburg to appoint him Chancellor. In other words, propaganda can be successful only under certain conditions, and with a state of readiness for it in the pre-existing attitudes of the people. This still leaves to it a tremendous influence in modifying these attitudes and directing them into certain channels rather than into others.

The growing concern of American social scientists and educators concerning the dangers of propaganda in this country is indicated by the founding of the Institute of Propaganda Analysis in 1934, with headquarters at Teachers College, Columbia University, and with Professor Clyde R. Miller as director. An official statement of the aims of the Institute describes it as "a non-profit corporation organized to assist the public in detecting and analyzing propaganda." It has issued many publications designed for this purpose, and although its success cannot be adequately gauged as yet, there can be no doubt that it represents an important step in the right direction.

The Experimental Modification of Attitudes. There have been many experimental investigations of the possibility of modifying attitudes. These have usually taken the form of giving to the subjects an attitude questionnaire, presenting to them controlled educational or propaganda material, and retesting after a period of time in order to determine what changes have taken place. One of the earliest studies of this type is that of Young (34), who had his students rank various groups before and after a course in race relations, and found little change. During the Manchurian "incident" Chen (35) presented pro-Chinese and pro-Japanese propaganda to student groups, and measured attitudes before and after the presentation. He found a definite though not very large change in the direction of the propaganda in each case. As was pointed out in connection with Suggestion, certain individuals reacted in the opposite direction from that which was expected, that is to say, became more pro-Chinese after being exposed to Japanese propaganda. This raises the important problem in this whole field of the nature of the audience. Unless a great deal is known about one's subjects, the results may be quite unpredictable. In connection with socio-economic attitudes a study by Rosenthal (36) showed some change in a pro-communist direction after the presentation of moving pictures illustrating slums and riots in America, and wonderful facilities for recreation and healthful living in Russia; in this case also, many subjects reacted in the opposite manner to that indicated by the propaganda.

The effect of moving pictures on attitudes has been studied by Thurstone (37) in a series of experiments. The five films used included one favorable to, and one unfavorable to the Chinese, a pro-German film, an anti-gambling film, and one illustrating the evils of bootlegging. The subjects were high school children in small towns not far from Chicago, and they answered the attitude questionnaires before and after seeing the pictures. In the case of the pro-Chinese film the change was 16.98 times its P.E.; the other pictures were not quite so effective, but in their case also some change was reported. Two films with the same type of propaganda were more effective than one, and three were more effective than two. Thurstone reports that most groups retain a large percentage of the change after intervals of time varying from 2½ to 19 months.

There have been many attempts to modify racial attitudes by experimental techniques. Reference has already been made to Young's study. Droba (38) found no significant change in attitude among a group of college students who had had a course on the Negro. Schlorff (39), on the other hand, gave to two equated groups of high school students a Social Distance Scale, and then exposed the experimental group to a modified curriculum "to increase tolerance toward the Negro." The topics included the Negro's origins and his history, his contributions, the prejudice against him, and so forth. The Negro was placed lowest on the Social Distance Scale at the beginning of the experiment, and retained that position for the control group. The experimental group, however, on the retest ranked the Negro above the Portuguese, Greeks, Russians and Hungarians.

After summarizing these and other studies, Murphy, Murphy, and Newcomb (18) suggest this hypothesis:

Instruction regarding a single race does not significantly change attitudes as measured on a scale involving that race only, nor does instruction regarding several races produce changes in the rank positions assigned to those races; but instruction concerning one race may significantly change the rank position of that race among others (p. 952).

A different technique was used by F. T. Smith (40) in his study of the modifiability of racial attitudes. Instead of merely telling his subjects, who were 46 Teachers College students, about Negroes and the reasons for developing a more favorable attitude toward them, he exposed them to two consecutive week-ends in Harlem. With the co-operation of Negro artists, writers and business men, he showed his White subjects the inadequacy of their stereotypes and brought them into contact with Negroes of a kind quite foreign to their previous experience. The change was much more marked than in the other experiments, and shows the great advantage of this over a purely verbal or "passive" propaganda.

It should be kept in mind that these studies cannot tell us a great deal about the limits of the experimental modification of attitudes. Material used by a single investigator is presented for a brief time only and is usually not repeated. Few of the principles of propaganda discussed above enter to any considerable degree. There can be no primacy, for example, since the work is usually done upon adults or older children who already have a varied background of experiences and attitudes. There can be no elimination of counter-propaganda emanating from other sources, nor is there much use of repetition in order to make perception certain. In other words, the laboratory situation is a weak imitation of that which obtains when the agencies of propaganda are all under the control of a central government body, or backed up by the resources available for a large advertising campaign. If therefore any positive results, no matter how slight, are obtained by the experimental techniques used, they bear testimony to the far greater power of propaganda when employed under optimal conditions.

In connection with the study of attitudes, the problem of the origin and meaning of race prejudice occupies so important a place in social relationships as to require careful and detailed consideration.

SUMMARY

An attitude is defined as a state of readiness for certain types of response. It may be adopted ready-made by imitation of others, or it may be due to personal experiences of various kinds. It expresses itself frequently in the form of a stereotype or "picture in our heads" which may have a marked influence upon perception and behavior; such stereotypes may apply to single individuals or to groups.

Attitudes have been measured in various ways, including (1) the simple census of opinions, (2) the construction of an *a priori* scale, and (3) the psychophysical or rational scale. Attitude scales usually have high reliability, but their validity constitutes a problem. One form of validity refers to verbal behavior alone, and this may frequently be attained; another form refers to the correspondence between verbal and overt behavior, and this has rarely been demonstrated. Attitude measurement may be useful in indicating in a quantitative manner some of the phenomena of social change, for example, increase or decrease in economic radicalism, racial prejudice, and so on.

The control or manipulation of attitudes is known as propaganda. It is usually distinguished from education, which is concerned with truth, whereas propaganda is indifferent to truth; in actual practice this distinction is often difficult to maintain. The principles of propaganda include those of (1) the Intention of the Propagandist, (2) Perception, (3) Type of Propaganda, (4) Related Attitudes, (5) Desired Integration, (6) Sphere of Unpredictability, (7) Counter-propaganda, (8) Persuasion. Propaganda has great influence in modifying attitudes, but it can be successful only under certain conditions. Experimental studies of the possibility of affecting attitudes have in general yielded positive results, although the changes have usually been of a small order of magnitude.

REFERENCES

1. Allport, G. W. "Attitudes," *Hdbk. Soc. Psychol.* (ed. by C. Murchison). 1935.

2. Thomas, W. I., and Znaniecki, F. *The Polish Peasant in Europe and America.* 5 vols. 1918-20.

3. Bogardus, E. S. *Social Psychology.* 4th ed. 1923.

4. Folsom, J. K. *Social Psychology.* 1931.

5. Moore, H. T. "Innate Factors in Radicalism and Conservatism," *J. Abn. and Soc. Psychol.*, 1929, 35: pp. 220-238.

6. Horowitz, E. L. "The Development of Attitude toward the Negro," *Arch. Psychol.*, 1936, No. 194.

7. Lasswell, H. D. *Psychopathology and Politics.* 1930.

8. Fromm, E. *Autorität und Familie.* 1936.

9. Klein, E. "The Relation Between One's Attitude to His

Father and His Social Attitudes," *Unpublished Master's Essay,* Columbia University, 1925.

10. Newcomb, T. M. *Unpublished study.* See Reference *18.*

11. Lippmann, W. *Public Opinion.* 1922.

12. Rice, S. A. *Quantitative Methods in Politics.* 1928.

13. Goring, C. *The English Convict.* 1913.

14. Lombroso, C. *Crime, Its Causes and Remedies.* 1911.

15. Hull, C. L. *Aptitude Testing.* 1928.

16. Katz, D., and Braly, K. "Racial Stereotypes of 100 College Students," *J. Abn. and Soc. Psychol.,* 1933, 28: pp. 280-290.

17. Bogardus, E. S. "A Social Distance Scale," *Sociol. and Soc. Res.,* 1933, 17: pp. 265-271.

18. Murphy, G., Murphy, L. B., and Newcomb, T. M. *Experimental Social Psychology.* Rev. ed. 1937.

19. Saadi, M., and Farnsworth, P. R. "The Degrees of Acceptance of Dogmatic Statements and Preferences for Their Supposed Makers," *J. Abn. and Soc. Psychol.,* 1934, 29: pp. 143-150.

20. Horowitz, E. L., and Horowitz, R. E. "Development of Social Attitudes in Children," *Sociometry,* 1937-38, 1: pp. 301-338.

21. Stagner, R. "Fascist Attitudes: an Exploratory Study," *J. Soc. Psychol.,* 1936, 7: pp. 309-319.

22. Thorndike, E. L. "The Nature, Purposes, and General Methods of Measurement of Educational Products," *Yrbk. Nat. Soc. Stud. Ed.,* 1918, 17: pp. 16-24.

23. Katz, D. and Allport, F. H. *Students' Attitudes.* 1931.

24. Thurstone, L. L. "The Method of Paired Comparisons for Social Values," *J. Abn. and Soc. Psychol.,* 1927, 21: pp. 384-400; "Theory of Attitude Measurement," *Psychol. Rev.,* 1929, 36: pp. 222-241.

25. Stouffer, S. A. "An Experimental Comparison of Statistical and Case History Methods of Attitude Research," *Unpublished Ph.D. thesis,* University of Chicago, 1930.

26. Katz, D. "Attitude Measurement as a Method in Social Psychology," *Soc. Forces,* 1937, 15: pp. 479-482.

27. Murphy, G., and Likert, R. *Public Opinion and the Individual.* 1938.

28. Moore, G., and Garrison, K. C. "A Comparative Study of Social and Political Attitudes of College Students," *J. Abn. and Soc. Psychol.,* 1932, 27: pp. 195-208.

29. Lumley, F. E. *The Propaganda Menace.* 1933.

30. Young, K. *Social Psychology.* 1930.

31. Doob, L. W. *Propaganda.* 1935.

32. Freeman, E. *Social Psychology.* 1930.

33. Biddle, W. W. "A Psychological Definition of Propaganda," *J. Abn. and Soc. Psychol.*, 1931, 26: pp. 283-295.

34. Young, D. "Some Effects of a Course in Américan Race Problems on the Race Prejudice of 450 Undergraduates at the University of Pennsylvania," *J. Abn. and Soc. Psychol.*, 1927, 22: pp. 235-242.

35. Chen, W. K. C. "The Influence of Oral Propaganda Material upon Students' Attitudes," *Arch. Psychol.*, 1933, No. 150.

36. Rosenthal, S. P. "Changes of Socio-economic Attitudes under Radical Motion Picture Propaganda," *Arch. Psychol.*, 1934, No. 166.

37. Thurstone, L. L. "Influence of Motion Pictures on Children's Attitudes," *J. Soc. Psychol.*, 1931, 2: pp. 291-305; "The Effect of a Motion Picture Film upon Children's Attitude toward the Germans," *J. Ed. Psychol.*, 1932, 23: pp. 241-246.

38. Droba, D. D. "Education and Negro Attitudes," *Sociol. and Soc. Res.*, 1932, 17: pp. 137-141.

39. Schlorff, P. W. "An Experiment in the Measurement and Modification of Racial Attitudes in School Children," *Unpublished Ph.D. thesis*, New York University, 1930.

40. Smith, F. T. "An Experiment in Modifying Attitudes toward the Negro," *Unpublished Ph.D. thesis*, Teachers College, Columbia University, 1933.

CHAPTER XIV

RACE PREJUDICE

INTRODUCTION

THE title of this chapter is in certain respects misleading. The type of group conflict which is usually termed "race prejudice" does not necessarily occur between groups with distinct physical features (see Chapter XI). In the United States the prejudice against the Negro may be regarded as racial, but even in this case it extends to many persons who are much less Negro than White, and who differ very little "racially" from the majority group. The hostility against the Oriental on the West Coast may also be expressed in terms of race. On the other hand, the prejudices of non-Jew against Jew, of American-born against immigrant, of one religious group against another, show essentially the same psychological phenomena even though race in the strict sense plays no part. Prejudice has been explained in many ways, and from many different points of view.

THE "CONSCIOUSNESS OF KIND"

One group of theories of the origin of prejudice lays stress upon a consciousness of kind, a feeling of solidarity with those like oneself and an accompanying "dislike of the unlike." It is the American sociologist Giddings who is mainly responsible for this concept and its use as a principle of explanation (1). The philosopher Royce (2) also spoke of a "natural antipathy" against those who differ from us. A similar point of view is expressed in the distinction between the in-group and the out-group, as well as by Sumner's (3) reference to ethnocentrism, or the feeling of loyalty to one's own group and of hostility against all who threaten it in any way.

374

The phrase "consciousness of kind" has little practical meaning until the term "kind" is adequately defined. Until we know, for example, the basis of similarity or likeness, we cannot use it as the explanation of actual group hostilities. The most common interpretation is the identification of kind with race, and the "high visibility" of the Negro or the ease with which he is recognized, is often mentioned as a sufficient reason for the prejudice against him. This is certainly an oversimplification. It is much more likely that the external visible characteristics are merely made the excuse or the occasion for the manifestations of a pre-existing prejudice.

The case of the Jews makes this clear. In spite of the fact that a certain proportion among them may be recognized as such, it remains true that in a very large number of cases they cannot be distinguished from the non-Jews among whom they live. As was indicated in Chapter XI, American and British anthropologists do not regard the Jews as a distinct race, and usually explain this degree of recognizability on the basis of cultural and social factors. Even Houston Stewart Chamberlain (4), who was certain of the existence of a distinctive Jewish race, admitted the frequent difficulties of identification, and fell back upon a childlike intuition as a means to that end. He wrote:

Very small children, especially girls, frequently have a quite marked instinct for race. It frequently happens that children who have no conception of what "Jew" means, or that there is such a thing in the world, begin to cry as soon as a genuine Jew or Jewess comes near them. The learned frequently cannot tell a Jew from a non-Jew; a child that scarcely knows how to speak notices the difference (Vol. I, p. 537).

As is well known, visibility can be artificially manufactured when it does not exist in nature. During the Middle Ages Jews were required to wear a distinctive cloak, sometimes marked with a yellow badge, so that they could be easily recognized. A recent German edict requires Jews and Jewesses to use distinctive personal names for the same purpose. There were of course many cases in which Jewish identity was unknown until brought to light by the painstaking investigations of the authorities. The fact that there is no Jewish race and no dependable visibility does not lessen the severity of the prejudice.

Even between groups of different racial characteristics a consciousness of kind may not always be presumed to exist. Pearl Buck tells an interesting story about being informed by her little daughter that a lady wished to see her. "Is it a Chinese or an American lady?" she asked. "I don't know, Mother," was the reply, "I didn't ask her." Mrs. Buck's explanation is that in a social environment in which racial differences mean nothing, they simply go unnoticed. Perhaps the child did notice the features of the visitor, but did not classify them in the usual manner. This experience has been duplicated by many persons who have had intimate contact with another race, the members of which then become distinguishable as individuals rather than as an alien group.

We live in a society in which skin color has been made the basis for distinguishing between groups, and in consequence we notice differences of this kind more readily than others. As was pointed out previously, however, at least one anthropologist, Sergi (5), regarded shape of the head as a more significant characteristic. Fouillée (6), a French writer, went so far as to say that in the future millions would be at each other's throats because of one or two points difference in their cephalic index. If this point of view were generally accepted, we would in all probability notice first the head shape of a new acquaintance instead of the color of his skin. Visibility depends largely on habit.

A special turn to the theory of the dislike of the unlike has been given by Embree (7) and Reuter (8), who interpret it as a kind of narcissism. It is because we like and admire ourselves so much that we react with hostility against those who differ from us. This still leaves open the question as to what kinds of differences between individuals are important, and what criterion we are to use for likeness and unlikeness.

The best indication, however, that dislike of the unlike is not a natural but an acquired trait comes from the fact that it is entirely absent in young children. Even in those parts of the South in which the color line is most rigidly drawn, there is the most intimate association between children of both races until that is prevented by parents or teachers. An observation by Horowitz (9) is pertinent here. During the investigation of race relations in a small Tennessee community, it was noticed that not only did White and Negro children play together until the former were forbidden to do so, but that they even attempted to continue the friendships in spite of parental opposition. There were many instances in which the White children had to be punished more than once before they finally accepted the mores of the group. In the sociometric studies of Moreno (10) in which children in school were asked which of their classmates they would like to have seated next to them, there was no noticeable racial cleavage in the first three or four grades; here, too, it is evident that prejudice is acquired and is not native to the child. This result proves clearly that the theory of the instinctive nature of racial hostility has no basis in fact.

It has often been suggested that the dislike of the unlike may express itself in connection with cultural rather than physical differences. It is probably true that in some cases a difference in folkways and in values may create certain misunderstandings that contribute to hostility. Lafcadio Hearn (11) goes so far as to suggest that the contrast between the emotional folkways of the Japanese and the Whites has played a large part in developing hostility between them, the Japanese smile appearing to the Whites to be insincere, whereas the White face in turn seems to the Japanese to be in a state of constant irritation. This is rather a small point upon which to base racial hostility, although it may play a part in individual cases. In general, cultural differences do not afford a satisfactory basis of explanation. In the South there appears to be the greatest hostility between Negroes and poor Whites between whom cultural differences are at a minimum, and the extent to which Jews in Germany identified themselves with German culture and made their contributions to it did not protect them from the development of animosity.

To the psychologist the whole notion of dislike of the unlike fails to carry conviction for the reason that most individuals show a desire for new experience, and curiosity and interest in what is novel. This tendency should at least counteract some of the opposition which Giddings regarded as natural under these conditions. Finally it should be kept in mind that between two scientists, let us say, of different race, we would expect more consciousness of kind than between either of these and a day laborer of the same race. We cannot use the concept without further definition, and this further definition removes from it any exclusively racial significance.

Ethnocentrism is a fact, in the sense that we do regard ourselves as belonging to one group, and that we usually show a certain amount of hostility against others. Huxley and Haddon (12) write: "A 'nation' has been cynically but not inaptly defined as a 'society united by a common error as to its origin and a common aversion to its neighbours'" (p. 5). This may have nothing to do, however, with any biological affinity, since we know of many instances both among animals and human beings in which the in-group is composed of dissimilar elements. Several examples of this were mentioned in Chapter II. In this same connection Murphy, Murphy and Newcomb (13) point out that dogs of very different breeds may in puppyhood become so friendly that dogs of their own kind are "outsiders." The same has been shown for ringdoves reared with carrier pigeons and for a goose reared with a crow. Among human beings also, "unless barriers imposed by social stratification are present, friendships as deep as any can grow where there is physical dissimilarity" (p 43). These authors suggest that the major clue to the formation of these in-groups is familiarity, but it must be understood that this does not always overcome the effect of pre-existing lines of demarcation established by society.

A final reason for rejecting this theory as an explanation of race prejudice is that it is by no means present in all groups. Hooton (*14*) states:

Primitive peoples are probably not race conscious to the deplorable or laudable extent which is characteristic of civilized populations. I mean that they are rather naively free from race prejudice until they have learned it from bitter experience. The American Indian was quite ready to take the European literally to his arms until he found out that a civilized embrace was inevitably throttling (p. 143).

This of course does not mean that primitive groups never showed hostility against outsiders, but this hostility did not take a racial form, and apparently was just as frequently directed against those who were physically similar to themselves. It is probable that in most cases there was fear of the unfamiliar, rather than dislike of the unlike.

NATIVE AGGRESSIVENESS

The notion of the instinctivist psychologist that pugnacity or aggressiveness is a part of human nature has recently been revived in somewhat different form by the psychoanalysts. Freud speaks of a "death instinct" as referring to a universal need to express hostility against someone, and recently Menninger (*15*) has used it also as an explanation of many cases of suicide, in which the aggression, although ostensibly directed against oneself, is really a means of revenge against some other person.

Other psychoanalysts, although accepting the notion of the existence of these aggressive tendencies, find their explanation in the actual life experiences of the individual. Franz Alexander (*16*), for example, believes that the early experiences of childhood create such emotional tensions that most individuals in later life tend to develop greater resentments and aggressions than are warranted by their actual life situations. A frequent result is projection of the hostile aggression upon others, that is to say, an ascription to others of the aggressive attitudes held by oneself. As Alexander puts it, "it is not that *I* hate *him*, it is not that *I* want to attack *him*, but *he* hates *me* and *he* wants to attack *me*. This projection leads to fear and mistrust of others and eventually to hate and supposedly self-protective aggressions" (p. 810).

This interpretation, which has direct implications for the problem of racial hostility, is applied by Dollard (*17*) to the question of Negro-White relations in the South. He accepts the notion that in all individuals there is frustration due to the very fact of growing up in a culture. There are many things which the child is not permitted to do and the resulting frustration calls into action an aggressive tendency. It is probable that as a consequence every mature person carries some generalized hostility toward his environment, but is unable to find a legitimate object on which the hostility may be directed. The aggressive tendencies are kept in check by the folkways of the group as well as by a direct fear of punishment. In the case of the southern White, however, there is presented in the person of the Negro a socially acceptable means for the expression of this latent hostility. "It is suggested that, when society does indicate an object, like the Negro whom one may detest with a good conscience, much of this irrational affect is drained off" (p. 442). In this case the visibility of the Negro serves as a sign which tells the prejudiced person whom to hate and makes easy and consistent discrimination possible.

This approach, in spite of its wide use by psychoanalysts and others who have been influenced by them, is in reality based upon a circular argument. It takes for granted the existence of the very phenomenon which it presumably sets out to explain. If society does indicate the Negro as a legitimate object of hostility, that hostility must be there before it may offer to the Whites a satisfactory outlet for their latent aggressiveness. We cannot make use of the concept of latent aggressiveness in order to explain race prejudice, and at the same time assume the existence of the race prejudice to start with. We are left with the fundamental problem of explaining how the race prejudice originated, and how it happened to be there as a socially acceptable means of draining off the stored hostility.

Dollard's theory, therefore, is not to be accepted as an explanation of the existence of race prejudice. It may, however, to a certain degree account for the variations in its intensity. Even when racial hostility exists in a society, it is not present equally in all regions or in all individuals. It seems highly probable that where frustration has been great and the opportunities for self-expression negligible, there would be a greater readiness to seek that outlet for aggressiveness of which Dollard speaks. This probably accounts for the fact that acts of violence against the Negro in the South are committed not by the propertied classes, but by those whose economic level is barely above that of their victims. It may also account for the fact that hostility against the Jew developed in a Germany which had acquired a violent aggressiveness due to frustration in the World War and in the ensuing peace. This leads us, however, to an interpretation of race prejudice not in terms of the psychological mechanisms operative in the individual so much as in the political and socio-economic conditions prevailing in the community or in the region. This approach will be developed more extensively below.

The theory of aggressiveness as a *native* trait is even less acceptable as an explanation of the phenomenon we are here discussing. The Freudians have made use of this concept not only to account for race prejudice, but also as a basis for the understanding of war as well as of class conflict. War, at least from this point of view, becomes inevitable. In our discussion of warfare and aggressiveness in connection with the classical instinct theory, we had occasion to point out not only that there are many communities in which war is unknown, but also that when it does occur adequate causes are usually to be found in the general life conditions in the social and geographical environment. Aggressiveness appears to be an effect and not a cause. As for class conflict, it seems highly probable that the underprivileged are influenced more by the actual inequalities and their consequences than by a native impulse to kill and to destroy. This is by no means a denial of the strength of aggressiveness as a motive in individual cases, nor of its possible influence in the behavior of whole communities or groups, but it is a denial of its universality and innate character.

PERSONAL EXPERIENCES

Another type of approach sees in race prejudice the result of individual experiences. In the discussion of Allport's theory (*18*) of the formation of attitudes, it was pointed out that three of the four conditions mentioned refer to personal experiences, either of a long-continued or a traumatic nature. Allport admits, however, that they may be conditioned by the acceptance of pre-existing attitudes current in the community. In the study by Lasker (*19*) of the development of racial attitudes, many cases are cited in which individuals explain their racial dislike and preferences in terms of their own experience with members of a particular race. A distinguished professor of sociology accounts for his own favorable attitude toward Norwegians as the result of his pleasant memories of a childhood nurse.

This whole approach is made explicit in the suggestion by House (*20*) of a method for the study of race relations.

. . . it is in the experience of individuals, their *subjective* experience as known to them and susceptible of being reported by them, that the data for the study of race relations . . . may be found. In other words, race relations, conceived as cultural, may profitably be studied from "life-history" documents, or by the method of "case-study," in the best scientific sense of the term (p. 3).

This method can help to answer such questions as how are the attitudes which are the elements of race relations formed? How are the cultural characteristics and reciprocal attitudes of Whites and Negroes changing?

It is highly probable that in the case of many individuals personal experiences may play a definitive part in the formation of attitudes. It is also probable that the study proposed by House would yield valuable information as to the manner in which individuals consciously react to members of other races, and as to regional and community differences, and the changes which have taken place in this respect. It would be of little value, however, for the discovery of the motives underlying the prejudice or of its exact origin.

This is indicated by the results of one of the experiments on "social distance" by Bogardus (*21*), to which reference has previously been made. The results showed that the students had the greatest prejudice against the Turks, although actually most of them had never seen a Turk, and had had no experiences which could account for their attitude. In his analysis of the reasons for the attitudes, Bogardus mentions first the acceptance of traditions and current opinions, second the personal experiences of childhood, and third the personal experiences of adult life. There can be no doubt that in the case of the Turks, at least, personal experiences played no important part. The investigation was conducted at a time when the stories of the Armenian massacres were receiving much space in the newspapers, and when the notions of the brutalities of the "unspeakable Turk" were prevalent. Without any direct knowledge of their own, the students who were subjects in these experiments merely adopted the current stereotypes.

Another example of the existence of prejudice apart from any direct personal experience is given by Bilgray (*22*), who was one of the guides at the Jewish Exhibit at the Chicago World's Fair in 1933. He writes that visitors stared openmouthed at the replica of the synagogue, and requested in a whisper to see the knives used for sacrifice. Some of them wished to know whether Jews really sacrifice children before the Passover. Many stared at him because they had never seen a Jew before. A village pastor from northern Wisconsin said: "I have been teaching the Gospel for 30 years and I have often mentioned the Pharisees; but until now I never knew what a Pharisee looked like. When my congregation asked me whether there were any Pharisees left, I told them I had heard there were some in New York" (p. 176).

The discussion of stereotypes in the preceding chapter has also indicated the frequent discrepancy between the actual experience and the "pictures in our heads." It has shown too that the presence of these stereotypes actually interferes with the acquisition of new experiences, frequently predetermining what we shall see and hear. It means little that many people think their attitudes are conditioned by their experiences, since we are in so many cases unaware of the sources of our attitudes. At most we may say that these personal experiences play a part in determining individual variations in the degree of prejudice, but they certainly do not account for its origin.

RATIONALIZATIONS

Among the mechanisms which the psychoanalysts have brought to our attention, none is more important in the present connection than that of rationalization. There seems to be in most of us a definite urge to give good reasons in support of our attitudes or behavior, though these reasons may not be the true ones. In the field of race relations this means in practice that the exploitation of a weaker group by a strong one is always justified by the latter, either in terms of the characteristics of the weaker people, or on the grounds that they will be benefited thereby. As Hooton (*14*) expresses it:

Man incessantly seeks to compromise with his conscience or with his innate humanitarianism, by rationalizing his predatory behavior. He must convince himself that the act of grabbing is somehow noble and beautiful, that he can rape in righteousness and murder in magnanimity. He insists upon playing the game, not only with an ace up his sleeve, but with the smug conviction that God has put it there (p. 151).

A survey of the historical material pertinent to the problem of ethnic contacts supplies a great many examples of this mechanism. When the Spaniards first came to America, several of their apologists, particularly Quevedo and Sepulveda, supplied them with the proper excuses for taking the land away from the Indians, and for treating them with complete lack of consideration. They developed the theory that the Indians had an entirely different origin from that of the Spaniards, that they were not human in the same sense, and that there was therefore no need to accord to them the same treatment as to one's fellow human beings. The familiar refrain of the "White Man's Burden," which was mainly of British manufacture and found its literary expression in the writings of Carlyle, Froude, Kingsley, and most recently and clearly in those of Kipling, made of imperialism a noble activity destined to bring civilization to the benighted members of other races. What the British stood to gain as a result was never mentioned. Almost exactly the same mechanism is at work at the present time in connection with the Japanese invasion of China (1939). The Japanese have asserted that this is purely to benefit the Chinese, who do not realize that it is to their advantage to live under Japanese authority. There are undoubtedly a great many idealistic Japanese who completely accept this explanation, and even outside of Japan it is not always recognized as a rationalization.

One of the best examples is the case of the Chinese on our own West Coast. Schrieke (23) has collected many of the descriptive phrases applied to them during the course of their residence in California. In the beginning, the Chinese were among "the most worthy of our newly adopted citizens," "our most orderly and industrious citizens," "the best immigrants in California"; they were spoken of as thrifty, sober, tractable, inoffensive, law-abiding. They showed an "all-round ability" and an "adaptability beyond praise." This was at a time when the Chinese were needed in California. Most of the White immigrants from other parts of the United States were anxious to make money quickly; they had no patience with domestic labor or with working in cigar factories or making boots and shoes. The Chinese were welcomed into these occupations, particularly during the hectic gold-rush period. Then came competition in the fields which the Chinese were occupying. In the elections of 1867 both political parties pledged themselves to enact legislation protecting Californians against Mongolian competition. The following phrases were now applied to the Chinese—"a distinct people," "unassimilable," "keeping to their own customs and laws," "they did not settle in America," "they carried back gold to their homes," "their presence lowered the plane of living," "they shut out White labor." They were spoken of as clannish, dangerous because of their secret societies, criminal, secretive in their actions, debased and servile, deceitful and vicious, inferior from a mental and moral point of view. They smuggled opium and spread the use of it, and Chinatowns were full of prostitution and gambling. They were "filthy and loathsome in their habits." They were "undesirable as workers and as residents of the country" (pp. 10-12). Here is an instance of a diametrical change in the alleged characteristics of a group without any actual change in the nature of the population. There were no new personal experiences to account for the contrast. There was no increase in native aggressiveness on the part of the White group. There was no heightening of an instinctive consciousness of kind. There was, however, a change in the economic conditions in California which made it to the advantage of the Whites to eliminate the Chinese as a factor in competition, and the attitude toward them was an effect of this situation.

Strong (*24*) points out an essentially similar mechanism operating in the case of the Japanese at a time when hostility against them had developed in California.

Every significant thing about the Japanese, whether favorable or unfavorable, was seized upon and twisted about until it made a suitable weapon for injuring the newcomers. Hence, if they asked less than the going wage, they were threatening the American standard of living; if they demanded better wages, they were avaricious; if they were successful in farming and saved enough to buy their own ranch, they were driving the whites out; if they were unsuccessful, they were "wearing out the land" (p. 125).

Recently a careful study of the place of rationalization in group antipathy has been made by LaPiere (*25*) in the case of Armenian immigrants to Fresno County in California. LaPiere states correctly that it is safe to disregard the explanation given by the members of an in-group for their antipathy toward the members of an out-group. Such explanation is in his opinion more in the nature of a justification than a reason for antipathy. It was alleged, for example, that the Armenians are "dishonest, lying, deceitful," but the records of the Merchants' Association give them as good a credit rating on the average as Americans. The Armenians were described as "parasitic," but they apply much more rarely for charity to the County Welfare Bureau. They were also said to have an inferior code of social morality and to show frequent cases of social friction, yet they appear in fewer legal cases than their numbers would lead one to expect. La-Piere concludes: ". . . these explanations for the antipathy towards the Armenians have this in common: they point to a cultural difference between the in-group and the out-group. But all have this further trait in common as well: they are not verifiable; in fact, they are definitely false" (p. 236).

In the case of the Negro many different types of rationalization have been used. The customary excuse for not giving to Negroes an equivalent occupational status to that of the Whites is that the Negro is constitutionally inferior. Charles Johnson (26) cites in this connection the fact that during slavery many skilled mechanical tasks were in the hands of Negro slaves, whose masters were quite content to entrust them with this work. After Emancipation, there was competition between Negroes and Whites for paid positions of this type. There followed the gradual growth of the idea that Negroes are fitted only for the simplest manual tasks and that complicated mechanical activity is outside the scope of their intelligence.

Rationalizations also play an important part in lynching. Many southerners, while deploring its occurrence, speak of it as a necessary check to the attacks of Negro men upon White women. They give the impression that actual or attempted rape is by far the most frequent cause of the lynchings. It has been shown, however, in a recent careful investigation (27) that out of 3724 people lynched between 1899 and 1930, four-fifths of whom were Negroes, there were actually fewer

than one-sixth who were accused of rape. This crime therefore can hardly be the cause of the lynchings. It should be
added that cases of rape occur even less frequently than this
would indicate, as it is certain that in many instances the
charge is false.

In the case of European immigrants to this country, the
hostility of the "hundred-percent Americans" usually expresses
itself less violently, but quite as clearly as in connection with
the Negro. It is illuminating to note the recurrence of this
same attitude even though the racial and the national composition of the immigrants may differ widely with the passage of
time. There is a tendency (28) to hold our immigrants responsible for a great deal of the crime of the country and to
regard them as representing the lowest elements in their respective mother countries. One reason given is that the character of the migration has changed in recent years and that at
least until the latest immigration restrictions, the "inferior"
countries of southern and central Europe were contributing a
major share. As Schrieke (23) points out, however, in the
early days of immigration there was also apprehension when
the "bands of homeless, houseless mendicants" from Ireland
invaded the country, and "the deluge of paupers from Germany," "the sweepings of English poor-houses and prisons"
were deposited upon American shores. In a speech before the
House of Representatives during the immigration debate of
1924, Congressman Meyer Jacobstein said:

You contend that the present foreign element is less desirable than
that of forty, fifty, sixty years ago. I call your attention to a report made to the House by a select congressional committee in
1838. It charged that "the country is being flooded with the out-
casts of the jails, almshouses, and slums of pauper-ridden Europe."
It asserted that at the time the jails of the capital were filled with
these foreign-born people. It described them as "the most idle and
vicious classes, in personal appearance most offensive and loathsome." But who were these "offensive and loathsome paupers and
criminals"? Why, they were the scrappy Irishmen and Germans
and British whose children today fear the influx of new "foreign
hordes" (29, p. 136).

Still earlier, in a letter dated May 9, 1753, Benjamin Franklin expressed his opinion of the Germans who were then migrating into Pennsylvania.

Those who come hither are generally the most stupid of their nation, and as ignorance is often attended with great credulity, when knavery would mislead it . . . it is almost impossible to remove any prejudice they may entertain. . . . Not being used to liberty, they know not how to make modest use of it. . . . I remember when they modestly declined intermeddling with our elections; but now they come in droves and carry all before them (*29,* p. 134).

Earlier still it was the Irish who were the objects of the hostility of the previous settlers. By 1720 there were many Irish in Massachusetts, and the General Court passed an ordinance directing that "certain families recently arrived from Ireland be warned to move off" (*30,* p. 89). The hostile attitude against the Irish was by no means restricted to this period, and it has flared up on many occasions throughout American history.

These various incidents show that in all probability it is not the characteristics of the immigrants which cause them to be disliked, but rather that those characteristics are ascribed to them which give the dislike an apparent justification. There may of course be differences in folkways which cause a certain degree of suspicion and distrust, but it is unlikely that these by themselves could ever lead to open and violent antagonisms. From this point of view it is illuminating to observe that the very groups which are scorned on their first arrival quickly join in the hostility against any newcomers.

The case of prejudice against the Jew is complicated by a succession of religious and historical factors which differentiate it in many respects from hostility against other groups. The phenomenon of rationalization is, however, as patent in this case as in any other. In Germany in particular there has been a series of explanations given, none of which is substantiated by fact. The Nazis have, for example, identified the Jews with communism, and have asserted that the communist "menace"

in Germany was largely a Jewish product. It has been pointed
out many times, however, that in the last free election in Germany in 1932 the communists obtained 5,980,240 votes,
whereas the total Jewish population—men, women and children—was barely 600,000. There was only one Jewish communist out of 89 in the pre-Nazi Reichstag. These facts do
not prevent the ascription to the Jews of responsibility for
opposition to the Nazis, not only in Germany but in the rest
of the world as well. Further than that, the Jews are condemned both for being communists at the one extreme and
capitalists on the other, so that as in the case of the Japanese
on the West Coast, whatever they do is held against them.
One other explanation given in Germany for the new anti-
Semitism is the alleged influx of Jews from eastern Europe
since 1918; the figures show, however, that there was actually a decrease in the number of Jews in Germany in 1925 as
compared with 1910, and only a slight increase since that time
(31). The further fact that the prejudice was directed against
all Jews no matter what their origin, and even against many
persons with so little Jewish blood as to be unaware of it,
shows that neither the number nor the characteristics of eastern European Jews could be responsible for the outbreak.

In connection with the Jews more than with any other
minority group, the presence of alleged racial characteristics
of behavior and mentality is frequently held responsible for
the hostility. Whatever these characteristics may be, it is
clear from our previous discussion in Chapter XI that we cannot regard them as racial or hereditary. First, the Jews are
not a race and their behavior cannot be explained on a racial
basis. Second, the so-called Jewish characteristics are by no
means universally found among Jews, and the hostility still
extends to those who show no trace of them. Finally, and
most important, the characteristics of the Jews as of other
minority groups are much more probably the effect than the
cause of prejudice. If it is true, for example, that aggressive
behavior manifests itself more frequently among Jews than
others, by far the most probable explanation is to be found

in the need for self-assertion in a group that has been kept in a subservient position. The same phenomenon appears among southern Negroes who experience for the first time the relative freedom of the North. If it is true that Jews play a comparatively large part in radical movements, this is certainly not due to any special genes for radicalism in their heredity, but is a reaction against a socio-economic system in which they have been oppressed. Even the economic distribution of the Jews, and their preponderance in the cities, are to be explained by the former legal restrictions against their ownership of land and their resulting concentration in trade and the professions. The suggestion by Browne (32) that de-urbanization would be a solution of the Jewish problem confuses the cause with the effect. At the most it may be said that a redistribution of the Jews would have a slight palliative effect. As in the case of other minority groups it is not likely that the behavior or the psychological characteristics of the Jews have very much to do with the hostility which is directed against them. These factors may in some cases help to keep the prejudice alive, but they cannot be regarded as responsible for its origin.

It is frequently suggested that the Jewish case is peculiar because of the religious issues involved. The story of the Crucifixion is part of the education of all Christian children, and it is sometimes told in such a way as to leave the impression that the Jews were responsible; the resulting attitude of hostility may never be overcome. Even this, however, presupposes some prejudice in the interpretation, since otherwise the decisive part played by the Romans, and the Jewishness of Jesus, could be emphasized. Here, too, there has been confusion between cause and effect.

THE BASIS OF PREJUDICE

The question remains as to the true causes of the prejudice which underlie the good reasons, or rationalizations, submitted in justification. It seems clear that prejudice exists because something is to be gained by it. In the examples given, the

gain which emerges most clearly and unmistakably is the economic. The attitudes of the Spanish Conquistadores, of the
British to the "White Man's Burden," of the Americans to the
Orientals on the West Coast, may all be explained in terms of
a direct economic gain resulting from the exploitation of a
weaker group or from its elimination as a factor in competition. Economic factors play a dominant part also in Negro-
White relations, the Negro being kept in a position of inferiority so that he will not become an active rival of the Whites.
As Dollard (17) points out, there have been frequent cases of
aggression against Negroes entirely as a consequence of their
economic success, even when they are willing to "keep their
place." As for the Jews in Germany, the economic motive
for their suppression is clear; long before the Nazis came into
power they promised their followers the jobs held by the Jews,
and to a certain extent that promise has been fulfilled. Owing
to the relatively small number of Jews in the country the
Nazis were forced to extend the concept of "Jew" to those
who were unable to prove a pure "Aryan" ancestry as far
back as January 1, 1800, in order to increase the possible
economic rewards to their supporters. The actual expropria-
tion of Jewish wealth is a further step in the same direction.
Although the economic motive may not be the only one, it is
probably the most important factor determining the origin
and the extent of prejudice. Where the weaker group has
"high visibility," as in the case of the Negro or the Oriental,
physical characteristics serve as a convenient distinguishing
mark between the members of the two groups; they indicate
at a glance those whom one may with impunity eliminate from
the field of competition. Where there is no such visibility, as
in the case of the Jews, the same purpose may be obtained by
other means. The underlying motive of the dominant group,
although not realized by all its members, is to appropriate
the best positions and the greatest wealth for itself.

A second purpose served by prejudice is allied to the economic motive, but sufficiently distinct from it to deserve special attention, namely, finding a scapegoat to blame for all

hardships and calamities. This mechanism is probably clearer in the case of anti-Semitism than in any other variety of prejudice. In a recent play by S. N. Behrman, *Rain from Heaven,* one of the characters is a German expatriate who has been forced to leave the country for writing a pamphlet, "The Last Jew." He says:

With the extermination of the Jews, the millennium has been promised the people. And with the efficiency of a well-organized machine the purpose is all but accomplished. They are all dead— but one—the last Jew. He is about to commit suicide when an excited deputation from the All-Highest comes to see him. There has been a meeting in the sanctum of the Minister of Propaganda. This expert and clever man has seen that the surviving Jew is the most valuable man in the Kingdom. He points to the Council their dilemma. Let this man die and their policy is bankrupt. They are left naked, without an issue, without a programme, without a scapegoat. The Jews gone and still no millennium. They are in a panic —till finally a committee is dispatched—and the last Jew is given a handsome subsidy to propagate. . . .

The economic motive underlying the need for a scapegoat is illustrated in a story reported by Gessner *(33).* Two German workers are reading an official bulletin. "I see where another anti-Jewish campaign begins on Monday," says one. The other replies, "That means another wage-cut on Saturday." They knew from experience that if conditions became worse so that another wage-cut was necessary, the blame would again be placed upon the Jews.

It is perhaps unnecessary to state that the writer is not using these stories and anecdotes to prove, but rather to illustrate, the scapegoat theory. There can be little doubt that this mechanism plays an important part in many of the manifestations of group hostility. Gessner has made a strong case for the theory that the famous forgery known as *The Protocols of the Elders of Zion* was published anew whenever a scapegoat was needed. It appeared in Russia in 1905 to prove that the Jews were responsible for the disaster of the war with Japan; in 1919 in England at a time of severe industrial distress; in 1921 in Damascus in connection with Arab-Jewish riots; and it was outlined in twenty pages of *Mein Kampf* to aid the campaign of the National Socialists.

The intimate relationship between economic conditions and the need for a scapegoat is indicated by the material on lynching collected by a southern sociologist (*27*). There appears to be a close correspondence between the level of real wages and the success of the cotton crop on the one hand, and the number of acts of hostility against southern Negroes on the other. When conditions are bad someone must be blamed for them, and the Negroes are convenient victims. It is difficult to know whether this is a conscious program, but the relationship is there. Hovland and Sears (*34*) computed the annual per acre value of cotton for 14 southern states for the years 1882 to 1930. The correlation between this index and the number of lynchings in these same 14 states was —.67, i.e., the aggression increased as the economic frustrations became more severe. This type of correspondence has been analyzed in detail by Gallagher (*35*).

The scapegoat mechanism does not always have a direct economic basis. It has frequently been used as a means for re-establishing feelings of national self-importance. Not only in the Germany of our own generation, but also in France after the defeat of 1870 there was the need to find someone to blame for the disaster. As Barzun (*36*) points out, the insecurity and relative helplessness of the French were expressed in the wave of anti-Jewish feeling which followed the Dreyfus Affair, and which was extended at times to include Protestants, atheists, Freemasons and all foreigners.

The Dreyfus affair . . . exhibited the full force of racial hysteria that we have come to associate with Nazi Germany. The only difference was that the anti-Semitic, anti-foreign, anti-Protestant group did not fully control the government (p. 206).

Indirectly, however, a case might be made for economic motives underlying all these expressions of group hostility. War itself in our complex society is certainly to a large extent the result of economic competition between nations, and it is probable that the exaggerated nationalism which is often the direct cause of conflict has originally an economic basis. The aftermath of war, with the resulting feelings of insecurity in the vanquished and the accompanying manifestations of hostility against minority groups, must also be ascribed to an original economic situation.

It must be kept in mind, however, that even those attitudes which are basically economic in origin acquire a dynamic quality of their own which results in their continued existence long after the economic causes have ceased to function, and that they may actually operate in a direction opposed to economic self-interest. As an example of the latter type, we have the refusal of southern White merchants to give to prospective Negro customers the title of "Mr." or "Mrs.," even though this refusal may alienate their patronage. It should be added, however, that as yet the economic loss resulting from this attitude has been slight, and it may be that greater buying power on the part of the Negro will do a great deal toward altering this form of behavior.

There is one other gain which may result from the existence of race prejudice or a "caste" situation, namely, the sex gain. In the contact between two different groups the usual pattern is for the men of the stronger to have access to the women of the weaker, and to resist violently any attempt by the men of the weaker group to obtain reciprocal privileges. As Dollard (17) and others have pointed out, this is the typical pattern in race relations in the South. "It may indeed be one of the functions of the caste situation to keep the Negro woman without a protector and therefore more accessible" (p. 146). It is difficult to estimate the importance of this gain in keeping the caste situation alive, but it undoubtedly enters to some degree.

In summary we may state that prejudice exists because there is something to be gained by it. This gain is usually directly economic, in that it eliminates the competition of members of the minority group and makes it easier for those of the dominant group to obtain jobs or advancement. It may also serve as an instrument in the hands of those in authority to persuade the people that a minority group is responsible for all of their misfortunes. It may similarly be the means of restoring feelings of security and self-confidence to those who have suffered defeat and failure, by providing a group to whom they may feel superior and of whom they may take advantage with impunity.

THE ELIMINATION OF PREJUDICE

In the light of this analysis, it seems clear that prejudice will continue just so long as it serves the interests of the dominant group. Its elimination, therefore, would seem to require some fundamental change in the socio-economic structure so that one person's success need not necessarily be at the expense of another's failure. In a society based upon competition, every excuse will be seized upon to reduce the possibility of failure. One such excuse is "race," and attention has been focused upon racial characteristics so as to reduce the fear of the competition of minority groups. If there were no competition there would be no need for such excuses, and physical differences between groups would not have the importance usually ascribed to them. The fact that in Soviet Russia the destruction of the capitalist economy appears to have been accompanied by the practical disappearance of the prejudice against minority groups is evidence in this direction.

It is important for students of social psychology to concern themselves with the possibility of modifying group antagonisms even under present conditions. There is hope in the fact that there are many individuals brought up in a "democratic" competitive society who feel little or no prejudice against members of groups different from their own. A careful study of their life histories might reveal certain characteristics of their education or family traditions which would explain why they do not share the common practice of using racial prejudice to decrease competition against themselves. There are similar variations between whole groups and nations which also indicate the possibility of a marked reduction in the amount of prejudice in a competitive society. As Bilden (37) has indicated, there is very much less prejudice against the Negro in Brazil than in the United States, and race mixture is countenanced to an extent unheard of in our own country. The same is true of the attitude toward Orientals in Hawaii as contrasted with California; Romanzo Adams (38) suggests that the marriage of many of King Kamehameha's White advisers to the Hawaiian ladies of his court set a pattern of interracial friendliness which extended to other racial groups as well. With some relatively rare exceptions, there is substantial equality between the racial groups on the Hawaiian Islands, and intermarriage has taken place there to an almost unprecedented extent.

Even as between France and England, the attitude toward Negroes differs markedly. In a comparative study by LaPiere (39) of race prejudice in these two countries, it was noted that out of 360 people questioned in France, 279 of them were apparently free from prejudice; the figures for England were 14 out of 315. Out of 31 French hotels, 24 admitted Negroes, whereas only 4 out of 20 English hotels admitted Negroes. LaPiere was careful to make the comparison between people of similar socio-economic status in the two countries. It may be added that the difference in French and English attitudes extends also to the colonization policies of the two countries, and that there has been much more intermarriage in the French than in the British colonial Empire. Bunche (40) indicates that this does not prevent the same degree of exploitation of African Negroes by the French as by the British administrators. As far as race is concerned, however, the French attitude is undoubtedly less prejudiced.

This means that there are customs and folkways with regard to race which create regional and national differences not understandable in terms of economics alone. To that extent they are subject to change even under relatively constant economic conditions. In our previous discussion of propaganda and the experimental modification of attitudes we saw evidence to the effect that even within a relatively short space of time and under limited laboratory conditions, a certain amount of change might still take place. If we could apply the principle of "primacy" of which Doob (*41*) speaks, so that relevant material on race would be presented to children at an early age, and followed up by the use of all available educational techniques in the field of race relations, it is probable that the effect would be substantial. In this field, perhaps more than in any other, the greatest possible care and intelligence are required in order that the effect may not be opposite to that in the mind of the propagandist or educator. In this connection the story is told of a group of children in a church school who had been studying the Negro, his history and his contributions to American life. At the conclusion of the period the teacher asked a 15-year-old girl who was a member of the class to lead in prayer. "She thanked God for the contributions of the Negro, enumerating them in some detail, and then concluded, 'Teach us to be tolerant and to keep the Negro in his place' " (*19,* p. 4).

Even under the best conditions, however, education may be expected to act only as a palliative, which reduces the severity of the disease, but does not really cure the condition. To continue with the medical analogy, the patient is not the person who has the prejudice, but the society in which he lives, and it is in the last analysis the sick society which requires treatment. As Lowenthal (*42*) expresses it:

. . . hatred and intolerance can never be banished, together with all the wanton miseries they provoke, until we can distinguish between men and their environment, until we can understand that the real enemies of humanity are not human beings—not members of sects, races, or nations—but social systems which breed and perpetuate injustice and exploitation (p. x).

In this whole field we have seen that what appears to be the psychological problem of the formation of attitudes within individuals cannot be understood in psychological terms alone. The existence of prejudice is not primarily a psychological problem, but a socio-economic one. Certain aspects of it, as, for example, individual differences in the nature of attitudes, their experimental modification, the conscious experiences or the unconscious rationalizations with which they are accompanied, constitute fields of investigation with which the psychologist may legitimately concern himself. A complete analysis, however, requires a consideration of historical backgrounds, of folkways, of regional and national traditions, of the sociological make-up of the community, and of the economic currents and cross-currents operative within it. In this area more than in any other it is impossible to draw a line between the preoccupations of the psychologist and those of other social scientists, and it is only a combined approach which will yield an adequate and comprehensive analysis of the whole phenomenon of prejudice.

SUMMARY

The type of conflict referred to as race prejudice is found between groups which differ from one another in various ways; it is not limited to distinct races. The explanation in terms of a natural antipathy must be rejected, primarily because an awareness of difference may be absent in those individuals who have not learned from others that the differences are to be taken seriously, and also because in-groups are frequently formed independently of physical characteristics. The notion of a native aggressiveness which finds an outlet in group hostility is also unsatisfactory. It is highly probable, however, that when frustrations are great, there is more readiness to engage in aggressive behavior, and fluctuations in the amount of group hostility may be accounted for on this basis.

Personal experiences may explain prejudice in some cases. More frequently, the attitudes of hostility against certain groups are taken over ready-made from the social environment. The standing of the Turks on the Social Distance Scale is evidence in this direction. It seems certain that in a large number of instances the nature of one's experiences with members of another group will be determined by the pre-existing attitude, rather than the attitude being determined by the experiences.

The reasons given for hostility against a particular group are commonly rationalizations. Many examples of this mechanism are available, including the White Man's Burden, the opposing characteristics ascribed to the Chinese on the West Coast, the alleged dishonesty of the Armenians, the assumption of Negro incapacity to do skilled labor, the justification of lynching because of the incidence of sex crimes, the identification of German Jews with communists, and so on. These rationalizations may be employed in order to justify economic exploitation, to find a scapegoat for one's misfortunes, to reestablish feelings of self-importance, in some cases also because of the sexual gains involved. Prejudice exists because there is something to be gained by it.

For this reason, prejudice may be completely eliminated only in a socio-economic system in which one person's success or security is not dependent upon another's failure. At the same time, the variations in the degree of prejudice found between different individuals in the same society, as well as between two different societies with approximately the same economic structure, indicate that education and training may reduce the amount of group hostility, even though they cannot succeed in eliminating it completely. *

REFERENCES

1. Giddings, F. H. *The Principles of Sociology.* 1896.
2. Royce, J. *Race Questions, Provincialism and Other American Problems.* 1908.
3. Sumner, W. G. *Folkways.* 1906.
4. Chamberlain, H. S. *The Foundations of the Nineteenth Century.* 2 vols. 1911.
5. Sergi, G. *L'Uomo, secondo le origini, l'antichità, le variazioni e la distribuzione geografica.* 1911.
6. Fouillée, A. *Tempérament et caractère selon les individus, les sexes et les races.* 1893.

7. Embree, E. R. *Brown America.* 1931.

8. Reuter, E. B. *The Mulatto in the United States.* 1918.

9. Horowitz, E. L., and Horowitz, R. E. "Development of Social Attitudes in Children," *Sociometry*, 1938, 1: pp. 301-338.

10. Moreno, J. L. *Who Shall Survive?* 1934.

11. Hearn, L. *Glimpses of Unfamiliar Japan.* 2 vols. 1894.

12. Huxley, J. S., and Haddon, A. C. *We Europeans.* 1936.

13. Murphy, G., Murphy, L. B., and Newcomb, T. M. *Experimental Social Psychology.* Rev. ed. 1937.

14. Hooton, E. A. *Apes, Men and Morons.* 1937.

15. Menninger, K. A. *Man Against Himself.* 1938.

16. Alexander, F. "Psychoanalysis and Social Disorganization," *Amer. J. Sociol.*, 1937, 42: pp. 781-813.

17. Dollard, J. *Caste and Class in a Southern Town.* 1937.

18. Allport, G. W. "Attitudes," *Hdbk. Soc. Psychol.* (ed. by C. Murchison). 1935.

19. Lasker, B. *Race Attitudes in Children.* 1929.

20. House, F. N. "Some Methods of Studying Race and Culture," *Soc. Forces*, 1936, 15: pp. 1-5.

21. Bogardus, E. S. *Immigration and Race Attitudes.* 1928.

22. Bilgray, A. T. "Alas, Poor Goy," *Hebrew Union College Monthly.* Oct., 1933.

23. Schrieke, B. *Alien Americans.* 1936.

24. Strong, E. K., Jr. *The Second-Generation Japanese Problem.* 1933.

25. LaPiere, R. T. "Type-Rationalizations of Group Antipathy," *Soc. Forces*, 1936, 15: pp. 232-237.

26. Weatherford, W. D., and Johnson, C. S. *Race Relations.* 1934.

27. Raper, A. F. *The Tragedy of Lynching.* 1933.

28. Armstrong, C. P. "Juvenile Delinquency as Related to Immigration," *School and Soc.*, 1933, 38: pp. 61-64.

29. Feldman, H. *Racial Factors in American Industry.* 1931.

30. Reilly, A. J. "Irish Americans," *Our Racial and National Minorities* (ed. by F. J. Brown and J. Roucek). 1937.

31. Tenenbaum, J. *Races, Nations and Jews.* 1934.

32. Browne, L. *How Odd of God.* 1934.

33. Gessner, R. *Some of My Best Friends Are Jews.* 1936.

34. Dollard, J., et al. *Frustration and Aggression.* 1939.

35. Gallagher, B. G. *American Caste and the Negro College.* 1938.

36. Barzun, J. *Race: A Study in Modern Superstition* 1937.

37. Bilden, R. "Brazil, Laboratory of Civilization," *Nation*, 1929, 128: pp. 71-74.

38. Adams, R.　*Interracial Marriage in Hawaii.*　1937.

39. LaPiere, R. T.　"Race Prejudice: France and England," *Soc Forces,* 1928, 7: pp. 102-111.

40. Bunche, R. J.　*A World View of Race.*　1937.

41. Doob, L. W.　*Propaganda.*　1935.

42. Lowenthal, M.　*The Jews of Germany.*　1936.

Part Five
PERSONALITY

CHAPTER XV

THE PROBLEM OF PERSONALITY

INTRODUCTION

THERE is considerable difference of opinion as to the extent to which problems of personality fall within the scope of the social psychologist. Theories range all the way from that of Berman (*1*) or Kretschmer (*2*), who see personality as determined by inherited body constitution, to F. H. Allport's (*3*) view that personality traits are entirely social, and that a hermit has no personality. As is usual in controversies of this kind, the truth probably lies somewhere between these extremes. It will be clear in what follows that the writer inclines more to a social than to a biological interpretation, but without going so far as to adopt Allport's position. Granting that what we call personality emerges mainly in a social situation and in terms of reactions between individuals, the fact remains that two hermits are not exactly alike and that they have some individuality in spite of their isolation. Biological factors undoubtedly play a part in shaping the individual, and they require the attention even of those psychologists whose concern is mainly with the social aspects of personality.

There have been many definitions of personality, and many different uses to which the term has been put. G. W. Allport (*4*) lists a total of 50 different ways in which the words "person" and "personality" have entered into our common speech; with original meanings derived from the use of "persona" as a theatrical mask, the terms have been extended to the physical self, to a moral ideal of perfection, to legal relationships, to esthetic qualities of attractiveness, and to many other uses, popular as well as academic. Among more recent and more

important definitions there are several which regard personality as the sum total of innate and acquired dispositions; this
usage is rightly criticized on the ground that the individual
is not a mere addition, but represents some form of integration or organization.   Allport suggests the following: "Personality is the dynamic organization within the individual of
those psycho-physical systems which determine his unique adjustments to his environment."   The word "unique" deserves
special emphasis; what we mean by personality is what makes
one individual psychologically different from every other.

In that sense, everyone has personality.   When popularly
we say "he has personality," we usually mean that he has some
positive quality which makes his presence felt by others, or
which makes him attractive to others.   May's (5) suggestion
than an individual who has "personality" is one whose presence or absence "makes a difference" to the group, is apparently an extension from this popular view.   He would presumably ascribe "personality" in this sense equally to the individual who is heartily disliked as to the one who is liked by
others.   This is a step in advance of the popular concept; we
would go further and insist that a person whom no one notices
still has personality in the same sense as anyone else.   There
is something in him as an individual which describes him,
which marks him off from others, even though he may have
little social stimulus-value.   The great differences in the "attractiveness" or "noticeability" of individuals are important
and demand the attention of psychologists, but they are not
part of the definition of personality.

The psychology of personality stresses the uniqueness of the
individual, and as such must be directly concerned with the
phenomenon of individual differences.   This was, however, the
subject matter of Chapter IX, and a word is needed to distinguish between the two approaches.   In the field of Differential Psychology, the individual is really not considered as
such, but rather in his relationship to the characteristics of
the population to which he belongs.   The interest is focused on
the nature and the causes of the variations, rather than upon

the individuals who vary. The findings deal with measures of central tendency, of range, of variability, of shape of the distribution curve, and so forth, but tell us nothing about the individual persons who have been measured and whose scores contribute to the total picture. It is true that in the studies of twins in connection with the nature-nurture controversy, case histories of individual twins are presented, but more for their bearing on the general argument than in order to throw light upon the twins as persons. It is the psychology of personality which re-discovers the individual, and makes him the center of attention.

The term "character" which in popular use is sometimes identified with personality, has a definitely moral connotation. It may be described as personality evaluated. Although this distinction should be kept in mind, it is true that early descriptions of differences in character constitute one of the important introductions to the study of personality. In the work of Theophrastus (6), for example, there is a delineation of character in terms of the dominant trait of typical individuals, and the characters are labeled the Flatterer, the Boor, the Loquacious Man, the Penurious Man, and so on. There is shrewd observation and literary skill in the descriptions, but no attempt to penetrate to the underlying factors responsible for these characteristics. The best-known imitators of Theophrastus were Earle (7) in England, and La Bruyère (8) in France. The latter in particular realized the greater complexity of his subjects and came close to an understanding of the total integration of a great many different motives and attitudes instead of drawing a simple unified picture. Although they may have started from the interest in moral evaluation, these characterologists approached the standpoint of the whole personality, and in that sense represent important forerunners of the more modern interpretations.

A distinction must also be made between personality and temperament. The latter term may be defined as an habitual emotional attitude; G. W. Allport (4) describes it as consisting of the characteristic phenomena of an individual's emotional nature. He adds that it is largely hereditary in origin, but this is debatable. It is usual to begin any discussion of temperament by reference to the famous doctrine of the Four Temperaments attributed to Hippocrates and Galen. These four are the Sanguine, the Choleric, the Melancholic and the Phlegmatic. The terms used indicate the belief that temperament is to be explained in terms of the preponderant influence of one or other of the body fluids or "humors"—the blood, the bile, the black bile and the phlegm, respectively. In this sense the theory may be regarded as foreshadowing the more recent approach in terms of the endocrine glands. The fact that these terms are used is, however, no proof that the true basis of temperament lies in the inherited biological constitution. There is some evidence in that direction, but also much material which indicates the strength of early experiences in determining the nature of emotional reactions which later become habitual. It seems desirable to use the term "temperament" to refer to such habitual emotional attitudes without making any assumptions as to the causal factors involved.

THE BIOLOGICAL APPROACH TO PERSONALITY

The point of view which sees in personality the reflection of the biological nature of the individual has its most direct and historically its earliest expression in the study of physiognomy. Even before Aristotle there were suggestions that physical characteristics were expressive of mentality, and it was usual to draw an analogy with the appearance of animals, a man with a leonine head having the courage and ferocity of a lion, and so on. Aristotle himself was skeptical of this tendency and believed that the parallels between animals and men should be carefully observed before they were used as a means of diagnosis. He was not very critical, however, of the whole physiognomic approach and believed that stub noses indicated love of pleasure; broad and flat noses, frivolity; broad nasal alae, courage; staring eyes, stupidity, and so on.

The most important attempt to place the study of physiognomy on a scientific basis was made by Lavater (9), who in

1804 published four volumes of photographs and sketches with his own interpretative comments. Lavater accepted and amplified the old notions, going so far as to ascribe psychological importance to the presence of warts and moles, as well as to the high forehead and prominent jaw popularly regarded as significant. He accepted also the notion that similarity to animals indicated the presence of corresponding qualities.

There have been many modern followers. Lombroso (10), to whom reference has already been made, used this approach in the study of the characteristics of criminals. Havelock Ellis (11) believed that blondness and brunetteness are associated with traits of personality, and studied the characteristics of many paintings in the National Portrait Gallery in London for evidence in support of this theory. He concluded that men of restless and ambitious temperament are blond, and scholars and men of letters are dark, although his own data fail to substantiate this view. Woods (12) believed that the size of the nose is psychologically significant, great men having noses larger than the average. Recently the physiognomical approach has been extended to vocational guidance through the writings of Katharine Blackford (13), who finds a difference not only between blonds and brunettes, but also between those with convex and concave profiles. It is safe to say that none of this material has any scientific validity. Several surveys have been made (14, 15, 16) of the experimental attempts to verify the physiognomic hypothesis, and they agree in their conclusion that the results are negative. Recently Healy (17) has reported a series of studies by means of composite photographs of individuals well known to him and his associates. He writes as follows:

I found that no one could distinguish the young sadist from a kindly youth, and often not even a misanthrope from a jovial fellow. By taking group photos I found . . . that feeble-minded adolescents in the picture could not be differentiated from the others. Kretschmer, the great student of body and personality types, once spoke of the face as the visiting card of the individual constitution . . .

he should have remembered that it is quite possible to find many misrepresentations recorded on even a visiting card (p. 132).

In one sense, however, physiognomy may be important. We may safely rule out characteristics like the shape of the head, the color of the skin and eyes, the size of the nose or the presence of warts or other blemishes. It is still possible that the face may reflect the personality to the extent that facial expression is affected by previous experience and habitual emotional reactions. The muscles of the face are used differently to express joy and sorrow, and the frequency of their use in one direction or the other will leave its imprint upon the face even under conditions of repose. It is even possible that in a society which regards a jaw thrust forward as a sign of determination, an individual may unconsciously put on a sort of bulldog expression whenever he is faced with difficulties, and as a result this physiognomical sign may have real significance. This type of physiognomical diagnosis applies, however, only to the soft parts of the face which may be affected by experience, or to movements which may be consciously made. The face then serves as a medium of expression rather than as an indication of an original biological relationship.

Phrenology may be regarded as another movement in this same direction, and the work of Lavater gave it a strong impetus. The attempt was made by Gall (*18*) toward the close of the eighteenth century, and by his pupil Spurzheim (*19*), to develop a system of personality diagnosis based upon brain localization, the details of which could be ascertained by an examination of the protuberances on the skull. The "science" which they originated had a great deal of success, and societies for the study of phrenology were formed in many parts of the world. In America the most outstanding follower was Fowler (*20*), whose maps of localization had a great vogue in the latter part of the nineteenth century. Experiments were performed, in one of the most famous of which an electric current was applied to the bump of "religiosity" on the skull of a woman who immediately took up a position of worship. This result is not mysterious, since the woman knew which bump was being stimulated. The whole phrenological approach has now only an historical interest. It can have no scientific validity, first because there is no brain localization of the detailed type that the theory assumes, and second because even if there were, there is so much difference between the contours of the brain and the external contours of the skull that the method would be useless. The phrenologists performed a useful function, however, in stimulating the study of brain anatomy and of the problem of cerebral localization.

The Endocrine Glands. The approach to personality in terms of the functions of the endocrines, or glands of internal secretion, is in a different category and is still regarded as potentially a valuable method. It has been discussed so frequently and in such detail in a great many psychological texts, that relatively brief comment should suffice here. In the writings of Berman (*1*) various types of personality are described in terms of the hyper- or hypofunctioning of a single endocrine gland, and outstanding figures in history are also analyzed in terms of their endocrine make-up. The interest with which Berman's theory was first received has given way to considerable skepticism as to the validity of such a specific relationship. At the present time there obtains a more conservative position to the effect that endocrine factors undoubtedly play a part, but that except in pathological cases the exact nature of their influence is still unknown. As far as normal personalities are concerned, the argument appears to depend upon an extension from the known changes which occur in diseased conditions. The fact that cretins, who are hypothyroid, show a sluggishness in behavior and a low mentality has led to the belief that even slight deficiencies in these respects may also be explained as conditioned by the thyroid. The actual experimental investigations, however, of the relationship between thyroid activity as measured by basal metabolic rate on the one hand, and differences in speed of reaction on the other, have failed to yield any conclusive results.

Lanier (*21*) gives evidence for a positive relationship, but Steinberg (*22*) and Levy (*23*) have reported findings in the opposite direction. The case of the thyroid is particularly important, because it is the only gland whose degree of activity may adequately be measured by experimental methods applicable to normal individuals.

In the case of the other glands, some of the evidence, though indirect, is suggestive. We know from the work of Cannon (*24*) that the adrenal medulla and the associated sympathetic nervous system are responsible for many of the physiological accompaniments of emotional excitement. There is some probability therefore that differences in the functioning of this gland may have something to do with the greater or lesser emotional excitability of individuals. The fact that the thymus remains large until the period of adolescence, and that it involutes or degenerates in the course of the acquisition of maturity, has suggested its possible influence in determining different rates of mental and physical development. Many additional examples of this type of argument could be given. It is probable that there is some relationship of the kind assumed, but its exact nature and extent have not yet been adequately determined.

In connection with the attempt to explain personality in terms of the endocrine glands, two critical considerations must be kept in mind. The first is that endocrine functioning is not entirely hereditary, but that social and environmental factors may enter to a considerable degree. In the case of the thyroid, for example, it is known that great emotional excitement of the kind experienced during an air raid, may raise the basal metabolism considerably and involve a permanent change in the condition of the gland. We know also that even less drastic experiences like a change in diet and habits of exercise may modify thyroid functioning to an appreciable degree. The fact that puberty may occur earlier in life in the tropics or under the influence of stimulating experiences indicates that the glandular changes accompanying adolescence may also be in part environmentally conditioned. The pituitary gland allegedly determines stature, but it is well known that more favorable socio-economic circumstances may cause an increase in stature, so that in all probability the pituitary is also affected by the environment. These facts illustrate the impossibility of completely separating biological from social influences in glandular functioning.

The other important consideration is that no endocrine gland functions in isolation, and that consequently the description of a personality in terms of the functioning of a single gland is undoubtedly misleading. The rate of sexual maturation, for example, appears to be influenced by the changes in the thymus and by the activity of the sex glands, as well as by the secretion of the adrenal cortex. Maturation may also be disturbed by hypofunction of the thyroid as well as in many cases of pituitary involvement in which the sex glands are also affected. Energy or "drive" is probably affected by the adrenal cortex, the thyroid and the gonads. Emotional excitability may be influenced by the adrenal medulla, the thyroid, the parathyroids, and in some cases also, the pituitary. This means that we must always consider the endocrine glands as an organized system, in which no element can be disturbed without the involvement of the remainder. Thyroid disturbance is not restricted to that gland, but alters the inter-relationships of all the glands with one another. It is probable that future research on the relation between the endocrine glands and personality will concern itself not so much with measures of the activity of single glands as with a technique for the study of the glandular system as a whole.

Constitutional Types. This has in a sense been attempted in the approach to personality in terms of general bodily constitution. The approach is clinical in origin, and has arisen from the observation of medical men that different individuals are not equally susceptible to various diseases. Hippocrates was probably the first to suggest a typology on this basis when he spoke of an "habitus phthisicus" predisposing to pulmonary tuberculosis, and an "habitus apoplecticus," predisposing to diseases of the heart and circulatory system. Since then many attempts have been made to relate physical type to the incidence of disease, the most recent being that of Draper (25), whose careful measurements have yielded some evidence in favor of a "gall bladder" type, a "gastric ulcer" type, etc.

For the psychologist the most important constitutional typology is that of Ernst Kretschmer (21), a German psychiatrist who has postulated a relationship between physical type and susceptibility to mental disorder. Taking as his starting point the two most common functional psychoses, dementia praecox, or schizophrenia, and manic-depressive or circular insanity, Kretschmer presents evidence for the theory that those who suffer from one or the other of these two diseases differ markedly in their physical constitution. There are four main constitutional types—the pyknic, who is relatively short and round, has considerable weight in relation to his height, and whose sitting height is a relatively large proportion of his standing height; the leptosome, tall for his weight, with a short trunk and long arms and legs; the athletic or muscular type, with a heavy frame and well-developed musculature; and the dysplastic, who shows some asymmetry, or physical deformity. The relationship between physique and personality may be expressed in the following table:

Constitutional Type	Mental Disease	Borderline Cases	Normal Biotypes
Pyknic	circular insanity	cycloid	cyclothyme
Leptosome ⎫ Athletic ⎬ Dysplastic ⎭	schizophrenia	schizoid	schizothyme

The description of the cycloid and schizoid temperaments is based upon the case histories of the early life of patients who later develop one or the other of the two psychoses. Cyclothyme and schizothyme are roughly equivalent to extravert and introvert types with the addition of other allied psychological tendencies.

With reference to the psychoses, Kretschmer's original data have been supplemented by a series of subsequent investigations in various parts of the world, the general result of which has been in favor of this theory. Recently, however, and particularly in America, a number of serious objections have been raised. The most important of these has to do with the effect of the age factor; it is argued that as people grow older they tend to become more pyknic. It is also true that schizophrenia usually appears early in life, and circular insanity relatively late. There might therefore be more leptosomes and more schizophrenia among young people, and more pyknics and manic-depressive insanity among older ones, without any necessary causal relationship between physique and mental disorder. This view has been tested by Garvey (26) and Farber (27), who found that when they equated the patients for age, Kretschmer's theory no longer held. A thorough study was made by Burchard (28) in which the psychotic subjects were divided into ten-year groups. The results showed that although much of the difference between the two psychotic groups may be attributed to age, there is still within each decade a slight difference in the direction favorable to Kretschmer's theory. The conclusion would be that age is an important factor which Kretschmer has unduly neglected, even though it may not account entirely for his findings.

A second serious criticism lies in the relative frequency of exceptions. In the various studies which Kretschmer reports, from one-quarter to one-third of the patients failed to fit into his scheme. Kretschmer explains this discrepancy in terms of mixed heredity, the constitution being inherited from one parent and the disease from the other. This explanation appears to be in flat contradiction to the rest of the theory. If there is a causal relation between physique and psychosis, it is difficult to understand how a case of schizophrenia could ever appear with a pyknic constitution.

As for normal personalities, a large amount of material has been accumulated by Kretschmer and his colleagues indicating that pyknics and leptosomes differ in a wide variety of psychological activities. Klineberg, Asch and Block (29) give the following summary of the main conclusions of the German studies.

Pyknics (cyclothymes) as contrasted with leptosomes (schizo-thymes) have a greater perception span, are more distractible, have less power to abstract, less "cleavage capacity" or "Spaltungs-faehigkeit," better incidental memory, respond "synthetically" (lep-tosomes "analytically") in the case of a difficult perception, are more sensitive to colors (leptosomes to forms), see colors as blends more quickly, respond as "extraverts" to the Rorschach test (lep-tosomes, "introverts"), diagnose themselves as cyclothyme (lepto-somes, schizothyme), give more chain associations in the word as-sociation test (leptosomes more perseveration and more meaning-less associations), show less marked psychogalvanic reactions except to pain stimuli, and are superior in motor tasks excepts those which require fine and delicate movements.   The handwriting differences are not clear, and the differences in intelligence negligible (p. 156).

This imposing list of differences appeared to make it worth while to repeat these experiments under controlled conditions, and this was done in two separate investigations (*29, 30*). The attempt was made to adhere as closely as possible to the psy-chological categories involved in the studies of the German psychiatrists and even to use identical techniques wherever possible.   The greatest care was exercised to choose those sub-jects who could unmistakably be diagnosed as pyknics or leptosomes.   As all the subjects were students, it was possible to equate the two groups for age, intelligence and socio-eco-nomic status, as well as sex, and in that way to avoid some of the errors of the German studies.   The results showed not a single psychological category in which the differences be-tween two constitutional groups were statistically reliable. The first of the two investigations concludes: ". . . the results of the present investigations, with the use of methods more careful than those of Kretschmer's group, have consistently failed to provide evidence for the existence of types which they claim to have found" (*29*, p. 215).

The general problem of what is meant by a "type" and whether this concept is a legitimate one for psychology will be discussed in greater detail later.   At this point it is im-portant to keep in mind that Kretschmer's use of the concept differs markedly from the one customary among American psychologists. For him, the description of types does not follow those cases which occur with the greatest frequency, and the conventional criticism that pure types are rare does not really affect his theory. Kretschmer willingly admits that the "classical cases occur only rarely" and states that the type as he understands it refers to the most "beautiful" cases (p. 16). One may draw an analogy between his procedure and that of medical books which describe a disease in terms of what is frequently referred to as the "text-book picture," and which may be only approximated in the actual experience of the physician. Just as the diagnosis of gastric ulcer may still be made even though some of the expected signs and symptoms are lacking, so Kretschmer makes the diagnosis of leptosome constitution in spite of the presence of certain pyknic or athletic characteristics in the individual. This is a concept of type which is difficult to handle statistically, and which is not in favor among most scientists. Even if we accept Kretschmer's use of it, however, we must still conclude that the significance of his theory has been overrated, and that it is not nearly so useful an approach to the understanding of personality as was formerly believed.

Body Chemistry. Another approach to a biological analysis of personality is in terms of body chemistry. The fact that psychological activities may be accompanied by changes in the contents of the blood has led to the hope that this might prove a valuable approach. It is known, for example, that in emotional excitement glycogen is liberated from the liver and is made available in the blood stream in the form of sugar. Chemical analysis of the sugar content of blood may therefore indicate the amount of immediately available energy, and also the presence of emotional excitement. It is known that violent convulsive effects may follow the presence of great alkalinity in the body fluids, and the possibility arises that even within normal limits differences in the acid and alkaline content not only of the blood, but also of the urine and the saliva, may be accompanied by variations in aggressiveness or submissiveness of personality. Some evidence in this direction has been reported by Rich (*31*). Another fact of body chemistry which may have psychological significance is the predominance of the fatty acids cholesterol and lecithin in the brain tissue, and it has been suggested that their excessive presence in the blood may indicate a marked degree of cerebral activity. Many investigations have been carried out in an attempt to establish some relationship between personality, normal and abnormal, and the chemistry of the blood and other body fluids (*32*).

A significant experimental attack has been made upon this problem by Goldstein (*33*), who also gives a careful summary of other investigations in this field. His most important result is that there are such great variations in the body chemistry of the individual from day to day that biochemical measures may not be used as an explanation of the relatively stable attributes of personality. The variations within the individual in this respect are almost as great as those between different individuals. The result indicates that the measures at present available have little value for the understanding of personality differences, although it is possible that further refinement in the techniques may bring greater success. The work now being done on the electro-encephalogram seems promising, but it is too early to say just where it will lead (*34*).

One positive result of Goldstein's study should be mentioned. He gives evidence to show that those subjects who are more variable in their day-to-day blood determinations also appear to be psychologically more unstable. This is in line with the finding by Hammett (*35*) that marked variations in basal metabolic rate are accompanied by similar variations in emotional responses, stability in the one apparently implying stability in the other. It may be that variations in body chemistry are more important for the diagnosis of personality differences than the actual chemical determinations themselves.

Bodily Diseases. The effects of bodily diseases on personality also give indication of a possible relationship between biological and psychological activities. Physicians, for example, who have had considerable experience with cases of pulmonary tuberculosis have found a frequent tendency for relatively mild cases to be accompanied by feelings of well-being or optimism—the "spes phthisica." It may be that the slight continuous fever exercises a mildly stimulating effect, so that the optimism persists even when the patient has good reason to feel otherwise. On the other hand cardiac cases, particularly those involving the coronary arteries of the heart as in angina pectoris, are often accompanied by strong depression and anxiety. The possibility arises that in less extreme cases there may still be a slight effect upon personality, so that a generally pessimistic or optimistic outlook may have a somewhat analogous explanation. The opposite effect, namely, of emotional attitude upon physical condition, is even better substantiated. It seems certain that chronic anxiety, for example, may give rise to gastric conditions leading to the formation of ulcer, and Alexander (36) and Chappell (37) among others have reported cures of these gastric conditions by psychoanalytic or psychotherapeutic methods. It is popularly believed that gastro-intestinal conditions in general may account for many instances of depression or irritability. This field is one in which much more careful experimentation and statistical study are needed. As in other types of pathological material, however, the application of the results to normal cases will have to be made with considerable caution.

In summarizing these various biological approaches to personality, it may be said that whereas no one of them by itself gives a satisfactory explanation of individual differences, there is considerable evidence to the effect that biological factors do play an important part. We may rule out phrenology as well as physiognomy in the narrower sense, but the findings of endocrinology and possibly also of blood chemistry appear to have some significance. Much further work is needed before the exact extent of such significance is determined.

There is one other way in which physique and personality may be related. As is well known, Alfred Adler (38) has attempted to explain personality formation as a reaction to bodily characteristics, particularly those related to organ inferiorities. This approach is only indirectly biological. Excessively short stature, ugliness, and a humped back do not directly determine personality characteristics, but are effective because of the attitudes held in connection with them. Short stature, for example, would have an entirely different effect upon personality if it were generally regarded as a desirable characteristic.

That this approach may also to some degree apply to Kretschmer's theory is indicated in a recent study by Cabot (39) who found that the "athletosomes" (Kretschmer's "athletics") possessed certain personality traits that have high social value. Because their physique is regarded as the most desirable, they tend to develop an ascendant, influential, and extraverted personality. This is in conflict with Kretschmer's position, but it reveals the possibility of an indirect association between bodily and mental characteristics.

THE PROBLEM OF EXPRESSION

The material summarized in connection with the biological approach to personality may be regarded from two points of view, first as an explanation of the nature of individual differences in personality, and second, as a means of diagnosing such differences. A leptosome constitution, for instance, may be thought of as furnishing the biological framework for the schizothyme temperament, or as an aid in discovering the presence of such a temperament. In certain psychiatric institutions there appears to be some tendency to regard the diagnosis of schizophrenia as a little more certain if the disease is found in a person of leptosome habitus. In this second sense, the biological approach leads directly to consideration of the problem of expression, or the outward manifestation of the presence of particular psychological characteristics.

The Interpretation of Handwriting. This aspect of personality study has attracted a great deal of popular attention, and expressive movements are widely accepted as having meaning for the understanding of personality. One of the methods in widest use is that of graphology, or the interpretation of handwriting, which is of special interest in this connection because of the number of experimental studies which have been directed toward a determination of its significance. A distinction must be made, however, between that form of graphology which is concerned with identity or differences between handwritings and which has medico-legal as well as literary and historical significance, and the other type which uses it as a means to the diagnosis of personality. It is with the latter use of the term that we are here concerned.

According to Saudek (40), the history of graphology really begins with Michon (41), who was the first to use this word in 1871. Michon interpreted character according to signs, and had no inkling of any direct causal connection which would explain the relationship. One of his important followers was Crépieux-Jamin (42), who did not take the signs quite so strictly, but whose work was still in the same general tradition. He reports an interesting experiment in which a nineteen-year-old student was hypnotized and given successive suggestions that he was a cunning peasant, a miser, an old man, etc., and his handwriting became modified according to the laws of graphology. A woman was given the suggestion that she was Napoleon, and her handwriting indicated an overbearing, manly personality with extraordinary will-power. Crépieux-Jamin believed it was possible to discover from graphology the amount and nature of intelligence, the moral character, will-power, esthetic sense, age, sex, and pathology of the individual. In Germany, Preyer (43) wrote on this subject in 1895, pointing out that handwriting was really brain-writing, and related to the fundamental neural structure of the individual. He had right-handed individuals use their left hand, and he found that the script was fundamentally identical in the two cases. Preyer gave a new turn to the problem by ignoring the signs used by his predecessors and formulating in their place certain general variables such as slant, duration, thickness of stroke and interruptions in the writing, which he regarded as more important.

In this respect he was followed by Ludwig Klages (44), who is sometimes spoken of as the founder of a scientific graphology. He concerned himself mainly with three characteristics of the handwriting—rapidity, which measured the psychological activity of the writer; expanse, which was an expression of will-power, designs, ambition; and pressure, which indicated the degree of individual energy. Saudek (40) is in general a follower of Klages, although he notes certain relationships which he cannot explain, such as the fact that pasty (fat and stumpy) writing, resulting from holding the pen far from the tip so that there is no up-and-down pressure, is a sign of sensuality, and is found, for example, in the handwriting of Casanova and Oscar Wilde. Saudek is careful to take into account all possible extraneous factors such as conditions of writing, penmanship instruction, materials used, date of writing, and so on.

Up to the present time probably the best study of graphology has been made by Allport and Vernon (45). They were interested in two distinct problems, first, the consistency, and second, the meaning of expressive movements. In connection with the first, they measured a large number of activities such as speed of writing and counting, speed of walking and strolling, estimation of known sizes and of distances and angles, speed of tapping, muscular tension, rapidity and expanse in drawing, etc. They found a considerable degree of consistency between groups of traits, with reliabilities in the neighborhood of +.70, which means that speed and expanse and similar characteristics are not accidental, but may be expected to reveal themselves with a fair degree of consistency.

In the second portion of the experiment two attempts were made to check the validity of the graphological hypothesis. In the first of these, ten male students copied a forty-word passage under uniform conditions. Brief character sketches, approximately 250 words in length, were written about each of the subjects by close acquaintances. The handwriting samples and the sketches were then "matched" by three groups of judges—students, faculty and three graphologists. This technique is known as the "matching method." By pure chance, one might expect one correct matching out of ten. The actual results gave for the students an average of 1.77, for the faculty, 1.80, and for the graphologists, 2.41 correct judgments. When the judgments of the whole group were combined, there were five cases out of ten in which the most frequent matching was also the correct one. These results indicate in the first place that even inexperienced judges have a success above chance, and in the second, that the greater experience of the graphologists really has an effect in terms of accurate judgments. It should be added that this method, admirable in other respects, fails to indicate how bad the errors were, and it may be that the mistakes made in matching were not serious ones. The wrong choice of a character sketch differing only slightly from the correct one is counted equally with an error involving a much greater contrast. If some correction could be made for the amount of error in each case, the accuracy of the judgments might be represented by a somewhat higher figure. On the other hand, the successful judgments in this study were far rarer than is claimed by popular graphologists, and this should impose great caution in the use of the method for vocational or other forms of psychological guidance.

In the second attempt to test graphology, two graphologists wrote case studies of 23 freshman students on the basis of their handwriting, and the psychologist, who knew the students well, attempted to identify them. The results were somewhat better than chance, but on the whole not very satisfactory. One of the graphologists explained his relative lack of success on the ground that the students were immature, and would later develop those traits which he saw reflected in their handwriting. This is, of course, a possibility, but can hardly be accepted as an adequate explanation of the failures. This whole study proves that some significance may be ascribed to graphology, though not nearly so much as is claimed by the graphologists.

Voice and Personality. There have been several studies of voice as an expression of personality. A careful analysis of the factors involved has been made by Sapir (46) in his discussion of speech as a personality trait. He points out that the basic or fundamental speech level is the voice, which is usually regarded as having an hereditary basis. The voice, however, has a social quality as well, since we imitate one another's voices to some extent, and if our voice is criticized we try to make it more acceptable socially. In deducing personality traits from voice we must disentangle social or cultural elements from purely personal ones.

A man has a strained or raucous voice, let us say, and we might infer that he is basically "coarse-grained." Such a judgment might be entirely wide of the mark if the particular society in which he lives is an out-of-door society that indulges in a good deal of swearing and rather rough handling of the voice. He may have had a very soft voice to begin with, symptomatic of a delicate psychic organization, which gradually toughened under the influence of social suggestion (p. 31).

Sapir goes on to point out that what we customarily call voice is not voice alone, but also the manner in which we use it, or voice dynamics. This may be described as the second level of speech analysis. One of its most important aspects is intonation, which is socially determined, and there are characteristic intonations, for example, in different parts of the country, as well as slight individual differences. Obviously we cannot make any inferences about personality on the basis of intonation without taking into consideration the speech habits of the community. The monotonous tone of a Japanese does not necessarily point to a personality of this type. In connection with voice dynamics, we must consider also rhythm and the relative continuity of speech. A third level of speech analysis is pronunciation, a fourth is vocabulary, and a fifth is style. In all cases in which speech is used as a means of diagnosing personality, we are able to arrive at individual differences only after having equated for social and cultural factors.

In the actual studies in this field conditions were controlled to some degree, but not sufficiently to take care of all the cautions which Sapir mentions. Pear (47) asked radio listeners to give physical descriptions of nine speakers whose voices they heard, and the descriptions were on the whole fairly accurate. The sex of the speaker was stated correctly except in the case of an eleven-year-old child, and the judgments of approximate age were usually correct. Even the vocation of the speaker was recognized in some cases. More recently, Cantril and Allport (48) conducted a series of experiments in which the speakers read uniform material from prepared texts. There were eight laboratory experiments in which students were the judges, and two over radio station WEEI, in which the public was asked to participate. The features of the individuals studied were age, height, complexion, appearance in photograph, appearance in person, handwriting, vocation, political preference, extraversion-introversion, ascendance-submission and dominant values. The last three of these were arrived at by means of the corresponding personality inventories or questionnaires. There were 24 male speakers, three in each of the eight experiments. The matching method was used. When photographs or handwriting samples were to be matched with the voice, they were shown on the screen during the experiment; when the matching was to be made with actual personal appearance, the speakers walked out in front of the judges after they had read their speeches behind a screen. The judges were also given brief personality sketches of the speakers to be matched with the voice. The results for the experiment as a whole were somewhat better than chance, though never strikingly so. As in the case of the graphological studies, the conclusion is that there is a relation between voice and personality.

Other Aspects of Expression. There have been other suggestions as to ways in which personality expresses itself. Gerstäcker (49) attempted character reading from the position of the hat on the head; a deeply tipped hat means frivolity and obstinate imperiousness; the hat at the back of the head suggests improvidence, conceit, sensuality and extravagance, etc. Popular use of this idea has been made on the stage and screen, the personality of the man who wears his hat jauntily over one eye differing markedly from that of the man who wears it straight on the middle of his head. Wolff (50) made a study of gait, the subjects walking under controlled conditions and with their faces hidden. The gait reflected buoyancy, dullness, pride, courage and other characteristics, and showed considerable agreement with impressions of personality, handwriting and voice. There have also been studies of style as a whole, or of personal idiom which reveals itself in a large variety of different activities. F. H. Allport, Walker and Lathers (51) were able to match two different groups of themes by the same students with considerable success, using the general "form quality" of the writing as a criterion. There is room here for a great deal of interesting research. It would be valuable to know, for example, to what extent the distinctive quality of Debussy's music has any parallels in his written style or in his social relationships, or whether on the other hand Michelangelo's robust sculptures reveal a style which is manifest in his other activities as well. It is likely that in these and other instances certain common qualities of style will be discovered. Woodworth (52) regards this individual style as the essence of personality. In this connection it is important to keep in mind Allport and Vernon's (45) suggestion that there may be "congruence" without "consistency," that is to say, apparently contradictory attitudes in an individual may be seen to supplement each other and actually to be unified. In one of their examples, it is pointed out that the same individual may exert great pressure in one motor experiment, and very little in another, and that this apparent inconsistency might be explained by the fact that the subject is an artist who realizes the importance of variations of pressure under different conditions. Similarly, in the broader aspects of personality, apparent conflicts may be explained in many cases on the basis of an underlying unity.

There has been an attempt to make practical use of the

study of motor expression in connection with mental disease. Jacobson (53) believes that much mental disturbance is related to the presence of neuromuscular hypertension, which reveals itself in "tenseness" either in specific muscles or muscle systems, or in the individual as a whole—the "high-strung" individual. The clinical evidence of nervous hypertension is seen in the increase of tendon reflexes, of mechanical muscle and nerve excitability, spastic conditions of smooth muscle, abnormal excitability of the heart and the respiratory apparatus, tremor, restlessness, volubility and other overactivity. The cure is "progressive relaxation." The patient is made aware of the tensions in his muscles, learns the forms these may take, recognizes them and counteracts them. Jacobson has reported cures by this technique, but it has not achieved any wide use at the hands of other psychiatrists.

PERSONALITY TYPES

Many attempts have been made to introduce some order or classification into the large variations between individual personalities. Granting that no two persons are alike, it has seemed worth while to many investigators to describe general types or categories expressing similarities or identities instead of differences. We have already had one example of this tendency in the theory of Kretschmer, but there have been many others, usually without the biological or physical background which Kretschmer has postulated.

Nietzsche (54), for example, on the basis of his studies of Greek tragedy, spoke of two different ways of life, the Apollonian and the Dionysian. Apollo "governs the beauteous illusion of the inner world of fantasy." He represents measure, number, limitation, the mastery of everything savage and untamed. The Dionysian represents the freeing of unmeasured instinct, nature unbridled, drunkenness in the highest sense. Although Nietzsche himself did not attempt to divide human beings on this basis, his dichotomy has often been employed in this manner. A recent application has also been made to types of culture by Ruth Benedict (55), who believes that the

Pueblo Indians of Arizona and New Mexico are Apollonian, and the surrounding tribes Dionysian in their general way of life.

William James suggested a distinction between "tender-minded" and "tough-minded" individuals (56), the former governed by ideas, the latter, by facts. This distinction was of some importance in connection with his system of pragmatism, since the notion that ideas could be regarded as true if they were emotionally satisfying would presumably appeal only to tender-minded individuals.

The best-known psychological typology is undoubtedly that of C. G. Jung (57) who is responsible for the division into extraverts and introverts. The fundamental difference between these is that in the one case there is an outward movement of interest toward the object, in the other, a movement away from the object toward the subject and his own psychological processes. The extravert gives the object the predominant value, and the subject is relatively unimportant; for the introvert the values are reversed. Jung has often been criticized on the ground that there are no pure types, but he himself recognizes and acknowledges this fact. For him, every human being possesses both mechanisms; usually one predominates, though there may be a rhythmical alternation of the two forms of psychic activity. If the predominance of one becomes chronic or habitual, a type is produced. The other is not completely suppressed, however, and there is merely a relative predominance of one mechanism over the other. Jung considers the decisive factor to be the inherited disposition of the child, although under abnormal conditions there may be a falsification of the type by the external environment. Plant (58) believes that these attitudes may arise from inherited factors, from acquired bodily conditions producing similar factors, from the environment, or from any combination of these.

Jung interprets the psychological systems of his distinguished colleagues, Freud and Adler, from the point of view of his typology. Adler's system is essentially introvert, since it emphasizes feelings of superiority and inferiority in the ego, and subjective values in general. Freud's system is essentially extravert, the craving for the sex object constituting its central drive whereas failures in this respect give rise to disturbances of various kinds.

There have been many experimental attempts to test Jung's theory. In a study by Heidbreder (59) a questionnaire was given to 200 students at the University of Minnesota, the items being so chosen that a positive answer meant introversion, and a negative, extraversion. There were altogether 54 items, and an individual who was completely extravert would therefore score —54, one who showed equal tendencies in both directions would have a score of 0, and so on. It was felt that the shape of the distribution curve would give evidence as to the validity of Jung's theory, since the existence of two distinct types in a population should yield a bi-modal curve. Actually, the curve obtained was a normal distribution curve, and Heidbreder therefore concludes that pure introverts or extraverts are rare, most individuals falling into an intermediate category. This conclusion is undoubtedly the correct one, but as we have seen, it does not really conflict with that adopted by Jung himself. One other interesting result of this study was that the average score was not 0 but —11.25, that is to say, the group as a whole showed a definite tendency in the extravert direction. This is probably to be expected from an American group, since the culture of the United States as a whole undoubtedly stresses extravert rather than introvert activities. As Plant points out:

Psychiatrists very generally have felt that a mild degree of extraversion represents the most healthy type of temperament. . . . This is no more than the statement that it is more healthy to live in the world as it is than in the world only as one wishes it to be (p. 115).

It should be added, however, that this notion of what is healthy is not necessarily shared by other cultures. There seems little doubt that in India, for example, introversion would be at a much greater premium than it is among ourselves. It may be that whole cultures may be characterized in terms of Jung's types. It is more probable, however, as in the case of individuals, that pure types are rare among cultures as well, and the use of these labels may therefore be misleading in many cases.

An ingenious study of introversion and extraversion in young children was made by L. R. Marston (60), the subjects ranging in age from 23 to 71 months, with an average of 51.3 months. The investigator manipulated an attractive toy, a teeter-tauter, in the presence of the child. He ignored the child (unless the child approached him) for 60 seconds. Then he looked up at the child, but said nothing, and did not smile. Thirty seconds later he looked up and smiled. Thirty seconds later he said: "Do you like the teeter-tauter?" If there was no response, after 30 seconds, he asked cordially: "Would you like to play with this teeter-tauter?" If the child failed to approach, he said: "You may; come over and play with it." If the child still refused, the investigator urged him persistently. According to their reactions in this experiment, the children were classified into 6 degrees of introversion, ranging from the one extreme in which the child refused unyieldingly to play with the toy or fled from the room, to those at the extravert end of the scale who did not wait for recognition, but promptly approached and played with the toy. The study is important because of the wide differences which it revealed in the children, and because it made use of an actual situation rather than a series of questions. It does not answer the question as to whether these differences represent relatively stable aspects of personality, or are conditioned by the particular, temporary situation. This was studied in a later investigation by Newcomb (61) on boys aged 10 to 16 who were observed in a camp situation over a period of two months, and there was no marked consistency of introvert tendencies at different times. It appears certain that an individual may vary in his degree of extraversion not only in different situations, but also in the same type of situation if an interval of time has elapsed. This strengthens the conclusion that pure types are rare or non-existent, except as extremes in a normal distribution.

There have been several questionnaires constructed in order to measure extraversion-introversion, the best known of which are those by Freyd (*62*) and Laird (*63*). The latter contains a graphic rating scale by means of which the subject indicates not only whether or not he engages in a particular activity (like daydreaming, for example) but also how frequently he does so. This technique would permit a certain degree of quantification of each response, but Laird has used it only in two segments, without any further subdivision. Conklin (*64*) has devised an interest questionnaire based upon preference for certain activities like baseball, listening to a lecture on classical music, visiting an auto show, talking with friends about literature, reading essays on literary criticism, and so on. There are 40 activities listed, some of an introvert and some of an extravert nature.

Another typological approach which has attracted considerable attention is that of Eduard Spranger (*65*). He starts out with the distinction between psychology as a "cultural science" (Geisteswissenschaft) and as a "natural science" (Naturwissenschaft). In the latter sense it is a psychology of elements, which may have a certain value but leaves out the kind of psychological understanding shown by the poet, historian, minister and educator. These may still be good psychologists even though they do not analyze a mental complex into the elements of which it is composed. From the cultural science point of view the significant whole is primary, and an analysis is significant and valid only if one thinks of the elements in relation to the whole. This type of psychology attempts to understand the meaning of experiences and acts for the individual; its goal is the understanding of the individual. There is in addition a field of differential cultural science psychology which establishes types of individuals according to the dominant meaning of the personality; this meaning is best discovered through an understanding of the principal value by which a man lives and shapes his own life.

From this point of view six types of values are distinguished: (1) the economic, in which the value is that of a utilitarian ethics, with everything being judged in terms of its practical usefulness; (2) the theoretic, interested in truth for its own sake, and valuing ideas for their objectivity and consistency; (3) the esthetic, in which the value is placed upon inner experience and harmony, and activities are judged in terms of their artistic quality; (4) the social, with stress upon humanitarianism and the virtues of love and loyalty; (5) the political, which emphasizes the will to power, self-control, and control over others; (6) the religious, with values based upon the spiritual meaning of life and the finding of blessedness in God.

An interesting test of personality known as the "Study of Values" has been devised by Allport and Vernon (*66*) in an attempt to place the measurement of these types on a more empirical as well as quantitative basis. Questions are asked in which the alternative choices represent one or another of these values; for example, a greater interest in the life of military leaders than of humanitarians points to a political rather than a social interest; a preference for an art magazine over a scientific one indicates an esthetic rather than a theoretic value, and so on. The method is ingenious, but the individual questions may not have quite the same significance for all subjects. A person with esthetic values may happen not to like *The Arts* magazine, or the theoretic person, *The Scientific American*. One with social values may happen not to find the life of Florence Nightingale particularly interesting. Although many of the items are well chosen, there are many which, at least on logical grounds, appear questionable. The authors report, however, that these particular items have as high a reliability and validity as the others in the test. "The Study of Values" has been of service in arriving not only at individual, but also at cultural differences. There have already been some attempts to use it for the study of group differences. Harris (*67*) found, for example, that Jewish students scored higher on theoretic and social, and lower on religious values than the non-Jews with whom they were compared. It need hardly be pointed out that the use of this method in different cultures would depend upon the possibility of discovering questions sufficiently broad in their implications to transcend the limitations of one particular community.

The psychoanalysts have also been concerned with the problem of personality types. Abraham (*68*), for example, regards early suckling habits as responsible for a distinction between two types of personality, the oral optimist and the oral pessimist. Where suckling in infancy is undisturbed and pleasurable, there develops an imperturbable optimism which may lead to carefree indifference and inactivity. Such individuals expect that they will be cared for, that the mother's breast will "flow for them eternally." Those who have had an unsatisfactory suckling period are pessimistic as a result of their failure to achieve gratification in early life. This may result in a later attitude of asking or demanding things of others and in a tendency to cling to them. Campbell (*69*) suggests that the great Osler may have had some premonition of this in a humorous speech which he made in honor of the pediatrician. He stated that the efforts to encourage breast feeding had been stimulated "by an exhaustive collective investigation which has been made on the future of bottle-fed babies, in which it is clearly shown that intellectual obliquity, moral perversion and special crankiness of all kinds result directly from the early warp given to the mind of the child by the gross and unworthy deception to which it is subjected" (p. 102).

An observation by Mead (*70*) makes it possible to apply this concept to group differences. In her study of temperamental differences in three Melanesian communities, she found one of them, the Arapesh, similar to the oral optimist type, and another, the Mundugumor, to the oral pessimist. In the former, children were fed frequently and liberally, and were caressed by their mothers while being suckled; as adults, the Arapesh were friendly co-operative individuals. The Mundugumor mothers, on the other hand, fed their children grudgingly, bending down so that they could take the breast for a brief period, and then drawing away; as adults, the Mundugumor were about as hostile and unfriendly a people as one could possibly find. In this type of material, however, the difficulty lies in separating cause and effect. If the Mundugumor mothers treat the children in this way, there must be a relatively unfriendly attitude among them to start with; we cannot assume that the adult behavior is the result of the feeding habits. In any case it is probable that early experiences do have an effect upon the later optimism or pessimism of the individual, but these early experiences are not restricted to the phenomenon of feeding. It is more likely that the general atmosphere in which the young child develops is of prime importance in determining his attitude toward the world.

Freud speaks also of an anal character type, developing from an unusual childish interest in the function and products of elimination. There are three personality traits which Freud explains on this basis; the first is orderliness, frequently accompanied by bodily cleanliness, reliability, conscientiousness and pedantry. Patterns of activity and work may develop on the basis of habits of elimination, so that there may be on the one hand thoroughness, persistence, general energy and on the other, inactivity, brooding, delay, postponement of work with final complete absorption and rapid productivity, and so on. A second trait is parsimony, which may become avarice. This is due to symbolization or to identification of the products of elimination with gifts or money. The third trait is obstinacy, which may become defiance and include irascibility and vindictiveness. This approach has also been applied to the understanding of a culture, in this case by Roheim (71) to the Australian Arunta. Roheim finds this triad of traits entirely absent among the Australians, who have at the same time a completely natural attitude toward elimination, without any taboos or restrictions whatsoever. It is important to check this on other communities before deciding whether the Australian material indicates a causal relationship. In any case this whole approach rests upon very inadequate evidence.

With reference to the general tendency to divide human beings into types, there are several critical considerations which should be mentioned. In the first place, as has already been indicated, types are unsatisfactory because so few individuals actually fit into the categories which the typology assumes. Most people are not completely introvert or extravert; theoretic or economic; Apollonian or Dionysian. Pure types are so rare as to make the whole procedure questionable. In the second place, there is the related fact that no two individuals are alike, and that the use of a single term to include the behavior of a large number of different persons ignores the wide variations among them. Finally, as in the case of racial classifications, the fact that one typology cuts across another throws doubt on the reality of any one of them. An introvert may be theoretic or religious, an oral optimist may be Apollonian or Dionysian, social values may be found both in tough-minded and tender-minded individuals. The notion of types is convenient, but misleading. Except in extreme cases, it probably subtracts from rather than adds to a thorough psychological understanding of the individual.

SUMMARY

Personality may be described as that which is unique in an individual, and which marks him off from others. It is not a mere sum of traits, but a dynamic integration. *Character* refers to the moral aspects of personality, and *temperament* to habitual emotional behavior.

Among the attempts to find a biological or organic basis for personality may be mentioned the study of physiognomy, which has some value as an aspect of expressive behavior; phrenology, which has been discredited; glandular secretions, undoubtedly of importance, although the exact nature and extent of the effects upon normal personality remain to be determined; general bodily constitution, which seems to show some relation to psychosis, but has not been demonstrated to have any consistent relation to the characteristics of the normal individual; body chemistry, from which conflicting results have so far been obtained, and others. The combined evidence is to the effect that biological factors do play a part.

There have been many attempts to classify individual personalities into types; the most significant is the introvert-extravert typology of Jung. This has been studied in various ways, by means of clinical observation, questionnaires and experimental techniques. Another interesting typology is that of Spranger, who describes six systems of values. Psychoanalysts have spoken of oral and anal types. Typologies are suggestive and useful, but they fit few individuals completely and they do violence to the uniqueness of personality.

REFERENCES

1. Berman, L. *The Glands Regulating Personality.* 1921.
2. Kretschmer, E. *Physique and Character.* 1925.
3. Allport, F. H. *Social Psychology.* 1924.
4. Allport, G. W. *Personality: A Psychological Interpretation.* 1937.
5. May, M. A. "The Foundations of Personality," *Psychology at Work* (ed. by P. S. Achilles). 1932.
6. Theophrastus. In R. C. Jebb's *The Characters of Theophrastus.* 1909.
7. Earle, J. *Microcosmographie.* 1628.
8. La Bruyère, J. de. *Les Caractères.* 1688.
9. Lavater, J. K. *Physiognomische Fragmente zur Beförderung der Menschenkenntniss und Menschenliebe.* 3 vols. 1783-1787.
10. Lombroso, C. *Crime, Its Causes and Remedies.* 1911 (Tr.).
11. Ellis, H. *A Study of British Genius.* Rev. ed. 1927.
12. Woods, F. H. "What is There in Physiognomy? I. The Size of the Nose," *J. Heredity,* 1921, 12: pp. 301-318.
13. Blackford, K. M. H., and Newcomb, A. *The Job, the Man, the Boss.* 1914.
14. Paterson, D. G. *Physique and Intellect.* 1930.
15. Viteles, M. S. *Industrial Psychology.* 1932.
16. Klineberg, O. *Race Differences.* 1935.
17. Healy, W. *Personality in Formation and Action.* 1938.
18. Gall, F. J. *On the Functions of the Brain.* 6 vols. 1835.
19. Spurzheim, G. *The Physiognomical System of Gall and Spurzheim.* 1815.
20. Fowler, O. S. *Human Science or Phrenology.* 1873.

21. Lanier, L. H., and Leedy, J. L. "Speed of Reaction in Relation to Basal Metabolism and Blood Pressure," *Psychol. Bull.*, 1933, 30: pp. 609-610.

22. Steinberg, J. "The Relation between Basal Metabolism and Mental Speed," *Arch. Psychol.*, 1934, No. 172.

23. Levy, J. "A Quantitative Study of the Relationship between Basal Metabolic Rate and Children's Behavior Problems," *Amer. J. Orthopsychiat.*, 1931, 10: pp. 298-310.

24. Cannon, W. B. *Bodily Changes in Pain, Hunger, Fear, and Rage.* 1929.

25. Draper, G. *The Human Constitution.* 1924.

26. Garvey, C. R. "Comparative Body Build of Manic-Depressive and Schizophrenic Patients," *Psychol. Bull.*, 1933, 30: pp. 567-568.

27. Farber, M. L. "A Critique and An Investigation of Kretschmer's Theory," *J. Abn. and Soc. Psychol.*, 1938, 33: pp. 398-404.

28. Burchard, E. M. L. "Physique and Psychosis," *Comp. Psychol. Monog.*, 1936, 13, No. 1.

29. Klineberg, O., Asch, S. E., and Block, H. "An Experimental Study of Constitutional Types," *Genet. Psychol. Monog.*, 1934, 16, No. 3.

30. Klineberg, O., Fjeld, H., and Foley, J. P. Unpublished study.

31. Rich, G. J. "A Biochemical Approach to the Study of Personality," *J. Abn. and Soc. Psychol.*, 1928, 23: pp. 158-175.

32. McFarland, R. A., and Goldstein, H. "Biochemistry of the Psychoneuroses—a review," *Amer. J. Psychiat.*, 1937, 93: pp. 1073-1095.

33. Goldstein, H. "The Biochemical Variability of the Individual in Relation to Personality and Intelligence," *J. Exper. Psychol.*, 1935, 18: pp. 348-371.

34. Jasper, H. H. "Electrical Signs of Cortical Activity," *Psychol. Bull.*, 1937, 34: pp. 411-481.

35. Hammett, F. S. "Observations on the Relation between Emotional and Metabolic Stability," *Amer. J. Physiol.*, 1921, 53: pp. 307-311.

36. Alexander, F. *The Medical Value of Psychoanalysis.* Rev. ed. 1936.

37. Chappell, M. N. *In the Name of Common Sense; Worry and Its Control.* 1938.

38. Adler, A. *The Study of Organ Inferiority and Its Compensation.* 1917.

39. Cabot, P. S. de Q. "The Relationship between Character-

istics of Personality and Physique in Adolescents," *Genet. Psychol. Monog.*, 1938, No. 20.

40. Saudek, R. *The Psychology of Handwriting.* 1925.
41. Michon, J. H. *Le Mystère de l'Écriture.* 1872.
42. Crépieux-Jamin, J. *"L'Écriture et le Caractère.* 4th ed. 1896.
43. Preyer, W. T. *Psychologie des Schreibens.* 1893.
44. Klages, L. *Prinzipien der Graphologie.* 3d ed. 1920; *Handschrift und Charakter.* 7th ed. 1923.
45. Allport, G. W., and Vernon, P. E. *Studies in Expressive Movement.* 1933.
46. Sapir, E. "Speech as a Personality Trait," *Amer. J. Sociol.*, 1927, 32: pp. 892-905.
47. Pear, T. H. *Voice and Personality.* 1931.
48. Cantril, H., and Allport, G. W. *The Psychology of Radio.* 1935.
49. Gerstäcker, F. See reference *45.*
50. Wolff, W. "The Experimental Study of Forms of Expression," *Char. and Pers.*, 1933, 2: pp. 168-176.
51. Allport, F. H., Walker, L., and Lathers, E. "Written Composition and Characteristics of Personality," *Arch. Psychol.*, 1934, No. 173.
52. Woodworth, R. S. *Psychology.* Rev. ed. 1929.
53. Jacobson, E. *Progressive Relaxation.* 1938.
54. Nietzsche, F. *The Birth of Tragedy.* 1924.
55. Benedict, R. F. *Patterns of Culture.* 1934.
56. James, W. *Pragmatism.* 1911.
57. Jung, C. G. *Psychological Types.* 1926.
58. Plant, J. S. *Personality and the Cultural Pattern.* 1937.
59. Heidbreder, E. "Measuring Introversion and Extroversion," *J. Abn. and Soc. Psychol.*, 1927, 21: pp. 120-134.
60. Marston, L. R. "The Emotions of Young Children: An Experimental Study in Introversion and Extroversion," *Univ. Iowa Stud. Child Welfare*, 1925, 3, No. 3.
61. Newcomb, T. M. "The Consistency of Certain Extrovert-Introvert Behavior Patterns in 51 Problem Boys," *Teach. Coll. Contrib. Educ.*, 1929, No. 382.
62. Freyd, M. "Introverts and Extroverts," *Psychol. Rev.*, 1924, 31: pp. 74-87.
63. Laird, D. A. "Mental Hygiene and Vocational Tests," *J. Ed. Psychol.*, 1925, 16: pp. 419-422.
64. Conklin, E. S. "The Determination of Normal Extrovert-Introvert Interest Differences," *Pedagogical Seminary and J. Genet. Psychol.*, 1927, 34: pp. 28-37.

65. Spranger, E. *Types of Men.* 1928.
66. Allport, G. W., and Vernon, P. E. *A Study of Values.* 1931.
67. Harris, D. "Group Differences in Values within a University," *J. Abn. and Soc. Psychol.*, 1934, 29: pp. 95-102.
68. Abraham, K. *Selected Papers.* 1927.
69. Campbell, C. M. *Human Personality and the Environment.* 1934.
70. Mead, M. *Sex and Temperament in Three Primitive Societies.* 1935.
71. Roheim, G. "Psychoanalysis of Primitive Cultural Types," *Internatl. J. Psychoanal.*, 1932, 13: pp. 2-224.

CHAPTER XVI

THE MEASUREMENT OF PERSONALITY

INTRODUCTION

THERE is probably no field of psychology which has attracted more attention in recent years than that of personality testing. The reviews of this material and the related bibliography (*1, 2, 3*) indicate the extent to which the subject has grown. In spite of that fact there is still considerable difference of opinion as to the value of this quantitative approach to personality. In 1927 Roback (*4*) wrote:

The empirical approach to the study of character is not to be belittled, and some of the experimental methods devised bespeak a considerable amount of ingenuity applied in such a manifestly elusive sphere. At the same time it is doubtful whether the combined efforts of all the experimental investigators have established half a dozen new facts or have placed the subject in a new light (p. 354).

Although considerable time has elapsed since this was written, many psychologists would subscribe to this opinion at the present time. Thorndike's (*5*) statement, to which reference has already been made, that "whatever exists, exists in some amount and can be measured" is widely accepted, but it is not agreed that in the meantime adequate methods have been devised for the measurement of personality.

The whole testing approach in this field has been criticized by clinicians and others whose attention is usually centered upon the individual patient. From their point of view testing does violence to the nature of the individual case. To the clinician each individual is unique and can be understood in terms only of a total life history which makes use of all the available information about him. The relatively isolated and piecemeal information supplied by a test consequently seems inadequate. On the other hand, the experimental psychologist believes with some reason that generalizations may be made only from a large number of cases and from adequately controlled data, and he regards the test as the only satisfactory means to that end. There is probably some truth in both positions, and the method to be used will depend in each case on the nature of the problem. There is no need to discard either method in favor of the other.

Personality tests in general may be divided into two groups —the so-called paper-and-pencil test and the performance test. In the former the subject is asked questions, or reports upon his personal impressions; in the performance test he is given the opportunity to show by his actions to what degree he possesses the trait which is being studied.

PAPER-AND-PENCIL TESTS

In the first group considerable attention has been paid to various rating methods. Individuals are rated, usually on a scale, for the amount of a given trait which they appear to possess. Sometimes the ratings are made by others, sometimes by the subject himself. A common method is to define the various steps on the scale and then ask the judge to determine what position the subject occupies; for example, an educator may be asked to rank his student for "originality" on a scale in which the one extreme represents the 5% of the most original students he has known, and the other extreme, the 5% least original. The intervening points may be assigned in various ways. It appears that a rating scale with seven divisions is the most satisfactory. There is almost no limitation to the wide variety of situations in which rating scales may be used, and they are a convenient tool in many research problems. In the experiments on physiognomy, for example, mentioned on page 409, blond and brunette students were rated for the possession of those traits regarded by Blackford (6) and others as related to pigmentation. Rating scales have also been widely used in the validation of other testing methods.

There are many pitfalls in the use of this method (*7*). The most important of these are the fact that the judge may not know all the subjects equally well so that the acquaintance factor may cause him to rate some of them too high and others too low, the "halo effect" which makes most judges believe that subjects who are superior in one respect will excel in others also, the subjectivity of the ratings, individual differences between standards used by different raters, and so on. This means that the validity of the rating scale is usually in doubt and it may be added that the doubt is all the greater when the scale makes use of self-ratings. The reliability of this method, arrived at usually by comparing the results of two different raters, is in the neighborhood of $+.55$ (*1*), which means that the method has a fair but not a high degree of consistency.

The most common type of paper-and-pencil test of personality is the questionnaire. The first important use of this method was made by Woodworth (*8*) in 1917 with his psychoneurotic inventory, or Personal Data Sheet. This was devised for use in the American Army by a Committee on Emotional Fitness of the National Research Council. Woodworth studied the actual symptoms of the war neuroses and chose from these 116 questions referring to the presence or absence of these symptoms. The subjects were asked, for example, "Do you get rattled easily?" "Did you ever have a strong desire to commit suicide?" etc. This questionnaire has given an impetus to the construction of many others, similar in general aim, though differing in detail. In 1921 Matthews (*9*) adapted it for use among school children. Laird (*10*) used it at the college level, but separated the questions into sub-groups so that he could obtain information as to the specific nature of the symptoms. One group had reference to psychasthenia, the items dealing with the presence of obsessions, morbid fears and doubts; the second to schizoid tendencies—social adjustments, daydreams and fantasy; the third to neurasthenic symptoms—aches, pains, fatiguability, anxiety regarding health and so on. House (11) revised the Woodworth inventory to include questions referring to childhood experiences. More recently, new inventories have been devised by Thurstone (12), Bell (13), Lecky (14), Bernreuter (15), and others.

The general purpose of questionnaires of this type is to discover the presence of neurotic symptoms in a latent or incipient form, so that the subject may be aided before he becomes a definite psychiatric case. With this aim they have been used widely in colleges and universities, as well as in connection with vocational guidance. One objection usually raised against them is that there is never any assurance that the questions are being answered correctly. This may of course be due to the unwillingness of the subject to admit the presence of neurotic symptoms, or to his inability to recognize them when they occur. Different subjects may interpret the questions differently, and it is difficult completely to exclude ambiguity in the expressions used (16). The temporary emotional attitude of the subject may also distort the picture and cause him to give answers which do not usually hold true. In the second place, there is always doubt as to the meaning of a total score in an inventory of this kind. One subject may have a great many symptoms to a mild degree, and may therefore not require psychiatric treatment; another may have only one symptom, but it may be so severe as to be really dangerous, as, for example, if thoughts of suicide are constantly present. The former of these two subjects would have a much higher neurotic score than the latter, and this would of course be misleading. Although these cases are purposely exaggerated, facts of this type probably account for the finding (17) that many "normal" individuals receive a higher neurotic score than some persons known to be neurotic. On the average, the results are in the direction claimed by the inventory, but there are many individual exceptions. The inventory may therefore be used to indicate the probability of a tendency to neurosis, but the results must always be interpreted with considerable caution. The reliability or consistency of the inventories in general use is usually good, but the validity has not been demonstrated to be high enough so that the results may safely be accepted as an adequate indication of tendency to neurosis.

Among the special inventories, designed to measure the presence of specific traits rather than of general tendency to neurosis, mention has already been made of those dealing with introversion-extraversion, and of "The Study of Values." One other which should be mentioned in this connection is the Allport (18) Ascendance-Submission Study. The questions deal mainly with social situations, and the subject is asked to report his usual reactions—whether, for example, he would walk to the front of a lecture room to take his seat if this would make him conspicuous, whether he takes an active part in classroom discussion, etc. This test is regarded by its authors as useful in vocational guidance, submissive individuals presumably being unfitted for tasks which require many aggressive social contacts. Recently Maslow (19) has devised a questionnaire on Dominance which is somewhat similar in intention, but which stresses the presence of dominant or submissive reactions mainly in connection with members of the opposite sex.

Another personality test of the paper-and-pencil type is the well-known Pressey X-O Test (20) for investigating the emotions. In the revised form there are four parts—(1) in which the subject crosses out all words which seem to him unpleasant; (2) all words which refer to things which he regards as wrong; (3) words which are associated in his mind with the key words given; (4) words referring to things about which he worries. Total affectivity is presumably measured by the total number of words crossed out, and idiosyncrasy scores may also be obtained by adding up the number of words crossed out which are not the same as those crossed out by the majority of other subjects. The test is interesting, but its reliability is not very high and its validity has not been adequately demonstrated.

It may be possible to use certain questionnaires in an indirect manner so that the purpose is hidden from the subject, in which case the questionnaire really functions as a performance test of personality. An example of this technique is Murray's Psychological Insight Test (*21*) which compares the subject's rating of himself with the estimate that others have of him. This method assumes that the ratings by others may be depended upon, and that any marked discrepancy of the self-rating indicates lack of psychological insight. A similar use may be made of Lennig Sweet's test (*22*) in which, for example, a subject's estimate of what "most boys" would do in a certain situation is compared with what the boys themselves say they would do; the amount of agreement is used as a measure of "Social Insight."

PERFORMANCE TESTS

Among the performance tests of personality the most significant are those employed by Hartshorne and May (*23*) in their studies of deceit, which form part of their general investigation under the Character Education Inquiry. They made use of a large number of different tests of honesty. One of these was the "duplicating technique" in which students were given an examination of the usual school type, after which their papers were taken away and the answers noted; the original papers were then returned to the students who were told the correct answers and allowed to mark their own papers. Comparisons were then made with the duplicates, and the amount of cheating was noted. A second method was the "improbable achievement" test, in which the subjects were required to perform difficult tasks with their eyes closed. Since such achievement was improbable, if not impossible, it was assumed that the successful ones had opened their eyes. There were also tests of overstatement in which the subjects were asked whether they had read certain books or knew the meaning of certain words, and since many of the titles and words were fictitious, the amount of cheating could be measured. Use was also made of the "double-testing technique," in which two equivalent forms of a test were given, one with a chance to cheat, the other without. It was assumed that when the second score was eight or more points lower, cheating had occurred. There were a number of cheating tests in connection with athletics; for example, the subject was given a dynamometer and his best score was noted by the experimenter. Then the subject was left alone and later asked about the record he had made in the interval. It was assumed that a marked improvement in the score indicated overstatement on his part. A second group of tests created opportunities for stealing by the "planting" of a coin in a puzzle-box given to the subject, who in many cases returned the box minus the coin. There were also tests of lying by means of the comparison of the actual scores obtained on the cheating tests, and the answers to questions concerning them.

The study yielded many interesting results, for example, a high correlation between honesty scores and intelligence, as well as between honesty scores and socio-economic status. There seemed little relationship to race or religion when socio-economic factors were controlled. Jewish children cheated more frequently than the average when they lived in a poor neighborhood, and less frequently than the average when their economic status was superior.

The most important conclusion from this investigation is that no single test of deceit has diagnostic significance for deceit in general. In other words, the fact that a child is dishonest in one situation gives very little information with reference to his behavior in another. The intercorrelations of different types of honesty tests vary from o to $+.45$, becoming progressively lower as the nature of the tests differs more widely. The behavior that we label honest or dishonest appears to be related to a specific situation rather than to a general character trait. Some individuals are consistently honest and others consistently dishonest, but most people seem to vary in this respect according to circumstances. The significance of the specific situation is also indicated by another finding to the effect that in one case cheating was more prevalent year after year with one particular teacher than with any of the others in the school. In fact, many of the pupils who cheated in this class had not cheated before and did not do so thereafter. Even within one particular type of honesty situation, therefore, the specific circumstances may alter the results.

Among other honesty tests, Maller's "Test of Sports and Hobbies" (24) may be mentioned. Ostensibly a test of information, it gives the subject an opportunity to cheat by looking at the answers printed at the end of the booklet. Half the questions are so difficult that they require information available to few if any subjects, and the number of such questions answered correctly is taken as a measure of dishonesty. Maller reports a correlation of +.82 between two alternative forms, and also significant differences between groups of delinquent and non-delinquent boys. H. W. James (25) has used bluffing as a measure of honesty, somewhat after the manner of the Overstatement Test of the Character Education Inquiry.

With reference to other performance tests of personality, mention has already been made of the various measures of suggestibility (see p. 323). In the series of experiments in this field conducted by Warner Brown (26) it was also noted that there was very little consistency in the results of the various tests. The average intercorrelation between them was only +.143. This again means that we cannot speak of suggestibility as a general character trait, since the ability to resist a suggestion varies with the nature of the performance involved.

Persistence has been studied by various methods. Morgan and Hull (27) recorded the time spent by the subjects in working on a partially concealed insoluble maze before they "gave up," and the Character Education Inquiry included a similar technique in connection with difficult puzzles. Howells (28) used a group of tests which involved the endurance of constantly increasing fatigue from holding a dynamometer, willingness to endure pain, and so forth. There was a high reliability (approximately +.90) in these tests with a median intercorrelation of +.50. The trait of perseveration is sometimes listed with persistence, but is quite distinct from it. It refers in a sense to the amount of inertia within the subject; a high degree of perseveration is taken to mean a high degree of sluggishness. In general the tests in this field involve the exercise of a thoroughly habituated activity, such as writing repeatedly a letter of the alphabet, and then attempting an activity closely similar to the habituated one. The amount of interference is presumably a measure of difficulty in shifting from one task to another (*29, 30, 31, 32*).

Attempts have been made to measure co-operation and other aspects of social interaction. The classical study in this field is that of Henning (*33*), who had two subjects work together, but recorded the work done by each, for example, by using a double ergograph. Another technique was to have the apparatus so set up that the work of one subject interfered with that of the other, and various relations between the subjects were revealed. Recently Rickers-Ovsiankina (*21*) attempted to use an actual life-situation as a test in this field. The subject was introduced into a room where he found another person (actually an assistant of the experimenter) and was told he would have to wait a short while for the experiment to begin. The subjects, observed through a one-way screen, displayed social attitudes varying from a companion-like reaction to a complete disregard of the existence of the other person.

The related traits of caution, speed of decision and recklessness have been studied by various methods. Henning (*33*) tested caution by giving the subject an elastic band and telling him to stretch it as wide as possible without breaking it, and a glass rod to bend as far as possible. Burtt and Frey (*34*) presented seven tasks designed to measure recklessness —pouring water into a beaker to a designed level, walking a maze with difficult hurdles as short cuts, placing nuts on screws, etc. Time and accuracy are recorded, so that the relation between care and haste may be noted. Intercorrelations range from .02 to .67. Speed of decision has been measured by Gibson (*35*), who presented a series of cards with varying arrangements of the four letters E, I, Y, K, the task being to name the letter which occurs most frequently on each card. The Downey Will-Temperament Profile (36) includes a test of speed of decision. Trow (37) also studied speed of decision in eight tasks, including some of those used by Downey. Intercorrelations ranged from —.25 to +.55.

Interesting work has been done on the "Level of Aspiration." Hoppe (38) defined this as "a person's expectations, goals, or claims on his own future achievement in a given task." Individual differences in reaction to success or failure seem to him to be related to ambition, caution, courage, self-confidence, fear of inferiority, as well as to the security of self-confidence and the courage to face reality. J. D. Frank (21) speaks of it more simply as "the level of performance in a familiar task which an individual explicitly undertakes to reach." He used a simple printing task and parts of Kelley's spatial relationships speed test. After being informed of his achievement in one trial, the subject states what he expects to do in the next one. Frank believes that this test can show among other things marked individual differences in objectivity toward one's own performance, in the ability to dismiss failures, in tenacity of purpose, etc. Gould (39) has indicated, however, that the same "level of aspiration" score may be due to very different factors in different subjects, and that some knowledge of the individual is necessary for the interpretation of his behavior in the test situation.

These and other personality tests show considerable ingenuity and the results obtained from them are of undoubted interest. They have the further advantage over paper-and-pencil tests in that there can be no doubt about their validity. A performance test of deceit actually measures deceit, at least in the specific situation studied. It is clear that the child has cheated in an examination or that he has exaggerated his performance or stolen the dime, and so on. There is, however, a serious criticism to be made of this whole technique. A performance test which sets out to measure deceit may actually be measuring deceit plus any one of a number of other factors. The honesty score of any particular child may be affected by his motivation; he may be ambitious and anxious to do well, or he may be indifferent to the marks he obtains on an examination. He may be intelligent enough to guess at the purpose of some of the tests, or he may be excessively afraid of detection. In a persistence test, there may be wide individual differences in the amount of interest in the task; the time spent in solving a crossword puzzle will depend at least in part on the enjoyment of the puzzle and not entirely on persistence as a personality trait. This interdependence of traits of personality and the consequent fact that no trait may be measured in isolation from others throws great doubt on the interpretation in any particular case. If deceit alone is to be measured, other factors must be controlled either by equating the subjects in every respect except the one to be measured, or by varying the conditions sufficiently so that these other factors cancel each other. Both techniques are difficult, but unless some such precaution is taken the results of the performance tests will be unclear. In this respect the Gestalt psychologists are correct in their insistence upon seeing personality in terms of total interrelationships rather than as a sum of separate and distinct traits.

The Rorschach Test. One other test of personality has recently attracted so much attention that it requires some comment at this point. This is the Rorschach Test (*40*), consisting of a series of symmetrical ink-blots presented to the subject, who reports what he "sees" in them. Hermann Rorschach was a Swiss psychiatrist who found this technique valuable for the understanding of the personality of his patients, on the principle that when we look at the ink-blots we see not what is there, but what is in ourselves. The usual procedure is to give the subject one card at a time (there are twelve in all) and allow him to look at it from any direction he wishes, holding it not further than arm's length away. There is no time limit, and the subject may be encouraged to look for more meanings in the ink-blot, if at first he gives only a few responses. The words of the subject are taken down verbatim, and the responses are divided into categories—responses determined by form, by color, by movement, whole responses, details, small details, etc. From the relative frequency of these various types, Rorschach and his followers believe that they can learn a great deal about the nature of the personality. Movement responses, for example, suggest intratensive (or introvert) reactions; color responses, extratensive (or extravert) reactions. Schizophrenics give a large number of detailed responses; intelligent subjects, a great many whole responses, and so on. As far as content is concerned, animal responses are frequent, but are found less often in intelligent subjects and those with rich fantasy than in persons whose thoughts and images are of a stereotyped nature. These are only a few of the inter-relationships suggested.

There have been several attempts to use the Rorschach Test in the study of group differences. A recent investigation in New York City by Hunter (*41*) showed that Negro subjects had a higher proportion of extratensive responses than a comparable group of White subjects; this is in agreement with the usual stereotype, but the difficulty of exactly equating the two racial groups in other respects throws some doubt on the conclusions. A study by Bleuler and Bleuler (*42*) of Moroccan subjects shows the importance of cultural factors even in a test of this type, and makes the use of norms obtained in our culture dubious. These Moroccans showed a tremendous interest in detail and gave detailed responses to a degree which would not occur in our society except in schizophrenic patients. The authors explain this result by the fact that Moroccan art and story-telling lay great emphasis upon detail and that this attitude expresses itself even in the test situation.

The Rorschach Test must be regarded as a promising approach to the understanding of the total personality. It is unfortunate that its use demands considerable experience, and that no objective rules can be established for the easy guidance of prospective testers. It is a test which does not conform to the usual criteria of objectivity and statistical exactness, but which, nevertheless, in the hands of a skillful investigator, does furnish valuable information.

The experimental approach known as "projective techniques" will be discussed in connection with the personality of young children.

SUMMARY

Personality tests are of two main types—paper-and-pencil tests and performance tests. The former include the rating scales, which have been used in a variety of research problems as well as in the validation of other testing techniques. Although useful in research, rating scales are subject to many pitfalls, some of which may be avoided by the careful choice of raters. Questionnaires have been directed mainly to the discovery of neurotic tendencies, the pioneer inventory of Woodworth being followed by many others with similar or related aims. Results must be interpreted with caution, since a high score indicates the probability but not the certainty that the subject has a tendency to neurosis.

Among the performance tests of personality, the most significant are those employed by the Character Education Inquiry in the studies of deceit. The results showed, among other things, that no single test could be used as a measure of deceit in general, and that the behavior of the subject varied in terms of the particular social situation. Performance tests have been used also as measures of suggestibility, persistence, co-operation, perseveration, speed of decision, aspiration level, and many other personality traits. The most important defect in all these measures is their specificity, and their consequent failure to take into adequate account the interdependence of various aspects of the personality.

The Rorschach test represents a promising attempt to understand the total personality.

REFERENCES

1. Symonds, P. M. *Diagnosing Personality and Conduct.* 1931.
2. Garrett, H. E., and Schneck, M. R. *Psychological Tests, Methods and Results.* 1933.
3. Maller, J. B. *Character and Personality Tests.* 1937.

4. Roback, A. A. *The Psychology of Character.* 1927.

5. Thorndike, E. L. "The Nature, Purposes, and General Methods of Measurement of Educational Products," *Yrbk. Nat. Soc. Stud. Ed.,* 1918, 17: pp. 16-24.

6. Blackford, K. M. H., and Newcomb, A. *The Job, the Man, the Boss.* 1914.

7. Allport, G. W. *Personality: A Psychological Interpretation.* 1937.

8. Woodworth, R. S. *Personal Data Sheet.* 1917.

9. Matthews, E. "A Study of Emotional Stability in Children," *J. Delinquency,* 1923, 8: pp. 1-40.

10. Laird, D. A. "Detecting Abnormal Behavior," *J. Abn. and Soc. Psychol.,* 1925, 20: pp. 128-141.

11. House, S. D. "A Mental Hygiene Inventory," *Arch. Psychol.,* 1927, No. 88.

12. Thurstone, L. L., and Thurstone, T. G. "A Neurotic Inventory," *J. Soc. Psychol.,* 1930, 1: pp. 3-30.

13. Bell, H. M. *The Adjustment Inventory.* 1934.

14. Lecky, P. *Individuality Record.* 1932.

15. Bernreuter, R. G. *The Personality Inventory.* 1931.

16. Benton, A. L. "The Interpretation of Questionnaire Items in a Personality Schedule," *Arch. Psychol.,* 1935, No. 190.

17. Landis, C., and Katz, S. E. "The Validity of Certain Questions Which Purport to Measure Neurotic Tendencies," *J. Appl. Psychol.,* 1934, 18: pp. 343-356.

18. Allport, G. W., and Allport, F. H. *A-S Reaction Study: A Scale for Measuring Ascendance-Submission in Personality.* 1929.

19. Maslow, A. H. "Dominance Feeling, Behavior and Status," *Psychol. Rev.,* 1937, 44: pp. 404-429.

20. Pressey, S. L. "A Group Scale for Investigating the Emotions," *J. Abn. and Soc. Psychol.,* 1921, 16: pp. 55-64.

21. Murray, H. A., et al. *Explorations in Personality.* 1938.

22. Sweet, L. *The Measurement of Personal Attitudes in Younger Boys.* 1929.

23. Hartshorne, H., and May, M. A. *Studies in Deceit.* 1928.

24. Maller, J. B. *Test of Sports and Hobbies.* 1933.

25. James, H. W. "Honesty as a Character Trait in Young People," *J. Educ. Res.,* 1933, 26: pp. 572-578.

26. Brown, W. "Individual and Sex Differences in Suggestibility," *Univ. Calif. Pub. in Psychol.,* 1916, 2: No. 6, pp. 291-430.

27. Morgan, J. J. B., and Hull, H. L. "The Measurement of Persistence," *J. Appl. Psychol.,* 1920, 10: pp. 180-187.

28. Howells, T. H. "An Experimental Study of Persistence," *J. Abn. and Soc. Psychol.*, 1933, 28: pp. 14-29.

29. Bernstein, E. "Quickness and Intelligence," *Brit. J. Psychol. Monog. Supplement*, 1924, 3, No. 7.

30. Cattell, R. B. "Perseveration and Personality: Some Experiments and a Hypothesis," *J. Ment. Sci.*, 1935, 81: pp. 151-167.

31. Stephenson, W. "Perseveration and Character," *Char. and Pers.*, 1935, 4: pp. 44-52.

32. Maller, J. B., and Elkin, J. *Attention Test.* 1933.

33. Henning, H. "Charaktertests," *Indus. Psychotech.*, 1927, 4: pp. 270-273.

34. Burtt, H. E., and Frey, O. C. "Suggestions for Measuring Recklessness," *Person. J.*, 1934, 13: pp. 39-46.

35. Gibson, S. M. "A Decision Study of 150 Young Men and Women," *J. Appl. Psychol.*, 1930, 4: pp. 364-374.

36. Downey, J. E. *The Will-Temperament and Its Testing.* 1923.

37. Trow, W. C. "Trait Consistency and Speed of Decision," *School and Soc.*, 1925, 21: pp. 538-542.

38. Hoppe, F. "Erfolg und Misserfolg," *Psychol. Forsch.*, 1930, 14: pp. 1-62.

39. Gould, R. "An Experimental Analysis of 'Level of Aspiration,'" *Genet. Psychol. Monog.*, 1939, 21: pp. 1-116.

40. Rorschach, H. *Psychodiagnostik.* 2d ed. 1932.

41. Hunter, M. "Responses of Comparable White and Negro Adults to the Rorschach Test," *J. Psychol.*, 1937, 3: pp. 173-182.

42. Bleuler, M., and Bleuler, R. "Rorschach's Ink-Blot Test and Racial Psychology: Mental Peculiarities of Moroccans," *Char. and Pers.*, 1935-36, 4: pp. 97-114.

CHAPTER XVII

GENETIC AND BIOGRAPHICAL APPROACHES TO PERSONALITY

PERSONALITY OF YOUNG CHILDREN

THE methods of studying personality described in the preceding chapter are usually not applicable to young children. The large majority of personality tests are of the paper-and-pencil variety and require considerable linguistic development and understanding. Many of them are as a matter of fact applied only to adults, and an experimenter who is studying school children may often be at a loss to discover adequate techniques. The Rorschach is one of the few tests which may be used with immature subjects. The performance tests may also be tried at younger ages, although they too require a certain level of maturity. As a result a number of techniques have been developed which are especially applicable to young children.

The study of personality differences in early childhood has a number of important implications. The observation of personality in the making may throw important light on the genesis of personality differences. That such differences are found at a very early age cannot be disputed. These may be constitutional in nature, with their origin in glandular and other physical factors to which reference has already been made. The fact that they appear so early, and that infants almost immediately after birth already differ in their reactions makes such a constitutional basis highly probable. It is also possible that factors in the early experience of the child, perhaps even before birth, may have causal significance. Genetic studies are of the greatest importance in this field. An investigation at present in progress in California is engaged in an extended survey which starts with the child before birth, that is to say, it studies the family environment into which the child will enter, and the reception which awaits him. It inquires into the marital relationships of the parents; it records the conditions of pregnancy and childbirth and the physical condition of the new-born infant. Thereafter it makes periodical examinations of the child so that his whole history during the early formative years is followed with the greatest care. Few results have as yet been reported (*1*), but a study of this kind should make a definite contribution.

Healy (*2*) has pointed to the wide variations observable in fetal behavior as possibly foreshadowing later personality differences. These variations occur particularly in the extent of reflex activity and output of energy. "Intelligent mothers of aggressively active children have in a few instances given us reliable histories of unusual activity, dating back to a considerable time before birth" (p. 71). The factors determining these differences are not well understood, and they may depend either upon constitutional make-up or upon the nature of the maternal environment. Unfortunately no method has as yet been discovered for the study in any detail of environmental conditions before birth.

There is ample evidence that personality differences are clear-cut from the earliest period of life. R. F. Washburn (*3*), for example, studied the reactions of fifteen babies to various laughter stimuli, the experiment being repeated at four-week intervals from the eighth to the fifty-second week level. There were very marked individual differences in the strength and frequency of the reactions. In another connection similar differences are reported by Charlotte Bühler (*4*), who observed the behavior of nursing children put together in small social groups. Some of the children were embarrassed and inactive; others were openly delighted; some pounced on the toys and paid no attention to the other children; others explored the general environment; some robbed their companions of all their toys, while others attempted to exchange their own toys for those of other children; some were furious in the new situation and showed definitely negativistic attitudes even in the first year of life.   It is difficult to be certain whether these differences are due to early association with the mothers and other people in the social environment, or to inherited dispositions.   Bühler regards the latter as the more likely explanation.

It appears to be true that individual differences in personality appear so early that drastic differences in conditioning have not yet had time to play an important part.[1]   The weight of evidence is definitely in favor of some sort of hereditary predisposition which plays a part in the causation of individual differences in very young children.   Whether it is more or less important than environmental factors, we are in no position to say.

Granting the existence of an hereditary factor, this does not mean that later adult personality is similarly determined.   We have here the important problem of consistency in the life history—namely, whether personality characteristics found in early life remain relatively unaltered by later experiences.   In the study by Washburn, to which we have just made reference, it was found that most children remained true to type from the second to the twelfth month.   Bonham and Sargent (5) studied the relationship between the personality of the newborn and that of the same child twenty-four to thirty months later.   They originally obtained ratings on 120 babies by the head nurse of the maternity ward, the traits rated including good-naturedness, restless motion, frequency of smiling and good looks.   The correlations with the later measures of personality were very low, good looks being the only one of the characteristics which showed definite consistency.

The problem of consistency of behavior has been subjected to careful critical analysis by Murphy and Murphy (6), who discuss some of the difficulties in the concept.   They point out that the terms "consistent" and "inconsistent" have been con-

---

[1] It may be added that those who have had experience in breeding dogs have been struck with the marked differences in activity and disposition in members of the same litter soon after birth.

fused with "invariable" and "variable," and they correctly insist upon keeping these concepts distinct from each other. Behavior which varies in its specific character may still be consistent from the point of view of the organization of the personality, and behavior which remains invariable in spite of alterations in the external situation may actually be inconsistent both from the point of view of logic and of personality organization. They suggest that confusion would be eliminated if the terms "consistency" and "inconsistency" were avoided.

It would be better to confine ourselves to the terms "variable" and "invariable" when we are referring to the objective records of stimulus-response units. On the other hand, when we are referring to qualitatively different behaviors appearing in different situations, yet arising from one psychologically intelligible attitude of the whole personality, the term "congruence" (Allport and Vernon, 1933) is preferable (6, pp. 1049-1050).

The possibility of altering personality characteristics by a change in the accompanying circumstances has been demonstrated by Jack (7) in an ingenious study of ascendant behavior among four-year-old children. Ascendant behavior is defined to include the pursuit of one's own purposes against interference and direction by others. After careful observation, 18 children were divided into three groups—ascendant, moderately ascendant, and non-ascendant. The differences between them seemed to be mainly a matter of self-confidence. The five most non-ascendant children were selected and given information regarding the opportunity to use certain materials, including complicated toys, etc. They were then put back with the others, and they made a tremendous gain in their ascendance scores. Apparently, the acquisition of new information and the ability therefore to take the lead in social situations altered their "personalities." The problem remains as to the permanence of this change and its transfer to other social situations. Jack's conclusions were verified in a subsequent study by Page (8), who found that ascendance could be increased by a "training series" and by attendance at a nursery school.   There was some tendency, however, for the effect to be less marked after the passage of time.   The results show clearly, nevertheless, the manner in which personality characteristics may be influenced by experience, and it is highly probable that the change would be permanent if the experience continued to act in the same direction.

Among the methods employed in the study of young children, one of the most widespread is the controlled observation technique developed by Dorothy Thomas (9).   One result of the establishment of a large number of pre-school laboratories and nursery schools has been the possibility of observing children in a free play-group situation.   In connection with the kind of behavior studied, observers are trained to record carefully the behavior of the child during a brief period of time. This is known as the "short-sample technique," the period of observation varying from one minute to half an hour, depending upon the nature of the problem.   Frequently a code is used so that all the relevant behavior may be recorded as quickly as possible.   Thomas used this technique in the study of contacts between children and found striking individual differences in the ratio of the number of contacts made by a child with others, as compared with the number others made with him.   The method has been used in connection with a large number of different problems.   It has the advantage of having usually a high reliability, the results obtained in one sample period agreeing quite closely with those obtained in another (10).   On the other hand, it is true that a tremendous amount of material of this type has been collected without any adequate analysis, and unrelated to any particular problem posed by the investigator.   The records of behavior are precise and complete, but they often have little meaning.   It is perhaps for this reason that the method has lost some of its former popularity.

Projective Techniques.   In recent years an entirely different approach—the projective technique—has been used in an attempt to see how the total personality of the child reveals itself in an imaginary situation.   David Levy (11) was per-

haps the first to use the method of having children play with
dolls which were labeled "Father," "Mother," "Brother," and
so on.   From the treatment of these dolls, as well as in the
verbal fantasy associated with them, Levy was able to obtain
a great deal of information about family relationships and
sibling rivalry.   In many cases, a hitherto unsuspected difficulty in the life of the child expressed itself in this way.   An
allied technique makes use of a number of pictures showing a
man engaged in different types of activity or with varying
emotional expressions and asking the child, "Which is your
daddy?"   In this way also, it may be discovered whether the
child habitually sees his father as a scowling or as a friendly
person (12, 13).   L. B. Murphy (14) has made an ingenious
use of this method in her study of sympathy in young children, and has shown the interesting variations between children in their manner of interpreting the same picture.   The
rich fantasy which occasionally emerges from such an interpretation of pictures has been used by Murray (15) as a kind
of abbreviated psychoanalysis.   He believes that the picture
functions mainly as the first item in a chain of associations,
and that the personality of the subject shows itself in the nature of the associations which follow.   He has made use of the
same technique in a variety of studies, and refers to it as
the Thematic Apperception Test.   The Rorschach Test (see
above) has a somewhat similar function, since it also creates
the opportunity for projection, although the results are different when the materials vary in meaning and definiteness.
Both methods are valuable, some subjects expressing themselves more freely in one situation, and others in the other.

Mention should also be made in this connection of the
puppet shows which have been used by the psychiatrists at
Bellevue Hospital.   One method is to present one of these
shows and to stop before the end, then leaving it to the children to decide what the end should be.   There is sometimes a
demand for a violently aggressive ending, whereas other children prefer that the enemies be reconciled.   This method not
only gives to the children an opportunity to express any latent

aggressiveness, but also uncovers existing emotional attitudes. As in the case of the pictures, the technique may be modified by having the puppets represent definite individuals in the environment of the child, and allowing him to express freely his emotions concerning them. This whole approach has great promise for therapy as well as for personality study and will probably be modified in many ways in future investigations. It cannot be used like a personality test and is not easily susceptible to quantitative or statistical treatment; on the other hand it has the great virtue of making use of a situation in which the whole personality of the child plays a part in the response, and which makes it possible to learn something of the underlying worries and preoccupations of the child. The one important caution which must be observed, however, is in the interpretation of the fantasy of the child as "real." It may be that the correspondence between fantasy and reality is not always so close as this method would assume.

Piaget (16) has made use of language as an index to the development of the social personality of the child. When two children are together, the language that they use may be of two different types—(1) egocentric and (2) socialized. In the former, the child does not bother to know to whom he is speaking, or whether anyone is listening to him. He makes no attempt to place himself at the point of view of the hearer, and anyone may serve as an audience. Egocentric speech consists of mere repetition, or a monologue, or a sort of dual or collective monologue in which the other child serves as a stimulus although his viewpoint is not taken into account. This type of language is the more frequent of the two until the age of seven or eight. In socialized speech, on the other hand, there may be a real exchange of information, criticism, commands and requests, questions and answers. In this type, the child shows his awareness of the other person, and the increasing frequency of socialized as compared with egocentric speech gives some indication of the degree of social development of the child.

An interesting approach to personality study among children

has been made by Moreno (*17*), in his development of "sociometry," by which he means in general the measurement of the social inter-relationships within a population. As applied in the classroom, for example, his technique consists in finding out from each child which member of the class he would like to have sit near him. In this way he is able to draw a chart indicating the positive and negative attitudes of these children toward each other. He finds that there are certain key individuals, or leaders, who have a positive attraction for a great many others in the class; others who are "isolates," not wanted by anyone; and others in between. This method makes it possible to rearrange the seating so that most children have neighbors whom they like, instead of being placed in a haphazard manner. The technique may be used not only in a classroom, but also in helping to create any harmonious community. One of the interesting results is that a person who is an isolate, and therefore very unhappy in one group, may find himself fairly well liked in another, and his whole personality will undergo a consequent change for the better. In the placement of girls in the cottages of the Home with which Moreno is connected, excellent results have been obtained by this method of reducing the possibilities of friction in any small group. One other aspect of Moreno's method is the Spontaneity Test, in which Moreno has his subjects take part in a sort of dramatic play in which they express spontaneously various emotional attitudes. It may happen, for instance, that when two girls act out "anger" or "hate" together, they put on such a convincing performance, that the observer has reason to suspect that this really represents their attitudes toward each other; so with the other emotions.[2]

THE BIOGRAPHICAL APPROACH

The review of the methods of studying personality in young children leads naturally to a consideration of the whole prob-

[2] For a comprehensive account of the process of socialization in young children, and of the varied research techniques used, see Murphy, Murphy, and Newcomb (*18*).

lem of personality genesis and development. In this connection the materials presented in biographies and autobiographies furnish a rich source of information as to the variations between personalities, and of the manner in which these variations express themselves. Since, however, these biographies have been written from many different points of view, and usually with little concern for those aspects of personality in which the psychologist is primarily interested, the approach through biography has not usually been regarded as a scientifically acceptable method. Use has been made of biographical material, but for the most part in piecemeal fashion, as illustrative of one or another general theory of personality.

Recently, an attempt has been made by Dollard (*19*) to place the writing of biographies upon a more scientific basis through the use of certain "criteria" for an acceptable life history. These criteria represent the most significant systematization in this field and will therefore be presented in detail with some critical comments.

1. *The subject must be viewed as a specimen in a cultural series.* Much is known about an individual merely from the fact that he is born into a certain community. We can foretell a great deal about the later personality of any individual at birth if we know the nature of the culture of his group. This is a criterion which has on the whole not received adequate consideration in the biographies which we possess. Most writers have taken for granted the folkways of the community and have not stressed sufficiently their direct effect upon the personality. The writings of the anthropologists satisfy this criterion better than do any others.

2. *The organic motors of action ascribed must be socially relevant.* Here Dollard, in spite of his predominantly cultural and sociological approach, appears to give some weight to the organic basis of personality. As a matter of fact, the organic motors of which he speaks appear to be those which are common to all individuals, rather than those which account for personality differences. There are of course biological motives related to hunger and sex, which to a considerable

extent condition the individual's response to his social environment and which play an important part in his personality development. There are also, however, glandular and metabolic factors which are "socially relevant" and which Dollard completely neglects. Although it is true that the organic basis of personality differences is not adequately understood, there seems little doubt that it exists, and it should be taken into account wherever possible. The biographical analysis of the endocrinologists and of Kretschmer and others who stress the significance of constitution may be said to satisfy this criterion, although the manner in which they do so is not universally regarded as valid.

3. *The peculiar role of the family group in transmitting the culture must be recognized.* There can be no doubt that the family is of the greatest importance in the development of personality, and it has been stressed by most biographers. Among the psychological systems, the Adlerian, and to a lesser extent the Freudian, have given to the family a very great significance. It should be kept in mind that this significance will vary in degree according to the nature of the culture. It is likely that in ancient China the large family really constituted the social environment of the individual to such an extent that outside influences were relatively unimportant (20). In our society also the influence of the family is undoubtedly very great. In modern Russia, on the other hand, as the result of what Frankwood Williams (21) calls "the emotional aeration" of the home, the other members of one's family are taken much more for granted, and their influence is apparently secondary to that of the prevailing ideology taught in the school and in the community generally. In Samoa (22), where a child who is dissatisfied with his own home may find a more congenial one with some of his relatives, there are obvious limitations to the role of the family. The hostility against the father, for example, which allegedly plays a dominant role in the development of certain types of personality, will not develop to nearly the same extent if the son may leave his father's house whenever he is so inclined. In this same con-

nection it is important to keep in mind that the nature of the family may vary in different cultures; we have already referred to the Trobriand Islanders (see p. 147) among whom authority is vested in the uncle, not the father. In the American Negro family it is probable that in large sections of the country the mother is the real head of the household, and the whole pattern of inter-family relationships may be altered as a consequence (23). We should add, therefore, to Dollard's criterion our insistence upon the recognition of variations both in extent and in kind of family influence, and also upon the fact that the family is important not only in transmitting the culture, but also in terms of the personal relationships which develop within its framework.

4. *The specific method of elaboration of organic materials into social behavior must be shown.* It is a little difficult to see why this criterion should have been separated from the second. The emphasis here seems to be on the need to show how the organic materials work, instead of remaining satisfied with their mere description or enumeration. The two criteria could easily be combined into one which has reference to the inclusion of the organic or biological approach to the understanding of personality.

5. *The continuous related character of experience from childhood through adulthood must be stressed.* This is an insistence upon seeing the total personality in terms of its development through life. The genetic approach should be carried back as far as possible so that any explanation of later behavior in terms of early experiences will have an adequate basis. Inconsistency, real or apparent, must be explained in terms of the specific situations which give rise to them. This criterion has on the whole been fairly well satisfied by most biographers, and has been stressed in particular by the Freudians, who see personality characteristics as directly related to the experiences of early childhood.

6. *The "social situation" must be carefully and continuously specified as a factor.* Behavior is not understood except in relation to the social situation; Dollard insists, however,

*t*hat the social situation as seen by an outside observer may not be the same as that seen by the subject himself. It is important always to keep in mind the standpoint from which the subject interprets his social environment.

7. *The life history material itself must be organized and conceptualized.* This criterion is perhaps the most controversial. Dollard is suggesting that a life history can be written only in terms of some conceptual system, and that it must not be a mere collection of facts. It is of course true that no biographer can write down everything that has occurred in the lifetime of his subject and therefore he must make a selection of the materials he wishes to present. Such a selection would undoubtedly be more coherent and logical if undertaken from the standpoint of a certain theory of personality which serves as a framework into which the details may fit. On the other hand it is precisely this conceptualization which has troubled the readers of biographies written, for example, from the Freudian or Adlerian point of view. In Freudian biographies, the choice of materials related to early sex life or to attitudes toward the parents may be stressed to the relative neglect of experiences which a non-Freudian might regard as having a decisive influence. There is no doubt that the same life history written from the Freudian and Adlerian standpoints, respectively, would stress different factors and that the actual content of the biography would differ markedly as a consequence. If a biography is to be generally useful, it seems clear that it ought not to be tied too closely to any one system of psychological interpretation. Perhaps here a compromise position is possible, permitting the organization of the material in terms of one particular system, but with the inclusion of materials which might possibly be relevant to any other theory of the nature of personality formation.

These criteria are in need of revision, but they represent a significant attempt to make the writing of biographies more useful. It would be worth while to examine the life histories which have appeared, or to write new ones with the use of these criteria in mind, in order to see the extent to which they are really applicable. Dollard has already made this attempt with six biographies which are written from various points of view, but he has been concerned mainly with pointing out their limitations in respect to the criteria. It would be advisable to repeat the process without any preconceptions as to the value of the criteria which Dollard has suggested.

THE GENIUS

For obvious reasons, the large majority of biographies have been concerned with individuals whose lives are of general interest because they stand out in some important way from their fellows. The problem of genius has attracted the attention of investigators in various fields of social science, and many attempts have been made to determine the essential characteristics of genius. Extensive use has been made of material available in biographies, although recently experimental techniques have also entered this field.

The term "genius" as first used in the ancient Italian religions was the god-like personification of the procreative power of man. Later it was extended to refer to his creative power in general and was considered responsible in particular for any activity of a rare and extraordinary character. It has been defined as "the highest conceivable form of original ability, something altogether extraordinary and beyond even supreme educational prowess, and differing, in kind apparently, from 'talent,' which is usually distinguishable as marked intellectual capacity short only of the inexplicable and unique endowment to which the term 'genius' is confined" (24).

We can distinguish two entirely different trends of opinion in connection with the nature of genius. The first regards the genius as differing only quantitatively from the normal or average person; the second insists upon a fundamental difference in kind. Of the first view Francis Galton (25) is perhaps the most outstanding exponent. His discussion of "Hereditary Genius" makes use of a strictly statistical criterion. The tremendous difference in human abilities from the idiot to the great man are to be regarded as deviations from the average ability. The genius represents one extreme of the normal probability curve. In this sense Galton defines an "eminent" man as one who has achieved a position attained by only 250 persons in each million of men, or by one person in each four thousand; an "illustrious" man is literally one in a million.

More recently Terman (26) has adopted a similar viewpoint. He defines genius as meaning the very exceptional, superior grades of ability, whether the ability in question be general or special. Talent refers to a superior grade of ability, exceptional, but less so than the grade constituting genius. The difference from the average is quantitative, not qualitative. "The genius and the moron are explained by the same psychological laws. Neither has any trait which the other, also, does not in some degree possess" (p. 406). In this sense the word "genius" has been applied to children with very high scores on intelligence tests, an I.Q. of 140 or more usually being regarded as the dividing line. In connection with the *Genetic Studies of Genius* by Terman and his collaborators (27), this criterion has been used in order to select those children in whom the characteristics of "genius" may be studied. As a research investigation the final results of this study may be of interest in revealing the proportion of children with a high I.Q. whose later achievement entitles them to be called geniuses. It is hardly possible, however, to start out with the assumption that a high score in the relatively simple tasks of an intelligence test is closely related to the extraordinary ability of a Shakespeare or a Michelangelo.

One other aspect of the study is even more doubtful from the point of view of acceptable scientific method. In the second volume the biographies of men of genius are studied for the light they throw upon the achievements of early childhood, and estimates are then made as to the probable I.Q. of these outstanding persons. From the fact that one of them wrote a letter far superior to what might be expected from a boy of his age, or that another showed an interest in mechanical things at an early period of life, their intelligence level is calculated. By this method the young Galton is given an I.Q. of 200, whereas at the other extreme among men of genius Raphael has an I.Q. little above the average. The determination of I.Q.'s from this type of material is hardly a justifiable procedure. It is difficult enough to know what reliance may be placed upon the I.Q. even when it has been obtained under the best experimental conditions, with the errors controlled as far as is possible; under the conditions of this study, the difficulties are multiplied. In any case, as has already been suggested, the whole concept of the I.Q. is inapplicable to cases of this kind.

Genius and the Abnormal. At the other extreme, the opinion is held that genius is qualitatively different from normality. This opinion is usually associated with the name of Lombroso (*28*), who carried further than anyone else the notion of the essential identity of genius and insanity. As Hirsch (*29*) has shown, Lombroso's theory was not new. Aristotle observed that many persons become poets, prophets and sibyls, and are fairly good poets while they are maniacal, but when cured can no longer write verse. Lamartine referred to "la maladie mentale qu'on appelle génie." Dryden wrote, "Great wits are sure to madness near allied." The immediate stimulus to Lombroso's theory came from the work of Moreau de Tours, who in his *Psychologie Morbide* in 1859 stated that all genius is a neurosis and often a psychosis. It was this thesis which was expanded by Lombroso and supported by much biographical material tending to show the frequency with which men of genius suffer from insanity. His theory received wide attention, and most of the succeeding books on the psychology of men of genius find their starting point in a discussion of his thesis.

Among the recent books in this field, one of the most interesting is that of Lange-Eichbaum (*30*), who brings modified support to Lombroso's theory. Geniuses may be healthy, and he mentions Titian, Raphael, Andrea del Sarto, Rubens, Leibnitz and a few others. These are a small minority. Among the very great geniuses more than 30 percent were psychotic at some time during their lifetime; more than 83 percent were, if not psychotic, at least markedly psychopathic, that is to say, they had a mental disorder less severe than a definite psychosis. About 10 percent of the remainder were slightly psychopathic, and only about 6.5 percent were healthy. Among those with genuine psychoses, Baudelaire and Donizetti had general paralysis of the insane, Tasso and Newton had schizophrenia, and so on. In general, however, it is not psychosis but psychopathy which is found most frequently among men of genius.

According to this theory, psychopathy tends toward genius for three main reasons. In the first place, it increases the strength of the emotional life and with it the responsiveness to minute stimuli; this, plus the lack of self-control, may result in experiences which average people do not have. In the second place, psychopaths experience great suffering and pain and a consequent feeling of inferiority which leads them to attempt some adjustment. This is accompanied finally by a tendency to dream and a rich fantasy life in which the creations of the genius find expression.

Kretschmer (*31*) holds similarly that mental diseases, especially psychopathic borderline cases, are definitely more common among men of genius than among ordinary men. People who are unadapted to their environment and who feel uncomfortable in it are more likely to do important things because they find their environment unbearable. There must of course be ability, but in genius there must also be the "daimonion," which has principally a psychopathic origin. "If we take the psychopathic factor, the ferment of demonic unrest and psychic tension away from the constitution of the genius, nothing but an ordinary gifted man would remain" (p. 28). Kretschmer goes on to apply his constitutional typology to men of genius, pointing to the qualitative differences in the achievement of pyknics and leptosomes. Among poets, for example, the cyclothyme pyknic will write narrative epic poems and the schizothyme leptosome will write subjective lyrics.

The Psychoanalytic Approach. The psychoanalysts have attempted to carry further this notion of unrest or psychic tension in the genius. Freud (*32*), for example, writes: "Happy people never make fantasies, only unsatisfied ones. Unsatisfied wishes are the driving power behind fantasies; every separate fantasy contains a fulfillment of a wish and improves an unsatisfactory reality" (p. 176). Similarly Healy (*2*) states that "many of the world's great achievements have come from those who were by no means happy about their own personality characteristics and responses— perhaps because in them burned the flame of divine discontent" (p. 138). Freud admits, however, that the fantasies may be transformed into artistic creations only if the individual who is displeased with reality is in possession of that artistic talent which is still a psychological riddle. While this general position of the Freudians seems essentially reasonable, the specific attempts made by psychoanalysts to explain the activity of individual geniuses seem in many cases far-fetched to the extreme. Jekels (*33*), for example, finds in the Oedipus complex a satisfactory explanation of the aims of Napoleon. "That astounding ambition that causes one half of the world to heap his memory with execrations and the other half to surround it with expressions of admiration," is explained as due to his wish to be in full possession of his mother—Mother Earth. Similarly, in an article "On Dante's Unconscious Soul Life" by Sperber (*34*), it is argued that Dante clung to authority in the form of the Church because of his love and reverence for his parents; his mild and non-interfering father aroused no revolt in him, and Dante had therefore no impulse to emancipate himself. This disregard of historical backgrounds in favor of doubtful psychoanalytic mechanisms is of little help in understanding the personality of the genius (*35*).

There is one Freudian mechanism which is, however, valuable as a principle of explanation in some cases, namely, sublimation. This refers to the fact that a man who has met frustration in the satisfaction of an instinctive impulse, usually sex, may find an outlet for the available energy in a socially more acceptable direction. This applies not only to cases of genius, but to all those in which a dissatisfaction in love presumably becomes the motivating force toward some other goal. Prescott (*36*), for example, finds that poetry may frequently be explained in this manner, and sees in the love lyrics of Heine a sublimation for a temporary failure in courtship. This mechanism undoubtedly functions in some cases, but it is questionable whether it explains many of the contributions of genius. There are too many instances in which men of genius showed a complete disregard of the usual sexual taboos, or produced their greatest achievements at a time when their love life was also giving them complete satisfaction.

The Freudian emphasis on the unconscious has also been directed toward an explanation of the products of genius, at least in certain fields. There have been many instances in which literature of the greatest value has been produced in a state resembling that of the trance; Coleridge's "Kubla Khan" is an outstanding example. Many writers certainly have the impression that their work is produced to some degree without conscious volition on their part. Henry James speaks of dropping an idea for a time "into the deep well of unconscious cerebration; not without the hope, doubtless, that it might eventually emerge from that reservoir . . . with a firm iridescent surface and a notable increase of weight" (*37*, p. 327). Nietzsche wrote, "If one had the least vestige of superstition, one could hardly refrain from supposing himself to be merely the incarnation, merely the mouthpiece, merely the medium of higher forces. . . . One hears, one does not search; one receives, one does not ask who gives; like lightning an idea flashes out, appearing as something necessary" (*37*, p. 329). The frequent accounts of literary production in the form of "automatic writing," the precise content of which is unknown to the writer until it has been completed, also testify to the importance of unconscious factors. This of course does not mean that creation is entirely unconscious; we know, for example, that even those of Tennyson's lyrics with the greatest air of spontaneity were worked over and polished before their publication. It is probable that the relative roles of conscious and unconscious factors vary in different individuals and with different kinds of creation.

An extreme use of the theory of the unconscious as an explanation of the products of genius is found in the writings of Mary Austin (38). For her, genius is simply the capacity to reach into the unconscious and make free use of the material which has been stored in it as the result of racial inheritance and one's own previous experience. She even goes so far as to suggest methods for making available the content of the unconscious, and freeing it from the inhibitions imposed by consciousness. The theory of the unconscious is here carried to an absurdity.

An interesting attempt to apply psychoanalytic principles to the interpretation of one particular type of creation has been made by Herzberg (39) in his *The Psychology of Philosophers*. After an examination of the biographical details in the life of the most important philosophers, Herzberg finds certain characteristics which he regards as typical. The philosophers were for the most part unadapted to their environment, found it difficult to earn a living, rarely made a satisfactory marital adjustment, and were in general dissatisfied with the reality in which they lived. As a consequence they found greater satisfaction in the constructs of their philosophical systems than in the world around them. Their philosophy may in the majority of instances be regarded as an escape. The "idealistic" philosophers went much further in this respect, since they denied the existence of the real or phenomenal world, insisting that the only reality was that of ideas. In this way they achieved the comforting conviction that the world in which they were unsuccessful was really nonexistent. This theory leaves unexplained the philosophic activity of men like Bacon and others who were also successful men of affairs.

The Adlerians regard significant achievements to be in many

cases the product of over-compensation for organ inferiority. We have already referred to the classical example of Demosthenes, who stuttered as a child and became one of the greatest orators the world has ever known. Wexberg (40) suggests that Beethoven's important works were composed after he became hard of hearing, and that even in early life he probably had hearing difficulties. "We may be certain that Beethoven focused his interest on auditory experiences from his earliest days, and that he began a process of intense training culminating in his remarkable success as a musician" (p. 119). Many other cases of such over-compensation have been cited; Theodore Roosevelt, for instance, was a sickly boy and developed in the direction of a "he-man." It is known that Glenn Cunningham, one of the greatest mile-runners of all time, suffered an accident in early life which left his legs in bad condition. He took to running to overcome this defect and achieved outstanding success.

Wexberg insists that there is absolutely no hereditary basis for genius. "It has been the experience of individual psychology that attainment is not the result of inherited talent, but a product of courage and training" (p. 142). Genius is not the product of the superman, but results from industry and drive of a compensatory nature. "The so-called 'genius' cannot be damaged by knowing that others can accomplish what he has done under certain circumstances" (p. 151). Differences in native ability do not exist; there are only differences in what one does with one's ability.

This is certainly an extreme position, and one which would be accepted by few psychologists. It leaves unexplained the large majority of cases of outstanding achievement. For one great musician who was deaf, there are easily a hundred with no known impairment of hearing; for one orator who stuttered in his childhood, there are many who never had any perceptible speech defect. On the other hand, hosts of people have poor hearing without developing into Beethovens, and few stuttering children later become famous orators. There must be some other factor differentiating the genius from the average individual. Exactly what this factor may be is in Freud's words "a psychological riddle," but it is apparently an ability which is in part inborn, and not to be explained entirely in terms of early training and experience or organ inferiority.

This does not necessarily mean that genius runs in families. There may occasionally occur a rare and happy combination of genes predisposing to great achievement without any earlier appearance of such a combination in preceding generations. Galton's studies are frequently taken to have indicated the hereditary nature of genius through the demonstration that an eminent person has many more eminent relatives than an ordinary one. The family histories given by Galton do not, however, separate hereditary from environmental factors; the son of a judge, for example, has a legal environment in addition to a "legal heredity," if there is such a thing. This method leads to some rather striking conclusions, as, for instance, that "a pious disposition is decidedly hereditary," although no geneticist today would accept the notion of the existence of special genes for the transmission of piety. Galton's view led to the development of his theory of eugenics, which he regarded as capable of adding to the number of geniuses. Lange-Eichbaum's material shows, however, that there are so many geniuses who were not only themselves psychopathic, but who came from families with an unmistakable history of disease, that any conscious manipulation of heredity in such cases becomes quite impossible. There are undoubtedly some instances, as that of the Bach family, which indicate the possibility that outstanding ability may be passed from father to son, but such instances are rare in every branch of achievement. More frequently genius arises from no known cause, sometimes in families where there is least reason to expect it.

There is no one statement of the nature of genius which can possibly do justice to the quality of those individuals who have made contributions in the various fields of art and science. These contributions have been made by all kinds of persons and under varying circumstances. It seems reasonably certain, however, that there can be no genius without great ability, and also that ability in itself is not sufficient. There must be in addition, as has so often been pointed out, some driving force which frequently results either from the presence of some psychopathic disturbance, or from unfulfilled wishes or from sublimation or compensation. The creations of a genius will appear only when there is a combination of this inborn ability with some powerful motive urging to creation. The contribution of psychopathic factors appears to be much more marked in artistic than in scientific genius.

There is one final problem in this field, namely, as to whether the outstanding individual is the product of his culture and society, or whether he himself does something to determine the nature of his society. There has been speculation, for example, as to what Shakespeare or Newton would have been in a different age or environment; whether Mussolini and Hitler are to be explained as the product of historical and political events or whether they themselves helped to shape the course of history. As evidence for the primacy of cultural over individual factors, reference is often made to the frequency with which important discoveries are made simultaneously by different men. Classical examples include the development of a theory of evolution by Charles Darwin and Alfred Russell Wallace, the nebular hypothesis by Kant and Laplace, the differential calculus by Leibnitz and Newton. In spite of these undoubted parallels in discovery, the opposition between the individual's contribution and that of his culture is a spurious one. The theory of biological evolution could not be placed upon a substantial and scientific basis until a great deal of previous work had been accomplished; such previous work prepared the way for a synthesis in terms of a general theory. In this sense the culture is responsible, since no individual can create except in terms of what has gone before him. The fact remains, however, that Darwin and Wallace did carry the work a step further. They made their mark on the future development of biological science, and without them science would for a time at least have been that much the poorer. Similarly, the rise to power of Mussolini demanded a certain set of political and economic circumstances; these did not create him, but provided the possibility for his activity. He is therefore the product of circumstances, but at the same time his personality is responsible for a further change in these circumstances. There can be no denying the role of the "great man" in every field of human activity.

INTEGRATION AND DISSOCIATION

In the discussion of the definition of personality, it was pointed out that the individual is not merely an aggregate or sum total of traits, but that he represents some form of personality integration or organization. It is also true, however, that individuals differ in the degree to which integration has been achieved. Even among normal individuals there are some who are characterized by consistency and dependability of behavior, whereas others vary considerably from day to day and from one situation to another. The frequency with which certain individuals engage in self-criticism, or wonder how they could possibly have acted as they did, testifies to the reality of this lack of integration. The alternations between joy and depression which are found to an extreme degree in manic-depressive insanity, occur also in normal human beings and indicate a lack of complete organization.

In the field of abnormal psychology the term "dissociation" has been used to refer to lack of integration. Dissociation may be expressed in many ways and in varying degrees. The familiar acts of absent-mindedness, in which an individual does something without complete consciousness of the act and frequently without any memory for it, represent perhaps the mildest degree of dissociation. Slightly more unusual is the phenomenon of automatic writing. Cases of hysteria, characterized, for example, by the paralysis of an arm or leg without any organic basis for such a disturbance, also represent a dissociation or splitting of that segment of the body from the control of the remainder. Janet (41) has described many cases of fugues and somnambulisms through which dissociation may express itself. In the somnambulism there is the performance of an act, usually representative of some emotional crisis in the past of the individual, with complete lack of consciousness or of subsequent memory. In the famous case of Irène, the patient had had a harrowing experience when her mother dropped to the floor dead, and she had to put her back into the bed. In her somnambulism Irène relived this experience over and over again. In the fugue there is usually a longer period of dissociation from the main stream of consciousness, and cases have been reported in which persons lose complete memory of their former selves and "wake up" some time later wondering what has happened to them. The newspaper accounts of amnesia victims probably refer to fugues in the majority of cases.

The most extreme form of dissociation is found in cases of multiple personality. Here we have the co-existence of two or more distinct personalities within the same organism, each with a relative degree of integration, but completely dissociated from the others. There is usually one-way amnesia, that is, the secondary personality is aware of the primary one, but the latter has no memory for what happens while the secondary personality is in possession. There may also be reciprocal amnesia. It is usually held by psychiatrists that unless some form of amnesia exists, the case is not a true instance of multiple personality. In spite of the attention which these phenomena have attracted, a relatively small number of such cases have been reported in the psychiatric literature. One of the most famous is that of Christine Beauchamp, described by Morton Prince (42), in which the original personality was a staid New England spinster with a somewhat neurotic history and a lifetime of repressions. There developed in her no less than three secondary personalities. The first, known as Sally, had the character of a mischievous youngster with a hearty contempt for Miss Beauchamp, whom she regarded as "living with her head in the clouds." Sally enjoyed playing tricks on Miss Beauchamp, such as unraveling the knitting upon which she was engaged, or hiding her money, and so on. Another secondary personality was that of The Woman, who apparently represented a certain freeing of repressions with reference to the opposite sex. The Woman would write letters to men suggesting appointments with them, and otherwise behave in a manner shocking to Miss Beauchamp. Still another secondary personality was known as the Saint, who was even more strait-laced and conventional than Miss Beauchamp herself. Although there are many aspects of this case which are too complicated to be explained in terms of one mechanism alone, it is probable that the secondary personalities of Sally and The Woman may be interpreted as the fulfillment of repressed wishes. In certain individuals such repressed wishes become sufficiently well organized and systematized to form distinct personalities. The Saint, on the other hand, may be regarded as a reaction against the excesses of the other two. This explanation in terms of wish fulfillment is borne out by another of Morton Prince's cases, in which a young woman who lived a drab and uninteresting life developed a secondary personality in which she was the reincarnation of a Spanish opera singer of earlier days. Investigation revealed that there were repressed wishes for the glamorous life of an opera star, but that all attempts to sing and act had been discouraged by her acquaintances. The secondary personality fulfilled these wishes in a dramatic fashion.

Even when there is no actual dissociation, there may be a marked change in personality so that the life-span as a whole gives the impression of a lack of integration. Healy (2) mentions an interesting example of this type.

When long ago for the Massachusetts State authorities I interviewed Jesse Pomeroy, notorious as having been a sadistic boy murderer, in order to render an opinion on what had been done to him by over forty years of solitary confinement, I was greatly impressed by his use of the third person singular when speaking of himself as a boy. This was obviously the result of his endeavor to dissociate a scholarly present, for during these years he had been an omnivorous reader and had acquired a smattering of four or five foreign languages, from a hideous past. When referring to his boyhood days, he usually made statements which, in effect, ran as follows: "I remember that he liked school"; "It seems to me that he was kind to animals"; "I think that he generally felt happy" (pp. 18-19).

These cases are of interest not only because of their striking and unusual character, but because they represent in marked degree what is a relatively common occurrence among normal individuals. Integration varies in amount and may be regarded as an ideal rather than as a universal characteristic of personality. It remains true, however, that there can be no personality without some degree of integration.

SUMMARY

Personality differences appear at such an early age that innate factors probably play an important part in their causation. These may of course be influenced to a tremendous degree by later conditioning and patterning, as is evidenced not only by common observation but also by the experimental modification of ascendant behavior in young children. Among the methods used in child study, the controlled observation technique with its short samples of behavior has attracted considerable attention. More recently projective techniques have become increasingly popular, and they hold great promise for future research as well as for child guidance. Social aspects of personality have also been studied in the development of language, particularly in the transition from egocentric to socialized speech. The techniques of sociometry have shown the manner and the degree to which personality is influenced by the social interrelationships within a population.

The writing of biographies has been subjected to analysis by Dollard, who has suggested several criteria for their improvement. These include attention to the cultural background, the organic motors of action, the role of the family group, the elaboration of organic materials into social behavior, the related character of experience from childhood to adulthood, the social situation, and the organization and conceptualization of the whole life history. Although the criteria are in need of modification, they represent a step in the direction of making biographies more useful to social science.

Approaches to the psychology of genius may be divided into two categories—those which see the genius as one extreme of the normal distribution curve of intelligence, and those which regard genius as qualitatively different from the normal. In this latter connection, the earlier theory that genius and insanity are closely related has been replaced by the belief that not psychosis but milder forms of psychopathic disturbance occur frequently among men of genius. The interpretations of Freudians and Adlerians and the emphasis upon the role of the unconscious, have thrown light upon certain individual cases, but are not universally applicable. Genius appears to have a multiple causation, but it seems probable that most frequently the combination of superior ability with some driving force of a psychopathic nature is responsible.

The definition of personality includes the concept of integration, but it is important to keep in mind that this is a matter of degree. Dissociation may range all the way from common acts of absent-mindedness to the striking phenomena of multiple personality. Personality must be integrated, but complete integration is an ideal rather than a reality.

REFERENCES

1. Bayley, N. *Studies in the Development of Young Children.* 1940.
2. Healy, W. *Personality in Formation and Action.* 1938.
3. Washburn, R. W. "A Study of the Smiling and Laughing of Infants in the First Year of Life," *Genet. Psychol. Monog.,* 1939, 6: pp. 397-537.
4. Bühler, C. "The Social Behavior of Children," *Hdbk. Child Psychol.* (ed. by C. Murchison). 1933.
5. Bonham, M. A., and Sargent, M. K. "The Behavior of Human Infants Twenty-Four and Thirty Months of Age." *Unpublished Master's Essay,* Catholic University, 1928.
6. Murphy, L. B., and Murphy, G. "The Influence of Social

482 APPROACHES TO PERSONALITY

Situations Upon the Behavior of Children," *Hdbk. Soc. Psychol.* (ed. by C. Murchison). 1935.

7. Jack, L. M. "An Experimental Study of Ascendant Behavior in Pre-school Children," *Univ. Iowa Stud. Child Welfare*, 1934, 9, No. 3.

8. Page, M. L. "The Modification of Ascendant Behavior in Pre-school Children," *Univ. Iowa Stud. Child Welfare*, 1936, 12, No. 3.

9. Thomas, D. S., et al. "Some New Techniques for Studying Social Behavior," *Child Develop. Monog.*, 1929, No. 1.

10. Robinson, E. W., and Conrad, H. W. "The Reliability of Observations of Talkativeness and Social Contact among Nursery-School Children by the 'Short Time Sample' Technique," *J. Exper. Educ.*, 1922, 2: pp. 161-165.

11. Levy, D. M. "Use of Play Technique as Experimental Procedure," *Amer. J. Orthopsychiat.*, 1933, 3: pp. 266-277.

12. Horowitz, R. E., and Murphy, L. B. "Projective Methods in the Psychological Study of Children," *J. Exper. Educ.*, 1938, 7: pp. 133-140.

13. Frank, L. K. "Projective Methods for the Study of Personality," *J. Psychol.*, 1939, 8: pp. 389-418.

14. Murphy, L. B. *Social Behavior and Child Personality.* 1937.

15. Murray, H. A., et al. *Explorations in Personality.* 1938.

16. Piaget, J. *The Language and Thought of the Child.* 1926.

17. Moreno, J. L. *Who Shall Survive?* 1934.

18. Murphy, G., Murphy, L. B., and Newcomb, T. M. *Experimental Social Psychology.* Rev. ed. 1937.

19. Dollard, J. *Criteria for the Life History.* 1935.

20. Latourette, K. S. *The Chinese, Their History and Culture.* 2 vols. 1934.

21. Williams, F. E. *Russia, Youth and the Present-Day World.* 1934.

22. Mead, M. *Coming of Age in Samoa.* 1928.

23. Frazier, E. F. *The Negro Family in the United States.* 1939.

24. "Genius," *Encycl. Britannica*, 1936, 10 (14th ed.): p. 116.

25. Galton, F. *Hereditary Genius.* 1869.

26. Terman, L. M. "Talent and Genius in Children," *The New Generation* (ed. by V. F. Calverton and S. D. Schmalhausen). 1930.

27. Terman, L. M., et al. *Genetic Studies of Genius.* 3 vols. 1925-1930.

28. Lombroso, C. *The Man of Genius.* 1891.

29. Hirsch, N. D. M. *Creative Intelligence.* 1931.

30. Lange-Eichbaum, W. *The Problem of Genius.* 1932.

31. Kretschmer, E. *The Psychology of Men of Genius.* 1931.

32. Freud, S. "The Relation of the Poet to Day-Dreaming," *Collected Papers,* 1925, Vol. IV.

33. Jekels, L. "The Turning Point in the Life of Napoleon I," *Imago,* 1914, 3: pp. 313-381.

34. Sperber, A. "Dante's Unconscious Soul-Life," *Imago,* 1914, 3: pp. 205-249.

35. Dooley, L. "Psychoanalytical Studies of Genius," *Amer. J. Psychol.,* 1916, 27: pp. 363-416.

36. Prescott, F. C. *The Poetic Mind.* 1922.

37. Chandler, A. R. *Beauty and Human Nature.* 1934.

38. Austin, M. "Making the Most of Your Genius," *Bookman,* 1923, 58: pp. 246-251; 1924, 59: pp. 171-178, 687-694.

39. Herzberg, A. *The Psychology of Philosophers.* 1929.

40. Wexberg, W. B. *Individual Psychology.* 1929.

41. Janet, P. *The Major Symptoms of Hysteria.* 1907.

42. Prince, M. *The Dissociation of a Personality.* 1906.

CHAPTER XVIII

CULTURE AND PERSONALITY

INTRODUCTION

THE problem of the relation between culture and personality, or of the nature and extent of the influence of the folkways upon the individual, is implicit in a great deal of what has been previously discussed. The material dealing with the fundamental drives and their cultural determination; emotions and their expression; differences between social and economic classes; personality attributes alleged to be determined by race, but in all probability of cultural origin; phenomena associated with the direct effect of the group upon the individual; the acceptance of attitudes current in the community; the variations between city and country, etc.—all belong in this general category. There remain a number of specific studies which have not so far been included and which deal directly with the problem. It is proposed to discuss in this chapter those that have more immediate reference to normal personality, reserving for a later chapter the question of culture and abnormality. This will be followed by a chapter on social factors in crime, which also has pertinence in this connection.

When the word "culture" is used by anthropologists, it usually has reference to a relatively well-defined system of folkways and customs effective throughout a community. From this point of view, however, a single culture may be spread over a very wide area. Western culture, for example, is now found throughout Europe, Australia, and America, and is spreading over substantial portions of Asia and Africa as well. It is true that there is a certain degree of homogeneity within this large area—among other things, an economic system based upon competition (with some exceptions) and the use of machines, the religion of Christianity, monogamy, and so on. From this point of view it is of course legitimate to contrast Western European culture with the simpler aboriginal cultures of Melanesia, Africa and Australia, and the more complex ones of India and China. There are in addition marked differences between the individual communities in the Western world, and these too fall under the head of cultural, or perhaps sub-cultural, differences. The folkways of Russia are not the same as those of the United States. Even within one country there are regional variations, as has recently been stressed by Odum (*1*); in the United States differences between north and south, city and country, professional and laboring classes, all are accompanied by sufficiently marked contrasts in folkways to warrant their inclusion under the head of variations in culture. It has been suggested that there is an urban culture as contrasted with a rural culture, and that there is a certain homogeneity in city life which transcends the particular characteristics of one national community; the people of Tokio and New York may in certain respects resemble each other more than they resemble the respective rural populations within their own country. These factors are of undoubted importance in understanding the nature of the individual members of a community and the manner in which they are influenced by society. There seems no valid reason why the concept of culture should not be used in cases of this type, as well as in connection with the more striking differences reported by ethnological field workers.

It happens that most of the material available for the study of the relation of culture and personality has been collected in the course of the study of distant peoples. There seems to be a real need for the application of similar methods, and the study of allied problems, within the sub-cultures with which we have more direct contact. This has certain advantages in that we have more ready access to the individuals concerned, and need not spend quite so much time learning the language or the background of our subjects; on the other hand, their very proximity makes it difficult to see them in perspective, and their resemblance to ourselves interferes with the attempts to separate cultural from "human nature" factors. At least one significant study has been made, however, in which an American community has been approached from this point of view.

The investigation to which we refer was conducted by Robert and Helen Lynd (2) and reported in two volumes, *Middletown* and *Middletown in Transition*. The community selected was a midwestern American city of about 40,000 population and regarded as more or less "typical," although it is admitted that this assumption may not be entirely justified. The authors list six main activities of the individuals in this community: (1) getting a living, (2) making a home, (3) training the young, (4) leisure, play and art, (5) religion, and (6) community activities. One of the peculiar aspects of American life as contrasted with many other cultures is the fact that earning a living is the dominant problem. This is a great concern of the individual from childhood on through life; it is often the cause of pessimism and worry about the future. It attaches fear to the prospect of growing old and not being able to keep one's place in the economic scheme. It is an important factor in determining the nature of law, which is concerned largely in maintaining the sanctions of "private property," "free competition" and "individual initiative." It results in the expenditure of much time and energy upon an education, since the uncertainty of the parents about the economic future makes them wish to give their children the best possible training. The authors point to the almost universal "dominance of the dollar" and to the fact that all are "running for dear life to make the money they earn keep pace with the rapid growth of their subjective wants" (*Middletown*, p. 76).

The other activities are by no means unimportant, but in the typical American community economic motives predominate. When we contrast this with the picture of a relatively simple Melanesian community in which there is no uncertainty about food and shelter, and in which the economic system consists mainly of reciprocal exchanges, our own preoccupation with earning a living becomes still clearer. When times are bad, as in a depression, the anxieties are multiplied, but even in relatively good times there are always many individuals whose economic security is so uncertain that it constitutes a constant worry. The fact that prestige is so often associated with economic level adds to the importance of economic activities.

In our society, growing old is regarded as a calamity, largely though not entirely because of the economic insecurity which it involves. In a society like that of the native Australians, old age is on the contrary a privilege. The government of an Australian tribe is really a gerontocracy, with the authority vested in the old men. Status and prestige, as well as the economic services of the rest of the tribe, are assured to individuals as they grow old. It is obvious that the whole attitude of the individual to his future would be modified as a result.

Evidence of the tremendous influence of economic factors upon personality in our culture is indicated by a series of investigations (3, 4, 5) on the effects of unemployment. These have shown that the whole personality may go to pieces under such conditions; there is a loss of self-respect, of sociability, of attention to one's personal appearance, even of an interest in one's future and in one's surroundings.

The Lynds have shown also the extent to which personality differences are determined by economic class. Membership in an occupational group, social status and relationships, income, education, membership in clubs and societies, all help to form the pattern of personality. Although of course there are many gradations within each class and transitions from one to another, class membership is still important. Old age, for example, although a calamity to a manual laborer is not such a handicap to men in business and the professions. In addition, the laborer can have only slight satisfaction in his work;

usually he has made only a minor contribution to the final product, and he has little opportunity to obtain dominance or status as the result of his industry.

In their second volume the Lynds give an interesting ac-count of the ideas, values and ambitions of the average American in Middletown.   There is in general a marked degree of conservatism and hostility to all radical ideas and movements, a belief in the "ladder of opportunity" and the possibility of rising above one's present position, there is a pride in the growth of one's community or of one's organization, there is a desire for prestige and the good opinion of one's neighbors, and so on.   This is by no means a denial of individual differences with respect to these attitudes, but there is sufficient homogeneity to enable us to speak of the influence of the culture of Middletown upon the large majority of its citizens.

CULTURAL INFLUENCES IN CHILDHOOD AND ADOLESCENCE

In recent years anthropologists have paid a great deal of attention to the study of children in various primitive socie-ties.   It has been thought that this would throw light not only on the differences between various groups of children, but also upon the manner in which the child is inducted into his cul-ture and becomes a member of a particular society.   The method has served also as a useful check upon the generaliza-tions which have too readily been extended to all children on the basis of studies in our own society.

We have already referred to some of the phenomena which have been reported in this field.   Primitive children in general are given responsibility and made to look after themselves at a much earlier age than those in more complex societies.   This is probably due to the greater simplicity of the demands which must be met, and to the much more limited knowledge re-quired to take one's place as a full-fledged member of society. More specifically, as Mead (6) points out, there may be a form of training which develops characteristics of a certain type.   In the Manus tribe in New Guinea much stress is laid upon physical proficiency. The early "education" of the child accustoms him from his first years to self-reliance as well as to a large number of manual and motor activities. "He grows up to be an adult wholly admirable from a physical standpoint, skilled, alert, fearless, resourceful in the face of emergency, reliable under strain" (p. 47). On the other hand, social discipline is very loose, and the children are pampered and spoiled to a considerable degree. They have everything their own way and show no obedience or deference to their parents' wishes. If the child is physically efficient, has respect for other people's property, and shows an adequate observance of the canons of prudery and shame, no other demands are made upon him.

It is perhaps unnecessary to point out that there are marked differences between primitive communities in respect to the training of children. The lack of discipline among Manus children is in striking contrast to the African Kaffirs described by Kidd (7). Among children in this group there is little disobedience, and the first lesson they learn is politeness and consideration for others. At the same time they are almost never punished, and they seem to catch the spirit of obedience and politeness by imitation of their elders. Sociability is strongly developed. In this connection there is one type of trauma which occurs rather frequently among children in our society, and which is rare in a primitive community; the primitive child is never "left out." There are no social gatherings from which he is excluded, and he is rarely if ever made to feel that he is not accepted by the others in his group. This has great significance in connection with feelings of personal security and with personality development generally.

Mead has indicated some of the factors contributing to the education of the child in Samoa (8). Responsibility is given at an early age, and a young girl of six or seven is expected to care for younger members of the family. The young child is pampered for a time, but soon it is disciplined and socialized through the task of caring for others. One of the interesting aspects of Samoan education is its condemnation of precocity.

The greatest social error a child can make is to "talk above his age," or in any way show advancement over his age-mates. In strong contrast with our own society, a child is not encouraged to progress as quickly as possible, and the parents would be ashamed to find their child ahead of the average. There is only one situation in which the community permits precocity, namely, in the dances. A child may then take the limelight and will gain prestige from any special proficiency he may show. A somewhat similar situation prevailed among the Plains Indians, where boasting of one's exploits was rare except in connection with prowess in war.

There has been much discussion of the nature of adolescence, and of the extent to which its manifestations are determined by biological and cultural factors, respectively. This interesting developmental period was studied particularly by G. Stanley Hall (9), and his theory has been the usual starting point for later investigations. Under the influence of the current doctrine of recapitulation, which sees the development of the individual as a reflection of the development of the whole human race, Hall regarded the adolescent as "neo-atavistic, prone to storm and stress," because of "ancestral prepotencies struggling with each other for predominance." He and his students circulated a large number of questionnaires dealing with the phenomena of this period and made a careful study of biographies from the same point of view. On the basis of this material ten characteristics of puberty were listed as typical—(1) inner absorption and revery, (2) the birth of imagination, illusions, dreams, etc., (3) self-criticism, skepticism, scruples, (4) the over-assertion of individuality, (5) imitation at its acme, (6) the assumption of dramatic roles, poses, affectations, (7) folly, absurdities, freakishness, (8) a new speech consciousness, (9) absorption in friendship, (10) impairment of orientation in time and place, intense fluctuations in energy, and emotional and intellectual plasticity. Hall regarded the adolescent stage as characterized especially by "a loosening of the bonds between the manifold factors of our ego." He likened the manifestations of adolescence to the symptoms of hysteria and insanity, and considered it a period particularly prone to religious conversions and other violent personality changes.

This dramatic description of the adolescent storm and stress has frequently been challenged even on the basis of material from our own culture. It is true that an early study by Starbuck (10) spoke of religious conversions as occurring rarely before adolescence, increasing in number rapidly from the age of thirteen to seventeen, and then falling off so that there were very few after the age of twenty. More recently, however, Clark (11) sent a questionnaire to students at many colleges, obtaining two thousand replies. Among these a sudden conversion had occurred in only 6.7% of the subjects, and the phenomenon did not appear to be particularly characteristic of adolescence. As for maladjustment in general, there is little indication of its greater frequency at adolescence than at other periods of life. Personality difficulties occur often in infancy and early childhood, as well as later (12). There are, however, certain problems which must be faced at or about the period of adolescence, even though these problems rarely result in definite psychotic disturbance.

Among these problems one of the most important is that arising out of the child's uncertainty as to his status. In our complex society there is no fixed age at which certain privileges are automatically obtained, and for a number of years an adolescent must fight for his independence. To take one example, a recent study by Butterfield (13) showed that in a relatively homogeneous community in a large city, the parents differed widely as to the age at which they permitted their daughters to go out unchaperoned; the range was from about fourteen years to twenty. Such a range might constitute a source of conflict and disappointment in all those children above the age of fourteen who were not allowed this privilege. This is one of many possible examples of variations in status among children of the same age which create uncertainty in the child's mind as to his true position, and make "becoming an adult" a source of continual struggle.

It seems apparent that a great deal of the difficulty in the life of the adolescent arises out of the physiological changes associated with sexual development. This does not mean that sex appears for the first time at this period. The material collected by the Freudians indicates its presence much earlier in the life of the child. It remains true, however, that sex as a problem is accentuated at adolescence, when the individual is prepared for a form of behavior that is denied him by society. We know that on the organic side there are actual tensions set up which demand some form of release, and that a psychological conflict may result from the inability to accomplish this in a satisfying manner. Even when some form of sexual satisfaction is discovered, there will be difficulties arising from the opposition between behavior on the one hand and the moral dictates of society on the other.

As Mead has shown, these difficulties need not arise in a different type of society. In her study of the adolescent girl in Samoa, she indicates that "storm and stress" during adolescence is rare. There is no conflict or revolt; no picture of neurotic or psychotic disturbance. The adolescent girl need have no worries either about her status in the community or about her sexual needs. The former is determined by rules and regulations which grant to members of certain age groups definite rights and privileges, and in these respects no one may progress more quickly than anyone else. On the sexual side, the girl engages shortly after adolescence in a series of affairs with the boys of the community, each affair lasting only a short time and being followed almost immediately by another. It is apparently rare for any girl except the "taupo," or princess, to be left out of such an arrangement. The adults in the community are of course perfectly aware of what is going on and make no attempt to interfere in any way.

Under such conditions there are no special problems characteristic of this period, and the adolescent girl differs from the non-adolescent only in the fact that certain bodily changes have taken place. Mead concludes that the difficulties associated with adolescence, whatever these may be, originate in the social situation and not in the physiological condition of the individual.

Undoubtedly this conclusion is in the main correct, but certain problems of interpretation in connection with the Samoan material still remain. There is, for instance, the fact that the adolescent girls do not engage in sex activity immediately after puberty; usually there is an interval of two or three years. Miss Mead writes that the adolescent girls were given this valuable interval in which to get accustomed to new work, greater isolation and an unfamiliar physical development. One wonders why this interval was not more often characterized by difficulties of adjustment, since the girls were now organically prepared for a form of behavior which nevertheless was postponed for a substantial period of time. The girls for whom difficulties were reported were principally, however, those who lived under missionary control, and who had special problems arising out of the imposition of foreign standards of morality. At any rate it seems clear that the situation of the Samoan adolescent girl contains much less stress and strain than Stanley Hall regarded as inevitable.

From another point of view, "coming of age" may constitute a severe trial in primitive communities. In a great many cases the appearance of puberty is the signal for special treatment which cannot fail to make a great impression upon the adolescent. Among other things, there may be change of dwelling, entrance into youth societies, ordeals, tests of skill and endurance, acquisition of a guardian spirit, separation from the family group, disappearance from home into the forest or desert, initiation into sexual life, freedom from childhood restraints, the symbolic use of decorations or mutilations as an indication of the enhanced status, ceremonies of initiation, and so on (*12*).

The initiation ceremonies, referred to by Van Gennep (*14*) as "rites de passage," may in some cases constitute a severe ordeal, and it is certain that the initiate is not undisturbed in the process. Among the Australian tribes the ordeal was particularly trying, and might be accompanied by circumcision, subincision, the knocking out of a tooth and other physically painful experiences. Since the adolescent had to bear his trial without any complaint or any indication of suffering, it was naturally a severe test of self-control. Among the African Masai, initiation was accompanied by circumcision in the case of the boys, and clitoridectomy for girls. In the Banks Islands in Melanesia, entrance into the men's society was not the occasion for any actual mutilation of the initiate, but he underwent all sorts of trials during a probationary period of 100 days, during which others threw his food into the fire, destroyed his possessions and set him all sorts of difficult tasks which he had to perform without complaining (15). Among a great number of American Indian tribes, as well as in other parts of the world, puberty in the girl resulted in her segregation as "unclean" for a varying period of time. There were, however, many primitive communities (Samoa is one example) in which adolescence was not marked in any important way, and in which coming of age was not attended by any special difficulties.

It is important to keep in mind, as Benedict has pointed out (16), that these initiation ceremonies and other activities indicating the transition from childhood to adult status, did not necessarily coincide with the period of the physical changes of puberty. They might come earlier or later, depending upon the customs of the community; they are to be regarded as a social rather than a biological coming of age. Even if they constitute periods of stress, the difficulties which they create are not to be explained by physiological instability, but by the need to meet the requirements set by custom and convention.

The comparative study of childhood and adolescence in various communities raises the question as to whether the stages of development described in our society are universally valid. There have been several attempts to arrive at a "developmental age," by analogy with mental age, which would indicate the level of development reached by the child apart from chronological or even physiological maturity. Furfey (17) has noted, for example, sudden changes in behavior among the boys under his observation; he regarded as a sign of maturity the growth of interest in members of the opposite sex, the relinquishment of gang activities, and so on. Doll (*18*) has made use of an elaborate system for the measurement of developmental age, with over one hundred items of behavior listed in the order of their usual appearance. These methods have not so far been applied to children in primitive communities, and it would seem worth while to discover the extent to which Doll's scheme would be applicable. It is highly probable that certain important changes would have to be made. The ability to fend for oneself would certainly appear earlier among many groups of primitive children, whereas many activities related to schooling in our complex society would of course not appear at all. As has already been indicated, the phenomena characteristic of adolescent changes would not be the same in all communities. To take an example at a later period of development, the traditional Chinese family made it possible for a young man to marry and have children long before he was able to earn his own living, and the developmental sequence is clearly different from that in the Western world. These are only a few indications of the possible results of research in this field.

PATTERNS OF CULTURE

Of direct pertinence to the problem of the relation between culture and personality is the attempt to describe whole cultures in terms of patterns or configurations. This is really an application to cultures of categories which have been found useful in the study of individual personalities. Reference has already been made (see p. 427) to Benedict's use of Nietzsche's Apollonian and Dionysian types in her analysis of the nature of American Indian cultures. She in turn admits her indebtedness to Dilthey (*19*), who stressed the importance of integration in the social sciences, and to Oswald Spengler (*20*), who characterized the great civilizations of the past and present in terms of a dominant value, or world view. The results of Benedict's study have been discussed elsewhere (*21*), and we shall content ourselves at this point with a mention of the more important implications for the study of personality.

There can be no doubt that for the understanding of a culture, as well as of an individual, it is of fundamental importance to realize the character of the integration, or of the inter-relationship of the parts with one another. As we have seen, an act of dishonesty may not have the same meaning for two individuals, and a vision experience may have functionally a quite different significance in two cultures. The analogy between individual and culture is in many respects a valid one, but the result is that the difficulties of understanding individual personality and its integration, and of classifying individuals into types, hold also, perhaps even more markedly, in the case of cultures. Not all cultures are integrated, for instance, or at least not all to the same degree; there may be contrasts and conflicts, and the culture is not understood unless these are taken into account. A striking example is found in the Hako peace ceremony of the Pawnee Indians. This consisted of a prayer to the Great Mother (Maize), requesting children, long life, the enjoyment of plenty, happiness and peace. There was not the slightest whisper of war or dissension; numerous ceremonies of the Pawnee were directed to this same end. Among these people, however, war in its most intensive form was the main preoccupation. They were the terror of their neighbors, and mothers in the adjacent tribes would frighten their children with "The Pawnees are coming!" As Radin (22) expresses it, "only in such introspective rites could they gain peace of mind and rid themselves of the evil effect of too much preoccupation with war. Only thus could a warrior civilization become balanced and save its soul" (p. 289). A similar phenomenon is found in the prevalence of the orgy which permits a periodic relaxation of social restraints. Here the behavior may be completely at variance with that which is normal or habitual for that particular community. To mention only one example, among the Hos of northern India during the period of the orgy "servants forget their duty to masters, children their reverence for parents, men their respect for women" (*23*, p. 108).

This does not mean that communities are not integrated. It does mean that integration is relative, that it varies in degree, and that it cannot be assumed to exist completely in every community. This makes it possible for two different observers to obtain from the same culture varying pictures of the nature of its integration. Many of the Plains Indian tribes, for example, whom Benedict describes as Dionysian, might still give an impression of calm and serenity throughout the major portion of their activities.

In the preceding discussion of personality types, it was pointed out that pure types are rare, and that most individuals fall somewhere between the extremes. Similarly in the case of cultures, the labels "Dionysian," "introvert," "ahistorical," and so on, do a certain amount of violence to the uniqueness of each particular culture. There is the allied difficulty that no typology makes possible a classification of all cultures, and that it is often impossible to describe a particular culture in terms of one or another alternative type.

To the psychologist interested in the nature of the individuals found in any particular community, the notion of patterns of culture is significant, but is in need of more objective treatment. One possibility in this field would be to list, for instance, those activities which may be described as Dionysian and Apollonian, respectively, and then to note what proportion of the individuals in the community show a definite predilection for one or the other type of behavior. This method would make it possible to decide between the varying characterizations of two different observers. Katz (*24*) has made this suggestion in connection with the study of attitudes as distributed in a culture; we would go further, however, and include if possible a study of the frequencies of various types of behavior as well as of attitudes. It would be of great interest, for instance, to know whether the vision experience occurs more frequently in one American Indian tribe than another, instead of merely describing it as an important component in the cultures of both. In other words, the psychologist is concerned with the range of individual variations in attitudes and behavior in addition to the uniformities determined by patterns of culture. This appears to be a fruitful field for further research and it is to be hoped that psychologically-minded ethnologists will soon supply the data needed in this connection.

It is not by any means suggested that ethnologists are unaware of the range of individual variations. It is rather that the emphasis which they have placed upon the general characteristics of a culture has tended to overshadow the character and the frequency of the exceptions, as well as the nature of the normal variations. The cultural viewpoint is of the greatest value to the psychologist, but it must be accompanied by a realization of the uniqueness of the individual.

BASIC PERSONALITY STRUCTURE

Certain of the difficulties in the typological approach to cultures are eliminated by means of the concept of *basic personality structure*, elaborated by Kardiner in association with Linton (*25*). This is an attempt to apply to cultures a psychoanalytic approach modified by a realization of the important part played by social factors in determining psychological phenomena. In view of the biological orientation of Freud and most of his followers, there can be no doubt that such a modification makes the theory much more acceptable to ethnologists and other social scientists. According to Kardiner and Linton, the ego or basic personality structure "represents the constellation of personality characteristics which would appear to be congenial with the total range of institutions comprised within a given culture" (p. vi). It includes techniques of thinking, or idea constellations; the security system of the individual; "super-ego" formation; and attitudes to supernatural beings. In general, it represents that which differentiates the personalities of members of two different cultural communities; it is distinguished from *character*, which is "the special variation in each individual to this cultural norm" (p. 132).

The volume describes in detail the basic personality structures of the Marquesans and of the Tanala tribe in Madagascar, in addition to giving briefer studies of the Zuñi, the Trobrianders and other communities. Kardiner's analyses of the ethnological data are exceedingly stimulating, but since it is impossible to do justice to them in a brief summary, the interested reader is referred to the original volume. It may be sufficient for our present purposes to point out that we have here an account, presented with caution but with considerable plausibility, of the manner in which the personality of the members of these groups may be related to the institutions by which they are surrounded and under the influence of which they live. The authors admit the need of more detailed study of the individuals in various societies, but point out that no satisfactory material of this type is yet available.

CULTURE AND THE "LIFE HISTORY"

One aspect of this problem receives direct expression in the life histories which have been collected by ethnologists as part of their work in the field. Among these the one that has attracted the most attention is the autobiography of Crashing Thunder, a Winnebago Indian. The autobiography was recorded in the native language by Paul Radin (26), who has published it with interesting editorial comments. This life history is important not only as a contribution to the study of the relation between culture and personality, but more particularly because it illustrates the dichotomy between a culture pattern and the experience of the individual. The Winnebagos, in common with many other American Indian tribes, stressed the importance of the vision experience as a focal point in personal development. Crashing Thunder received an education similar to that of the other young men in his tribe and was taught that fasting and praying and careful attention to the ritual procedure would bring him the vision and the attendant blessing. It is probable that many if not most of the other members of the group did obtain a vision under such conditions; Crashing Thunder tried twice and failed. As a result he became a convert to the peyote cult, obtaining his vision under the influence of the drug.

This account indicates that some persons are unwilling or unable to accept the suggestions given by their culture. Psychologically this raises the important problem as to what there is in personality which determines deviation from the norm in this and other respects. As a matter of fact, there may be many others who deviate in the same manner and do not confess their failure. The problem necessitates the understanding of individual personalities as well as of cultures.

Recently Linton (27) has attempted to introduce some order into the individual variations by means of the concept of the "status personality." In addition to the common factors operative in the culture, there are specific factors related to status—either natural status, determined by age and sex, for instance, or acquired status, due to prowess in war, wealth or other types of achievement. The position in the community resulting from status determines the habitual reactions and experiences of the individual and has direct effect upon the characteristics of his personality. From this point of view we would expect men of high rank to differ from those of low rank, older men to differ from younger, girls to differ from boys. This analysis is excellent as far as it goes, and there is no doubt that differences in status determine variations in personality. We need to go further, however. It seems certain that two different men with exactly the same status, whether natural or acquired, may still have contrasting personalities. To put it another way, there is no reason to assume that status, and status alone, accounts for all the individual variations.

It is impossible to say with any definiteness what other factors are responsible. As has been noted in a previous discussion (see Chapter XV), organic make-up, early conditioning, real and fancied inferiorities, sibling rivalries and other aspects of the family constellation, habitual and traumatic experiences, all help to determine the unique nature of the person. There is no more important problem in social psychology than the separation of these factors from the general impact of a culture upon all the members of a community. More detailed research in this field through the combined efforts of ethnologists, psychologists and psychiatrists, or by investigators trained in these distinct disciplines, is needed for the complete elucidation of the inter-relationships between culture and personality.

This discussion is incomplete without a consideration of abnormality as related to cultural and social influences. The wealth of material in this field, and the complexity of the problem make it advisable to reserve this for a separate chapter.

SUMMARY

The manner in which individual personality reflects the culture of the community was partially indicated in earlier chapters. There are many investigations which have attacked this relationship more directly. Within a typical American community, for example, the problem of earning a living takes precedence over other activities and determines many of the anxieties with which individuals in general are concerned. Studies of children in primitive communities show how personality characteristics are formed by the training specific to the culture. The "storm and stress" said to accompany adolescence in our society may not appear under different social and cultural conditions.

Whole cultures may be described in terms of a pattern or configuration, and this would undoubtedly be reflected in the personality of individuals; the notion of cultural types has been criticized, however, because it may neglect the uniqueness of each culture. Recently the concept of basic personality structure, described in terms of a modified psychoanalysis, has been applied to this problem. The approach is of interest, since it gives a picture of the common personality characteristics of a community as related to the total range of institutions.

502 CULTURE AND PERSONALITY

There remains the problem of individual variations in spite of the uniformities imposed by the culture. This would seem to be the area most in need of further investigation.

REFERENCES

1. Odum, H. W., and Moore, H. E. *American Regionalism.* 1938.
2. Lynd, R. M., and Lynd, H. R. *Middletown.* 1929; *Middletown in Transition.* 1937.
3. Lazarsfeld, P. F. "An Unemployed Village," *Char. and Pers.,* 1932, 1: pp. 147-151.
4. Zawadzki, B., and Lazarsfeld, P. F. "The Psychological Consequences of Unemployment," *J. Soc. Psychol.,* 1935, 6: pp. 224-251.
5. Eisenberg, P., and Lazarsfeld, P. F. "The Psychological Effects of Unemployment," *Psychol. Bull.,* 1938, 35: pp. 358-390.
6. Mead, M. *Growing Up in New Guinea.* 1930.
7. Kidd, D. *Savage Childhood.* 1906.
8. Mead, M. *Coming of Age in Samoa.* 1928.
9. Hall, G. S. *Adolescence.* 2 vols. 1908.
10. Starbuck, E. D. *The Psychology of Religion.* 1900.
11. Clark, E. T. *The Psychology of Religious Awakening.* 1929.
12. Van Waters, M. "Adolescence," *Encycl. Soc. Sci.,* 1930, 1: pp. 455-459.
13. Butterfield, O. McK. *Love Problems of Adolescence.* 1939.
14. Van Gennep, A. *Les rites de passage.* 1909.
15. Lowie, R. H. *Primitive Society.* 1925.
16. Benedict, R. F. *Patterns of Culture.* 1934.
17. Furfey, P. H. *The Growing Boy.* 1930.
18. Doll, E. A. *The Vineland Social Maturity Scale.* Rev. ed. 1936.
19. Dilthey, W. *Gesammelte Schriften.* 1914-1931, vol. 2.
20. Spengler, O. *The Decline of the West.* 1932.
21. Klineberg, O. *Race Differences.* 1935.
22. Radin, P. *The Story of the American Indian.* 1934.
23. Crawley, E. *Studies of Savages and Sex* (ed. by T. Besterman). 1929.
24. Katz, D. "Attitude Measurement as a Method in Social Psychology," *Soc. Forces,* 1936, 15: pp. 479-482.
25. Kardiner, A. *The Individual and His Society.* 1939.
26. Radin, P. *Crashing Thunder.* 1926.
27. Linton, R. *The Study of Man.* 1936.

Part Six
SOCIAL PATHOLOGY

CHAPTER XIX

SOCIAL FACTORS IN ABNORMALITY

INTRODUCTION

THE relationship between abnormality and the society in which it occurs is a problem of the greatest practical significance. The opposition between the biological and social approaches to mental disorder represents not only two different systems of explanation, but also two divergent attitudes to therapy. There is no unanimity in this field, but it is largely true that the recent history of abnormal psychology represents something of a movement away from a biological to a social interpretation.

Although our own emphasis is in the same direction, this by no means signifies that biological or physiological bases of abnormality are unimportant or that they should be neglected. There can be no denying that a great deal of mental disorder is determined by causes which are not directly social. There are psychological consequences of brain injury, alcoholism, drug addiction, syphilis and other physical diseases. At the same time it must not be forgotten that even these factors have a social aspect. Alcoholism and drug addiction, for example, are not only the causes but also the effects of personality difficulties; they represent in many cases an escape from a social world which is otherwise unbearable. Syphilis, too, is in large measure a result of an economic system which makes early marriage impossible, and of a moral code which prevents the free mingling of the sexes outside of marriage. Similarly the Freudian emphasis on the thwarting of the biological sex urge as a cause of maladjustment should be accompanied by the realization of its relation to social and economic factors. As Freeman (1) points out:

505

. . . even sex and other economically remote maladjustments, which may occur under any conditions of restriction, are frequently due to economic causes. Marriage is prohibited to those who are old enough to be sexually active, but not old enough to have achieved the economic means of supporting a mate and children. Economic dependency often forces women to marry and remain with incompatible mates (p. 62).

The separation, therefore, of biological from social factors in the causation of abnormality may frequently be artificial.

These and allied considerations have led many social scientists to conclude that mental abnormality is to be regarded as a disease of the society rather than of the individuals who compose it. This concept of "society as the patient" or of the "sick society" has recently been analyzed by L. K. Frank (2). Such an approach has many advantages over the more usual emphasis upon disturbances in the individual, the most immediate gain being that of simplifying the problem.

Instead of thinking in terms of a multiplicity of so-called social problems, each demanding special attention and a different remedy, we can view all of them as different symptoms of the same disease. . . . If, for example, we could regard crime, mental disorders, family disorganization, juvenile delinquency, prostitution and sex offenses, and much that now passes as the result of pathological processes (for example gastric ulcer) as evidence not of individual wickedness, incompetence, perversity or pathology, but as human reactions to cultural disintegration, a forward step would be taken (p. 336).

The problem of social and cultural factors in abnormality is, however, much wider than that included in the concept of a sick society. There are at least four distinct ways in which culture and abnormality may be said to be related. In the first place, the very concept of normality and abnormality may vary from one community to another. Secondly, there may be variations in the relative frequency of abnormality. Thirdly, and allied to this, the situations precipitating mental disturbance may differ because of social patterning. Finally, there may be differences in the nature of the disturbance; we might speak of "fashions in abnormality" in this connection.

These various approaches to the problem are closely inter-related, but for the sake of convenience the relevant material will be presented under the four distinct headings. Certain aspects of the material have been discussed elsewhere (3) and these will here receive only brief mention.

VARIETIES OF NORMAL BEHAVIOR

A good discussion of the relativity of the concept of the abnormal is to be found in the work of Ruth Benedict (4). She points out that there are a number of societies in which the usual pattern of behavior corresponds rather closely to what in our society would be regarded as abnormality. The Kwakiutl Indians of British Columbia, for example, act in a manner which she characterizes as paranoid—they show megalomania, or "delusions of grandeur," in their self-glorification during the speeches made in the potlatch, and also "delusions of reference" in their interpretation of accidents and untoward events as deliberate "insults" directed against them by the universe. Similarly, the intricate system of taboos in Polynesia is regarded as analogous to the extension of the neurosis known in our culture as "défense de toucher," characterized by an avoidance of certain objects. Other examples are the "normal" occurrence of trance and ecstasy among the shamans of many California tribes, and the cataleptic seizures among the Siberian shamans; the continual and excessive fear found among the Dobuans of Melanesia; and the homosexual practices of many American Indian and Siberian communities. These examples lead Benedict to the conclusion that the limits of the normal and abnormal are culturally defined and vary markedly between one group and another.

From a strictly behavioristic standpoint there can be no doubt that the concept of the normal demands restatement for each culture. It is obvious that going about unclothed would not be diagnosed as exhibitionism in an Australian native, or strict avoidance of the mother-in-law as a neurosis in the case of Navajo Indians. Examples of this kind could easily be multiplied. Benedict's instances are somewhat different, since they refer to feelings and attitudes as well as to overt behavior. Even in their case, however, it is debatable, whether terms like "paranoid" or "défense de toucher" may legitimately be applied to the phenomena she describes. As Horney (5) points out:

If we regard a neurosis only from the sociological point of view as a mere deviation from the behavior pattern common to a certain society, we neglect grossly all we know about the psychological characteristics of a neurosis, and no psychiatrist of any school or country would recognize the results as what he is accustomed to designate a neurosis (p. 27).

A deviation must be considered both in its objective or manifest picture and in the dynamics of the psychic process. It may be that in this latter respect there is something common in the concept of a neurosis or other form of abnormality no matter where it is found; it may be, as Horney suggests, that there are always fears, and defenses against these fears, as well as attempts to find compromise solutions for conflicting tendencies. If this is true, the similarity between the behavior of the Kwakiutl and that of the paranoid patient in our society may be more superficial than real, and may not require a redefinition of the normal except in connection with the overt behavior patterns. The same considerations apply to Franz Alexander's (6) suggestion that the Buddhistic self-absorption of mystics in India, accompanied by the physical phenomena of rigidity and immobility, is to be interpreted as an artificial schizophrenia of the catatonic type. As is well known, schizophrenia represents among other things an extreme form of withdrawal from reality, and the catatonic type of schizophrenia is frequently characterized by phenomena of rigidity, stupor and immobility. Superficially there are obvious similarities, but the ability of the mystics to control their behavior and their consequent rapport with the physical environment, separate them sharply from the schizophrenic patient. It remains true that the argument of Benedict, supported by the further data of Alexander, is important as showing the variability in normal *behavior*. In those cases in which the abnormality consists entirely of a form of behavior, as in homosexuality, trance states, etc., Benedict's point is clearly proven. In those abnormalities, however, which contain subjective components of fear, maladjustment, conflict, autistic fantasy and so on, the analogy must not be pressed too far.

This material raises the interesting possibility that an individual whose personality determines him to behave in a specific manner may find his behavior accepted in one society and rejected as abnormal in another. A tendency to daydream, for example, may be looked upon as reprehensible in an American classroom, and as a sign of potential holiness in India. The occurrence of epileptic seizures has always been regarded by Mohammedans as conferring a special virtue upon the individual. Among many Siberian tribes, the transformed shaman who took on the habits of the opposite sex, often to the extent of homosexuality, acquired added power as a consequence; in this case, however, the shaman was feared and disliked and apparently regarded as a deviant, even though he was accepted by the community.

A person who has a desire to withdraw from the world would find it hard to fit into our American culture. Even among Catholics, escape to a monastery or a convent is not always considered a satisfactory solution. Such a person would have a relatively simple problem if he lived in a country in which Buddhism was an accepted religion, since Buddhism regards the external world as unimportant. In the psychopathic hospital in Peking the writer observed several cases in which people suffering from a mild form of schizophrenia showed simultaneously an increased interest in Buddhism and the Buddhist classics. In one such case the physician in charge noticed a marked improvement in the symptoms whenever the patient was given an opportunity to express this interest. Although this observation could not be checked by any statistical investigation, it seems to point to the possibility that an individual with the desire to withdraw from the world may find Buddhism, with its insistence upon the unimportance of external reality, particularly palatable. It is probable that many persons may actually be saved from the disease of schizophrenia because their introvert tendencies find in Buddhism a satisfactory outlet.

On the basis of her experience with psychotic patients in our society, Horney (5) arrives at a similar conclusion. She points out that in Western civilization there are few if any cultural patterns in which the drives toward withdrawal or oblivion, regardless of their neurotic character, may be satisfied.

Religion, which offers such a possibility, has lost its power and appeal for the majority. Not only are there no effective cultural means for such satisfaction, but their development is actively discouraged. for in an individualistic culture the individual is expected to stand on his own feet, assert himself, and if necessary fight his way. In our culture to yield realistically to tendencies toward self-relinquishment involves the danger of ostracism (pp. 278-9).

There is suggested here a research problem of the first importance. In India, China or Japan, there are possibilities for the careful study of the behavior of the psychotic or neurotic from this point of view. A psychiatrist trained to observe the significance of cultural factors could give us valuable insight into the extent to which the religions of the Far East afford a satisfactory diversion of these tendencies toward oblivion.

There is another possibility in this field which should not be overlooked. Granting that there are individuals who would be normal in one society and abnormal in another, there may still be some who would be abnormal anywhere. This is probably true of extreme cases of feeble-mindedness, although where the demands of the culture are simple, such defect may not be conspicuous. More important, however, is the possibility that some individuals are so constituted, whether as a result of biological factors or of early conditioning, that they rebel against the customs and dictates of their society, whatever these may be. It is conceivable, for example, that a person who has the urge to express his contempt of society, or who wishes to attract attention to himself, may indulge in precisely that form of activity which his society condemns. If further investigation proves this to be the case, we should still have to insist with Benedict that the majority of individuals are patterned by the form of their culture; we should have to add that some individuals are, by their very nature, deviants.

SITUATIONS DETERMINING ABNORMALITY

Associated with the phenomenon of cultural relativity in the meaning of abnormality is the fact that in different cultures there will be variations in the situations in which abnormality develops. This really follows from certain of the considerations discussed in the preceding section. A special defect or inhibition in the individual may escape notice if there is nothing in his social environment which demands the presence of the corresponding ability. Among the African Bantu, for example, almost every man and woman is a fluent and sustained speaker, and Dr. Gordon Brown has observed (7) that "the most prevalent mental disturbance is in youths who realize that they are unable to become finished speakers" (p. 55). It is hardly necessary to point out that in our own society such inability causes only temporary inconvenience on special occasions.

The family situation in our culture may give rise to conflict and mental disturbance in many ways (8). There is the usual pattern of obedience to parental authority and the consequent taboo upon criticism of parents by their children. One possible consequence is the violent revolt of the child against the parent; another is the guilt-feeling which accompanies the reflection that if the parents are necessarily right it must be the child himself who is in the wrong. In either case—and there are many other possibilities—the pattern of authority in the family may contain inherent contradictions. As has previously been pointed out, another type of family, in which the authority is not nearly so pronounced, will not precipitate the same type of conflict.

There are other contradictions in the demands and the values of our culture which constitute possible sources of disturbance. According to Horney (5) these contradictions are of three main types—(1) between competition and success on the one hand, and brotherly love on the other; (2) between stimulation of our needs and our factual frustrations in satisfying them; (3) between alleged freedom of the individual and all his factual limitations.

These contradictions embedded in our culture are precisely the conflicts which the neurotic struggles to reconcile: his tendencies toward aggressiveness and his tendencies toward yielding; his excessive demands and his fear of never getting anything; his striving toward self-aggrandizement and his feeling of personal helplessness. . . . It seems that the person who is likely to become neurotic is one who has experienced the culturally determined difficulties in an accentuated form. . . . (pp. 289-290).

It has been pointed out that the present cultural pattern in our own community may disturb certain of the characteristics of behavior and of personality regarded by psychiatrists as essential to healthy individual development (9). There is a threat to feelings of security because of constant migration to new social environments which necessitate new adaptation; to extraversion, through the marked reduction in the opportunity for physical expansion of the play life of children as well as by the rapidly changing mental content due to the radio and the newspaper; to the inviolability of the self, as a result of crowding; to personal integration, because of clashing patterns of behavior; and to the family matrix, since the duties of the family have been taken over by so many other agencies. There are, however, compensatory mechanisms, so that there is the possibility that a new form of adaptation may be discovered which may still satisfy the basic needs of the individual.

In a changing culture the possibilities of difficulty and conflict become increased. In China, for example, the transition between the old family pattern and the new Western one has constituted serious difficulty for many young people (10). The traditional Chinese family demanded complete submission of a young wife to her mother-in-law, and the girl brought up in the accepted Chinese fashion found little or no difficulty in adapting to such an arrangement. In those cases, however, in which there had been exposure to the Western notion of the independent small family, marriage into the large one might easily produce friction. There were some cases in the Peking psychopathic hospital in which this was apparently the precipitating cause. Other types of culture change may have equally unfortunate consequences, as is indicated by Margaret Mead's study of "the changing culture of an Indian tribe" (11). In our own society, the adjustment of immigrant groups to American folkways may be difficult, particularly for the children, who are caught between two ways of living, and who must effect some sort of compromise between the authority of their parents and their desire to be like other Americans. This problem will be discussed more fully in the following chapter.

AMOUNT OF ABNORMALITY

The discussion of the situations giving rise to abnormality leads directly to a consideration of its frequency, since it appears certain that the more numerous such situations are, the more often does disturbance of one sort or another ensue. This is of course a problem of the greatest practical importance. The effect of the social environment in determining the incidence of abnormality is sometimes considered to be proven by the far greater frequency in reported cases of psychosis and neurosis in the city than in the country (12). This fact is difficult to interpret, however, since it may be due to a difference in the ease of diagnosis and of hospitalization in the city rather than to a direct increase resulting from urban living conditions (13). That the social environment is important, however, can hardly be questioned. Healy (14) reports a number of almost miraculous changes in problem children as the result of their transfer to foster homes, and Plant (9) tells of a child who gave an uneasy picture of tension in her own home as a result of competition with an elder sister, and whose symptoms cleared up entirely upon association with a group of companions of her own age. A survey of the incidence of abnormality in large cities has revealed a concentration in certain areas rather than others, and has indicated the relation of mental disease to economic factors (15).

The most striking account of a reduction in the extent of abnormality following social and economic changes is that by Frankwood Williams in the case of Russia (16). This has been discussed elsewhere (3), but it is worth repeating that Williams believes that the reduction of "anxiety pressures" has meant that hundreds of thousands of people have been saved from the development of mental disturbance. Although economic worries may not be the only ones precipitating a breakdown, they are so important that their elimination will affect for the better the mental health of the community. Accurate statistics are difficult to obtain, but Williams points to the fact that hospital beds for psychotic patients are largely unoccupied, and that cases of certain types of mental disease are actually difficult to discover.

This report by Williams is of the greatest significance, but his conclusions have not uniformly carried conviction. It has been urged that his visit to Russia was too brief and too superficial to permit such far-reaching inferences, and that actually mental diseases may be more frequent in Russia than he believed. It has also been suggested that whereas the disturbances consequent upon economic worries may have been reduced, there are other sources of difficulty which are still present to the same or even to a greater degree; the speeding-up process in many factories, for example, may conceivably lead to an increase in neurasthenia and other fatigue neuroses, and fear of denunciation to the police for failure to live up to accepted party standards may be the source of strong anxiety feelings. If the Freudians are right in their insistence upon sex problems as the main source of neurotic disturbance, we should hardly expect these to disappear entirely in the Russian system, although the greater ease of marriage and divorce would perhaps reduce this danger. There is badly needed in this field a detailed statistical analysis of the incidence of mental disease in Russia, and of the specific types of disturbance which occur with greatest frequency. In the meantime we may accept Williams' conclusions as probable, although it may be that the picture which he gives is painted in too favorable colors.

According to the Freudians, a certain amount of neurotic disturbance is apparently inevitable in a civilization as complex as ours. Freud (17) regards culture as primarily the result of the action of biological urges which are denied their natural expression and consequently sublimated; the energy which would be directed to the satisfaction of biological urges is used for the production of culture. Since, however, not all individuals possess the ability to sublimate their drives in these socially valued directions, repression will in many instances lead to neurosis. If there were no repression there would be no neurosis, but at the same time there would be no culture. This is what Roheim (18) has in mind when he says the culture is produced at the expense of the woman, man's energy being diverted from her to the creation of cultural products. From this point of view, the growth of civilization necessarily implies an increase in the amount of neurosis, the more complete repression of instinctive urges being accompanied by a higher development of culture. This direct relationship between the amount of sexual repression and the level of cultural development is not, however, substantiated by the findings of anthropology. There are many "primitive" cultures, it is true, which allow a degree of freedom in sexual activity far greater than that permitted in our society. On the other hand, the Veddas of Ceylon, with an exceedingly simple material culture, are very strict in their insistence upon a rigid monogamy, and any infraction of the moral code is dealt with severely (19). Many other examples could be given. Malinowski (20) contrasts the Amphlett Islanders and the Trobrianders with respect to their sexual morality; the former are very puritanical, regard pre-nuptial intercourse with disapproval, and have no institutions to support sexual license. This apparently results in a greater incidence among them of neurasthenic and other neurotic tendencies, but it has evidently not resulted in raising their cultural level above that of the Trobrianders. The creation and development of culture are certainly more than the sublimation of repressed sexual impulses.

VARIETIES OF ABNORMALITY

In a previous section we discussed the variations in the concept of the normal, and the fact that behavior regarded as normal in one society may be abnormal in another. We turn now to an allied problem, namely, that of the manner in which abnormality expresses itself when it does occur. It is possible to speak of "fashions of abnormality" from this point of view, except that these manifestations have a continuity and a permanence in social life with which the concept of fashion is not usually associated.

The writer has discussed some of these phenomena in another connection (3). Familiar examples include the Arctic hysteria of the Siberian tribes, characterized by heightened suggestibility and an irresistible impulse to imitate the words or the acts of others in the vicinity; a similar disturbance among the Malays known as latah; running amok, also most frequent among the Malay peoples, and so on. Even in the history of our own culture, there are many instances of such fashions in abnormality. Bromberg (21) tells of an epidemic of convulsions of an erotic nature which occurred among the nuns in the Convent of Nazareth in Cologne about 1565. These nuns would lie on their backs with their eyes closed and their abdomens elevated; after the convulsion passed, they "opened their eyes with apparent expressions of shame and pain." The "charming invalid" of the Victorian era, who made up a good portion of the doctor's practice in the latter part of the nineteenth century, is another instance of this phenomenon.

It was not uncommon for women of gentle birth to be afflicted with a mysterious ailment that kept them languishing in bed behind drawn curtains, sipping as their only nourishment some anemic fluid like skim milk or port wine diluted with water. The bizarre types of hysteria described by medical writers of seventy years ago are for some unfathomable reason almost a rarity nowadays. It is almost as if nervous diseases succumb to the rule of fashion, at least in their outer appearances (*21*, pp. 200-1).

The well-known examples of the dancing mania and of the various forms of religious possession and ecstasy reported throughout the Middle Ages may also be cited in this connection.

An interesting observation is reported by a psychiatrist with much experience in the German city of Weimar, the home of Goethe and Schiller and long the center of drama and opera. The patients in this city were apparently influenced by the cultural traditions of the community, and their psychotic manifestations had a theatrical and dramatic aspect which distinguished them from similar psychoses elsewhere. It was as if they "declaimed their symptoms." The writer speaks in this connection of a "psychosis vimariensis," and states that the Weimar psychiatrists discounted these characteristics in their approach to the disease (*22*).

The Chinese writer Lin Yu-t'ang (*23*) mentions a similar phenomenon. He reports that there is a peculiarly Chinese disturbance referred to popularly as an "opera psychosis," in which the patient, apparently otherwise normal, has an impulse to sing long passages from the Chinese musical plays. Such an individual may be seen at a street corner in Peking singing and acting for hours at a time, though at other times he may be perfectly normal. During the present writer's stay in Peking no cases were observed of exactly this type, but there were some patients at the psychopathic hospital who showed this form of behavior as part of a more general disturbance. It may be added that in the psychoses of the Chinese, rich use is apparently made of mythological and traditional themes in connection with their delusions and hallucinations. Among these, possession by a fox spirit, a recurrent motif in the popular tales known to most Chinese, occurred with some frequency. This is reminiscent of the "werewolf" stories in our own tradition. In this case also there were many people whose hysterical disturbance evidently took the form of the belief that they were occasionally transformed into a wolf or other animal.

Among neurotics in our own society Horney (5) finds the striving for power to be a frequent symptom of the disturbance. This also involves a cultural factor. In our society individual power and prestige play an important role; this may be achieved by wealth, and the compulsive striving for possession occurs with some frequency among neurotics. This compulsion may disappear as soon as the anxieties determining it are diminished or removed. Wealth is, however, only one of the possible means of acquiring power, and the neurotic may use other methods to protect himself from his feeling of helplessness or humiliation. In other cultures such a striving for power is normally absent, and therefore plays no special part in neuroses. In an earlier discussion it was pointed out that certain communities, for example, the Pueblos, laid no particular stress upon individual prestige or power. Among such groups, says Horney, "it would be meaningless to strive for any kind of dominance as a means of reassurance. That neurotics in our culture choose this way, results from the fact that in our social structure power, prestige and possession can give a feeling of greater security" (p. 163). This raises the important problem of the manner in which neurotics in other societies may express their feelings of insecurity and the situations which determine such feelings; this field is one in which the combination of psychiatric and ethnological analysis may make a significant contribution.

An interesting example of a "fashion in abnormality" is the windigo psychosis among the Ojibwa Indians (24). The windigo is a mythological giant made of ice, who is also an insatiable cannibal. The psychosis expresses itself as the belief that one has been transformed into a windigo. The immediate cause is usually threatened starvation, and the disease begins with a melancholia which may give way to violence and compulsive cannibalism. In this final stage the patient may kill and eat the members of his own family. Recovery may occur, but often for the protection of the community the sufferer is put to death. This disturbance, which has also been described by Cooper (25) for the northern Cree, is clearly a culturally determined variety of abnormality. One other observation made by Landes (24) is significant in this connection. "A group of women who in our culture are thought simply eccentric are regarded by the Ojibwa not as merely abnormal but as criminally abnormal. These are the women who refuse to marry, spoiling the sexual sport of men and handicapping them in gaining a livelihood" (p. 29).

Many other examples have been collected. Powdermaker (26) reports the occasional occurrence in Buka of "states of hysterical dissociation" with considerable excitement and threats to kill; this is said by the natives to be due to possession by the "urar" or spirits of the dead. It is much like amok, though apparently not so serious in most cases, and the sufferer is not "out to kill" as in the case of the amok-running Malay. The people of Buka, incidentally, are Melanesians, and racially quite distinct from the Malays among whom amok is said to occur with some frequency. Among the Saultaux of the Berens River in Manitoba, Hallowell (27) tells of a case of zoophobia which took the form of an intense fear of toads. This occurred in an Indian who had spent most of his life in the bush, and had been a good hunter apparently unafraid of the most dangerous animals, but became panic-stricken when a toad hopped toward him. Toads are evil creatures in native lore, and the old belief had returned as a cause of this disturbance under certain precipitating circumstances.

This material raises a general problem of considerable interest. Wells (28) writes that "a special interest of comparative psychiatry is that, in so far as symptom-pictures vary according to culture, the influence of psychogenesis might be separated from that of organic or constitutional factors" (p. 890, n.). More work is needed on the underlying mechanisms of the disturbances as distinct from the external manifestations, before such a separation is possible on the basis of comparative material. As far as the external aspects are concerned, however, there can be no denying the tremendous importance of cultural influences.

CONCLUSION AND INTERPRETATION

The material summarized in this chapter amply demonstrates the significance of cultural factors for the understanding of abnormality. Such factors aid in determining the meaning we attach to normal and abnormal, the situations giving rise to abnormality, its frequency, and the nature of its manifestations. We must again caution, however, against the generalization from this material to the effect that all abnormality is culturally determined and that the personality is entirely at the mercy of prevailing cultural patterns. As has been frequently pointed out, not all individuals react similarly to the influences of the social environment; some may accept these influences readily, while others resist them. Even in a simple laboratory situation we may never be certain that the same external stimulus has an identical meaning for two different subjects, since the whole pattern of previous experience may contribute to the response. Piéron (*29*) speaks in this connection of an "envelope" surrounding the personality and varying in its permeability from one individual to another.

In a recent analysis of the relation between personality and culture, Plant (*9*) distinguishes three contributing elements.

There is a growing changing personality made up at any moment of the total of its own contributions and those of the environment. There is a cultural pattern which itself grows and changes in answer to the interests of all those personalities which make it up and in answer to a series of forces engendered precisely by the fact that it is made up of great numbers of personalities. There is a selective process occurring at the place where the pattern impinges upon the personality, which controls the material accepted. . . . (p. 233).

This means that although culture does shape and mold the personality, the individual still has an effect upon his cultural and social environment. He is not a mere passive recipient, but a reacting and interacting organism.

In connection with both the normal and the abnormal personality, therefore, it is important to study not only culture but also the individual. The available ethnological accounts of abnormality have made important contributions through their analysis of cultural phenomena, but they have so far taught us little about the individual who is considered abnormal. It may be argued that this has been done sufficiently by psychiatrists in our own culture, but in their case the concomitant emphasis upon the role of culture has usually been lacking. The relative influence of the culture on the one hand, and the attributes brought to it by the individual on the other, may be separated only by attention to both. There is no branch of social psychology more important as a field of potential investigation, and the material is relatively accessible. The combination of psychiatric and ethnological techniques in this field should yield data of the greatest significance. In the meantime, this chapter has emphasized the role of the culture because it is one that has not been sufficiently recognized in the customary psychiatric approach to the individual in our society.

SUMMARY

Without denying that many types of abnormality may be the result of organic disorders, the present emphasis is upon the influence of social and cultural factors. This influence may be effective in various ways.

In the first place, the concept of abnormality may vary from one society to another. Behavior resembling paranoia is normal for the Kwakiutl, withdrawal from reality is permitted to a Buddhist, homosexuality and trance states are accepted in many communities. Behavioristically, therefore, the relativity of the abnormal has been demonstrated, although the possibility remains that there are underlying problems—conflicts, fears, etc.—which constitute the real nature of neurosis wherever it is found.

There are variations in the situations in which abnormality develops. These include differing types of family organization, contradictions in the demands of the culture, conflicts

arising out of culture change, etc. The frequency of occurrence of such situations is at least partly responsible for the
incidence of abnormality; it seems certain that points of
strain, particularly with reference to economic and sexual
problems, are found more often in our society than in many
other communities, particularly those of relatively simple
character.

There are also varieties or fashions of abnormality determined by the folkways. Among others may be mentioned the
imitative mania of the Siberian natives, running amok among
the Malays, the windigo psychosis of the Ojibwa, and the
striving for power among neurotics in Western society.

These findings should not be interpreted as meaning that all
abnormality is culturally or socially determined.

REFERENCES

1. Freeman, E. *Social Psychology.* 1936.
2. Frank, L. K. "Society as the Patient," *Amer. J. Sociol.,* 1936, 42: pp. 335-344.
3. Klineberg, O. *Race Differences.* 1935.
4. Benedict, R. F. *Patterns of Culture.* 1934.
5. Horney, K. *The Neurotic Personality of Our Time.* 1937.
6. Alexander, F. "Buddhistic Training as an Artificial Cata-
tonia," *Psychoanal. Rev.,* 1931, 18: pp. 129-145.
7. Thomas, W. I. *Primitive Behavior.* 1937.
8. Fromm, E. *Autorität und Familie.* 1936.
9. Plant, J. S. *Personality and the Cultural Pattern.* 1937.
10. Lamson, H. D. *Social Pathology in China.* 1935.
11. Mead, M. *The Changing Culture of an Indian Tribe.* 1932.
12. White, W. A. "Social Significance of Mental Disease,"
Arch. Neur. and Psychiat., 1929, 22: pp. 873-900.
13. Landis, C., and Page, J. D. *Modern Society and Mental
Disease.* 1938.
14. Healy, W. *Personality in Formation and Action.* 1938.
15. Faris, R. E., and Dunham, H. W. *Mental Disorders in
Urban Areas.* 1939.
16. Williams, F. E. *Russia, Youth and the Present-Day World.*
1934.
17. Freud, S. *Civilization and Its Discontents.* 1930.

18. Roheim, G. "Psychoanalysis of Primitive Cultural Types," *Internatl. J. Psychoanal.*, 1932, 13: pp. 2-224.
19. Seligman, C. G., and Seligman, B. Z. *The Veddas.* 1911.
20. Malinowski, B. *Sex and Repression in Savage Society.* 1927.
21. Bromberg, W. *The Mind of Man.* 1937.
22. Binswanger, O. "Betrachtungen über Volksart, Rasse und Psychose im Thüringer Lande," *Archiv f. Psychiatrie u. Nervenkr.*, 1925, 74: pp. 218-240.
23. Lin Yu-t'ang. *My Country and My People.* 1935.
24. Landes, R. "The Abnormal Among the Ojibwa Indians," *J. Abn. and Soc. Psychol.*, 1938, 33: pp. 14-33.
25. Cooper, J. M. "Mental Disease Situations in Certain Cultures: A New Field for Research," *J. Abn. and Soc. Psychol.*, 1934, 29: pp. 10-18.
26. Powdermaker, H. *Life in Lesu.* 1933.
27. Hallowell, A. I. "Culture and Mental Disorder," *J. Abn. and Soc. Psychol.*, 1934-35, 24: pp. 1-9.
28. Wells, F. L. "Social Maladjustments: Adaptive Regression," *Hdbk. Soc. Psychol.* (ed. by C. Murchison). 1935.
29. Piéron, H. *Principles of Experimental Psychology.* 1929.

CHAPTER XX

SOCIAL FACTORS IN DELINQUENCY AND CRIME

INTRODUCTION

CRIME has been variously defined. It has sometimes been identified with behavior which is immoral, or which results in some harm to society. Actually, the one common characteristic of crime is the fact that it is prohibited by the criminal code. It follows, as Michael and Adler (1) have pointed out, that the criminal law is the formal cause of crime; if there were no law, crime would automatically disappear. In establishing our criminal law therefore, we are at the same time deciding what kinds of crime we wish to cause, paradoxical as this may sound. Delinquency has the same meaning, except that it refers to crimes committed by persons below a certain age, this age being determined by law and varying from one society to another. Delinquency and crime do not differ with regard to the seriousness of the act, in spite of popular belief to this effect, although the delinquency may be regarded less seriously by the court in view of the youth of the offender.[1]

It is clear from the above definition that crime is relative, and that an act regarded as criminal in one society may be unobjectionable in another. Offenders against the prohibition law in the United States furnish an example of behavior which is criminal at one time and later ceases to be so. Ethnological material is rich in examples of this variation. Patricide and matricide are among the most heinous crimes in our society, but under the influence of certain religious beliefs as in the

---

[1] The term "delinquency" is used in other senses as well, but the meaning here ascribed to it is the customary one.

Fijian notion of the virtue of an early death, killing a parent may be a pious act. Homosexuality is no crime among the Siberian Chuckchee, and "stealing" ceases to occur in a community with no notion of private property. This consideration in itself throws doubt upon the possibility of arriving at a "psychology of the criminal," since no single type of behavior may be taken as a universal characteristic.

This difficulty is also reflected in the study of the criminal in our own society. As Osborne (2) expresses it:

> To list men who commit all sorts of different crimes arbitrarily in a group and proceed to generalize about them, is as ridiculous as it would be to generalize about the habits and character of any chance assortment of men—legislators or theater-goers; or to draw conclusions as to the psychological characteristics of blue-eyed men, or those who wear tan shoes. "The criminal," as he is usually described, has about as much real existence as the equator (p. 19).

Osborne's rich and varied experience with all types of criminals in the penal institution of which he was in charge lends added weight to this conclusion.

It is almost universally assumed that crime represents a serious disease of society which should at all costs be eradicated. The problem of crime is in essence that of crime prevention. Dunlap (3) has, however, argued that crime is a necessary characteristic of a progressive civilization.

> Social progress . . . seems possible through two procedures. 1. The violation of conventions, leading to the formation of new conventions. 2. Where the conventions have the form of law, there crime (the breaking of law) is the indispensable method of progress. All great reformers have been law breakers, and wherever laws limit progress, the systematic and conscientious infraction of law is the only possible progressive method. Flouting of conventions and infraction of laws seem to constitute the essential spirit of civilization. Where a population shall have become universally law-abiding, civilization will have died (p. 58).

Adoption of this extreme position would necessitate a radical change in the usual attitude toward crime. It seems, however, to be something of an exaggeration. Admitting that there are certain infractions of the law which do point the way to an improvement in society, it is hard to justify the majority of them on the same ground. To most of us the elimination of crime would seem desirable even if this should impede slightly the process of social change.

CHARACTERISTICS OF THE CRIMINAL

In spite of the relativity of the concept of crime and the consequent variability in the nature of the individual criminal, there have been many attempts to discover general features typical of the criminal as such. The theory which has aroused the greatest comment and controversy is that of the Italian criminologist Cesare Lombroso (4), who in the latter part of the nineteenth century developed his view of the relation between criminality and physical or anatomical characteristics. In his early years Lombroso was in the medical service of the Italian army, and he noted the prevalence of tattooing among criminals; this appeared to indicate their greater degree of physical insensibility, and Lombroso concluded that moral insensibility is the result of its physical counterpart. Later he had occasion to make a post mortem examination of the brain of a brigand and he found that in certain respects it was like that of the lower vertebrates. This gave rise to the general theory of the atavistic nature of the criminal. Among the characteristics indicative of this atavism, Lombroso listed prognathism, woolly hair, a scant beard, oxycephaly (high, pointed head), oblique eyes, prominent cheekbones, prominent supraorbital ridges, a receding forehead, an unusually large or unusually small head, a long or narrow head, a high pointed palate, large ears, characteristics of the opposite sex type, and asymmetries of the skull, face or body. When several of these features are found combined in the same individual, the diagnosis of criminality may be made with some assurance. These features were spoken of as "stigmata of degeneration."

It is often stated that Lombroso failed to make any adequate comparison between criminals and non-criminals in the population. One such comparison was, however, made by Ferri (5) working under Lombroso's direction, and it was discovered that about 10% of prisoners and 37% of soldiers were without these stigmata. This result shows that even though the stigmata may occur more frequently among criminals, the exceptions are numerous. Lombroso attempted to explain this fact by the suggestion that when the stigmata "are found in honest men and women, we may be dealing with criminal natures who have not yet committed the overt act because the circumstances in which they have lived protected them against temptation." This is of course an admission that the social environment may play an important part in the occurrence of crime, and to that extent doubt is thrown upon the validity of the original theory.

Lombroso's work attracted great attention and at the same time bitter opposition. He himself suggested a crucial experiment which would determine whether he or his critics were right; he proposed a selection by his antagonists of one hundred criminals and one hundred honest men whose anatomical characteristics should be carefully studied. It would seem to us now that this was an exceedingly small number of cases with which to test a theory of such scope. In any event, the comparison was never made because no agreement could be reached as to the manner of selection of the individuals to be examined. Such a study was carried out, however, by Charles Goring (6) in England, with the co-operation of the biometrician Karl Pearson, and the results were published in *The English Convict* in 1913. Goring made a large number of measurements on 3000 prisoners, all recidivists, and compared them with groups of students and army men. He reported that stigmata of degeneration were just as frequent in Oxford and Cambridge as in the penal institutions of London. The only difference noted was that criminals were inferior in height and weight, and this was attributed to their lower economic status and inferior opportunities for bodily development.

There have been other attempts to describe the criminal in terms of physical features (1). Galet speaks of degenerative defects in the ears; Vervaeck states that criminals are taller and stronger than others. There have been many suggestions that the criminal may be distinguished by his glandular make-up; Schlapp speaks of a glandular imbalance, Reynolds, of the presence of abnormal thyroids in murderers, and Berman goes so far as to attach specific criminal propensities to varying glandular diagnoses. In his scheme, for example, thieves, hoboes, and liars are of the pituitary type; perverts and exhibitionists are thymus-adrenal; cases of impulsive assault are due to excessive activity of the parathyroid, and so on. It seems clear that these characterizations in terms of endocrine activity are made on insufficient evidence and are not to be accepted as valid until further proof is forthcoming.

In recent times the consensus has been against the point of view represented by Lombroso and his followers. His theory has, however, been revived as the result of an extensive investigation by Professor E. A. Hooton (7) of Harvard, who regards it as probable that the physical and mental features of an individual, both due to heredity, may be associated with each other, and that physical features may therefore afford clues as to mentality and disposition. If such a relationship could be established, it would be of practical benefit in the apprehension and identification of criminals, in the examination of persons suspected because of their bodily form, and in providing a better basis for the selection of immigrants. In connection with the study there were examined 17,680 inmates of penal institutions and 1976 non-criminals. On each individual a large variety of anthropometric measurements was made, as well as a visual appraisal of morphological features. The results showed significant differences between the criminal and civilian populations. One portion of the study dealt with "old Americans," that is, persons whose parents were American-born. In this group the comparison revealed "the smaller size of the felon, his inferior weight and poorer body build, his smaller head, straighter hair, absolutely shorter and relatively broader face, with prominent but short and often snubbed nose, his narrow jaws and his rather small, and relatively broad, ears" (p. 128). Hooton points out, however, that there is considerable overlapping, and that no single feature is peculiar to the criminals. He concludes nevertheless that "whatever the crime may be, it ordinarily arises from a deteriorated organism. . . . You may say that this is tantamount to a declaration that the primary cause of crime is biological inferiority—and that is exactly what I mean" (p. 130).

This conclusion is exceedingly important, and if verified it would have the most far-reaching implications for the attitude toward crime and the treatment of the criminal. There is, however, a fatal methodological defect in the whole approach which relieves us of the necessity of taking the results seriously. In any comparison between two groups, it is essential that they be equated for all characteristics except those in which they are being compared—in this case, criminality and physical characteristics. Since apparent biological inferiority may be due to socio-economic conditions, the two groups must at least come from comparable backgrounds. Actually, the "old American" criminals were taken from a number of different states and represent in general a selection at a low economic level. The civilian "controls" included 146 firemen from Nashville, Tennessee, who were "inclined to be fat" (!), and a heterogeneous Massachusetts sample taken from hospitals, drill-halls and beaches, and representative of the "lower and lower middle economic classes." No more precise indication is given of their comparability with the criminal group, though we are told that they have had more schooling, and the indications are that in other respects also the differences between the two groups are marked. For this reason, Hooton's study fails entirely to carry conviction; his conclusions may be correct, but they have not been demonstrated.

These criticisms do not apply in the same degree to Hooton's mention of physical variations within the criminal population itself according to the kinds of crime committed. One is struck, however, by the inconsistencies in these results for the separate racial and ethnic groups studied. For one thing the differences between criminals and non-criminals noted for the

White population do not hold in the case of Negroes; Negro homicides do not show the greater stature and more powerful physique said to be characteristic of Whites in the same category. It seems unlikely, if Lombroso is right in his contention that physique and criminality are somehow related, that such a relationship should hold for one racial group and not for the other. The writer is inclined to feel that the differences which Hooton has noted have no far-reaching significance.

There is, however, an indirect manner in which physical "stigmata" may be related to criminality. As Sutherland (8) and others have pointed out, personal appearance may play an important part in determining whether an individual will make a satisfactory social adjustment, or will seek gratification by devious and frequently illegal methods. This is probably true especially of women. Obvious deformities and asymmetries might therefore occur with greater frequency in criminal groups, not because of the relationship postulated by Lombroso, but because of the social and individual attitudes toward these defects. "It is easy to imagine the rebuffs and failures which offensive-looking individuals are likely to encounter in attempting to pursue many of the socially desirable walks of life and to understand why such individuals are prone to gravitate to the 'underworld' " (9, p. 122).

Many studies have been made of the social and psychological characteristics of criminals and of their families. A report of the U. S. Census Bureau for 1923, for example, indicates that there is a much larger proportion of illiteracy in the criminal group and a far greater frequency of divorce among the parents. This finding that crime is related to broken homes in a large percentage of cases, is verified by several other studies. There is considerable indication also that criminals and delinquents include a rather large proportion of neurotic and psychopathic individuals. Anderson (10), for instance, found that in his mental hygiene survey of 4326 school children in Cincinnati only 2.6% were psychopathic, whereas among the juvenile delinquents there were 31.2% who could be so described. Slawson (11) reports the occurrence among delinquent boys of a tendency to morbid depression and similar abnormal phenomena, together with an overwhelming preponderance of psychoneurotic responses to the questions on the Matthews revision of the Woodworth Personal Data Sheet. Perhaps the best recent study of psychiatric aspects of delinquency has been made by Healy and Bronner (*12*) in their survey of cases brought before the child guidance clinics of Boston, New Haven and Detroit from 1929 to 1933. They made an intensive examination of 105 pairs of seriously delinquent and non-delinquent siblings; that is to say, the delinquents were compared with their own siblings so that factors of heredity and socio-economic environment were adequately controlled. They report that about 91% of the delinquents showed major emotional disturbances, such as feelings of insecurity in affectional relationships, deep feelings of being thwarted, emotional disturbances over family discipline, marked feelings of inferiority, sibling jealousy or rivalry, deepset internal emotional conflicts, and unconscious feelings of guilt and the need for punishment. Among the control group, on the other hand, only 13% of the cases showed similar evidences of inner stress.

Alexander and Staub (*13*) also speak of a neurotic type of criminal whose transgressions are often of a compulsive nature and carried out under the strong pressure of unconscious motives. One type, for example, may have a sense of guilt of unknown origin; a crime is committed and the sense of guilt is then connected with it and becomes easier to bear as a consequence. In the case of such a criminal, punishment has of course no deterrent effect, since the expected punishment is the main motive for the transgression.[2] According to these writers, however, not all criminals are neurotic, and they distinguish three additional types. (1) Those who commit crimes as the result of toxic or other organic destructive processes, for instance, idiots, sufferers from organic mental disease,

---

[2] It is probable, as Healy (*14*) and others have pointed out, that punishment is no great deterrent in the majority of cases of criminal behavior, since the possibility of apprehension is rarely contemplated.

alcoholics and drug addicts. (2) Normal, non-neurotic criminals, including tramps, beggars, gangsters, professional criminals like pickpockets and burglars, etc. (3) Genuine criminals without any inhibitions whatsoever. In addition, there are crimes resulting from temporary emotional conditions, and usually forgiven by the community. The psychoanalytic approach to the neurotic criminal deserves careful consideration, since there can be little doubt that many criminals require psychiatric help rather than incarceration in a penal institution. This does not mean, however, that the psychiatric treatment must necessarily be psychoanalytic in character.

SOCIAL FACTORS IN CRIME

Among the many studies dealing with social factors determining the incidence and the nature of criminal and delinquent behavior, those of Shaw and his co-workers (15) in Chicago have attracted the greatest attention. In a careful survey of juvenile delinquency in Chicago among boys from 11 to 17 years of age, it was found that the city could be divided into a number of zones or delinquency areas, starting with the central or Loop district and progressing to the residential suburbs. In all, seven such zones were mapped at one-mile intervals from the center. It was found that there was a progressive decrease in the proportion of delinquency from the center to the periphery of the city. The study extended over a considerable period of years during which the population of the central area changed completely without affecting this relationship. There were, for example, successive waves of migration from various European countries, as well as of Mexicans and Negroes, but the delinquency rate remained substantially the same. This has usually been interpreted as meaning that the social and economic setting, rather than the nature of the people concerned, has a definitive influence upon the delinquency rate. The technique has been applied to other cities as well, although not all of them lend themselves geographically to this same regular division into concentric zones. In New York, for example, the careful surveys by

Maller (*16*) have shown a number of distinct delinquency areas rather than a single center; there is, however, a close relationship between delinquency and such factors as density of population and economic level. In London, Burt (*17*) demonstrated a correlation of +.77 between delinquency and density of population, and of +.67 between delinquency and poverty. It seems clear that even though the distribution may differ from one city to another, the relationship between delinquency and economic status remains certain.

There are other studies whose conclusions point in the same direction. Bonger (*18*) noted that in Italy between 1887 and 1889, 60 percent of the population was classified as indigent or poor and this group contributed 88 percent of the convicts in the Italian prisons at that time. Shaw and McKay (*19*) in connection with the Chicago delinquency area study found that when the city was divided into square mile areas, the delinquency rate (in 1931) correlated +.74 with the rates of financial aid to families. There was also a correlation of +.82 between the number of delinquency cases and dependency cases in the juvenile court, and +.63 between delinquency cases and mother's pension cases. These correlations are all high and indicate the close correspondence between economic conditions and crime. This is shown also (*20*) by the fact that criminality tends to increase during periods of depression and to decrease when there is relative prosperity. Sellin's research memorandum on crime in the depression demonstrates this relationship very clearly. It is pertinent also in this connection that in the *Studies in Deceit* by Hartshorne and May (*21*), dishonesty in the tests used was found to increase regularly with a decrease in economic level.

In a recent study by Dollard, Doob and others (*9*), it is suggested that the high rate of crime in underprivileged groups as well as its increase during bad times is to be understood as a reaction to frustration. Their theory is that frustration inevitably leads to aggression, and that acts of crime represent merely one of the possible types of aggressive behavior. There is considerable plausibility to this hypothesis, but it must be

534 FACTORS IN DELINQUENCY AND CRIME

borne in mind that economic crimes may in part result directly
from economic disabilities, rather than indirectly as a more
general response to a dissatisfied or frustrated condition.

In the same connection, these writers refer to the preponderance of males in the criminal population. Although the
proportion varies markedly from one country to another—3:1
in Belgium to 22.5:1 in Finland—there is a consistent difference in this direction (8). It is barely possible that biological
factors are responsible, but in the light of the earlier discussion
(see Chapter X), it seems more probable that the cause is to
be found in social and educational influences. For one thing,
aggressiveness is regarded as a legitimate masculine trait, but
as highly undesirable in a woman, and it has been suggested
that this may be the underlying factor.

A fundamental causative factor seems to be our socially conditioned
concepts regarding masculinity and femininity. Thus, passivity is
felt to be feminine, aggressivity, masculine. A male needs to fight off
any sense of femininity by physical activity—a masculine trait (22,
p. 408).

Crime and Race. The problem of the relation between
crime and race has attracted considerable attention and has
given rise to many popular misconceptions. As has been
pointed out in a previous discussion, it is usually believed that
the foreign-born contribute much more than their share to the
crime in this country; actually, the opposite is true. The
figures for Negroes are far in excess of those for Whites, but
as Woofter (23) and others have indicated, there is such a
great discrepancy in the readiness with which Negroes and
Whites, respectively, are accused and convicted that the statistics as such are meaningless. Even if the Negro rate is actually higher, the interpretation of this fact would have to take
into account his lower economic status, and some allowance
would have to be made for the consequent difference in the
predisposing factors. It seems unlikely that race as such
plays any significant part.

There is, however, a definite problem arising from the status of the native-born of foreign parentage. Glueck (24) has pointed out that the crime and delinquency rates for this group are definitely higher than those for comparable groups with native-born parents. The explanation cannot be a biological one, since the foreign-born parents themselves have a relatively low incidence of crime, and Glueck suggests the hypothesis of "conflict of cultures" as responsible. A case history of one such instance was reported by Shaw (25) in 1930; the subject of the study, Stanley, was born into a disorganized community situation where the *mores* of his family of Polish origin could not be maintained. The result, according to Shaw, was the freeing of the boy from traditional controls, making him accessible to delinquency patterns. Many similar cases have been reported, with the suggestion that where the conflict between the old European culture pattern and the new American one is great, delinquent behavior is a frequent consequence.

A recent study by Taft (26) gives an analysis of crime-rate data from 26 states and indicates that for these 26 states as a whole, the sons of immigrants actually show lower commitment rates than the sons of natives; in nine of these states, however, the rate is higher. These nine states are relatively more industrial, are concentrated in the northeast section of the country, except for Illinois, and are much more highly urbanized. They contain also a larger number of foreign-born, and these foreign-born come mainly from southern and eastern Europe. The cause, therefore, of the higher delinquency rate is not the fact of having foreign parents, but the degree of conflict between the two cultures as well as the attendant economic circumstances. This interpretation is supported by the finding of Carlson (27) that in Iowa the native-born of foreign-born parents have less than the expected proportion of delinquency. As he points out, "the process of assimilation has probably been smoother and more gradual in Iowa than in more industrial states." We must agree, therefore, with Sellin (28) that the concept of culture conflict by itself is not sufficient as an explanation of variations in crime rate, but that it must be seen within the total complex of social and economic factors. This does not mean, however, that culture conflict may not play an important part within the complex.

Apart from the question of culture conflict it is certain that the folkways of any particular group also contribute to the amount and the nature of the crimes committed. This is indicated by the statistics for homicide in various European countries. The following table gives the number of deaths by homicide per hundred thousand persons of all ages (*29*, p. 241).

Year	England and Wales	Scotland	Germany
1921	.7	.4	2.71
1922	.5	.4	2.50
1923	.6	.4	2.60
1924	.6	.5	2.22
1925	.7	.4	2.29
1926	.7	.4	2.17
1927	.5	.4	2.06
1928	.5	.7	1.99
1929	.5	.4	1.84
1930	.5	.5	1.91
1931	.5	.5	2.07
1932	.5	.5	

The remarkable consistency from year to year within any one country, and in spite of undoubted variations in economic conditions, indicates that there must be certain attitudes toward homicide prevalent in a community and that these are to be explained by the folkways or the culture generally.

In the Wickersham report (*30*) on crime in New York State in 1930, it was noted that Mexicans were convicted in great numbers of the crime of carrying concealed weapons; it is obvious that the habits of many Mexicans in their own country have merely been transferred to this one. Beynon's (*31*) study of Hungarians in Detroit illustrates a similar mechanism. The Hungarian peasants have transferred to coal-stealing from the railroad their old attitude toward the stealing of firewood from a nobleman's estate. Gangs of boys who steal coal receive therefore a sort of social approval in the community, even though this form of behavior may get them into trouble with the authorities. With the passage of time and the consequent acceptance of American *mores* there is a change in the social patterning of crime. Stofflet (*32*) has indicated that American-born sons of Italian parents commit homicide less frequently than do their fathers, and for different reasons. Whereas in the immigrant group, homicide often results from family quarrels or from threats to the family honor, in the next generation it is more likely to be a concomitant of predatory crimes like robbery or burglary.

Economic and Psychological Factors. It is not easy to separate the cultural from the more directly economic factors operating in this field. Ross (*33*) points out that rural areas have a lower crime rate than cities, independently of whether they are populated by foreign groups or children of immigrants or by native Americans. He concludes that the broad socio-economic environment rather than the characteristics of the culture is mainly responsible for crime. It is his hypothesis that all peoples on the same socio-economic level have approximately the same crime rate.

The second generation is not a group culturally adrift with neither the culture of their parents nor of their new environment to guide them, but is a group with a very definite culture, a culture of a socio-economic level that is determined by irregular, poorly paid employment and results in broken homes, inadequate education and recreational opportunity and a general stunted environment (p. 208).

This strictly economic viewpoint has recently received emphasis in a book by Rhodes (*34*) entitled significantly *The Criminals We Deserve*. His thesis is that crime grows directly out of the forms of our social organization, or more specifically, from the particular capitalistic economy of our time.

Without quarreling with this emphasis upon economic factors, we must still point out that they do not serve as a universal principle of explanation. The economic approach fails, for example, to explain those crimes which are committed by people in the most favored economic circumstances, and these constitute a substantial minority of all crimes. As was suggested at the beginning of this chapter there are so many different kinds of crime and criminals that it is exceedingly doubtful whether any one explanation will serve for all of them (we have already referred to the classification by Alexander and Staub, *13*). Recently Hopkins (*35*) has also attempted a classification into four varieties—(1) political crimes, or those regarded as treasonable by the state, (2) civic crimes, such as being drunk and disorderly, or failing to take out a driver's license, (3) economic crimes, due to want, and (4) psychological crimes, due to passion, sex and other emotional drives. Hopkins, whose approach is primarily psychoanalytic, believes that in all of these, with the possible exception of the third, psychological causes are the determining factors. It is certain that his emphasis goes too strongly in this direction, but there can be no doubt of the reality of those crimes which are psychological rather than primarily economic in their etiology. Both the socio-economic and the psychological approaches must receive adequate consideration. It may be that Dollard and his collaborators (*9*) are right in their assumption that the frustration-aggression hypothesis applies to all cases of criminal behavior, but more data are needed before such a conclusion can be accepted. In the meantime it seems more reasonable and more in keeping with the known facts to look upon crime as heterogeneous in nature and subject to multiple causation.

CRIME IN PRIMITIVE SOCIETIES

The variations in possible attitudes toward crime and the criminal, referred to above, are further illustrated in the material collected from primitive societies. This material raises a number of important psychological problems. The first of these is the question of individual responsibility. In our society we are accustomed in general to place the blame upon the person who commits the crime, but in many other societies responsibility appears to be vicarious. The Hupa Indians, for example, killed any member of a murderer's family, and among the Crow the grief of the parents at the death of a son in battle was at once assuaged when vengeance had been wreaked on any member of the hostile people (*36*). Hobhouse (*37*) gives many instances of this collective responsibility; among the Kaffirs, the Loango and other African tribes any of the criminal's relatives might be held responsible. Among the Papuans of the Gazelle Peninsula, a man whose wife has been stolen goes into the bush and kills the first man he meets. Lowie regards this collective responsibility as an instance of a type of social solidarity which considers a murder or any other offense as an encroachment of one state on the sovereignty of another, so that the group as a whole is responsible for the offense of any of its members. A striking instance of this type of responsibility is found among the Tlingit of Alaska, who regarded crime as a clan affair.

Immediately after a murder was committed spokesmen from both clans met to decide who was to die in compensation for the murder. If the murdered man happened to be of low rank and of poor reputation, a payment of goods could satisfy the injured clan. There was generally much haggling over the rank of the murdered man and the rank of the one who was to die in compensation (*38*, p. 147).

It is to be noted that the particular individual who committed the murder was not more likely to be put to death than any other member of the clan. There were, however, many primitive groups which did make a distinction similar to our own.

There are instances in which responsibility is centered in someone who bears a special relationship to the offender. Spencer and Gillen (*39*) report that among the Central Australians an avenging party set out on one occasion to kill a man to whose magical practices they imputed the death of one of their friends. Failing to find him, they killed his father on the pretext that he knew of the practices and did nothing to prevent them. Among other Australian groups it is the elder brother who is responsible. When an avenging party has judicially condemned a man to death the penalty falls not upon him, but upon his elder brother (40).

In a recent article on "Society as the Patient," L. K. Frank (41) finds an interesting parallel between this early tendency to hold the group responsible for the misdeeds of any one of its members and the current habit of placing the blame for crime and mental disturbance not upon the individual, but upon society. In this respect he believes that we are in a very real sense completing a cycle.

In the early period of Western European culture, especially Anglo-Saxon culture, the group was responsible for the individual, and he, in turn, shared the common responsibilities, even legal guilt for the misconduct of other members of the group. Then, slowly and haltingly, came the emergence of the legal doctrine of individual responsibility and guilt. . . . To-day, we are moving toward a reinstatement of the ancient doctrine of group responsibility . . . with increasing individual subordination and allegiance to the group (p. 343).

This parallel is striking, but it must not be carried too far. The present tendency to blame society instead of the individual results from the conviction that the criminal is created by an environment over which he has little or no control, whereas the attitudes noted among many primitive peoples indicate that other individuals (rather than the social environment) may be held responsible for the offenses committed by any one person.

Intent and Accident. Of perhaps greater psychological interest is the fact that among many primitive societies criminal *intent* is not nearly so important as among ourselves; the distinction between deliberate and accidental injury may not be regarded as significant. Goddard (42) cites a case among the Hupa in which a child was burned to death in a fire built by a woman for heating water out of doors; although the woman was in no way at fault the life of her son was sought as recompense. Westermarck (43) points out that blood-revenge followed both willful and accidental homicide among the Ondonga of South Africa, the Marshall Islanders and the

Nissan of the Bismarck Archipelago. The Kafirs of the Hindu Kush made no distinction between murder and killing by inadvertence in a quarrel. Perkins (*44*) reports a case among the tribesmen of Abyssinia in which a boy fell on the head of a comrade, killing him; he was punished in the same way by the victim's brother. The Kameroons in West Central Africa say, "He who kills another accidentally must die. Then the friends of each are equal mourners" (*43*, Vol. I, p. 219).

In this connection Hartland (*45*) in his discussion of primitive law expresses the belief that this lack of distinction between intentional murder and accidental or even justifiable homicide is characteristic of a primitive, undeveloped stage of society. He believes that considerable progress in civilization must be made before this distinction may be drawn. This interpretation is negated, however, by the fact that the distinction *is* frequently made by so-called primitive groups. Among the Ifugao of the Philippines, for example, voluntary and involuntary deeds are carefully differentiated. Among the Ashanti the penalty is reduced if the crime is unpremeditated, and among the African Kaffirs there is no penalty whatsoever (*37*). Intent, therefore, may be ignored, but it may also be carefully considered by the so-called simpler societies.

There is, as a matter of fact, considerable logic behind the evaluation of an act by its consequences rather than by its motivation. From the point of view of the victim or his family, the important thing is the effect, and questions of intent may appear to be irrelevant. We may go further than this and state that, as psychoanalysts in particular have demonstrated, many "accidents" have their basis in the unexpressed wishes of the person acting, and are not really devoid of intent. From this point of view it is striking to find an old Bantu remarking that "if we pardon one man who kills by accident there will be nothing but accidents" (*46*, p. 557). If punishment has any deterrent effect whatsoever, it should act to prevent carelessness as well as deliberate and intentional crime.

It will be argued, however, that there are undoubtedly cases of real accidents expressing neither conscious nor unconscious wishes on the part of the person involved, and that punishment under these conditions is unjustified. As a matter of fact one's judgment in this matter will be determined by one's view of the nature and significance of punishment. The popular viewpoint is that it is a form of retaliation, and therefore appropriate to deliberate but not to accidental injury. This attitude in turn assumes a belief in "freedom of the will," and the offender is punished because he performed an act from which he could have refrained, if he had so "willed." We do not exact the death penalty from minors, the feebleminded and the insane, because they are presumably not responsible for what they do. The science of psychology proceeds, however, on a deterministic rather than a "free will" basis. It is assumed that behavior results from the interaction between the organism and his environment, and that it is to be explained by the nature of the individual and of the internal and external forces acting upon him. If that is so, no one can act except as a consequence of these factors, and retaliatory punishment is never justified. If, on the other hand, punishment is determined by the social consequences of the offense, or even by the belief in its use as a deterrent, primitive peoples may be right in adopting a similar attitude to accidental and to premeditated offenses.

When use is made of the principle of retaliation, the so-called "lex talionis," there are many societies which apply it much more strictly and more literally than our own. Hobhouse and Westermarck have collected many examples. If, for instance, a man kills the son of another, he may himself go free, but his son will be put to death on the principle that he must suffer as he has made another suffer. In the Hammurabic code of ancient Babylon it is stated that "if a man has struck a gentleman's daughter and caused her to drop what is in her womb, he shall pay ten shekels of silver for what was in her womb. If that woman has died, one shall put to death his daughter." This latter penalty makes it clear that the "eye for an eye" principle is interpreted very strictly, and in a sense more logically than among ourselves.

In the actual imposition of punishment for crimes the material from primitive societies contains many instances of psychological interest. The Wachagga of East Africa take the view that a man who betrays the adultery of a woman to her husband must himself pay as much as the adulterer pays. "It is argued that it was not his business to watch another man's wife, and that by so doing he usurps the rights of a husband, which in point of fact is the essence of the offense of adultery" (46, p. 552). In primitive societies generally, although punishment may take the form of blood revenge or of material compensation as among ourselves, rich and varied use is made of the principle of humiliation or ridicule. In Samoa, for example, the death sentence may be pronounced and then modified in the form of binding the hands and feet of the culprit "like a pig prepared for slaughter" and carrying him thus suspended through the whole village and laid before the house of the injured person. The offender is "morally destroyed" because he is handled as a pig (47). The Sea Dyaks of Borneo have an ingenious method of punishing a liar.

Soon after his dishonesty is discovered, the people begin to pile twigs and branches near the place where the offense occurred, and always thereafter all passers-by throw their contributions of sticks on the heap. Some of these "liars' heaps" are very old, but the name of the offender is not forgotten, living on in perpetual disgrace as the name of his monument of shame (48, p. 463).

For the Crow Indians Lowie (49) gives striking examples of the manner in which ridicule is used as a social corrective. An offense against the customs of the group is commented upon so freely and so unpleasantly that the culprit, after he has suffered this ridicule, may wander away from the camp and never be heard of again. Similarly the Eskimos will do nothing to a thief except to laugh when his name is mentioned. As Linton (50) points out, this may not sound like a severe penalty, but it is sufficient to make theft almost unknown.

Since almost every primitive group lays stress upon individual prestige and status, the ridicule of the community is a very serious punishment. Among the American Indians in particular the use of ridicule in this manner was highly systematized and in the large majority of cases made a more direct, and from our point of view more drastic, punishment quite unnecessary. In more extreme cases there might be ostracism or expulsion from the group. The use of ridicule as a social corrective is probably universal, but its efficacy will vary with the size of the community. In a small group, in which every individual is known to every other, ridicule is a very severe punishment, particularly since escape to another community is usually impossible. In a large modern society, it is probably effective as a punishment only for minor infractions of the social code.

The Ordeal. The methods used in certain primitive societies for determining the guilt or innocence of the accused also raise an interesting psychological problem. In many parts of the world, particularly in Africa, some form of ordeal is used. Commenting on this practice, Lévy-Bruhl (51) points out that it indicates the "prelogical mentality" of the natives, since, for example, a poison will have an effect because of its strength or quantity rather than because the person who takes it is guilty. From what we know, however, of the effects of suggestion, it may very well be that certain forms of ordeals may work effectively in the majority of instances. In Samoa, for example, the suspected persons are summoned by the chief, grass is laid on the sacred stone of the village, and each person places his hand upon it saying, "I lay my hand on the stone. If I stole the thing may I speedily die" (52, p. 293). Similarly, among the African Lango a man accused of theft or witchcraft eats the food of a dog and it is believed that if guilty he will die within a year. An accused man among the Tungus is given a drink which will poison him if he is guilty and presumably leave him unharmed if he is innocent. In all these cases, it seems highly probable that the knowledge of one's own guilt or innocence coupled with a firm belief in the efficacy of the ordeal will actually succeed in attaching the punishment to the guilty person.

That suggestion may work in this way is attested by a number of instances reported from primitive as well as more complex communities. One example may be given, cited by Dundas (53) for the Bantu.

An incident related to me as absolutely authentic, told of a man who, having speared his father, was cursed by the dying parent, and forbidden ever to drink water or eat food excepting from remote localities. For some time the unhappy man lived on sugar-cane juice, but one day, forgetting the curse, he drank water from the river, and being unable to swallow it, died of suffocation (p. 266).

Similar instances could be multiplied. This does not mean, however, that all ordeals are in this category and that they will all work effectively because of the beliefs of the accused. One method used by the Lango, for example, in connection with the crime of adultery is to make the accused spit on his hand and rub the head, back and stomach of a he-goat; if the goat urinates, the man is convicted on the assumption that the urine is identical with the ejection of semen. In connection with this whole problem it would be interesting to know whether natives have more faith in those ordeals which appear to us to be subject to the principles of suggestion than in those which from our point of view are entirely matters of chance.

These few indications of the psychological problems arising in connection with the administration of criminal law in primitive societies are not to be regarded as exhaustive, but rather as pointing the way to further research in this field of ethnological psychology.

SUMMARY

The relativity of crime to the laws of a particular society, and the variations in the nature of behavior which is termed criminal, make it impossible to speak of *the criminal* as such, or to ascribe specific characteristics to him. The attempt by Lombroso to relate criminality to physical appearance may be regarded as a failure. The recent revival of the theory by

Hooton is unconvincing, mainly because the two groups compared, namely, the criminal and civilian populations, were not adequately equated. Certain "stigmata" may be related indirectly to crime, not because they are signs of biological inferiority, but because of the attitudes which such defects may arouse. There is evidence that many delinquents and criminals show signs of neurotic disturbance, and that they require psychiatric assistance rather than punishment.

Among the social factors related to criminal and delinquent behavior, the demonstration of the existence of delinquency areas and of the relation to crowding and poverty may be regarded as particularly significant. Races probably do not differ in innate criminal propensities, although there may be differences in crime rate because of economic and cultural backgrounds. The cultural conflicts in the native-born of foreign parentage contribute to the greater incidence of crime and delinquency in this group, although other factors undoubtedly enter.

The study of crime in primitive societies illustrates some of the possible variations in the attitude toward crime. There may be emphasis on collective as opposed to individual responsibility, lack of distinction between deliberate and accidental injury, different degrees of rigidity in the application of the principle of retaliation, and the use of ridicule as an institutionalized social corrective. The dependence upon the ordeal as a means of guilt detection may in some instances give accurate results because of the effect of suggestion upon those who are forced to participate.

REFERENCES

1. Michael, J., and Adler, M. J. *Crime, Law and Social Science.* 1933.
2. Osborne, T. M. *Society and Prisons.* 1924.
3. Dunlap, K. *Civilized Life.* 1934.
4. Lombroso, C. *Crime, Its Causes and Remedies.* 1911.
5. Ferri, E. *Criminal Sociology.* 1917.
6. Goring, C. *The English Convict.* 1913.

7. Hooton, E. A. *Crime and the Man.* 1939.

8. Sutherland, E. H. *Principles of Criminology.* 3d ed. 1939.

9. Dollard, J., et al. *Frustration and Aggression.* 1939.

10. Anderson, V. V. "Feeblemindedness as Seen in Court," *Ment. Hygiene,* 1917, 1: pp. 260-265.

11. Slawson, J. *The Delinquent Boy.* 1926.

12. Healy, W., and Bronner, A. F. *New Light on Delinquency and Its Treatment.* 1936.

13. Alexander, F., and Staub, H. *The Criminal, the Judge and the Public.* 1931.

14. Healy, W. *The Individual Delinquent.* 1915.

15. Shaw, C. R., et al. *Delinquency Areas.* 1929.

16. Maller, J. B. "The Trend of Juvenile Delinquency in New York City." *J. Juv. Res.,* 1933, 17: pp. 10-18.

17. Burt, C. *The Young Delinquent.* 1925.

18. Bonger, W. A. *Criminality and Economic Conditions.* 1916.

19. Shaw, C. R., and McKay, H. D. "Social Factors in Juvenile Delinquency," *Report on the Causes of Crime,* No. 13, Vol. II.

20. Sellin, T. *Research Memorandum on Crime in the Depression.* N. Y. Social Science Research Council, 1937.

21. Hartshorne, H., and May, M. A. *Studies in Deceit.* 1928.

22. Bender, L., Keiser, S., and Schilder, P. "Studies in Aggressiveness," *Genet. Psychol. Monog.,* 1936, 18: pp. 357-564.

23. Woofter, T. J., Jr. "The Status of Racial and Ethnic Groups," in *Recent Social Trends,* N. Y., 1933. Vol. I, Chap. II: pp. 553-601.

24. Glueck, E. T. *One Thousand Juvenile Delinquents.* 1934; "Culture, Conflict, and Delinquency," *Ment. Hyg.,* 1937, 21: pp. 46-66.

25. Shaw, C. R. *The Jack-Roller.* 1930.

26. Taft, D. R. "Nationality and Crime," *Amer. Sociol. Rev.,* 1936, 1: pp. 724-736.

27. Carlson, H. S. "The Incidence of Certain Etiological and Symptomatic Factors Among a Group of Iowa Delinquents and Felons," *Univ. Ia. Stud. Child Welf.,* 1937, 13, No. 4: pp. 61-98.

28. Sellin, T. "Culture Conflict and Crime," *Amer. J. Sociol.,* 1938, 44: pp. 97-103.

29. Huxley, J. S., and Haddon, A. C. *We Europeans.* 1936.

30. Wickersham, G. W., et al. *National Commission on Law Observance and Law Enforcement.* Report No. 10, Washington, 1933.

31. Beynon, E. D. "Crime and Custom of the Hungarians of Detroit," *J. Crim. Law Criminol.,* 1934-1935, 25: pp. 755-774.

32. Stofflet, E. H. "A Study of National and Cultural Differences in Criminal Tendencies," *Arch. Psychol.*, 1935, No. 185.

33. Ross, H. "Crime and the Native Born Sons of European Immigrants," *J. Crim. Law Criminol.*, 1937-1938, 28: pp. 202-209.

34. Rhodes, H. T. F. *The Criminals We Deserve.* 1937.

35. Hopkins, P. *The Psychology of Social Movements.* 1938.

36. Lowie, R. H. *Primitive Society.* 1925.

37. Hobhouse, L. T. *Morals in Evolution.* 3d ed. 1915.

38. Oberg, K. "Crime and Punishment in Tlingit Society," *Amer. Anthrop.* N. S., 1934, 36: pp. 145-156.

39. Spencer, B., and Gillen, F. J. *Northern Tribes of Central Australia.* 1904.

40. Howitt, A. W. *The Native Tribes of South-east Australia.* 1904.

41. Frank, L. K. "Society as the Patient," *Amer. J. Sociol.*, 1936, 42: pp. 335-344.

42. Goddard, P. E. "Life and Culture of the Hupa," *Univ. Cal. Publs. Amer. Archaeol. and Ethnol.*, 1903, 1: pp. 1-88.

43. Westermarck, E. A. *The Origin and Development of the Moral Ideas.* 2 vols. 1908-1912.

44. Perkins, J. *A Residence of Eight Years in Persia.* 1843.

45. Hartland, E. S. *Primitive Law.* 1924.

46. Thomas, W. I. *Primitive Behavior.* 1937.

47. Von Bülow, W. "Das Ungeschriebene Gesetz der Samoaner," *Globus*, 1896, 69: pp. 191-195.

48. Kennedy, R. *The Ethnology of the Greater Sunda Islands.* Manuscript quoted in *46*.

49. Lowie, R. H. *The Crow Indians.* 1935.

50. Linton, R. *The Study of Man.* 1936.

51. Lévy-Bruhl, L. *Primitive Mentality.* 1923.

52. Turner, G. *Nineteen Years in Polynesia.* 1861.

53. Dundas, C. "The Organization and Laws of Some Bantu Tribes," *Jour. Anth. Inst.*, 1915, 45: pp. 234-306.

CONCLUSION

IT may seem premature to speak of an Applied Social Psychology, or to attempt to relate our findings to the problems of human welfare. The goals of civilization are not adequately defined, nor are satisfactory techniques available for a constructive program of social engineering. At the same time, the social psychologist has a contribution to make. If there is one general conclusion which may be said to emerge from this survey of the available knowledge in the field, it is that most of the characteristics as well as the institutions of modern society are to be explained in terms of social rather than biological factors. This has far-reaching practical implications. Without denying the significance of man's biological nature or the importance of the physical organism in determining individual differences in personality, it remains true that improvements are to be sought more profitably in an amelioration of the social environment than in the creation of a superior genetic stock.

More precisely, the following statements may with some safety be made. Criminality and mental abnormality may best be attacked by social betterment, and not by sterilization; wars and conflicts are not inherent in human nature, but in the structure of our social and economic system; racial hostilities are not due to the innate characteristics of biologically distinct groups, but to historical and economic forces; the functioning intelligence and achievement of a people may be raised by making the best education available to the largest number, rather than by selective breeding. The list might be continued, but the additions would merely be variations on this same theme. Man is primarily a social animal, and his hope for the future lies in the improvement of his society.

INDEX OF NAMES

INDEX OF SUBJECTS

INDEX OF SUBJECTS
569

Race (*Cont.*)
classification, 286-288
cultural contributions, 292-297
definition, 282
and language, 283-286
mixture, 306-311
and nation, 282-283
"primitive," 288
Race prejudice, 88, 346, 348, 352,
353, 356, 370, 374-402
causes, 391-396
modification, 368, 369, 396-399
see also Rationalizations
Racial differences, 13, 47, 173, 282-
316
crime, 534
intelligence tests, 297-303
personality tests, 303-306
Radicalism, 326, 327, 357, 359, 391
Rating scales, 441-442
Rationalizations, 385-391, 399
Rats, 68, 157, 228-229
Regional differences, 485
intelligence, 253-259
Religion, 10, 13, 38, 77, 82, 83, 121,
170, 389, 391, 485, 490, 491,
507, 509, 510, 517
Repression, 515, 516
Responsibility, criminal, 538-540
Ridicule, 192-193, 543, 544
see also Laughter
Rivalry
see Competition
Romantic love, 125, 131
Rorschach test, 450-452, 455
Russian, 10, 93, 212, 277, 359, 368,
369, 393, 396, 464, 514

Samoa, 464, 489-490, 492, 493, 543
Samurai, 114, 195
Sanskrit, 44, 284
Scandinavian, 286
Scapegoat, 340, 341, 392, 393, 394
Schizoid, 414
Schizophrenia, 414, 415, 420, 451,
508, 509
Schizothyme, 414, 416, 420, 471
Sea Dyaks, 543

Selective migration
see Migration, selective
Self, 97
Self-assertiveness, 83, 95, 96, 97,
104-110, 159, 161, 337, 391,
487, 488, 518
Self-preservation, 60, 110-115, 121,
161
Self-submission, 159, 161, 417
Semang, 154
Semitic, 284
Sense perception, 4, 40, 203-214,
362
color, 204-205
smell, 209
sound, 208-209
taste, 209
see also Pain
Sentiment, 57, 134
Sex, 20, 21, 22, 67, 74, 121-149,
158, 161, 170, 275, 276, 395,
463, 492, 493, 515-516, 519
Sex differences, 72, 265-281
crime, 534
occupations, 272-273
Shame, 122, 123, 145, 170, 182
Short-sample technique, 459
Siberian, 45, 77, 93, 100, 112, 113,
134, 169, 295, 509, 516, 525
Siblings, 234-236, 301
Sicilian, 171, 283
"Sick society," 398, 506
Signaling reflex, 29
Sleep, 150, 161
Smile, 194-195
Social decrement, 337
Social distance, 356, 369, 383
Social facilitation, 24, 335-339
Social increment, 336-337
Social mobility, 251-253
Social norms, 205, 206
Social organism, 330-331
Social psychology, history, 8-13
Social time, 212
Sociology, 3, 5, 55, 346, 399
Sociometry, 377, 461-462
Sorrow
see Grief